Dana Facaros & Michael Pauls

NORTHERN SPAIN

W9-AAT-977

Cadogan Books plc
London House, Parkgate Road, London SW11 4NQ, UK

Distributed in North America by The Globe Pequot Press
6 Business Park Road, PO Box 833, Old Saybrook,
Connecticut 06475–0833

Copyright © Dana Facaros and Michael Pauls 1996
Illustrations © Alex Manolatos 1996

Design and cover illustration by Animage
Maps © Cadogan Guides, drawn by Map Creation Ltd

Editor: Dominique Shead
Series Editors: Rachel Fielding and Vicki Ingle

Proofreading: Philip Ward
Indexing: Isobel McLean
Production: Book Production Services

A catalogue record for this book is available from the British Library
Library of Congress Cataloguing and Publication data available
ISBN 0–94–7754–89–X

The author and publishers have made every effort to ensure the accuracy of the information in this book at the time of going to press.
However, they cannot accept any responsibility for any loss, injury or inconvenience resulting from the use of information contained
in this guide.
Printed and bound in Great Britain by Redwood Books Ltd.

About the Authors

Dana Facaros and Michael Pauls have written over 20 books for Cadogan, including a guide to Spain and one to Southern Spain. They live in an old farmhouse in southwest France with their two children and assorted animals.

Acknowledgements

The authors would like to extend a big thank you to all the tourist office staff of northwest Spain, to Victor and Kate who loaned us their beast, Ricky the Renault, to Jackson and Lily who kept us company, and to Rachel, Sid, Alexander and Tristram who kept the home fires burning and fed Binkley and Atilla. Thanks too to Dominique Shead for fearlessly plunging into the mysteries of Basque spelling and obscure Spanish saints.

The publishers would like to thank Alex Manolatos for the illustrations, Amanda Purves for extra research, Philip Ward for proofreading, Isobel McLean for indexing, Stewart Wild for travel information, Map Creation for the maps and Adrian McLaughlin for DTP support.

Please help us to keep this guide up to date

We have done our best to ensure that the information in this guide is correct at the time of going to press. But places and facilities are constantly changing, and standards and prices in hotels and restaurants fluctuate. We would be delighted to receive any comments concerning existing entries or omissions.

All contributors will be acknowledged in the next edition, and will receive a copy of the Cadogan Guide of their choice.

Contents

Old Castile and León 215–268

Galicia 269–324

Language 325–333

Glossary of Terms, Further Reading 334–336

Index 337–344

Maps

The north is the alternative Spain, the 'Green Spain', where all national stereotypes collapse, or at least those stereotypes we acquire on the Med. Northern landscapes can be just as spectacular, and beaches just as plentiful, with blue and emerald colours in the ocean and along the estuaries that bite into the coast; the mountains—the western Pyrenees, the Cordillera Cantábrica and the Picos de Europa—are

Introduction

endearingly lovely and inviting to linger and walk in, unlike much of the austere, dry *meseta* to the south. Here are sheep in the meadows, cows in the corn and storks on every spire—the biggest colony of these, over a hundred, live atop Calahorra cathedral. The northwest is as rich and lush as the rest of Spain is traditionally hard and dry; here you'll find Spain's finest cheer: Galician seafood, La Rioja wine, Asturian cider, Cantabrian cheese, Navarrese garden vegetables, Castilian sucking-pig and roast lamb, and the chefs with the best reputation for putting it all together— the Basques. Of course much of the north's luxuriance comes from the fact that no matter how Eliza Dolittle pronounces it, the rain in Spain does not fall mainly in the plain, but rather right on its head.

Northern Spain has the knack of acquiring a plethora of 'firsts' and then discreetly retiring into the background. The earliest settlers in Iberia found it convivial and left one of the world's great Palaeolithic masterpieces, at Altamira; the Basques, the oldest race in Europe, found it just as cosy and have called it home since the beginning of time. After the conquest of the Moors, the embryo of modern Spain, its architecture and language—Castilian—were formed in the mountains of Asturias and crystalized in Burgos. With the discovery of the relics of St James in Galicia, the northwest became the forerunner of European tourism, inventing the pilgrimage to Santiago de Compostela, now going on its second millennium. Even though Spain's centre of gravity gradually moved south to Madrid, the cities and countryside of the north have been adorned with a generous helping of magnificent architectural treasures, from the Visigothic to the most florid Baroque, not to mention a few works by the great Catalan *modernista* master Antoni Gaudí.

The Spaniards, especially the *madrileños*, have in the past few decades guarded the northwest as a secret for themselves, although they only come in July and August, when it rains less. But even then you have to look hard to find beaches blighted by Benidormish excess (Laredo and Zarautz are the only ones that come close); tourism in northern Spain is more low key, and by the nature of its short 'season' is probably destined to remain so. To let the threat of a shower or two keep you away would be to miss out on the best preserved and most idiosyncratic corners of old Europe, a place that has kept a sense of place in the face of creeping homogeneity, one full of unexpected pleasures: a Roman bridge over a brook, the fishmarket in A Coruña, a tableland in northern Castile abruptly cut away by a canyon filled with eagles, a spontaneous party that lasts until dawn in an outdoor *sidrería*, old women herding their cows home by twilight, the walls of stained glass in León, a Basque tug-of-war match, and a sunset at Finisterre, the end of the world.

Travel

By Air

There is an astounding variety of flight options these days to Spain, especially from the UK; even Spain's national airline, **Iberia**, offers tempting discounts—bargain fly-drive deals, as well as an unlimited domestic flight option for purchasers of regular flight tickets. No matter how you go, you can always save by going off-season (15th September–early June). APEX fares, purchased at least two weeks in advance, and for a stay of 7–180 days, offer a discount, especially if you're travelling mid-week. Ask, too, about their UK deals: 'Moneysaver' weekend specials, 'Countdown' second-ticket discounts, 'Citysaver' reductions, and discounts for children under 12. Discounts are also available for domestic flights; enquire about the 'Visit Spain' offer.

Three airlines serve northern Spain with non-stop flights from London: **British Airways** (℅ 0345 222111), **Iberia** (℅ 0171–830 0011) and Iberia subsidiary **Aviaco** (℅ 0171–830 0011). British Airways and Iberia serve Bilbao from London Heathrow, and Iberia has a daily service from Manchester to Bilbao via Barcelona. Iberia also has a daily service from Heathrow to Santiago de Compostela. Aviaco flies non-stop to Oviedo from London Stansted three times a week. Aviaco also flies to San Sebastián, Pamplona, Vitoria, Santander, A Coruña and Vigo from Madrid and Barcelona.

British Airways has four offices in London; check locally for regional locations. Iberia's office is at Venture House, 27–29 Glasshouse Street, London W1R 6JU (open Mon–Fri, 9–5.30)

charter flights

These can be incredibly cheap, and offer the added advantage of departing from local airports. Companies such as **Thomson, Airtours** and **Unijet** offer return flights ranging from £130–220. This theoretically includes *basic* accommodation, but nobody expects you to make use of this facility. Some of the best deals have return dates limited strictly to one or two weeks, sometimes four, the maximum allowed by law. Check out your local economy agent or bucket shop, your local paper or, if you're in London, *Time Out.*

Get your ticket as early as possible, but be doubly sure of your plans, as there are no refunds for missed flights—most travel agencies sell insurance, so that you don't lose all your money if you become ill. Students and anyone under 26 have the additional option of special discount charters, departing from the UK, but make sure you have proof of student status. An STA Youth card costs £4; if you teach at a recognized educational institution, an STA Academic card is available for £6.

discount and youth travel specialists

STA Travel: 117 Euston Road, London NW1 and 86 Old Brompton Road, London SW7 are the main London centres, ℅ (0171) 937 9921.

Campus Travel: 52 Grosvenor Gardens, London SW1, ℅ (0171) 730 3402.

By Sea

The **Plymouth–Santander** ferry, operated by Brittany Ferries, is a good way to go if you mean to bring your car or bicycle. Prices for passengers are just a bit lower than a charter flight; children from 4–13 go for half-price, under 4s free. Prices for vehicles vary according to size and season—it's most expensive from 28 June–1 September: one adult (without vehicle) pays £46–76 one way; one adult with vehicle pays £146–254 depending on the length and type of vehicle. In the high season, on-board accommodation goes from £6 for a simple Pullman seat, to £23 to share a four-berth cabin, finishing at £110 for a deluxe twin-berth cabin. There are also 8-day return specials, where one adult plus car comes to £198–345. The 24-hour crossing is made twice a week, with departures from Plymouth usually on Mondays and Wednesdays, and from Santander on Tuesdays and Thursdays. For information, contact your travel agent or Brittany Ferries, Millbay Docks, Plymouth PL1 3EW, ✆ (0990) 360360. In Santander the address is the Estación Marítima, ✆ (942) 214 500.

The alternative is P&O's **Portsmouth–Bilbao** run, which is in service year-round, and usually departs Portsmouth on Tuesday and Saturday evenings. Prices are comparable to the Plymouth–Santander ferry, though with either there is tremendous variation between seasons and between services on offer: getting a car to Bilbao and back can go from £145 to £470, with an additional £80–140 per person; children pay half fare. Cabins cost an additional £60–150. P&O offer a special discount rate for a one-week return trip, and a 'family rate' of £404–715 for a car and up to five passengers. Note that the Spanish terminal is at the port of Santurzi, 13km from the centre of Bilbao. The ferry can be booked through travel agents, or else the number for information and reservations is ✆ (0990) 980980. In Bilbao, see Ferries Golfo de Vizcaya, Cosme Echevarrieta 1, ✆ (94) 423 44 77.

By Rail

From London to San Sebastián it's a full day's trip, changing trains in Paris and maybe at Bordeaux or Hendaye in the small hours of the morning. The TGV service from Paris to Bordeaux can cut some hours off the trip if the schedule works right for you. Time can also be saved by taking the Eurostar (✆ 0345 881881) rail service through the Channel Tunnel to Paris. Services are very frequent and take three hours from London (Waterloo) to Paris (Gare du Nord). Fares are lower if booked at least 14 days in advance.

If you've been resident in Europe for the past 6 months and are under 26, you can take advantage of the 'two-zone' **InterRail Pass**, available at British Rail or any travel agent, giving you a month's rail travel for £220, as well as half-price discounts on Channel cross-ings and ferries to Morocco, where the pass is also valid. **Bookings:** rail tickets to Spain from England or vice versa, can be obtained from British Rail International, Ticket and Information Office, PO Box 29, Victoria Station, London SW1V 1JX, ✆ (0171) 834 2345. Take your passport. Tickets for local Spanish services can be obtained from certain UK travel agents, but bookings must be made weeks in advance. For *couchette* and sleeper reservations in France, contact French Railways, 179 Piccadilly, London W1, ✆ (0171)

495 4433. If you're taking a car, ℭ (0171) 409 3518. French Railways are also agents for the American EurRail pass. Note that neither InterRail nor EurRail passes are valid on Spain's numerous narrow-gauge (FEVE) lines.

By Bus or Coach

One major company, **Eurolines,** offers departures several times a week in the summer (once a week out of season) from London to Spain, along the east coast as far as Alicante, or to Algeciras via San Sebastián, Burgos, Madrid, Córdoba, Granada and Málaga. From either San Sebastián or Burgos, it will be relatively easy to find further connections to any other town in the northwest. Journey time London–San Sebastián is 21 hours (19 hours on the Saturday express service). The fare to San Sebastián is from £115 return, to Vitoria and Burgos from £127. Peak season fares between 22 July and 4 September are slightly higher. There are discounts for anyone under 26, senior citizens and children under 12. The national coach companies operate services that connect with the continental bus system. In the summer, the coach is the best bargain for anyone over 26; off-season you'll probably find a cheaper charter flight. **Information and booking**: Eurolines, 52 Grosvenor Gardens, London SW1, ℭ (0171) 730 8235; National Express, ℭ (0171) 730 0202; Caledonian Express, (0141) 332 4100. Details of all UK–Spain bus services can be obtained from the Spanish Tourist Office in London.

By Car

From the UK via France you have a choice of routes. Ferries from Portsmouth cross to Cherbourg, Caen, Le Havre and St Malo. From any of these ports the most direct route takes you to Bordeaux, down the western coast of France to the border at Irún, and on to San Sebastián, Burgos and Madrid. The route takes an average of a 1½ days' steady driving. You may find it more convenient and less tiring to try the ferry from Plymouth to Santander (*see* above), which cuts out driving through France and saves expensive *autoroute* tolls.

For something different, opt for one of the routes the old Santiago pilgrims followed over the Pyrenees, through Puigcerdà and Somport-Canfranc, or the classic route through Roncesvalles and the Vall d'Aran—you can get warmed up for Spain by inspecting the French side of the Basque country along the way (it's actually more fun on the French side: see the *Cadogan Guide to Southwest France*). In high season, and really any time of year when bored customs officers decide to act up, there can be long backups at the busy autoroute at the Hendaye-Irún border—a three-hour wait is not impossible.

Getting There from the USA and Canada

By Air

There are numerous carriers that serve Spain. Most regular flights from the US or Canada are to Madrid or Barcelona. **Iberia,** the national airline, offers fly-drive deals and discounts: enquire about the 'Visit Spain' offer. From anywhere in the US, you can use Iberia's toll-free line ℭ (800) 772 4642.

Iberia Offices in the US and Canada

USA:

20 Park Plaza, Boston, MA 02116, © (617) 426 8335

509 Madison Avenue, New York, NY 10022, © (212) 644 8797

1725 K. Street NW, Washington, DC 20006, © (202) 293 6970

Suite 1308, 150 S. E. Second Avenue, Miami, FL 33131, © (305) 358 8800

8111 LBJ Freeway, Suite 941, Dallas, TX 75251, © (214) 669 3336

Canada:

102 Bloor Street West, Toronto, M5S 1M8, © (416) 964 6625

2020 University Street, Montreal, H3A 2A5, © (514) 849 3352

other airlines with direct routes to Spain

American Airlines: toll-free © (800) 433 7300

Continental Airlines: toll-free © (800) 231 0856

TWA: toll-free © (800) 892 4141

United Airlines: toll-free © (800) 538 2929

Air Canada: toll-free © (800) 268 7240

other airlines with routes via Europe

British Airways: toll-free © (800) 247 9297

KLM: toll-free © (800) 777 5553

Lufthansa: toll-free © (800) 645 3880

TAP Air Portugal: toll-free © (800) 221 7370

Virgin Atlantic: toll-free © (800) 862 8621

charter flights

These require a bit more perseverance to find, though you can save considerably on the cost of a regular or APEX flight—currently a charter from New York to Madrid varies between $400–700 depending on the season. You may want to weigh this against the current transatlantic fares to London, where in most cases you can get a low-cost flight to Spain departing within a day or two of your arrival. This is an especially cheap way to go off-season. The Sunday *New York Times* has the most listings.

some major charter companies and consolidators

Council Charters: 205 East 42nd Street, New York, NY 10017, toll-free © (800) 800 8222; uses Air Europa

DER: toll-free © (800) 782 2424

Spanish Heritage Tours: 116–47 Queens Blvd, Forest Hills, NY 11375, © (718) 520 1300; uses Air Europa

TFI: 34 West 32nd Street, New York, NY 10001, © (212) 736 1140, toll-free © (800) 745 8000

By Rail

The American **EurRail Pass,** which must be purchased before you leave the States, is a good deal only if you plan to use the trains every day—though it's not valid in the UK,

Morocco or countries outside the European Union. A month of travel is around $508 for those under 26; those over 26 can get a 15-day pass for $460, a 21-day pass for $598 or a month for $728. **Contact:** CIT Tours, 342 Madison Avenue, Suite 207, New York 10173, ✆ (212) 697 2100, or toll-free ✆ (800) 248 7245.

In Spain you'll have to pay supplements for any kind of express train and the EurRail pass is not valid on Spain's numerous narrow-gauge (FEVE) lines.

Specialist Tour Operators

The **Spanish Tourist Office** is located at 57 St James's Street, London SW1A 1LD, ✆ (0171) 499 0901. They stock a number of brochures and leaflets on main towns and cities as well as information on a variety of holiday options.

General

CV Travel: 43 Cadogan Street, London SW3 2PR, ✆ (0171) 581 0851. Country house accommodation and tailor-made holidays throughout Spain.

First Choice: First Choice House, London Road, Crawley, West Sussex RH10 2GX, ✆ (01293) 588405. General beach holiday programme; also winter programme for over 50s to beach destinations, with mystery tours, dancing, bingo etc.

Mundi Color Travel: 276 Vauxhall Bridge Road, London SW1V 1BE, ✆ (0171) 828 6021. Tailor-made city break and *parador* holidays.

Specialtours Ltd: 81a Elizabeth Street, London SW1W 9PG, ✆ (0171) 730 2297. Short city breaks (members of National Art Collections Fund only).

Unicorn Holidays Ltd: 2 Place Farm, Wheathampstead, Hertfordshire AL4 8SB, ✆ (01582) 834400. Tailor-made fly-drive and self-drive touring holidays featuring the *paradores* and other excellent hotels.

Cultural Tours

Martin Randall: 10 Barley Mow Passage, London W4 4PH, ✆ (0181) 742 3355. Lecturer-accompanied cultural tours throughout Spain.

Page & Moy Ltd: 136–140 London Road, Leicester LE2 1EN, ✆ (0116) 250 7000. Cultural guided tours throughout Spain.

Plantagenet Tours: 85 The Grove, Moordown, Bournemouth BH9 2TY, ✆ (01202) 521895. Historical tour every April of Castile, Galicia and Asturias.

Prospect Music & Art Tours Ltd: 454–458 Chiswick High Road, London W4 5TT, ✆ (0181) 995 2151. Fully-escorted tours led by art historians to Andalucía, Santiago, Catalunya, Castile, Madrid and Extremadura.

Saga Holidays (Discover Europe): The Saga Building, Middleburg Square, Folkestone, Kent CT20 1AZ, ✆ (01303) 711111. Guided cultural coach tours for the over 50s.

Specialtours Ltd: 81a Elizabeth Street, London SW1W 9PG, ✆ (0171) 730 2297. Fully-escorted cultural tours to major cities and sites throughout Spain (members of National Art Collections Fund only).

Tandem, Spanish courses and cultural exchanges in Oviedo: Naturlengua, C/ Teodoro Cuesta, I Bajo A 33012 Oviedo, ✆ (98) 529 0739 and San Sebastián: Centro Intercultural Tandem, Apdo. 1075, E-20080 Donostia, ✆ (943) 42 51 57

Walking Tours

Alternative Travel Group: 69–71 Banbury Road, Oxford OX2 6PE, ✆ (01865) 310399. Pilgrimage to Santiago de Compostela on foot or by bike.

Exodus Travel: 9 Weir Road, London SW12 0LT, ✆ (0181) 675 5550. Walking tours throughout Spain.

Explore Worldwide Ltd: 1 Frederick Street, Aldershot, Hants GU11 1LQ, ✆ (01252) 344161. Small-group exploratory holidays and treks in the Picos de Europa and elsewhere.

Ramblers Holidays: Box 43, Welwyn Garden City, Herts AL8 6PQ, ✆ (01707) 331133. Walking tours in the Picos de Europa and Pyrenees.

Sherpa Expeditions: 131a Heston Road, Hounslow, Middlesex TW5 0RD, ✆ (0181) 577 2717/✆ (0181) 572 9788. Eleven-day guided walks in the Picos de Europa.

Waymark Holidays: 44 Windsor Road, Slough, SL1 2EJ, ✆ (01753) 516 477. Guided walks along the Camino de Santiago.

Special-interest Holidays

Andante Travel: Grange Cottage, Winterbourne Dauntsey, Salisbury SP4 6ER, ✆ (01980) 610555. Archaeological and historical study tours of Altamira cave paintings.

Arblaster & Clarke Wine Tours: Clarke House, The Green, West Liss, Hants GU33 6JQ, ✆ (01730) 893344. Tours to the Rioja, Navarra, Jerez and Penedes regions, escorted by a wine expert and with lunches and visits at leading and lesser known *bodegas*.

Naturetrek: Chautara, Highton, Alresford, Hampshire SO24 9RB, ✆ (01962) 733051. Birdwatching and botanical tours in the Picos de Europa, the Pyrenees, Extremadura, Andalucía and Coto Doñana.

Entry Formalities

Passports and Visas

There are no formal entry requirements for EU passport holders travelling to Spain, regardless of the purpose or duration of the visit. If you intend staying for more than 3 months, you must report to the Foreign Nationals Office (*Oficina de Extranjeros*) at the local police station and apply for a community resident's card (*tarjeta de residente comunitario*). If you fly to Gibraltar you'll have no trouble getting into Spain. Holders of US or Canadian passports can enter Spain for up to 90 days without a visa; holders of Australian or New Zealand passports need a visa, available from any Spanish consulate.

Spanish Consulates

Canada: 1 West Mount Square, 1456 Montreal, H3Z 2P9. ✆ (514) 935 5235

Ireland: 17a Merlyn Park, Ballsbridge, Dublin 4, ✆ (1) 691 640

UK: 20 Draycott Place, London SW3 2RZ, ✆ (0171) 589 8989

1a Brooks House, 70 Spring Gdns, Manchester M22 2BQ, ✆ (0161) 236 1233

63 North Castle Street, Edinburgh EH2 3LJ, ✆ (0131) 220 1483

USA: 545 Boylston Street, Boston, MA 02116, ✆ (617) 536 2506

180 North Michigan Avenue, Chicago, IL 60601, ✆ (312) 782 4588

1800 Berins Drive, Houston, TX 77057, ✆ (713) 783 6200

6300 Wilshire Blvd, Los Angeles, CA 90048, ✆ (305) 446 5511

2102 World Trade Centre, 2 Canal St, New Orleans, LA 70130, ✆ (504) 525 4951

150 East 58th Street, New York, NY 10155, ✆ (212) 355 4090

2080 Jefferson Street, San Francisco, CA 94123, ✆ (415) 922 2995

2700 15th Street NW, Washington, DC 20009, ✆ (206) 265 0190

Customs

Spanish customs are usually polite and easy to get through—unless you come through Morocco, when they'll search through everything you own. EU limits of duty free are 1 litre of spirits or 2 litres of liquors (port, sherry or champagne) plus 2 litres of wine and 200 cigarettes. Much larger quantities, bought locally and provided you are travelling between EU countries (up to 10 litres of spirits, 90 litres of wine, 110 litres of beer), can be taken through customs if you can prove that they are for private consumption only.

If coming from the UK or the USA, don't bother to pick up any duty-free alcohol—it's cheaper on the supermarket shelves in Spain. It may be worth buying cigarettes if you are fussy about the flavour of your tobacco.

Getting Around

By Air

Internal flights in Spain are on Iberia, Aviaco, Viva and Binter. These are nationally run and all operate under the Iberia Group umbrella, almost always sharing the same office in the cities. You'll find airports in the following cities: Oviedo, Bilbao, Burgos, A Coruña, Logroño, Pamplona, Santander, Santiago de Compostela, Vigo and Vitoria. Bilbao, the largest city, is logically the main air hub, with about seven daily flights to Madrid and four to Barcelona, as well as a daily flight to Santiago and three a week to Vigo. More typical is Oviedo/Gijón's airport, with several daily flights to Madrid and one or two a week to Santiago, Vitoria and A Coruña.

Prices are inexpensive compared to most of Europe, and if you shop around and are willing to travel at night on slow days you can pick up some bargains, especially if you're going on a round trip. Also, check out the national charters in Spanish travel agencies.

Iberia/Aviaco Bookings and Information

Bilbao: C/ Ercilla 20 ✆ 44 24 43 00, Sondika airport ✆ 44 71 12 10

Vitoria: Avda. Gasteiz 84, ✆ 22 41 42

Gijón: C/ Alfredo Truán 8, ✆ 535 18 46
Oviedo: C/ Ventura Rodríguez 6, ✆ 524 24 46
A Coruña: Plaza de Galicia 6, ✆ 29 38 55
Santiago de Compostela: Calvo Sotelo, ✆ 59 41 04

By Rail

If you're using public transportation, there is usually an even choice between the bus and train. The slight difference in price normally favours the train, while buses can be a bit faster.

Democracy in Spain has made the trains run on time, but western Europe's most eccentric railway, **RENFE**, still has a way to go. The problem isn't the trains themselves; they're almost always clean and comfortable, and do their best to keep to the schedules. Steam engines, country families picnicking on mortadella sandwiches in the aisles, and drunken conductors are now only items for nostalgia, but the new efficient RENFE remains so phenomenally complex it will foul up your plans at least once if you spend much time in Spain.

To start with there are no fewer than 13 varieties of train, from the luxury **TEE** (Trans-Europe Express) to the excruciating *semidirecto* and *ferrobús*. Watch out for these; they stop at every conceivable hamlet to deliver mail. The best are the **Talgo** trains, speedy and stylish beasts in gleaming stainless steel, designed and built entirely in Spain; the Spaniards are very proud of them. **TER** trains are almost as good. Note that a majority of lines are still, incredibly, single-track, so whatever train you take, you'll still have to endure delays for trains coming the other way.

Every variety of train has different services and a different price. RENFE ticket people and conductors can't always get them straight, and confusion is rampant. Prices are never consistent. There are discounts for children (under 4 years old, free; 4–12 pay 50 per cent), large families, senior citizens (50 per cent) and regular travellers, and 25 per cent discounts on *Días Azules* ('blue days') for round trip tickets only. 'Blue days' are posted in the RENFE calendars in every station—really almost every day is a 'blue day'. Interpretations of the rules for these discounts differ from one ticket-window to the next, and you may care to undertake protracted negotiations like the Spaniards do. There is a discount pass for people under 26, the *tarjeta joven*, and BIGE or BIJ youth fares are available from TIVE offices in the large cities. There is also a *tarjeta turística*, similar to the EurRail pass, available to anyone resident outside Spain, with unlimited travel for periods of 8, 15 or 22 days (price depending on period), but again, it's not worth it unless you intend to do extensive travelling.

Every city has a **RENFE travel office** in the centre, and you can make good use of these for information and tickets. Always buy tickets in advance if you can; one of RENFE's little tricks is to close station ticket-windows 10 minutes before your train arrives, and if you show up at the last minute, you could be out of luck. Other stations don't open ticket-windows until the train is a couple of minutes away, causing panic and confusion. Don't rely on the list of trains posted; always ask at the station or travel office. There may well be an earlier train that makes an obscure connection at some place like Medina del Campo, Bobadilla, or Miranda del Ebro, big junctions where several lines cross. Fares average 500 pts for every 100km (63 miles)—750 pts first class—but there are supplements on the faster trains that can raise the price by as much as 80 per cent.

RENFE has plenty of services you'll never hear about—like car transport to all parts of Spain. If you plan to do a lot of riding on the rails, buy the *Guía RENFE*, an indispensable government publication with all the schedules, tariffs, and information, available for a pittance from any station newsagent. It's heavy, but you can always tear out the pages you need. To add to the confusion, northern Spain has two private narrow-gauge railway lines: **FEVE**, which has tracks along the north coast of Spain connecting Bilbao to Oviedo via Santander; and, in Euskadi, the **Eusko Trenbideak** (Basque Railways) connects Bilbao and San Sebastián by way of Zarautz and Zumaya. Both these lines show off rural Spanish life and scenery at their best, and both are fun to ride, though slow and more expensive than the bus.

rail excursions

RENFE has inaugurated a series of special trains especially designed to attract tourists. One of these, the **Transcantábrica,** takes in some of the loveliest parts of northern Spain, including the Picos de Europa. For full details contact Marsans Travel, 7a Henrietta Place, London W1M 9AG, ✆ (0171) 493 4934; the same company in the USA: 205 East 42nd Street, Suite 1514, New York, NY, ✆ (212) 661 6565; or in Spain, contact RENFE direct. The Basque Railways narrow-gauge line maintains an electric train from the 1920s with wooden carriages, and runs it in summer for excursions around San Sebastián; ask at the ET station there for details.

left luggage

After disappearing for many years because of terrorism, left luggage facilities are reappearing in Spanish stations; the word in Spanish is *consigna.*

By Bus

With literally hundreds of companies providing services over Spain, expect confusion. We have included all of the important lines and stations to make things easier. Not all cities have bus stations; in some, such as Vitoria or Bilbao, there may be a dozen little offices spread around town for each firm. Like the trains, buses are cheap by northern European standards but no memorable bargain; if you're travelling on the cheap you'll find that transportation is your biggest expense. Usually, whether you go by train or bus will depend on simple convenience: in some places the train station is far from the centre, in others the bus station is.

Small towns and villages can normally be reached by bus only through their provincial capitals. Buses are usually clean and dependable, and there's plenty of room for baggage in the compartment underneath. On the more luxurious buses you even get air conditioning and a movie (Kung Fu, sappy Spanish flicks from the Franco era or locally produced rock videos). Tourist information offices are the best sources of information. They almost always know every route and schedule.

By City Bus and Taxi

Every Spanish city has a perfectly adequate system of public transportation. You won't need to make much use of it, though, for even in the big cities nearly all the attractions are within walking distance of each other. City buses usually cost 100 pts, and if you intend to use them often there are books of tickets called *abonamientos* or *bono-Bus* or *tarjeta* cards to punch on entry, available at reduced rates from tobacco shops. Bus drivers will give change if you don't have the correct amount (within reason; don't give them a 1000-pts note). In many cities the bus's entire route will be displayed on the signs at each stop (*parada*).

Taxis are still cheap enough for the Spaniards to use them regularly on their shopping trips. The average fare for a ride within a city will be 700–1000 pts. Taxis are metered, and the drivers are usually quite honest; they are entitled to certain surcharges (for luggage, night or holiday trips, to the train or airport, etc.) and if you cross the city limits they can usually charge double the fare shown. It's rarely hard to hail a cab from the street, and there will always be a few around the stations. If you get stuck where there are none, or in a small village, call information for the number of a radio taxi.

By Car

This is probably the most pleasurable way of getting about, though the convenience is balanced by a considerably greater cost; petrol is as expensive in Spain as anywhere else in Europe. In cities, parking is always difficult; another problem is that only a few hotels—the more expensive ones—have garages or any sort of parking. Spaniards may still have a reputation as hotheads behind the wheel, but you will find that northerners potter about rather serenely, and on the whole they are as careful and courteous as you could wish.

Spain's highway network is adequate and in good repair, and many major cities are now linked by dual carriageways. The government is currently investing trillions of pesetas on a full-scale highway system, but until it is completed you will often have to be content with the two-lane roads that blanket the country. The good news is that a proper road is finally being built following the entire length of the northern coast. The bad news is that this difficult undertaking will not be complete for a few years yet—in western Asturias or Galicia, the new road will suddenly disappear, leaving you stranded on a hellish two-lane road little better than a mule track, crammed with heavy trucks. The other motorist's nightmare is the Bilbao area; even if you're just passing through, you'll probably get good and lost among the bizarre topography and endless roadworks. Tolls on the motorways (*autopistas*) are pure highway robbery: about £12 from Bilbao to Burgos, or £8 for the short trip from Bilbao to San Sebastián.

To drive in Spain you'll need an **International Driver's Licence**, available through the AA or RAC in the UK, or any auto club in the USA, and a **green card** proving limited liability insurance, together with a **bail bond**, an extra precaution which your insurance company will provide in case your car is impounded after an accident. Seat belts are mandatory. The speed limit is 100km (62 miles) per hour on national highways, unless otherwise marked, and 120km (75 miles) per hour on motorways.

This is moderately cheaper than elsewhere in Europe. The big international companies are expensive, but ATESA, the government-owned Spanish firm, offers cheaper rates. Prices for the smallest cars begin at about £80 per week with unlimited mileage, but insurance adds considerably to the costs. Small local firms can sometimes offer a better deal, but these should be treated with some caution. Local firms also rent **mopeds** and **bicycles**, especially in tourist areas. **Hitchhiking** involves a long wait anywhere; few Spaniards ever do it.

Ask your travel agent about the 'Tour Spain' package that offers an inclusive price for ATESA car hire and accommodation in any of Spain's *paradores* for seven nights or more. The plan is for a minimum of two people or maximum of four in one car; savings are considerable. Car rental can also be booked through British Airways and Iberia.

Practical A–Z

Fiesta de la Virgen Blanca, Vitoria

Children

Spaniards love children, and they'll welcome yours almost everywhere. Baby foods, etc. are widely available, but don't expect to find babysitters except at the really smart hotels; Spaniards always take their children with them, even if they're up till 4am. Nor are there many special amusement for kids—though these are beginning to spring up with Spain's new prosperity, for better or worse; traditionally Spaniards never thought of their children as separate little creatures who ought to be amused. Ask at a local tourist office for a list of attractions in its area geared towards children.

Climate and When to Go

You get just one guess to figure out what makes the north coast of Spain so luxuriantly green. The Cordillera Cantábrica stops all the weather fronts coming over the Atlantic and squeezes out all the precipitation; the coast gets between three and four inches of rain in *August*—and the real rainy season doesn't start until September. Galicia seems to get a bit less rain than the coastal regions to the east, and the high Castilian plains are climatically another world altogether—hot and dry most of the year, chilly and strange in winter; La Rioja enjoys a more reasonable climate between the two extremes, which is very good for the vines. For the coast as a whole, rain is spread around the calendar; plenty of it from September until January, with July by far the most reliable month (only an inch or two). The rain champion is the Basque coast, which can get seven or eight feet of the stuff a year, as much as Wales or the west of Ireland.

Spring and summer are the best times to visit; the winter can be pleasant, though damp and chill (you'll probably feel more uncomfortable outside than in; Spanish homes—and hotel rooms—are not made for the winter). Even with the rain, the high season is squeezed in between June and September, when the ocean is warm enough for water sports, the fiesta calendar is in full swing and everything is open. The chart below shows the highest and lowest temperatures in °C (°F) you're likely to encounter in each season, along with average rainfall.

Seasonal temperatures in °C (°F)

	Jan		April		July		Oct	
	max	min	max	min	max	min	max	min
San Sebastián	15 (59)	-10 (14)	27 (80)	5 (41)	34 (93)	14 (57)	24 (75)	8 (46)
A Coruña	16 (60)	-3 (27)	25 (77)	6 (42)	27 (80)	14 (57)	26 (78)	8 (46)

Average monthly rainfall in mm (in.)

	Jan	April	July	Oct
San Sebastián	142 (6)	84 (3)	92 (4)	142 (6)
A Coruña	125 (5)	78 (3)	35 (1)	135 (5)

Facilities for disabled travellers are limited within Spain, and public transport is not particularly wheelchair-friendly, though RENFE usually provides wheelchairs at main city stations. You are advised to contact the Spanish Tourist Office, which has compiled a two-page fact sheet and can give general information on accessible accommodation, or any of the organizations that specifically provide services to people with disabilities.

Some Specialist Organizations in Spain

ONCE (Organización Nacional de Ciegos de España), Paseo de la Castellana 95, Planta 28, Madrid, ✆ (91) 597 47 27, is the Spanish association for blind people; they offer a number of services to blind travellers (such as braille maps).

ECOM, Balmes 311, Barcelona, ✆ (93) 200 19 80, the federation of private Spanish organizations offering services for disabled people. Ask for Emilio Grande who speaks good English.

Some Specialist Organizations in the UK

Holiday Care Service, 2 Old Bank Chambers, Station Road, Horley, Surrey RH6 9HW, ✆ (01293) 774535, for travel information and details of accessible accommodation and care holidays. All sites have been visited and assessed by Holiday Care representatives.

RADAR (The Royal Association for Disability and Rehabilitation), Unit 12, City Forum, 250 City Road, London EC1V 8AF, ✆ (0171) 250 3222, has a wide range of travel information.

Royal National Institute for the Blind, 224 Great Portland Street, London W15 5TB, ✆ (0171) 388 1266. Its mobility unit offers a 'Plane Easy' audio-cassette which advises blind people on travelling by plane. It will also advise on accommodation.

Some Specialist Organizations in the US

American Foundation for the Blind, 15 West 16th Street, New York, NY 10011, ✆ (212) 620 2000; toll free ✆ 800 232 5463. The best source of information in the US for visually-impaired travellers.

Federation of the Handicapped, 211 West 14th Street, New York, NY 10011, tel (212) 747 4262. Organizes summer tours for members; there is a nominal annual fee.

Mobility International USA, PO Box 3551, Eugene, OR 97403, ✆ (503) 343 1248, offers a service similar to that of its sister organization in the UK.

SATD (Society for the Advancement of Travel for the Disabled), Suite 610, 347 5th Avenue, New York, NY 10016, ✆ (212) 447 7284, offers advice on all aspects of travel for the disabled, on an ad hoc basis for a $3 charge, or unlimited to members ($45, concessions $25).

Travel Information Center, Moss Rehabilitation Hospital, 1200 West Tabor Road, Philadelphia, PA 19141, ✆ (215) 456 99 00.

Electricity

Current is 225 AC or 220 V, the same as most of Europe. Americans will need converters, and the British will need two-pin adapters for the different plugs. If you plan to stay in the less expensive *hostales*, it may be better to leave your gadgets at home. Some corners of Spain, even some big cities, have pockets of exotic voltage—150 V for example—guaranteeing a brief display of fireworks. Big hotels have the standard current.

Embassies and Consulates

Australia   Paseo de la Castellana 143, Madrid, ✆ (91) 579 0428

Canada   Núñez de Balboa 35, Madrid, ✆ (91) 431 43 00

Ireland   Claudio Coello 73, Madrid, ✆ (91) 576 35 09

New Zealand Plaza de la Lealtad 2, Madrid, ✆ (91) 523 02 26

UK   Calle de Fernando el Santo 16, Madrid, ✆ (91) 319 02 00

US   Calle Serrano 75, Madrid, ✆ (91) 577 40 00, consular office for passports, around the corner at Paseo de la Castellana 52

Entertainment and Nightlife

Bars and **cafés** soak up most of the Spaniards' leisure time. These are wonderful institutions, where you can eat breakfast or linger over a glass of beer until 4 in the morning; in any of them you could see an old sailor delicately sipping his camomile tea next to a young mother, baby under her arm, stopping in for a beer break during her shopping. If you aren't familiar with a town, walking into any of them can be an adventure. Some bars put on Parisian airs; others, including the *chigres* (another word for *sidrerías* in Asturias) are resolutely proletarian. Some have great snacks, or tapas, some have pinball machines or digital one-armed bandits, doling out electronic versions of *La Cucaracha* whenever they get lonely. Some keep the music on, while others have no tape player and are dedicated to serious snacking, newspaper reading and coffee drinking. Where there's music, you may hear gormless, saccharine Spanish rock, but then again you may hear Django Reinhardt or Camarrón or Celia Cruz or arias from the *zarzuela* (operettas from the Madrid stage); you will probably never have to suffer East 17 or the Beach Boys, which is an important reason for visiting Spain in the first place. Out along the highways you will find hundreds of truck-stop bars in lonely settings, where you can eat a factory-made doughnut and a Coke and pretend you're in Oklahoma.

At night, some bars will have live music—jazz, rock or flamenco, or maybe *salsa* in the styles of Colombia, Cuba and New York, an increasingly popular genre here. Many nighttime bars and clubs are totally invisible in the day, exploding into blue-light noise palaces punctually from midnight until 6 am. This is the twilight world of *la marcha* , the all-night pub crawl of Madrid and Barcelona that finds a reflection in any Spanish city, especially if it has a university. Spots that stay open late tend to congregate in one area of the city centre, accompanied by a few restaurants to satisfy nocturnal binges. Cities that can nourish a proper *marcha* include Santander, San Sebastián, Oviedo, Santiago, A Coruña, Pontevedra, Pamplona and León. Industrial, hard-working Bilbao does its best, while Burgos and Vigo are a little too staid to try very hard at all.

Discos and **night clubs** are easily found in the big cities and tourist spots; most tend to be expensive. Ask around for the current favourites, which change as quickly as those in New York or Paris. Watch out for posters for **concerts** and **ballets**; every year brings more acts to the touristy cities. Santander and San Sebastián in particular are known for their music festivals.

Also keep an eye open for **circuses**. The little travelling Spanish troupes with their family acts, tents, tinsel and names like 'The National Circus of Japan' will charm you; they often gravitate to the major fiestas throughout the summer. Beyond the slot machines in the bars and petrol stations, there will be plenty of other opportunities to lose money pointlessly. Every Spaniard is a gambler; there seem to be an infinite number of lotteries run by the State (the *Lotería Deportiva*), for the blind (ONCE), the Red Cross, or the church, and there are casinos in major resorts.

Festivals

One of the most spiritually deadening aspects of Francoism was the banning of many local and regional fiestas. These are now celebrated with gusto, and if you can arrange your itinerary to include one or two you'll be guaranteeing an unforgettable holiday. Besides those listed below, there are literally thousands of others, and new ones spring up all the time.

The big holidays celebrated throughout Spain are *Corpus Christi* in late May; Holy Week (*Semana Santa*), the week preceding Easter; 15 August, the Assumption of the Virgin and 25 July, the feast day of Spain's patron, Santiago. No matter where you are, there are bound to be fireworks or processions on these dates, especially for *Semana Santa* and *Corpus Christi*. Beware that dates for most festivals tend to be fluid, flowing towards the nearest weekend; if the actual date falls on a Thursday or a Tuesday, Spaniards 'bridge' the fiesta with the weekend to create a four-day whoopee. If there's a fiesta you want to attend, check the date at the tourist office in advance.

Many village patronal fiestas feature *romerías* (pilgrimages) up to a venerated shrine. Getting there is half the fun, with everyone in local costume, riding on horseback or driving covered wagons full of picnic supplies. Music, dancing, food, wine and fireworks are all necessary ingredients of a proper fiesta, while the bigger ones often include bullfights, funfairs, circuses and competitions. In the Basque lands and Navarra, summer fiestas often feature a loose bull or two stampeding through the streets—an *encierro*. 'Giants' (10ft-tall dummies of Fernando and Isabel and a Moor) and 'fat-heads' (comical or grotesque caricatures) pirouette through the throngs and tease the children.

Semana Santa is a major tourist event, though not as much as in southern Spain; unless you're prepared to fight the crowds to see the *pasos* (ornate floats depicting scenes from the Passion) carried in an excruciatingly slow march to lugubrious tuba music, and accompanied by children and men decked out in costumes later copied by the Ku Klux Klan, you may want to skip it; the real revelry takes place after Easter.

The listing below is hardly complete: during the summer every village has its own special fiesta, with a wheezing brass band to serenade the statue of the patron saint on his or her annual airing through the streets, a few bulls or heifers to chase the young bloods in the street, a market and fun fair (with the volume of the latest disco or techno hits turned up full blast), food and dancing into the night and perhaps even some fireworks if the Ayuntamiento's pot is full of *pesetas*.

Note that many of these dates are subject to change (to fit weekends, etc.); a call ahead to the tourist office is always a good idea.

Calendar of Events

January

1	Huge livestock fair, **Betanzos** (A Coruña)
6	*Los Reyes* (the three Magi) procession, **Baiona** (Pontevedra)
15	San Mauro, big fiesta with fireworks, **Villanova de Arousa** (Pontevedra)
19–20	**San Sebastián**'s *Tamborrada*, marches of the Basque pipe-and-drum corps.
20	San Lesmes, patron of **Burgos**
Third Sunday	San Vicente, bachelors' party at **Los Arcos** (Navarra)
22	Fiesta at **San Vicente de la Barquera** (Cantabria)
28	San Tirso, with dances and the burning of a paper maché *falla*, in **Villafranca del Bierzo** (León)
End January	**Ituren** and **Zubieta** (Navarra), dances of the *ioaldunak* with pointed hats, fur vests, and big bells.

February

Carnival: Feb/ early March	A big affair anywhere in Spain. Some of the biggest are in Bilbao, San Sebastián, Vitoria and Tolosa. The entire week before Lent, Asturias puts on the biggest show in the northwest: at **Avilés** on Saturday and Tuesday; at **Gijón** on Monday; and in **Oviedo** on Tuesday, or Mardi Gras, the day before Ash Wednesday

March

1	Fiesta de San Rosendo, **Celanova** (Ourense)
Two Sundays after the 4th	The *Javierada*, two important pilgrimages for St Francis Xavier at **Javier** (Navarra)

April

Palm Sunday	Procession at Monte San Tecla, **A Garda** (Pontevedra)
Semana Santa (Holy Week)	In the north, it's the Castilians who really get into the processions, especially at **León** and **Covarrubias** (Burgos). In **Avilés** (Asturias), Easter and Easter Monday are celebrated with the **Fiesta del Bollo**, with folklore groups, cake eating and regattas.
	Good Friday brings *Los Picaos*, medieval style self-flagellants, **San Vicente de la Sonsierra** (La Rioja); Descent from the Cross, **Vivero** (Lugo); mystery play, **Balsameda** (Vizcaya), processions in **Fuenterrabía** and **Segura** (Guipúzcoa)
19	Festival of Santísimo Cristo, **Finisterre** (A Coruña)
First Sun Easter	**San Vicente de Barquera**'s *La Folía*, where the sailors transport an after image of the Virgin at night in an illuminated maritime procession (Cantabria)
2nd Sun after Easter	Fiesta de San Isidoro, **León**
2nd Mon after Easter	Fiesta de San Telmo, **Tui** (Pontevedra)
25	San Marcos, **Noia** (A Coruña)
End of month	Wine Festival, **Ribadavia** (Ourense)

May

10–15	Saint's day and parades, **Santo Domingo de la Calzada** (La Rioja)
22	Santa Rita, **Vilagarcía de Arousa** (Pontevedra)
23	Anniversary of the battle of **Clavijo** (La Rioja)
Corpus Christi	usually falls at the end of May or early June (Thursday after Trinity Sunday), initiating four days of festivities. Also, *Procesión del Olé*, with dances, **Frómista** (Palencia); Flower carpets in the streets, **Ponteareas** (Pontevedra). On the first day after Corpus Christi, Los Corpillos dances and celebrations at Las Huelgas, **Burgos**; Maragato festivals, **Astorga** (León) and around

June

11	San Bernabé, with the distribution of grilled fish, **Logroño** (La Rioja)
12	San Juan, with *encierros*, giants and Maragato bagpipers, **Sahagún** (León)
21–24	San Juan, bonfires and fishwives' festivities in **Laredo** (Cantabria); La Magdalena, with Basque sports, **Bermeo** (Vizcaya), followed by a

	nautical *romería* to the isle of Izaro. For midsummer's day, 'bonfires of San Juan' in many Basque villages. **León** celebrates St John's Day with parties and bullfights, bonfire in Plaza Alfonso II, **Oviedo** (Asturias)
24	Vueltas de San Juan, **Nájera** (La Rioja); Fiesta de San Juan, **Laguardia** (Álava)
26	Fiesta de San Pelayo, **Zarautz** (Guipúzcoa)
29	Wine battle, **Haro** (La Rioja)
End June	San Felices de Bilibio at **Haro** (La Rioja), pilgrimage and drunken 'wine battles'. **Cudillero** (Asturias), *La Amuravela*, satirical poems on the year's events in the local dialect and lots of drink.
29	**Burgos**, San Pedro, beginning of two weeks of International Folklore Feria. Fiesta de San Pedro, **Orio** (Guipúzcoa)
30	*El Coso Blanco*, processions and fireworks, in **Castro Urdiales** (Cantabria); fiesta of San Marcial, **Irún** (Guipúzcoa)

July

All month	**Santander** holds its International Music Festival
First Sunday	*Rapa das Bestas*, (Gallego wild horse round-ups, races and shearings) **Viveiro** (Lugo) and **San Lorenzo de Sabucedo** (Lugo). **Zumaya** (Euskadi), Basque sports and dancing by the sea. At **La Estrada** (Pontevedra), another *Rapa das Bestas*, with big festivities from Saturday till Monday.
7–14	**Pamplona** (Navarra) the famous running of the bulls and mad party for San Fermín.
11	San Benitiño de Lérez, with river races and pagentry, **Pontevedra** (Galicia)
15	**Comillas** (Cantabria), 'catch the goose' and other country fair-type festivities and humour. **Avilés** (Asturias) has dances, entertainment and bullfights.
Last half	Historical sound and light pageant, **Nájera** (La Rioja)
16	Virgen del Carmen with boat processions, **Muros** and **Concubión** (A Coruña)
Third Week	Jazz festival, **Vitoria**
Around last 10 days	International Jazz Festival, the biggest in Spain, **San Sebastián**
22	**Anguiano** (La Rioja), fiesta with the dance of the *Zancos*, down the streets and steps on stilts; **Bermeo** (Vizcaya), boat races, Basque sports and dancing. Fiesta de Santa María Magdalena, **Rentería** (Guipúzcoa).

24	**Tudela** (Navarra), music and dancing for a week for Santa Ana
25	**Santiago de Compostela**, great celebrations for Santiago—national offering to the saint, the swinging of the *Botafumeiro*, burning of a cardboard replica of Córdoba's Mezquita, fireworks and more; Romería de Saniaguiño do Monte, with bagpipes and a sardine and pepper feast, **Padrón** (A Coruña); **Cangas de Onís** (Asturias), shepherds' festival. Also **Vitoria** and **Bilbao**'s saint's day, Santiago
Last Sunday	Fiesta de la Playa, **Langosteira** (Finisterre); *Fiesta de los Vaqueros*, La Brana de Aristebano, by **Luarca** (Asturias)
29	**Luarca** (Asturias), Vaqueiro festival, mock wedding and dances; **Santa María de Ribarteme** (Pontevedra), pilgrimage made in coffins by people who narrowly escaped death the year before. Octopus-eating festival, **Villanova de Arousa** (Pontevedra) Fiesta de San Pedro, **Mundaka** (Vizcaya)
31	Fiesta de San Ignacio, **Getxo** (Vizcaya) and **Azpetia** (Guipúzcoa)

August

Throughout month	International Music Festival, **Santander**
3–9	**Estella** (Navarra), ancient fiesta, with giants and the only *encierro* where women can run with the bulls
First Sat	**Arriondas-Ribadesella** (Asturias), great kayak race on the Río Sella
First Sun	**Gijón**, Asturias Day celebrations, with lots of folklore. Festival of Albariño wine, **Cambados** (Pontevedra); Santa Cruz, at **Ribadeo** (Lugo)
5–10	**Vitoria**, giants, music, bonfires and more for the Virgen Blanca—one of Spain's best parties (*see* p.153).
6	Fiesta de San Salvador, **Getaria** (Guipúzcoa)
10	San Juan Dantzak, procession and traditional dancing at **Berástegui** (Guipúzcoa)
9–11	**Foz** (Lugo), San Lorenzo festivities, folklore and kayaking
Second Sun	**Cabezón de la Sal** (Cantabria), Mountain Day folklore, song contests; **Carballino** (Ourense), octopus-eating festival and bagpipe music. Romería to the Ermita de Oca, **Villafranca de Montes de Oca** (La Rioja)
15–16	Assumption of the Virgin and San Roque festivities at: **Sada** (A Coruña) with a big sardine roast, also fiesta de San Roque at **Gernika** (Vizcaya); **Llanes** (Asturias), bagpipes and ancient dances; on the Saturday after the 15th, **Bilbao** has its *Aste Nagustia* ('Great Week'), with Basque sports and races; International Fireworks festival, **San Sebastián**; *El Rosario*, fisherman's fiesta, **Luarca** (Asturias)

15–19	Battle of flowers at **Betanzos** (A Coruña)
Third week	San Zoilo, **Carrión de los Condes** (Palencia)
25	San Ginés, **Sangenxo** (Pontevedra)
Last Sunday	**Vivero** (Lugo), pilgrimage and music; *encierro*, **Calahorra** (La Rioja)
31	**Loyola** (Guipúzcoa), St Ignacio de Loyola Day; Battle of Flowers, **Laredo** (Cantabria)

September

First week	**San Sebastián**, Basque food festival
2	**Lekeitio** (Vizcaya), Basque 'goose games', including contest to pull the head off a goose with a greased neck
6–10	Fiestas del Portal, **Ribadavia** (Ourense)
7–10	Pilgrimage of Nostra Señora da Barca, **Muxía** (A Coruña)
7–8	*Encierro*, **Ampuero** (Cantabria)
8	Fiesta of the Virgin of Guadalupe, **Fuenterrabía** (Guipúzcoa); Fiesta de la Virgen de la Encina, **Ponferrada** (León); pilgrimage at **Cebreiro** (Lugo); San Andreu, **Cervo** (Lugo)
8–10	Fiesta of Santa Eufemia at **Bermeo** (Vizcaya)
8	Virgin's Birthday with celebrations in many places
12	**San Sebastián**, International Film Festival
2nd week	**Zarautz** (Euskadi), Basque fun and games
16	Folk festival, **Llanes** (Asturias)
19	**Oviedo**, big Americas Day celebration, wtih floats and bands from all over Latin America; **Logroño** has the *Vendimia* wine festival of La Rioja
Third weekend	Americas Day, celebrating the many immigrants to the Americas from Asturias, **Oviedo**
Last weekend	San Cosme y San Damián, with antique dances, **Covarrubias** (Burgos)
27	Theft of the saints procession, **Arnedo** (La Rioja)
29	Fiesta de San Miguel, **Oñati** (Guipúzcoa), traditional Basque dancing at **Markina** (Vizcaya)

October

First Sunday	*Las Cantaderas*, with medieval song and a sacred dance, **León**
Second Sunday	Shellfish festival, **O Grove** (Pontevedra)
13	Fiesta de San Fausto, **Durango** (Vizcaya)
18–20	**Mondoñedo** (Lugo), *As San Lucas*, big horse fair dating from the Middle Ages

November

11	Fiesta de San Martín, **Bueu** (Galicia)
19	Fiesta de San Andrés, **Estella** (Navarra)
Last Sunday	Oyster festival, **Arcade** (Pontevedra)

December

6	San Nicolás Obispillo, **Segura** (Guipúzcoa)
13	Santa Lucía fair, **Zumárraga** (Guipúzcoa)
21	Santo Tomás fair, with processions, **San Sebastián**, **Bilbao**, **Azpeitia**
Last week	*O Feitoman*, handicrafts fair, **Vigo** (Pontevedra); *Olentzero* processions in many Basque villages
31	The National Offering to the Apostle—a major religious ceremony with the *botafumeiro* in **Santiago de Compostela**

Food and Drink

Eating Out

The massive influx of tourists has had its effect on Spanish kitchens, but so has the Spaniards' own increased prosperity and, perhaps most significantly, the new federalism. Each region, each town even, has come to feel a new interest and pride in the things that set it apart, and food is definitely one of them. The best restaurants are almost always those specializing in regional cuisine, though at the upmarket end of the scale you'll find plenty of new restaurants with innovative dishes heavily influenced by what the Basques call their *cocina nueva*—as with French *nouvelle cuisine* expect a lot of surprising combinations, peculiar sauces and an obsession with appearances. There are still thousands of old-fashioned restaurants around—and many of the sort that travellers have been complaining about for centuries; Spanish cooking still usually comes a bit on the heavy side. The worst offenders are often those with the little flags and ten-language menus in the most touristy areas, and in general you'd do better to buy some bread, Cabrales cheese and a bottle of Rioja red and have a picnic. But the regions along the northern coast have a repertoire of traditional dishes as gratifying as any in the country, and seafood is undoubtedly the star of the show.

The Atlantic has much more and better seafood than has the Mediterranean, and the ardent fishermen of Spain's northern coast are perfectly positioned to nab the best of it. They have plenty of practice cooking the stuff—archaeologists have found remains of sea urchins in settlements 10,000 years old. The bounty of the sea finds expression in famous fish soups from the western *caldereta Asturiana* to the Basque *ttoro*, and there are any number of prized delicacies in every region: surprising things like *cocochas*, 'cheeks' of the hake, or Galician *vieiras de Santiago*, scallops cooked with almonds. On the whole though, Spaniards try to keep their seafood simple. Galicians like to cook fish with potatoes and garlic; Basques do it with simple garlic and parsley sauces. In any coastal town or village, the best seafood restaurants will be around the harbour. The fancier ones will post set menus, while at the rest you'll find only a chalkboard with prices listed for a plate of grilled fish, or prawns or whatever else came in that day. It's a convivial arrangement; just choose a plate, or negotiate a full dinner with the waiter. Don't expect seafood to be a bargain though; a plate of prawns in garlic all by itself usually goes for about 800–1000 pts.

By popular acclaim, the champion cooks of northern Spain—really of all Spain—are the Basques. They shine with seafood of all kinds, and they are fond of red peppers, cider and a light green wine called *txakoli*; a full discussion of such matters can be found on p.125. The Galicians too have their talents in the kitchen, with the best of the best seafood, including some delicacies found nowhere else in the world (*see* p.272).

Inland, though you'll still find plenty of seafood, the cuisine is an entirely different world. Cooking can be heavy, almost medieval, with plenty of roasts and chops, stews and game dishes—partridge and pheasant are special favourites. Local dishes include *cochinillo asado* (roast sucking-pig), the most prized speciality of Castile, *chuletas de cordero a la navarra* (lamb chops), *truchas con jamón* (trout stuffed with ham) or, for something out of the ordinary, *liebres con chocolate* (hare with chocolate), washed down by the good strong wines from Tudela and Estella. Asturias and Cantabria are the dairylands of Spain, and produce a number of cheeses, notably the *Cabrales* of Asturias, made from cow's, sheep's and goat's milk all mixed together. Asturias has its famous dishes too, including hake in *sidra* (the ubiquitous local cider) or *fabada*, an enchanting mess of beans usually served with pork.

If you dine where the locals do you'll be assured of a good deal if not necessarily a good meal. Almost every restaurant offers a *menú del día*, or a *menú turístico*, featuring an appetizer, a main course, dessert, bread and drink at a set price, always a certain percentage lower than if you had ordered the items *à la carte*. These are always posted outside the restaurant, in the window or on the plywood chef by the door; decide what you want before going in if it's a set-price menu, because these bargains are hardly ever listed on the menu the waiter gives you at the table. Unless it's explicitly written on the bill (*la cuenta*), service is *not* included in the total, so tip accordingly.

Tapas Bars and Cafeterías

Going to Spain, you may have to learn to eat all over again; dining is a much more complex affair here than in many countries. The essential fact to learn is that Spaniards like to eat *all day long*—this scheme spreads the gratification evenly through the day, and it facilitates digestion, which in Spain can be problematic. Give it some consideration. Start out with a big coffee, a *doble in vaso* and a pastry (mostly French clones, with extra sugar) or find a progressive-looking bar where you might find a more fitting breakfast—a glass of wine or brandy, and a salami sandwich or *pincho*, or a glazed American doughnut. These bars will be around all day, their piles of treats under the glass cases on the bar growing by the hour, an eternal alternative to a heavy sit-down dinner. Ask around for the one that does seafood tapas. As if the bars weren't enough, there are *pastelerías* in the towns with all sorts of savoury pastries, *merenderos* (snack stands) in the countryside, and ice cream everywhere. You will never be more than a hundred feet from ice cream in a Spanish town. For a mid-morning or mid-afternoon energizer, there are sweet n' greasy *churros* (those inscrutable fried things that look like garden slugs) sold in bars and *churrerías*, dipped in thick cups of rich chocolate, for most non-Spaniards a once in a lifetime gut-gurgling experience.

If you are travelling on a budget you may want to eat one of your meals a day at a **tapas bar** or **tasca**. Tapas (*caxuelitas* in Basque) means 'lids', and they started out as little saucers of goodies served on top of a drink; along with these go *pinchos*, a word for any kind of small sandwich or hors d'oeuvre. They have evolved over the years to form a main part of the world's greatest snack culture. Bars that specialize in them have platter after platter of delectable titbits, from shelfish to slices of omelette or mushrooms baked in garlic or vegetables in vinaigrette or stews. All you have to do is pick out what looks best and order a *porción* (an hors d'oeuvre) or a *ración* (a big helping) if it looks really good. It's hard to generalize about prices, but on average 1000 pts of tapas and wine or beer really fill you up. You can always save money in bars by standing up; sit at that charming table on the terrace and prices can jump considerably.

Another advantage of tapas is that they're available at what most Americans or Britons would consider normal dining hours. Spaniards are notoriously late diners; in the morning it's a coffee and roll grabbed at the bar, a huge meal at around 2 or 3pm, then after work at 8pm a few tapas at the bar to hold them over until supper at 10 or 11pm. After living in Spain for a few months this makes perfect sense, but it's exasperating to the average visitor. On the coasts, restaurants tend to open earlier to accommodate foreigners (some as early as 5pm) but you may as well do as the Spaniards do. Galicians are the early diners of Spain (8 or 9pm); Basques do it from 9 to 11—if you can find a restaurant at all. In non-touristy areas they will be inconspicuous and few. Just ask someone, and you will find a nice *comedor* with home cooking tucked in a back room behind a bar—if you hadn't asked you never would have found it.

Such **comedores** (literally, dining-rooms), where the food and décor are usually equally drab but cheap, are common everywhere, along with **cafeterías**, those places that feature photographs of their *platos combinados* (combination plates) to eliminate any language problem. Dinner will go for between 800 and 1200 pts, and you'll find as many good ones as real stinkers. **Asadores** are restaurants that specialize in roast meat or fish; **maris-querías** serve only fish and shellfish. Try and visit one in the country on a Sunday lunchtime when all the Spanish families go out to eat and make merry.

There are also many **Chinese restaurants** in Spain which are fairly good and inexpensive (though all pretty much the same), and **American fast-food outlets** in the big cities and resort areas; while Italian restaurants are 98 per cent dismal in Spain, you can get a good pizza in many places. Don't neglect the rapidly disappearing shacks on the beach—they often serve up roast sardines that are out of this world. Vegetarians are catered for in the cities, which always manage to come up with one or two veggie restaurants, usually rather good ones too. In the countryside and away from the main resorts, proper vegetarians and vegans will find it hard going, though tapas make it easier to get your nutrition than in some other southern European countries. Fish-eaters will manage just about everywhere. Menu and restaurant vocabulary are included in the 'language' section at the end of the book.

Prices quoted in the 'Eating Out' sections throughout this book are for a three-course meal, including wine:

expensive	over 4000 pts
moderate	2000–4000 pts
cheap	under 2000 pts

Often we've just put in the price of the set menus; in those cases, it's safe to double it for the price of an average à la carte meal.

Drink

No matter how much other costs have risen in Spain, **wine** has remained refreshingly inexpensive by northern European or American standards; what's more, the northwest produces much of Spain's best—the famous reds of La Rioja and a number of good whites from Galicia. A restaurant's *vino del lugar* or *vino de la casa* is always your least expensive option while dining out; it usually comes out of a barrel or glass jug and may be a surprise either way.

There are 30 areas in Spain under the control of the *Instituto Nacional de Denominaciones de Origen (INDO)*, which acts as a guide to the consumer and keeps a strict eye on the quality of Spanish wine (*DO*, or *denominación de origen*, is the same as French AOC). *La Rioja* is the best known and richest area for wine in Spain, producing a great range from young whites to heavy, fruity reds; its *vino de gran reserva* spends three years ageing in American oak barrels, and then another in bottles, before release to the public. Look for the fine Viña Cumbrero '85 and Monte Real '85, and the aristocratic Marqués de Villamanga '73. La Rioja is divided into several sub-districts, including the *Rioja Alavesa*, in the Basque province of Álava north of the Ebro. East of Logroño, there is an extension of the La Rioja wine belt in Navarra; *DO Navarra* has some excellent reds (Magaña Merlot '85).

Euskadi is known for its very palatable young 'green' wine called *Txacoli* (not yet a *DO*), which is poured into the glass with bravura from a height like cider. Txakoli is made along the coast, around Getaria and Zarautz, as well as in small regions in Vizcaya and Álava provinces. In addition, there is a small, recently declared *DO* region around León, *El Bierzo*, with light and fruity reds (Casar de Valdaiga is a good one). Galicia's excellent *Ribeíro* (west of Ourense), made from aromatic Albarino grapes, resembles the delicate *vinho verde* of neighbouring Portugal; other good wines from the region are *Rías Baixas* (areas on the coast near Pontevedra, and south of Vigo on the Portuguese border), and *Valdeorros* (east of Ourense), pleasant light vintages that complement the regional dishes, seafood in particular.

Of course you'll find plenty of other Spanish wines present. Much of the inexpensive wine sold throughout the country comes from *La Mancha* or the neighbouring *Valdepeñas DO* regions. And then there is *Jerez*, or what we in English call sherry. When a Spaniard invites you to *tomar una copa* (glass) it will nearly always be filled with this Andalucían sunshine. It comes in a wide range of varieties: *manzanillas* are very dry, *fino* is dry, light and young (the most famous is *Tío Pepe*); *amontillados* are a bit sweeter and rich; *olorosos* are very sweet dessert sherries, and can be either brown, cream or *amoroso*.

Spanish brandy (mostly from Jerez too) is excellent; the two most popular brands, *103* (very light in colour) and *Soberano*, are both drunk extensively by Spanish labourers and postmen about 7am. *Anís* (sweet or dry) is also quite popular. *Sangría* is the famous summertime punch of red wine, brandy, mineral water, orange and lemon with ice, but beware—it's rarely made very well, even when you can find it. Each region has its wine and liqueur specialities and nearly every monastery in Spain seems to make some kind of herbal potion or digestive liqueur that tastes more or less like cough syrup.

In the areas in this book north of the Cordillera Cantábrica, where apples grow better than vines, they produce hard **cider**, or *sidra*, which can come as a shock to the tastebuds in the first five minutes, and then goes down just fine. One bottle is usually enough if you mean to do any walking afterwards. Cider means as much to Asturians as milk to babies, and the ritual of drinking it can make your evening. In any proper restaurant the waiter will hold the bottle over his head and pour it into a pint glass held behind his hip. The ones with the most *duende* do it without looking, splashing the stuff all over you, the floor, themselves, and people at three or four adjacent tables. This is done to air the stuff out; for the same reason they never put more than an inch in the glass, but it's a point of honour among them never to let your glass stay empty longer than fifteen seconds. In most bars they'll just leave the bottle (green, without a label and returnable) on the table and let you try it yourself. *Sidrerías* are the social centres of every Asturian town and village; to find one just follow your nose. In summer they migrate out onto the streets, and whole families gab around them until one in the morning, with small children bicycling between the tables. Basques are fond of cider too, and claim to have invented it, but among them it is not quite the cult it is with the Asturianos.

Many Spaniards prefer **beer**, which is generally nondescript. The most popular brand is *San Miguel*, but try *Mahou* Five Star if you see it. Imported whisky and other spirits are pretty inexpensive, though even cheaper are the versions Spain bottles itself, which may come close to your home favourites. Coffee, tea, all the international soft-drink brands and the locally-made *Kas* round off the average café fare. Spanish coffee is good and strong and if you want a lot of it order a *doble* in a *vaso*; one of those will keep you awake even through the guided tour of a Bourbon palace. In summer look for the bars that make *blanco y negros*—coffee and ice cream treats that quickly become addictive in the hot sun. Ground almonds whipped to create *horchata de chufa* are also refreshing in summer.

Official Classification of Spanish Vintages

District	80	81	82	83	84	85	86	87	88	89	90	91	92	93	94
Navarra	A	A	E	VG	VG	G	G	G	—	VG	G	G	G	VG	VG
Rías Baixas (Galicia)									G	E	G	G	G	G	G
Ribeiro (Galicia)									G	VG	G	G	G	A	—
Ribera del Duero (Castile)	G	E	VG	VG	A	VG	VG	G	VG	E	G	VG	G	A	VG
Rioja	G	VG	E	G	A	G	G	VG	G	G	G	VG	G	G	E

P: poor A: average G: good VG: very good E: excellent —: statistics not available
Source: Instituto Nacional de Denominaciones de Origen (INDO).

Health and Insurance

There is now a standard EU agreement for citizens of EU countries, entitling you to a certain amount of free medical care, but it's not straightforward. You must complete all the necessary paperwork before you go to Spain, and allow a couple of months to make sure it comes through in time. Ask for a leaflet called *Before You Go* from the Department of Health and fill out form E111, which on arrival in Spain you must take to the local office of the *Instituto Nacional de Seguridad Social*, where you'll be issued with a Spanish medical card and some vouchers enabling you to claim free treatment from an INSS doctor. At time of writing the government is trying to implement a much easier system. In an emergency, ask to be taken to the nearest *hospital de la seguridad social*. Before resorting to a *médico* (doctor) and his £20 ($34) fee (ask at the tourist office for a list of English-speaking doctors), go to a pharmacy and tell them your woes. Spanish *farmacéuticos* are highly skilled and if there's a prescription medicine that you know will cure you, they'll often supply it without a doctor's note. (*El País* and the other national newspapers list *farmacías* in large cities that stay open all night, and most pharmacies post a rota card in the window with the addresses.)

No inoculations are required to enter Spain, though it never hurts to check that your tetanus jab is up-to-date, as well as some of the more exotic inoculations (typhoid and cholera) if you want to venture on into Morocco. The tap water is safe to drink in Spain, but at the slightest twinge of queasiness, switch to the bottled stuff.

You may want to consider travel insurance, available through most travel agents. For a small monthly charge, not only is your health insured, but your bags and money as well, and some will even refund a missed charter flight if you're too ill to catch it. Be sure to save all doctor's receipts (you'll have to pay cash on the spot), pharmacy receipts, and police documents (if you're reporting a theft).

Maps

Cartography has been an art in Spain since the 12th-century Catalans charted their Mediterranean Empire in Europe's first great school of map-making. The tourist offices hand out beautifully detailed maps of every town. Unfortunately, for rural areas you will not find the detail you need for serious exploration of the countryside and signposting isn't all it could be. All the maps available in Britain and America simply aren't very good, and you won't find much better general maps in Spain itself. On most, the road system in particular will be out of date, thanks to Spain's ambitious road improvement programmes.

If in London, visit Stanfords at 12 Long Acre, WC2 for the biggest selection. In Spain, find a big bookstore that stocks the IGN (*Instituto Geográfico Nacional*) maps, comparable to the Ordnance Survey or US Geodetic Survey map; they come in several different scales.

Media

The Socialist *El País* is Spain's biggest and best national newspaper, though circulation is painfully low. Spaniards just don't read newspapers; *¡Hola!*—the Spanish version of *Hello!*—and the little magazine with television listings and scandals are by far and away the best-selling periodicals. Films are cheap, and the Spaniards are some of the world's great cinema-goers, and though half of the great cinemas have been converted into discos, others are still magnificent. There are also lots of cheap outdoor movie theatres in the summer. Look for new films by Carlos Saura (*Carmen, Blood Wedding, El Dorado*), who is regarded as Buñuel's natural successor, or Victor Erice, or most incredibly, Marx Brothers movies dubbed in Spanish. The bright new light is Pedro Almodóvar (*Women on the Verge of a Nervous Breakdown; Tie Me Up! Tie Me Down!*).

The other big papers are *Diario 16* (centrist), *ABC* (conservative, in a bizarre '60s magazine format), and the *Alcázar* (neo-fascist). Major British newspapers are usually available in all tourist areas and big cities in summer; the American New York *Herald Tribune*, the *Wall Street Journal*, and the awful *USA Today* are harder to find. Most hit the newsstands a day late; issues of *Time* and *Newsweek* often hang about, fading in the sun, till they find a home.

Money

Spanish **currency** comes in notes of 1000, 2000, 5000 and 10,000 *pesetas* (pts), all in different colours, and coins of 1, 5, 10, 25, 50, 100, 200 and 500 pts. There are several different styles of each in circulation, which can be confusing. Don't be surprised to see Generalísimo Franco's scowling mug staring at you from the older coins. At street markets and in out-of-the-way places, you may hear prices given in *duros* or *notas*. A *duro* is a 5-pts piece, and a *nota* is a 100-pts piece.

Exchange rates vary of course, but unless any drastic changes occur, £1 is 190 pts, and $1 equivalent to 115 pts. Spain's city centres seem to have a bank on every street corner, and most of them will exchange money; look for the CAMBIO or EXCHANGE signs and the little flags. Beware of private exchange offices in tourist areas (one chain, called *Exact Change*, charges a hefty 9.5 per cent commission on all transactions). You can sometimes change money at travel agencies, fancy hotels, restaurants and big department stores like El Corte Inglés. There are 24-hour *cambios* at most of the big train stations. Wiring money from overseas entails no special difficulties; just give yourself two weeks to be on the safe side, and work through one of the larger institutions (Banco Central, Banco de Bilbao, Banco Español de Crédito, Banco Hispano Americano, Banco de Santander, Banco de Vizcaya). All transactions have to go through Madrid.

Credit cards will not necessarily be helpful for purchases unless you rent cars, fly a lot, or patronize the most expensive hotels and restaurants; perhaps the handiest way to keep yourself in cash is by using the automatic bank tellers that have appeared on every street-corner in most towns and gorge out thousands of pesetas as long as you can remember your PIN number. A Eurocheque card will make your British bank cheques good, though it may not be easy. **Travellers' cheques**, if they are from one of the major companies, will pass at most bank exchanges.

Opening Hours

Most **banks** are open Mon–Thurs 8.30–4.30, Fri 8.30–2 and Sat (sometimes) 8.30–1.

Most of the less important **churches** are always closed. Some cities probably have more churches than faithful communicants, so many churches are unused. If you're determined to see one, it will never be hard to find the *sacristán* or caretaker. Usually they live close by, and would be glad to show you around for a tip. Don't be surprised when cathedrals and famous churches charge for admission—just consider the cost of upkeep.

Shops usually open from 9.30am. Spaniards take their main meal at 2pm and, except in the larger cities, most shops close for 2–3 hours in the afternoon, usually from 1pm or 2pm. In the evening most establishments stay open until 7pm or 8pm.

Museums and historical sites tend to follow shop opening hours too, though abbreviated in the winter months; nearly all close on Mondays. We have tried to list the hours for the important sights. Seldom-visited ones have a raffish disregard for their official hours, or open only when the mood strikes them. Don't be discouraged: bang on doors and ask around.

Public Holidays

The Spanish, like the Italians, try to have as many as possible. Everything closes on:

1 January	New Year's Day
6 January	Epiphany
March	Holy Thursday and Good Friday
1 May	Labour Day
May/June	Corpus Christi
25 July	Santiago Apóstol (St James' Day)

15 August	Asunción (Assumption)
12 October	Día de la Hispanidad (Columbus Day)
1 November	Todos los Santos (All Saints' Day)
6 December	Día de la Constitución (Constitution Day)
8 December	Inmaculada Concepción (Immaculate Conception)
25 December	Navidad (Christmas Day)

Photography

Film is quite expensive everywhere; so is developing, but in any city there will be plenty of places—many in opticians' shops (*ópticas*) or big department stores—where you can get processing done in a hurry. Serious photographers must give some consideration to the strong sunlight and high reflectivity of surfaces (pavements and buildings) in towns. If you're there during the summer, use ASA 100 film.

Pilgrim Facts

To be considered a pilgrim you have three choices of transport: foot, horse or bicycle. By foot, if you're reasonably fit and can clock off 30km a day, expect a journey of six weeks from Roncesvalles to Santiago; to enjoy the experience and take in all the monuments along or just off the way, give yourself two months. To get the Compostellana certificate in Santiago (and the time off purgatory that goes with it) genuine pilgrims are expected to bring a letter of accreditation from their parish priest or from the Confraternity of Saint James UK, c/o Marion Marples, 45 Dolben St, London, SE1 OUQ. If you pass through Roncesvalles or the Col de Somport, the letter will get you a 'pilgrim passport', which entitles you to stay for free or very cheaply in the *refugios* run by towns, churches or monasteries along the way, although the accommodation is often little more than a place to lay a sleeping bag; note that they often have fairly early curfews.

The walking path has recently been well marked, though bear in mind that in most parts of the trip, especially in Castilla y León, you won't have a walking path at all, but a dusty verge along a busy highway. July and August may have the best weather for the trip, but also bring the most traffic.

Spanish organizations devoted to helping pilgims and answering questions include the *Confradía de Santiago de Compostela del Camino*, Calle Mayor, 26250 Sto Domingo de la Calzada, La Rioja, and the *Amigos del Camino*, Marqués de Santillana 10, 2°, Carrión de los Condes.

Police Business

Crime is not really a big problem in Spain, and Spaniards talk about it perhaps more than is warranted, though there are signs that the country is gradually catching up with the rest of us. Pickpocketing and robbing parked cars are the specialities; except for some quarters of the largest cities walking around at night is no problem—partly because everybody does it. Crime is also spreading to the tourist areas; even there, though, you're generally safer in

Spain than you would be at home: the national crime rate is roughly a quarter of that in Britain. Note that in Spain less than 8 grams of reefer is legal; anything else may easily earn you the traditional 'six years and a day'. In Galicia, the traditional smuggling business has created a growing drug problem at home, along with some fierce vigilante efforts by locals to stop it.

There are several species of **police**, and their authority varies with the area. Franco's old goon squads, the Policía Armada, have been reformed and relatively demilitarized into the *Policía Nacional*, whom the Spaniards call 'chocolate drops' because of their brown uniforms; their duties largely consist of driving around in cars and drinking coffee. They are respected more than the Policía Armada, at least since their first commander, Lt. General José Antonio Sáenz de Santa María, ordered his men to surround the Cortes to foil Tejero's attempted coup in 1981, thereby proving that they were strongly on the side of the newly-born democracy.

The *Policía Municipal* (*Udaltzainzoa* in Basque) in some towns do crime control, while in others they are limited to directing traffic. Mostly in rural areas, you will see the *Guardia Civil*, with green uniforms; only in the conservative northwest do they still wear their archaic black patent-leather tricorn hats, once a hated symbol of oppression. The Guardia is now most conspicuous as a highway patrol, assisting motorists and handing out tickets (ignoring 'no passing' zones is the easiest way to get one). Most traffic violations are payable on the spot; the traffic cops have a reputation for upright honesty.

The Basques don't want anything to do with any of these. So far, they are the only community to take advantage of the new autonomy laws and set up their own police, the *Ertzantza* . You'll see them looking dapper in their red berets, waiting by the roadsides for motorists in a hurry.

Post Offices

Every city, regardless of size, seems to have one post office (*correos*) and no more, all open 8am–9pm and 9–1 on Saturdays. It will always be crowded, but unless you have packages to send, you may not need ever to visit one. Most tobacconists sell stamps (*sellos*) and they'll usually know the correct postage for whatever you're sending. Post everything air mail (*por avión*) and don't send postcards unless you don't care when they arrive. Mailboxes are bright yellow and scarce. The post offices also handle telegrams, which normally take 4 hours to arrive within Europe but are very expensive. There is also, of course, the poste restante (general delivery). In Spain this is called *lista de correos*, and it is as chancy as anywhere else. Don't confuse post offices with the *Caja Postal* , the postal savings banks, which look just like them.

Sports and Activities

Football has pride of place in the Spanish heart, though you will not often find Atlético Bilbao or any of the other northern teams except A Coruña challenging the dominance of Real Madrid and Barcelona. **Bullfighting** and **cycling** vie for second place; all are regularly shown on television which, despite a heavy fare of dubbed American shows, everyone is inordinately fond of watching. Euskadi has its own stations, and on some rainy night in your hotel you may have the treat of seeing John Wayne dubbed into Basque.

Cycling

Cycling is taken extremely seriously in Spain and you don't often see people using a bike as a form of transport. Instead, Lycra-clad enthusiasts pedal furiously up the steepest of hills on weekends, causing dire traffic hazards while they strive to reach the standards set by Miguel Indurain, the Navarrese winner of the *Tour de France* for three years running. If you want to bring your own **bicycle** to Spain, you can make arrangements by ferry or train; by air, you'll almost always have to dismantle it to some extent and pack it in some kind of crate. Each airline seems to have its own policy. In summer the moderate climate of the Basque Lands, Cantabria, Asturias and Galicia, with their greenery and network of coastal secondary roads, make them perfect spots for cycling. It's probably the current transport of choice among pilgrims to Santiago; pedalling across the frying pan of northern Castille in the August is appropriately a lot like purgatory.

Fishing and Hunting

Fishing and hunting are long-standing Spanish obsessions, and you'll need to get a licence for both. Freshwater fishing permits (*permisos de pesca*) are issued on a fortnightly basis from the municipal ICONA office, or from the Jefatura Provincial del ICONA, Licencia Nacional de Caza y Pesca, Jorge Juan 39, Madrid, © (91) 225 59 85. **Information:** for a list of the best trout streams (there are many), write to the Spanish Fishing Federation, Navas de Tolosa 3, 28013 Madrid, © (91) 532 83 52.

Deep-sea fishermen need to obtain a 5-year licence from the provincial Comandancias de Marina. **Information** on the best fishing waters and boat rentals can be obtained from the Directorate General of Sea Fishing, Subsecretaria de la Marina Mercante, Ministerio de Comercio, Calle Ruiz de Alarcón 1, Madrid.

You may bring sporting guns to Spain, but you must declare them on arrival and present a valid firearms certificate with a Spanish translation bearing a consulate stamp. Hunters (boar and deer are the big game, with quail, hare, partridges and pigeons, and ducks and geese along the coasts in the winter) are obliged to get a licence (*permiso de caza*) from the local autonomous community, presenting their passports and record of insurance coverage. **Information:** the Spanish tourist office, or the Spanish Hunting Federation, Avenida Reina Victoria 72, 28003 Madrid, © (91) 253 90 17.

Golf

English settlers built Spain's first golf course at the Rio Tinto mines in the 19th century, and since the advent of Severiano Ballesteros (whose home course is the Real Golf de Pedreña in Santander) Spaniards too have gone nuts for the game. The sunny warm winters, combined with greens of international tournament standard, attract golfing enthusiasts from all over the world throughout the year. Any real-estate agent on the coast hoping to sell villas to foreigners, especially Scandinavians and the latest newcomers, the Japanese, stands little chance of closing a deal unless his property is within 10 minutes of a golf course. It's a rage that's unlikely to diminish now that the 1997 Ryder Cup is to be held in Andalucía. Most places hire out clubs. Green fees have taken a leap in recent years, however and even the humblest clubs charge 3000 pts. Many hotels cater specifically for the golfer and there are numerous specialist tour operators. **Information**: any Spanish tourist office, or the Royal Spanish Golf Federation, Capitán Haya 9–5, 28020 Madrid, ✆ (91) 555 27 57.

Hiking and Mountaineering

Spain's sierras attract thousands of hikers and mountaineers. Los Picos de Europa and the Pyrenees are by far the most popular, though there are also some lovely hikes in El Bierzo of western Léon and Os Ancares of eastern Galicia. The tourist office or the Spanish Mountaineering Federation provide a list of *refugios*, which offer mountain shelter in many places. Some are well equipped and can supply food. Most, however, do not, so take your own sleeping bags, cooking equipment and food with you. Hiking boots are essential, as is a detailed map of the area, issued by the Instituto Geográfico Nacional, or the Servicio Geográfico Ejército. **Information**: Spanish Mountaineering Federation, Alberto Aguilera 3, 28015 Madrid, ✆ (91) 445 13 82.

Tennis

There is equal fervour for tennis as for golf, inspired by international champion Arantxa Sánchez Vicario, and more recently by Conchita Martínez, both of whom can be mentioned in the same breath as Graf, Seles and Sabatini. Every resort hotel has its own courts; municipal ones are rare or hard to get to. **Information**: Royal Spanish Tennis Federation, Avenida Diagonal 618, 08021 Barcelona, ✆ (93) 201 08 44.

Telephones

Emergency numbers: proteccíon civil ✆ 006   police ✆ 091

Spain has long had one of the best telephone systems in Europe. During the Civil War it kept running no matter what; commanders used it to keep in touch with their troops, and called towns on the front during offensives to check if they had fallen to the enemy. Today, calls within Spain are comparatively cheap (15–25 pts for a short local call), and Spain is one of the few countries where you can make an international call conveniently from a phone booth—within Europe at least. In newer phone booths there are complete instructions (in English) and phonecard slots. In most there will also be a little slide on top that holds coins; keep it full of 25 pts pieces—the newer ones also take 100 pts— and you can chat all day like the Spaniards do. This can be done to the USA too, but take at least 3000 pts in change with you in 100s. Overseas calls from Spain are among the most expensive in Europe: calls to the UK cost about 250–350 pts a minute, to the US substantially more. There are central telephone offices (*telefónicas*) in every big city, where you call from metered booths (and pay a fair percentage more for the comfort);

they are indispensable, however, for reversed charge or collect calls (*cobro revertido*). *Telefónicas* are generally open 9–1 and 5–10pm and closed on Sundays.

Expect to pay a big surcharge if you do any telephoning from your hotel or any public place that does not have a coin slot. Cheap rate is from 10pm–8am Monday–Saturday and all day Sunday and public holidays.

For calls to Spain from the UK, dial 00 followed by the country code (34), the area code (remember that if you are calling from outside Spain you drop the '9' in the area code) and the number. For international calls from Spain, dial 07, wait for the higher tone and then dial the country code, etc.

Toilets

Apart from bus and train stations, public facilities are rare in Spain. On the other hand, every bar on every corner has a toilet; don't feel uncomfortable using it without purchasing something—the Spaniards do it all the time. Just ask for *los servicios* and take your own toilet paper to be on the safe side.

Tourist Information

After receiving millions of tourists each year for the last two decades, no country has more information offices, or more helpful ones, or more intelligent brochures and detailed maps. Every city will have an office, and about two-thirds of the time you'll find someone who speaks English. Sometimes they'll be less helpful in the big cities in the summer. More often, though, you'll be surprised at how well they know the details of accommodation and transportation.

Many large cities also maintain **municipal tourist offices**, though they're not as well equipped as those run by the Ministry of Tourism, better known as **Turismo**. Hours for most offices are Monday to Friday, 9.30–1.30 and 4–7, Saturday mornings and closed on Sundays.

Spanish National Tourist Offices

Canada: 102 Bloor Street West, Toronto, Ontario, M5S 1M8, © (416) 961 3131, ✉ 961 1992

Japan: Daini Toranomon Denki Building, 4F, 3-1-10 Toranomon, Minato Ku, Tokyo 105, © (813) 34326141, ✉ 34326144 (provides information for Australia and New Zealand nationals)

UK: 55–58 St James's Street, London SW1A 1LD, © (0171) 499 0901, ✉ 629 4257

US: Water Tower Place, Suite 915 East, 845 North Michigan Avenue, Chicago, Illinois, 60611, © (312) 642 1992, ✉ 642 9817

8383 Wilshire Boulevard, Suite 960, Beverly Hills, California, 90211, © (213) 658 7188, ✉ 658 1061

665 Fifth Avenue, New York, NY 10022, © (212) 759 8822, ✉ 980 1053

1221 Brickell Avenue, Miami, Florida 33131, © (305) 358 1992, ✉ 358 8223

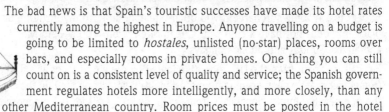

The bad news is that Spain's touristic successes have made its hotel rates currently among the highest in Europe. Anyone travelling on a budget is going to be limited to *hostales*, unlisted (no-star) places, rooms over bars, and especially rooms in private homes. One thing you can still count on is a consistent level of quality and service; the Spanish government regulates hotels more intelligently, and more closely, than any other Mediterranean country. Room prices must be posted in the hotel lobbies and in the rooms, and if there's any problem you can ask for the complaints book, or *Libro de Reclamaciones*. No one ever writes anything in these; any written complaint must be passed on to the authorities immediately. Hotel keepers would always rather correct the problem for you.

The prices given in this guide are for double rooms with bath (unless stated otherwise) but do not include VAT (IVA) charged at 15 per cent on five-star *hoteles*, and 7 per cent on other *hoteles*. No VAT is charged on other categories of accommodation. Prices for single rooms will average about 60 per cent of a double, while triples or an extra bed are around 35 per cent more. Within the price ranges shown, the most expensive are likely to be in the big cities, while the cheapest places are always in provincial towns. On the whole, prices are surprisingly consistent. No government, however, could resist the chance to insert a little bureaucratic confusion, and the wide range of accommodation in Spain is classified in a complex system. Look for the little **blue plaques** next to the doors of all *hoteles*, *hostales*, etc. which identify the classification and number of stars. If you're travelling around a lot, a good investment would be the government publication *Guía de Hoteles*, a great fat book with every classified hotel and *hostal* in Spain, available for only 750 pts in many bookshops. The government also publishes similar guides to holiday flats (*apartamentos turísticos*) and campsites. Local tourist information offices will have a complete accommodation list for their province, and some can be very helpful with finding a room when things are tight.

Price categories for a double room with bath in the 'Where to Stay' sections in this book are as follows:

luxury	17,000 pts and up
expensive	10,000–17,000 pts
moderate	4000–10,000 pts
inexpensive	2500–4000 pts
cheap	under 2500 pts

Paradores

The government, in its plan to develop tourism in the 1950s, started this nationwide chain of classy hotels to draw some attention to little-visited areas. They restored old palaces, castles and monasteries for the purpose, furnished them with antiques and installed fine restaurants featuring local specialities. *Paradores* for many people are one of the best reasons for visiting Spain. Not all *paradores* are historic landmarks; in resort areas, they are as likely to be cleanly designed modern buildings, usually in a good location with a pool and some sports facilities. As their popularity has increased, so have their prices; in most cases both the rooms and the restaurant will be the most expensive in town. *Paradores* are classed as three- or four-star hotels, and their prices range from 8000 pts in remote provincial towns to 17,000 pts and upwards for the most popular. They are open all year round and offer substantial off-season discounts. If you can afford a *parador*, there is no better place to stay. We've mentioned most of them throughout this book.

Advance Booking

Spain: Head Office, Requena 3, Madrid, ☎ (91) 559 00 69, ✉ (91) 559 32 33

UK: Keytel International, 402 Edgware Road, London W2 1ED, ☎ (0171) 402 8182, ✉ (0171) 724 9503

US: Marketing Ahead, 433 Fifth Avenue, New York, NY 10016, tel (212) 686 9213, ✉ (212) 686 0271

Hoteles

Hoteles (H) are rated from one to five stars, according to the services they offer. These are the most expensive places, and even a one-star hotel will be a comfortable, middle-range establishment. *Hotel Residencias* (HR) are the same, only without a restaurant. Many of the more expensive hotels have some rooms available at prices lower than those listed. They won't tell you, though; you'll have to ask. You can often get discounts in the off season but will be charged higher rates during important festivals. These are supposedly regulated, but in practice hotel-keepers charge whatever they can get. If you want to attend any of these big events, book your hotel as far in advance as possible.

Hostales and Pensiones

Hostales (Hs) and *Pensiones* (P) are rated with from one to three stars. These are usually more modest places, often a floor in an apartment block; a two-star *hostal* is roughly equivalent to a one-star hotel, but not always. *Pensiones* may require full- or half-board; there aren't many of these establishments, only a few in resort areas. *Hostal Residencias* (HsR), like *hotel residencias*, do not offer meals except breakfast, and not always that. Of course, *hostales and pensiones* with one or two stars will often have rooms without private baths at considerable savings.

Some cheap *hostales* in ports and big cities can be crummy and noisy beyond belief—as you lie there unable to sleep, you can only marvel at the human body's ability to produce such a wealth of unidentifiable sounds, coming through the paper-thin walls of the room next door. Don't worry too much though: the vast majority will be clean, welcoming places run by nice families that go out of their way to keep up the place.

Fondas, Casas de Huéspedes and Camas

The bottom of the scale is occupied by the *fonda* (F) and *casa de huéspedes* (CH), little different from a one-star *hostal*, though generally cheaper. Off the scale completely are hundreds of unclassified cheap places, usually rooms in an apartment or over a bar and identified only by a little sign reading *camas* (beds) or *habitaciones* (rooms). You can also ask in bars or at the tourist office for unidentified *casas particulares*, private houses with a room or two. In fact, in most towns and resorts you will not have to look at all. Someone will probably find you in the bus or train station, and ask you if you need a room. Almost all of these will be pleasant enough. Prices are usually negotiable (before you are taken to the place, of course). Always make sure the location of the place suits you— 'five minutes away' can mean five minutes walking, or ten minutes in a car with a hell-bent Spanish driver.

In many villages these rooms will be the only accommodation on offer, but they're usually clean—Spanish women are manic housekeepers. The best will be in small towns and villages, and around universities. Occasionally you'll find a room over a bar, run by some-body's grandmother, that is nicer than a four-star hotel—complete with frilly pillows, lovely old furnishings, and a shrine to the Virgin Mary. The worst are inevitably found in industrial cities or dull modern ones. It always helps to see the room first. In cities, the best places to look are right in the centre, not around the bus and train stations. Many inexpensive establishments will ask you to pay a day in advance.

Alternative Accommodation

Youth hostels exist in Spain, but they're rarely worth the trouble. Most are open only in the summer; there are the usual inconveniences and silly rules, and often hostels are in out-of-the-way locations. You'll be better off with the inexpensive *hostales* and *fondas*—sometimes these are even cheaper than youth hostels—or ask at the local tourist office for rooms that might be available in **university dormitories**. If you fancy some peace and tranquillity, the national tourist office has a list of 64 **monasteries** and **convents** that welcome guests. Accommodation and meals are simple and guests can usually take part in the religious ceremonies.

Camping

Campsites are rated from one to three stars, depending on their facilities and, in addition to the ones listed in the official government handbook, there are always others, rather primitive, that are unlisted. On the whole camping is a good deal, and facilities in most first-class sites include shops, restaurants, bars, laundries, hot showers, first aid, swimming pools, telephones and, occasionally, a tennis court. Caravans (campers) converge on all the more developed sites, but if you just want to pitch your little tent or sleep out in some quiet field, ask around in the bars or at likely farms. Camping is forbidden in many forest areas because of fears of fire, as well as on the beaches (though you can often get close to some quieter shores if you're discreet). If you're doing some hiking, bring a sleeping bag and stay in the free **refugios** along the major trails.

Information: the government handbook *Guía de Campings* can be found in most bookstores and at the Spanish tourist office; further details can be obtained from the Federación Española de Campings, Gran Vía 88, Grupo 3 10–8, Madrid, ✆ (91) 242 31 68; or Camping and Caravan Club, Greenfields House, Westwood Way, Coventry CV4 8JH, ✆ (01203) 694 995 (membership necessary £24–8). **Reservations** for sites can be made through Federación Española de Empresarios de Camping, General Oraa 52, 2° d, 28006 Madrid. ✆ (91) 562 99 94.

Private Homes and Self-catering Accommodation

With the rise in hotel prices, this has become an increasingly popular way of vacationing in Spain. Write ahead to any provincial tourist office (addresses in the various sections of this book) for the area you're interested in; most will send you complete listings, with detailed information and often photos. Self-catering is usually lumped together with what the Spanish call *Agriturismo*, or *Turismo Rural*, or in Basque (wait for it) *Nekazalturismoa*, because almost all the places are in rural areas. Accommodation can be anything from modern bungalows to the bottom floor of a traditional half-timbered cottage; some places are simply large, purpose-built houses with a number of rooms. Kitchen facilities may or may not be available, and prices generally fall in the range of 3000–5000 pts per day for a double room. Here are a few firms that arrange self-catering holidays in the north:

In the UK

Casas Cantabricas, 31 Arbury Road, Cambridge, CB4 2JB, ✆ (01223) 328721, ✉ 322711.

Individual Travellers, Bignor, nr Pulborough, West Sussex, RH20 1QD, ✆ (01798) 869461, ✉ 869381. Village and rural accommodation in farmhouses and cottages.

Keytel International, 402 Edgware Road, London, W2 1ED, ✆ 0171 401 8182, ✉ 724 9503.

Magic of Spain, 227 Shepherd's Bush Road, London W6 7AS ✆ (0181) 748 4220, ✉ 748 6381. Apartments and hotels along the coast.

Secret Spain, Model Farm, Rattlesden, nr Bury St Edmunds, Suffolk, IP30 0SY, ✆ (01449) 736096, ✉ 737850. Traditional houses and special small hotels.

Travellers' Way, Hewell Lane, Tardebigge, Bromsgrove, Worcs, B60 1LP ✆ (01527) 836791, ✉ 836159. Self-catering and hotels along the coast, in mountain villages and in the cities.

In the USA

EC Tours, 10153 1/2 Riverside, Toluca Lake, CA 91602, ✆ 800 388 0877. Pilgrimages and city accomodation.

Ibero Travel, 109–19 72nd Street, Forest Hills, NY 11375, ✆ 800 654 2376. Apartments and fly-drive offers.

Women

On the whole, the horror stories of sexual harassment in Spain are a thing of the past—unless you dress provocatively and hang out by the bus station after dark. All Spaniards seem to melt when they see blondes, so if you're fair you're in for a tougher time. Even Spanish women sunbathe topless these days at the international resorts, but do be discreet elsewhere, especially near small villages. Apart from the coast, it often tends to be the older men who comment on your appearance as a matter of course. Whether you can understand what is being said or not, it is best to ignore them.

The Women's Travel Advisory Bureau, © (01386) 701 082, has recently been launched in the UK. It provides information for women travelling alone and can research a specific destination or provide contact names and numbers recommended by other women travellers. The service costs between £6 and £30.

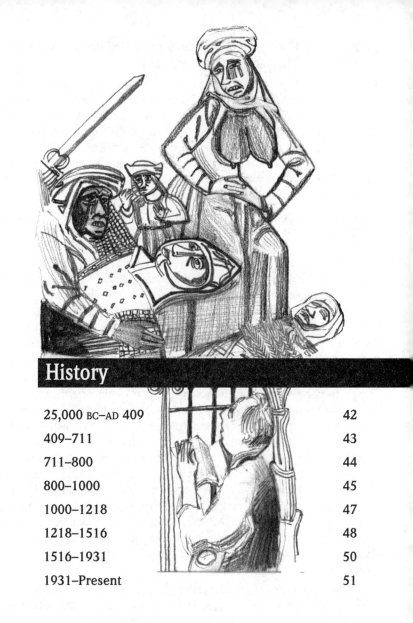

History

A fresco from Galicia depicting the Moors and Christians at war

25,000 BC–AD 409: In which a cultural early bird slows down and gets carved up for lunch by Romans and Carthaginians

Along with southwestern France, this corner of Spain can claim itself as home to the world's oldest known culture. About 25,000 BC, in the Palaeolithic age, the peninsula's many caves began to fill up with Palaeospaniards (or perhaps the ancestors of the Basques, *see* p.120), living well enough off herds of bison and deer to create impressive works of art on cave walls from Cantabria to the western Pyrenees and Périgord. Scholars generally divide these people into the earlier Aurignacian and later Magdalenian cultures. The latter reached their height around 15,000 BC and created some of the Stone Age's finest art, notably in the caves of Altamira near Santander.

It's a long dull stretch from the Palaeolithic masters to the next interesting period in Europe, the Neolithic age. Neolithic culture, with settled farming, trade and megalithic building, may have come to Spain as early as 5500 BC, and it enjoyed a long and relatively peaceful reign over the peninsula, lasting until roughly 2000 BC. This culture, extending from Spain to Scandinavia, distinguished itself by creating Europe's first architecture, with its dolmens, other burial chambers, standing stones and stone circles. Neolithic peoples, though probably a matriarchal society, were sailors and traders, and liked to live near the coasts, including the northern coasts; large concentrations of megalithic monuments are found in the Basque country and Galicia. The latter seems to have been unusually prosperous; dolmen burials here included plenty of gold jewellery, rare for the time.

About 2000 BC, many of the peoples of Iberia learned the use of bronze and started using it to make weapons, while spending their spare time building fortresses to protect the bronze. In an Iberia increasingly turned towards the Mediterranean, the northern coast seems to have been spared most of this progress, and people carried on in their sweet old Neolithic way. About 800 BC, the native Iberians were joined by other peoples, notably the Celts from over the Pyrenees. These got along well enough with the Iberians; in many cases they gradually merged with some tribes, creating a new people, the Celtiberians, who occupied much of the centre and north of the peninsula. The heritage of the Celts everywhere is the *castro*, or as it is called in France and sometimes here too, the *oppidum*. Asterix's lot didn't care much for towns, but wherever there was some trade to be conducted, or treasure to be guarded, the Celts would have a sort of tiny urban centre, perched on a hilltop and surrounded by walls—more a castle than a town.

Meanwhile, the Phoenicians were making their presence felt in the south. Their traders and colonists began taking over parts of coastal Andalucía *c*.1200, but evidence is lacking and it remains an open question just how much time the Phoenicians spent in the north. Several of the port towns have a height called 'Atalaya'; this is believed to be a Phoenician word meaning 'tower', etymologically related to *talayot*, the old word for the fortress keeps of the Phoenicians' neighbours on Minorca (*Spain* is another Phoenician word, meaning 'land of rabbits'). We can imagine that the northern coast was part of a fairly busy trade route, monopolized by Phoenician ships, bringing tin from Cornwall to make bronze in the Mediterranean—the Phoenicians were understandably secretive about the world they discovered outside the Pillars of Hercules, and they probably made up all the stories of sea monsters and such to scare off potential competitors.

Overlordship of Iberia fell to Rome in 202 BC, the big prize for the victory over Hannibal and Carthage in the Second Punic War. But just as the Carthaginians had never really controlled the wild northwest, Roman rule here was mostly a vain boast for another two centuries. The Romans found the region inhabited by a people they called the *Vascones*, the Basques, and further west the Celtiberian *Cantabri, Asturi* and *Gallæci*. Unlike the Carthaginians, the Romans couldn't bear a messy map, and they spent those two centuries methodically grinding down Celtiberians and Basques alike. One highlight of the endless campaigns was the epic siege of Numancia, a Celtiberian stronghold in what is now northern Castile (near Soria). After beating off Roman attacks for nineteen years, the Numancians escaped the dishonour of final defeat by burning the town with themselves inside it. To subdue Spain Rome had to send its best—Cato, Pompey, Caesar and Augustus were all commanders in the Spanish conquest—and the job was not finished in some isolated areas until 20 BC.

The rest of Spain had metal ores to make it worth the trouble, and even in the far north-west Rome probably broke even, thanks to the gold mines of El Bierzo. Only a few towns were founded: *Pallantia* (Palencia) was probably the biggest, followed by *Clunia* (an abandoned site near Aranda de Duero), *Pompaelo* (Pamplona), *Asturica Augusta* (Astorga), *Brigantium* (A Coruña), and *Lucus Augusti* (Lugo). Nor did the Romans break the bank building roads here, although the most important one, linking Zaragoza to León, would one day become the *camino de Santiago*. No town ever managed a population of more than about 5000. So while the rest of Spain got a good washing and a Latin grammar to study, the peoples of the north were pretty much left alone. Compared to the rest of the western Empire, relatively few wealthy villas have been discovered here, a sign that the Roman elite, which bought up or stole all the land elsewhere and gradually turned the native peoples into serfs or slaves, had barely penetrated the region.

Throughout most of the imperial era, the north was a forgotten corner of the province of Tarracona, with its capital on the Mediterranean, modern Tarragona. In one of the reforms of Diocletian, this sprawling province was split up, the far western part gaining the name of *Gallaecia* after its Gaulish inhabitants—the future Galicia. Christianity spread quickly in Spain, at least among the officials and landlords in the south, so much so that the peninsula held its first Church council in 313. The only representative from the north was a bishop of a little town called Lanobriga (León).

409–711: In which the northwest dozes fitfully through a depressing parade of barbarian hordes

The first Germans had found their way into Iberia during the great barbarian raid of the 260s, though the legions gradually recovered and threw them out again. When the Rhine frontier collapsed in 407, some of the Germans storming westwards were probably already thinking of Spain. Vandals, Alans and Suevi all made it over the pass at Roncesvalles by 409, and they separately ranged the peninsula looking for land and swag. To try and restore order, what was left of the Empire sent in another horde, the Visigoths, as allies to sort their cousins out. They smashed the Alans and Vandals, but let the Suevi keep the remote northwest. Rome, now worrying that the cure might be worse than the disease, talked the Visigoths into crossing the Pyrenees again to have some fun in southern Gaul. In the resulting vacuum, a new horde of Vandals (the Siling Vandals) broke in in 422. They did what Vandals will do, seven years of it, before crossing the Straits of Gibraltar in search of richer lands and towns in Africa.

That left the field clear for the Suevi (or Swabians—their stay-at-home relations gave the name to a region of southwestern Germany). Under their chief Rechila, they made a little kingdom for themselves, centred at Astorga, and by 448 controlled much of the peninsula. In 456, however, the Visigoths came back and defeated them near Astorga, bottling the remnant up in remote Galicia. The Visigoths thought they were just adding some Iberian possessions to their kingdom of southern Gaul—but when the Franks in turn defeated them at the great Battle of Vouillé in 507 and chased them over the Pyrenees, they found themselves in a position they would have to be content with—as rulers of Spain.

As Teutonic barbarians go, the Visigoths were a cut above the rest. They did not drink out of skulls, like the Lombards, or smear bear grease all over their bodies, like the Franks. The line of their kings went back to Alaric I, the Goth who had sacked Rome. For the next two centuries, the Visigoths ruled their Spanish kingdom from Toledo, building churches and inventing a rather blunt code of laws in vulgar Latin; in the northwest, they engaged in endless desultory fighting with the Suevi until 585, when the great King Leovigild finally put an end to their kingdom. Meanwhile, up in their mountains, the Basques lapsed into *de facto* independence, meeting in democratic assembly around the oak of Guernica to make their own laws. They were gradually expanding in all directions, and especially present in what is now Navarra—peacefully colonizing lands laid waste by too many hard times and too many armies. The kings sent frequent expeditions up north to try and squeeze some tribute money out of them, with occasional success. Asturias and Galicia proved just as hard to control, and the Visigothic kingdom probably had no more influence here than the Romans had.

711–800: In the middle of the Dark Ages, Spanish history records one of its most frantic centuries ever

At the dawn of the eighth century, it seemed that the Visigothic kingdom had truly established itself: a stable state, by the standards of the time, with a strong Church and some modest cultural achievements (in architecture and literature especially, Spain was more than holding its own). In fact, riven with clan feuds and religious bigotry, the kingdom was a plum waiting to be picked. Of all the luck, this happened to be the first century of Islam, with the explosive bursts of the Arab armies across the Middle East and North Africa. After digesting North Africa, Spain was the only place to go on Islam's western front, and the first small force under Tariq ibn-Zayad landed at Gibraltar in 711. The last Visigothic king, Roderick, was defeated and killed in a great battle near Toledo, and within three years the Muslims were in control of the entire peninsula—except, as you might have guessed by now, parts of the north.

The Arabs surged across the Pyrenees, only to be defeated and driven back by the Franks at Poitiers in 732, but what really kept them from consolidating their hold over northwest Spain was a short but intense revolt of the Muslim Berber troops in 740 against their Arab leaders. To hear the Spaniards tell the story though, the turning of the tide came with a legendary prince of Asturias named Pelayo, who defeated the Moors at the 'Battle of Covadonga' in 718 and kept Asturias free and Christian. Now, there seems to have really been a historic Pelayo, a Visigothic baron, but no reliable record of such a battle is preserved anywhere, and Asturias like the rest of the region was still largely pagan. Spanish history and national mythology are becoming inextricably intertwined; a little inconsequential skirmish in the mountains that Iberia's new masters didn't even notice would someday, in retrospect, appear as the beginning of a national history. Nearly forty years after the Battle of Covadonga, the *Chronicle of 754*, written by a Christian in al-Andalus, had never heard either of the battle or the new Christian 'kingdom' in the north.

Later legends in Cantabria and Asturias spoke of the 'Foramontanos' who fled into the mountains from the Moors and 'returned to repopulate Castile'. And it seems likely that a number of die-hard Visigothic nobles took refuge up in inaccessible parts of Asturias. But the romantic legend of the last few defenders of the faith, heroically holed up in the Asturian mountains—the seed from which Spain would grow—is only partially true. The records say that, only four years after the invasion began, the Moors were pretty much in control of Asturias and most of the rest of the northwest. Gijón, on the coast, fell to the Muslims in 715 and had an Arab governor for years afterwards, as did Pamplona. Galicia too was in Arab hands for some time.

While all this was happening, other neglected fringes of the Iberian world were beginning their careers, including the little state of Navarra. Pamplona freed itself from Muslim rule in the Berber revolt of 740, and the Basques were independent once again. Once again, though, they had to fight to stay that way. After beating the Moors at Poitiers, the self-confident Franks soon came over the Pyrenees looking for new lands to conquer. One of their raids gave birth to the famous legend of Roland and Oliver. These famous knights of Charlemagne perished at the hands of the Basques in an ambush at the pass of Roncesvalles in 778.

800–1000: The northern mountain boys tweak the moustaches of a powerful Emirate, and then found some kingdoms

The endless conquests and confusions of the 8th century set the pattern for centuries of Spain's history to come. The new Emirate of al-Andalus developed a policy of insulating itself from the wild north by a band of marches—no-man's-lands with military governors. At the beginning, these included what is now León, Castile and much of Aragón. The emirs might raid them every few years, but they could not keep Christian settlers from gradually filling in the empty spaces, laying the groundwork for the Reconquista.

While the Emirate (Caliphate after 929) was developing a brilliant Spanish-Muslim civilization in the middle of the Dark Ages, the northern kingdom was prospering and growing too, while economically and culturally drawing closer to Christian Europe. Not only was Asturias slowly and gradually expanding, but new centres of power appeared as well. In 800, the year Charlemagne was proclaimed emperor, the first written mention is made of the County of Castile, the 'Land of Castles'. The north may not have been so backward at all, comparatively speaking. The sophisticated and urbanized society of al-Andalus had a constant need for raw materials and food, and it spread prosperity and learning beyond its borders. One of the surprises of the Christian north was its pre-Romanesque architecture, as expressed in the famous 9th- and 10th-century churches around Asturias and Cantabria, built at a time when the rest of Europe was hardly building anything in stone. Design and clothing, however, were still heavily influenced by the latest fashions in Moorish Córdoba, Granada and Sevilla, and such educated princes as there were would more likely know Arabic than Latin.

In the 9th century, Muslim al-Andalus entered the golden age of its prosperity and power. Campaigns against the Christians in the north were frequent though inconclusive: Pamplona was taken again in 842, and Léon in 848, but neither could be held for long. Under ineffectual caliphs such as Abd Allah, the late 9th century was a time of civil strife and confusion in the south, and it permitted the new kingdom of Asturias to take its first steps on the way to the Reconquista—the retaking of all Iberia for Christianity that had already been predicted, against all odds, in a Christian work called the *Prophetic Chronicle*. Christians began to resettle and hold lands south of the Cantabrian mountains; they also managed to found or refound a number of towns in the no-man's-land of the Duero valley, notably Burgos (884). The reign of Alfonso III (866–910) was a watershed for the north-erners, in which they pushed their boundaries into Portugal and resettled much of northern Castile (for convenience' sake historians call Asturias the 'Kingdom of Léon, after that city was taken in 913, though interestingly for centuries the kingdom had no name at all, and such kings as could write would sign documents simply *Yo, el Rey*).

As for the Basques, by 824 Pamplona had chased the Franks out once and for all, forming the county of Navarra under a leader named Jimeno Aritza and his descendants. The Basques seem to have got on well enough with the Moors, and were often in alliance with them against the famous clan of the Banu Qasi—renegade Visigoths who had turned Muslim, and who held Zaragoza and much of Aragón not for the Emirate, but for them-selves. Later, Basques would provide many of the favourite women in the palace harem at Córdoba, and consequently more than a few of the emirs were at least half Basque.

The reign of Abd ar-Rahman III (912–961), who declared himself Caliph, marked the high point of the power of al-Andalus, and a setback for the northerners, though the caliph could do little to stop the resettlement of the new northern lands. Abd ar-Rahman's notable contemporary in the north was Fernán González, *El Buen Conde*, the 'Good Count' of Castile (923–970) who, despite continuous war with the Moors, made his land into a kingdom independent of Asturias. More troubles for the north came with the rule in al-Andalus of al-Mansur, 'the Victorious', an ambitious vizier who had locked the weak young caliph Hisham II away in the palace at Córdoba and pulled all the strings himself. Al-Mansur defeated the Asturians and sacked Léon in 988, and Burgos in 1000. He forced most of the northerners to pay tribute, and on one raid his armies even occu-pied Santiago de Compostela, carrying off the church bells as a prize for the Great Mosque of Córdoba.

1000–1218: The northerners persist, and find that constant bellicosity brings big rewards

The Muslims definitely still held the real power in the peninsula, but the same al-Mansur who had won so many battles for them was unwittingly to be the downfall of the caliphate. By assuming personal power, he removed the main prop of the legitimacy of the state. When he died, his sons attempted to carry on in his place, leading to a revolution in 1009 that put an end to the political unity of al-Andalus forever, leaving a collection of small states quarrelling amongst themselves. That was all the opportunity the warriors of the north needed. Especially under Alfonso VI (1065–1109) they extended their boundaries ever farther; Alfonso crowned a long string of victories with the capture of Toledo in 1085, securing permanent control of the central *meseta*. Alfonso was the first Castilian king to mint coins (instead of using Moorish currency); he collected tribute money from the little kings of al-Andalus, and he began calling himself 'Emperor of All Spain', but he never would have done it without the help of the Castilian adventurer El Cid, Rodrigo Díaz de Vivar.

The new millennium had definitely got off to an auspicious start for Christian Spain. But for a while it looked as if the big victor among the Christian states would be little Navarra. Still Basque but becoming increasingly hispanicized and feudalized, Navarra had reached its zenith under Sancho el Mayor (1000–35), capturing all of La Rioja and even much of Castile. But like so many of the transient empires formed in the free-for-all of the Reconquista, Sancho's proved to be only a house of cards, and Alfonso VI cut Navarra down to size in the 1070s. In fact, every Christian state was taking advantage of al-Andalus's disarray to expand its boundaries: León/Castile (united by marriage), Navarra, Portugal and Aragón. Aragón and León/Castile eventually emerged as the main rivals for dominance in the new Spain that was building. Under Alfonso I, *El Batallador*, Aragón emerged as a major power; in the 1110s Alfonso briefly controlled parts of Castile, including Burgos.

The new states could afford such rivalry; the new frontier life created by conditions on the *meseta* gave the Christians one particular military advantage: a class of hard men doing well enough to afford heavy armour and a horse. The Spanish cavalry was small in number, but they could cover ground quickly, raid everywhere and often carry the day in pitched battles against Moorish forces that were numerically superior. Another advantage was the spirit of the Crusader, both in reinforcing morale and attracting fresh blood; early on, the popes had declared Spain a legitimate sphere of Crusading activity, as much as was the Holy Land.

Al-Andalus, however, was not finished yet. Before the Christians could completely swallow it up, the various little states were swept away by the new Almoravid (Murabit) empire. Originally an Islamic fundamentalist movement among the Berbers, dominated by a few powerful tribes, this grew into an emirate that controlled all of Morocco. After the fall of Toledo the Almoravids were invited into Spain, where they stopped the Christian tide—and added al-Andalus to their dominions. They lasted until 1147, falling into decay and being replaced by a nearly identical African sectarian empire, that of the Almohads (Muwahhid). Although Muslim art and culture continued to shine, the Almohads suffered the same decay of reforming zeal as had the Almoravids, once introduced to the pleasures of Córdoba and Sevilla. The great disaster for al-Andalus came in 1212: the Battle of Las

Navas de Tolosa, where a Christian alliance led by Alfonso VIII of Castile destroyed the Almohad power forever. The great cities of the south were gobbled up soon after, leaving the Muslims only the little kingdom of Granada, which held out by careful diplomacy and heavy tributes until 1492. Six years after Las Navas de Tolosa, in 1218, Léon and Castile merged once and for all under Fernando III el Santo.

1218–1516: In which medieval Spain creates a fat and happy civilization, and pride goes before a fall

It's the great historical paradox of the Reconquista, one of the examples of Cervantean irony that Spain is always bountiful in providing: the northwest, previously little more relevant to Spain's history than Novgorod or Baluchistan, suddenly takes centre stage in creating a new Spain, and then with success finds itself left behind on the periphery again with nothing to do. After Las Navas de Tolosa, all the money was to be made in the centre and south, in *New* Castile around Madrid, and in al-Andalus—now Spanish Andalucía.

Castile had tripled in size, and its kings, now by far the most dangerous ones on the chessboard, began spending much more of their time in central towns such as Toledo and Valladolid, and less in Léon or Burgos. For simple geographical reasons, the northwest would never be the real heartland of a nation. But for the time being it managed to share fully in western Europe's blossoming during the 12th and 13th centuries. Particularly striking was the growth of towns. Trade came back in the Atlantic in a big way, for the first time since the Romans, and little ports from A Coruña to San Sebastián reawakened from 600 years' slumber. Increasingly, they sent wool to England, France and Flanders. That was the big-money commodity of the age, and the northern plains were perfectly suited for raising sheep. Run under a sophisticated sort of royal cooperative called the *mesta*, this trade fuelled most of medieval Castile's remarkable prosperity, and the annual fair at Medina del Campo became one of the biggest in Europe. Many of the northern cities at least doubled in size in the 12th century, the biggest boom in all history for places such as León and Burgos. Though doomed never to make a rôle for themselves as capitals or great trade centres, both these cities took advantage of the good times to create notable monuments, including the finest Gothic cathedrals in Spain. León began theirs in 1205, and Burgos followed in 1221.

With money came increasing power for the growing towns, and nearly all of them in this period were able to gain a high degree of independence from the kings, bishops or nobles who had formerly bossed them around. All over Spain, the towns were organizing themselves into *comunes*, as in the rest of Europe. A good example of the new type of medieval *comune* is Vitoria-Gasteiz, founded by King Alfonso VI of Navarra in 1181, soon after he had conquered the territory from Castile. Alfonso wanted a loyal town to consolidate his hold, and to keep the new settlers' loyalty, he granted it a charter of *fueros* (literally 'outsides', or exceptions to royal law) that gave the town rights of self-government and exemptions from some taxes and feudal responsibilities. This story was repeated literally hundreds of times across Christian Spain.

The *fueros* gave Spain a less oppressive government than most countries. They were made possible by the good example of the Basques. It was a good time for this incurably indus-

Alfonso the Wise supervising the compilation of an illustrated history of Spain in Castilian

trious people too, as they began to turn their talents to the sea. In 1296 a kind of Hanseatic league of Basque ports was founded, the *Hermandad de las Marismas*; shipping Vizcaya's iron and Castile's wool northwards, the *Hermandad* grew to control a disproportionate share of the Atlantic trade. But as in Navarra, the Basque language and culture were being pushed further into the background, in a world increasingly dominated by Spanish-speaking nobles and merchants. Navarra, condemned by geography to lose out in the Reconquista land grab, was now in full decline. French involvement in the kingdom dated from 1284, when an heiress of the kingdom, Juana I, married King Philip the Fair of France. Members of the Capetian dynasty ruled Navarra as a quaint Pyrenean Ruritania from then on.

Throughout the 14th and 15th centuries, the peninsula occupied itself with consolidating the gains of the Reconquista and trying to make some sense out of all the commotion that had occurred. Burgos and Léon got their tremendous cathedrals finished, but economically and culturally the northwest was increasingly left on the periphery of a Spain that was growing very large and complex. And already, some of the forces that would make this Spain go to pieces were in their larval forms—the big winners of the Reconquista, a bloated nobility and a dangerous but morally decayed Church, both exempt from taxes and loaded with privileges. On the whole, the experience of the Reconquista coarsened the life of Castile, creating a pirate ethos where honest labour was scorned, and wealth and honour were things to be snatched from one's neighbours.

The climax of unification came in 1469 with the marriage of *los Reyes Católicos*, Fernando of Aragon and Isabel of Castile. Under their reign Spain's borders were rounded out. Not only did they finally conquer the kingdom of Granada, the last remnant of al-Andalus, but Fernando's campaigns put an end to that medieval relic up north, the kingdom of Navarra. Spain was also embarking on its career as a grand imperialist, invading Italy and colonizing the Americas. All this cost a good deal of money, which

Fernando and Isabel's ministers extorted out of the towns and cities of Castile. They whittled away at the communal lands and the *fueros*, and towns that had run their own affairs for centuries now found their assets carved up little by little among the crown and the local nobles. The religious bigotry of the 'Catholic Kings', Isabel in particular, put a perverse twist on Spanish life that was to last a long time. Under their reign the Inquisition was reintroduced, and the Jews expelled.

1516–1931: The north's history is dissolved into that of united Spain, and it isn't a pretty story

Worse was still to come. Whatever cash and valuables were left in Old Castile were soon relentlessly sucked out by Fernando and Isabel's grandson, the Habsburg Carlos I. Better known to history as Charles V, his title as Holy Roman Emperor, this rapacious megalomaniac gained the throne by declaring the rightful queen, his mother Juana, insane, and locking her up in a windowless cell for the next forty years. Charles and his Flemish minions then started squeezing Spain dry, to raise the gargantuan bribes that were necessary for an Imperial election in those days (even though there were only seven voters!). To accomplish the looting of his new country, Charles rescinded or ignored most of the remaining municipal *fueros*, wrecked the trade fairs and invented new taxes everywhere. The church and nobles jumped in for a share of the spoils, and Spain embarked on a rather remarkable and ultimately successful attempt to destroy its own economy.

A national financial collapse came in 1519, and an outraged Castile finally rose up in rebellion. The Comunero Revolt, a brave last attempt of the *comunes* to defend their purses and their liberties, began in 1520 and quickly spread through the towns of Old Castile. Charles' foreign troops put it down the following year, and though the king took a conciliatory line towards the rebels, there was no doubt now about who was boss. Castile was finished, its trade ruined and its once-thriving towns condemned to be the backwater relics they remain today.

Ripping out the heart of his country meant relatively little to Charles, who now had gold and silver flowing in from America to finance his endless aggressions across Europe. For a final note on one of history's bigger rotters, we see Charles after his abdication in 1556, living in a monastery at Yuste, in Extremadura, praying for his soul and gorging himself continually on eel pies. His favourite recreation in the later days was rehearsing his funeral, and at one practice session he caught a chill and died. For Spain, still worse was yet to come. Under Charles's neurotic son Felipe II, Spain reached the height of its book- and heretic-burning frenzy, while the economy stayed wrecked and military defeats piled up on every side. A particular blow against the northwest, motivated by corrupt ministers, was Felipe's decision in 1573 to allow Sevilla to monopolize trade with the New World. The northern ports dwindled, and all the poor souls whose prospects had been ruined even had to find their way to the south to catch a boat just to emigrate.

This state of affairs lasted until 1788, by which time the northern towns had already undergone a steep decline along with the rest of Spain. Nevertheless, the northwest found ways to wring a penny from the Americas. The enterprising Basques, for example, created the *Compañía Guipuzcoana de Caracas*, which wangled a monopoly over the chocolate trade and brought a lot of money home to the Basque country. For generations, Basques and Spaniards alike contributed their share to Spain's colonial adventures. Sons who went overseas to make their fortunes were called *indianos*—and *indianos*, or *casas de indianos*, is also the name for the houses built by the lucky ones who came home well off; you'll see them everywhere in the northwest, as early as 1650 and as late as 1920.

If little good happened in these centuries, at least the north was usually spared the curse of armies and wars. That is, until Napoleon crossed the Pyrenees in 1808. French occupation led to a spontaneous national revolt—the Spaniards call it their 'War of Independence'. The British pitched in to fight their mutual nemesis, at first catastrophically as their army under Sir John Moore, pursued by Maréchal Soult, beat a desperate retreat across the northwest to flee from A Coruña. When the British returned under Wellington, it was their turn to chase the French from Cádiz to Paris, the result as much a disaster for Napoleon as his winter in Moscow. Wellington is well remembered by the Spanish for kicking the French out (they made him a duke too), but his boys dealt with conquered land far worse than Napoleon or any contemporary army would have dreamed, distinguishing themselves notably at the sack of San Sebastián. The French had been content with simply looting all the gold crucifixes and bad paintings.

But as the great chef Escoffier later expressed it, the only worthwhile thing France got out of the Peninsular War was the recipe for pheasant *à la Alcántara*. That did not stop the French from sending their army down again in 1823, with the blessing of the English and Austrians, to stamp out a democratic revolt against the despotic Bourbons. Nineteenth-century Spain became quite a wild place, often the very image of the banana republics that had just gained their independence from it in Latin America. The Basques, especially those of Navarra, did their best to keep the pot boiling. Supporting the claims of the pretender Don Carlos, they sided with the church and reactionaries in the Carlist Wars of 1833–39 and 1872–6. Many Carlists only took up the cause in defence of what was left of their *fueros*, which liberal reformers in Madrid were trying to abolish. The generals of Isabel II put down both revolts, though there were some close moments, as in the Second Carlist War when the insurgents briefly besieged Bilbao.

Isabel II presided over the confusing height of the banana monarchy where rival generals and politicians could compete for her favours while issuing *pronunciamientos* and plotting backstage coups. But while the country as a whole was becoming an increasingly inconsequential backwater in Europe, some signs of life were stirring in unlikely places—not in the moribund Castilian centre, but on the periphery. Along with the Catalans, the Basques were doing their best to give the country a boost into the Industrial Revolution. Bilbao became a noisy boomtown around its ironworks and shipyards, while a small echo was heard from tiny Asturias, which grew into Spain's most important mining region.

1931–Present: The northerners choose sides, fight it out, and most finally conclude that pluralism isn't so bad after all

Along with industrialization came political change. The Basque Nationalist Party, or PNV, appeared to speak up for Basque concerns at the Cortes in Madrid, while Asturias with its strong unions became increasingly radicalized. The boom years of the First World War, provided by Spain's neutrality, were followed by a steep depression that brought social problems to a head, especially after the Second Republic was proclaimed in 1931. One famous event of the time, a prelude to the Civil War, was the bloody revolt of the Asturian miners in 1934, crushed by army troops under a general named Franco.

When the Civil War broke out in July 1936, the Basques and Asturians sided enthusiastically with the Republic, while Old Castile supported Franco. Until the end of the war the Nationalists kept their capital at Burgos. Most Galicians took the Nationalist side too— Franco was after all a native son, from Ferrol—and so did the Navarrese, whose politics still revolved around Carlism. Franco's armies soon reduced Republican territory in the northwest to a chain of small pockets along the coast. The Basques held out until 1937, when they succumbed to a campaign distinguished by the terror bombing of Guernica, performed by Franco's Nazi allies.

After the war the Basques suffered more than anyone for their loyalty to the Republic. As in Catalunya, the government suppressed even the casual use of the native language, forbade most festivals and cultural manifestations, and sent thousands of intellectuals to prison or exile. State industrial schemes were consciously planned in a way to bring in large numbers of Spanish job-seekers to dilute the Basque population. The Basque response was the growth of the terrorist ETA, beginning in the '50s. As the only active resistance to the dictatorship, the ETA attracted widespread sympathy within Spain and elsewhere, especially in 1973 when they blew the car of Franco's hand-picked successor, Admiral Carrero Blanco, over the roof of a Madrid church.

In striking contrast, plenty of Navarrese, mostly Carlists, found posts in Franco's army and government until the end of the regime in 1975 (the Spanish fascists even borrowed the Carlists' yoke-and-arrows symbol for their own party). There are Carlists to be found even today, even though the current pretender, Prince Hugo de Borbón, has tacitly acknowledged King Juan Carlos by paying him a social visit. Navarra remains the most politically reactionary part of Spain, maybe of all Europe; Pamplona, its bright and prosperous capital, is the Mecca of the Opus Dei, the sinister, secret Catholic organization that in Franco's later years attempted to gain control of the Spanish government by insinuating its members into high positions.

In Galicia, Cantabria and Castile, politics remain quietly Neanderthal; these are the only parts of Spain where you're still likely to see statues and streets named after Nationalist heroes. Since the restoration of democracy in 1977, the most dramatic change in Spain has been the reversal of centuries of centralization, with the creation of autonomous regional governments throughout the country, including Galicia, Asturias, Cantabria, the Basque country (Euskadi), Navarra and Old Castile—the latter the only part of Spain where a majority didn't want autonomy, and had it forced upon them by Madrid. The Basques got a special autonomy statute, and they have made the most of it, with their own schools, television and police force. It isn't enough for the die-hards of the ETA, who demand total independence, and they continue their murderous bombing campaigns to this day, almost always in other parts of Spain.

Topics

I. The Official History

No saint on the calendar has as many names as Spain's patron—Iago, Diego, Jaime, Jacques, Jacobus, Santiago or, in English, James the Greater. James the fisherman was one of the first disciples chosen by Jesus, who nicknamed him Boanerges, 'the son of thunder', after his booming voice. After the Crucifixion, he seems to have been a rather ineffectual proselytizer for the faith; in the year 44 Herod Agrippa in Caesarea beheaded him and threw his body to the dogs.

But Spain had another task in store for James: nothing less than posthumously leading a 700-year-old crusade against the peninsula's infidels. In fact, the evidence suggests that it was really the French who put him up to it: the first mention of the Apostle's relics in Spain appear in a 830 annexe to the *Martirologio de Florus*, written in 806 in Lyon; after the fright of 732, when the Moors invaded as far as Poitiers and settled a good portion of France's Mediterranean coast, the French were ready to pull out all the stops to encourage their old Christian neighbours to rally and defeat the heathen. A new history of James emerged, one with links to Spain. First, before his martyrdom, he went to Zaragoza to convert the Spaniards and failed. Second, after his martyrdom, two of his disciples piously gathered his remains and sailed off with them in a stone boat (faith works wonders). The destination was Iria Flavia in remote Galicia, and the disciples buried Boanerges in the nearby cemetery of Compostela. In 814, a shower of shooting stars guided a hermit shepherd named Pelayo to the site of James' tomb; the bones were 'authenticated' by Bishop Theodomir. Another legend identifies Charlemagne (who died in 814) with the discovery of James' relics: in the Emperor's tomb at Aachen you can see the 'Vision of Charlemagne', with a scene of the Milky Way, the *Via Lactea*, a common name for the pilgrims' road.

In 844, not long after the discovery of the relics, James was called into active duty in the battle of Clavijo, appearing on a white horse to help Ramiro I of Asturias defeat the Moors. This new role as Santiago Matamoros, the Moor-Slayer, was a great morale booster for the forces of the Reconquista, who made 'Santiago!' their battle cry. In the churches along the Camino, James is portrayed either as a humble pilgrim himself or as a mighty warrior trampling the Moors underfoot. Ramiro was so pleased by his divine assistance that he made a pledge, the *voto de Santiago*, that ordained an annual property tax for St James' church at Compostela.

Never mind that the bones, the battle and the *voto* were as bogus as each other; the story struck deep spiritual, poetic, and political chords that fit in perfectly with the great cultural awakening of the 10th and 11th centuries. The medieval belief that a few holy bones or teeth could serve as a hotline to heaven made the discovery essential. After all, the Moors had some powerful juju of their own: an arm of the Prophet Muhammad in the Great Mosque of Córdoba (possession of it was Abd ar-Rahman's justification for declaring himself Caliph in 929). Another factor in the early 9th century was the Church's need for a focal point to assert its doctrinal control over the newborn kingdoms of Spain, especially over the Celts in Galicia, stubborn followers of the gnostic Priscillian heresy (*see* p.281). A third factor must have been the desire to re-integrate Spain into Europe—and what better way to do it than to increase human, commercial and cultural traffic over the Pyrenees? Pilgrimages to Jerusalem and Rome were already in vogue; after the long centuries of the Dark Ages, the Church was keen on re-establishing contacts across the old Roman empire it had inherited for Christianity.

The French were the great promoters of the *Camino de Santiago* (the Way to Santiago), so great in fact that the most commonly tramped route became known as the *camino francés*. The first official pilgrim was Gotescalco, bishop of Le Puy, in 950; others followed, including Mozarab Christians (those living under Moorish rule) from Andalucía, who emigrated north and put themselves under the protection of Santiago, founding some of the first churches and monasteries along the road in the province of León.

In the next century, especially once the frontier with the Moors was firmly pushed back to the south bank of the Duero, the French monks of the reforming abbey of Cluny did more than anyone to popularize the pilgrimage, setting up sister houses and hospitals along the way. Nor were the early Spanish kings slow to pick up on the commercial potential of the road; Sancho the Great of Navarra and Alfonso VI of Castile founded a number of religious houses and institutions along the way and invited down French settlers to help run them. It was at this time too, that the French stuck another oar in with their *Chanson de Roland,* which made Charlemagne something of a proto-pilgrim, although his adventure into Pamplona happened decades before the discovery of James' relics.

The 12th century witnessed a veritable boom along the *camino francés*: the arrival of new monastic and military orders, including the Templars, the Hospitallers, and the Knights of Santiago, which all vowed to defend the pilgrim from dangers en route. In 1130, the Abbey of Cluny commissioned Aymery Picaud, a priest from Poitou, to write the *Codex Calixtinus*, the world's first travel guide, chock full of prejudices and practical advice for pilgrims: he describes the four main roads through France and tips on where not to drink the water, where to find the best lodging, where to be on guard against 'false pilgrims' who came not to atone for crimes but to commit them. The final bonus for Santiago de Compostela came in 1189, when Pope Alexander III declared it a Holy City on equal footing with Jerusalem and Rome, offering a plenary indulgence—a full remission from Purgatory—to pilgrims on Holy Years (if you're planning a trip the next will be 1999 and 2004; other years you'll only get half time off). The favourite song they would sing along the way was the *Ultreya*:

> *Dum Pater familias, rex universorum*
> *donaret provincias ius apostolorum*
> *Jacobus Hispanias lux ilustrat morum*
> *Primus ex apostolis, martyr Jerosolimis*
> *Jacobus egregio, sacre et martyrio.*
> *Herru Sanctiagu, grot Santiagu*
> *e ultreia e suseia, Deus adiuva nos*

(Our father, King of the Universe/Concede the land to apostolic right/Santiago of Spain is the light illuminating tradition/First among the Apostles, martyr of Jerusalem/Distinguished Santiago, holy and martyred/Lord Santiago, Great Santiago!/And Forward! and Onward! God help us!)

The Tour de Saint-Jacques in Paris was a traditional rallying point for groups of pilgrims (there was more safety in numbers); from there the return journey was 800 miles and took a minimum of four months on foot. It was not something to go into lightly, but for many it was more than an act of faith, a chance to get out and see the world. By the time of Aymery Picaud the French had been joined by pilgrims from across Europe. Many were ill (hence the large number of hospitals), hoping to complete the pilgrimage before they died. Not a few were thieves, murderers and delinquents condemned by the judge to make the journey for penance. Sometimes dangerous cons had to do it in chains. To keep them from cheating or stealing someone else's indulgence (the *Compostellana* certificate), pilgrims had to have their documents stamped by the clergy at various points along the route, just as they do today (as a nice touch, the old stamps and seals have recently been revived).

An estimated half a million people a year made the trek in the Middle Ages (out of a European population of about 60 million) and, even in the 18th century, the so-called century of Enlightenment, the pass at Roncesvalles still counted 30,000 pilgrims a year. But in the 19th century numbers fell dramatically; most of the monasteries and churches were closed forever in the confiscation of church lands in 1837; many were converted into stables or simply pillaged for their building stone. In the 1970s, just when it seemed as defunct as a dodo, the pilgrimage made a remarkable revival, due to a number of factors—the modern world's disillusionment with conventional religion; the search for something beyond what overorganized day-to-day life and church attendance can offer and, more prosaically, the growth of ecological and alternative tourism. In 1982 John Paul II became the first Pope ever to visit Santiago; in 1985, Unesco declared it the 'Foremost Cultural Route in Europe', helping to fund the restoration of some of the Romanesque churches that punctuate the trail. Although modern roads have changed the face of the pilgrimage forever, efforts have been made to create alternative paths for pedestrians, marked every 500m with a stylized scallop shell; new free or inexpensive *hostales* have sprouted along the way for walkers or cyclists. The pilgrims' quest is back in business.

II. A Field of Stars

In the Middle Ages it took real courage to leave home and make such an arduous, perilous journey west to *Finis Terra* ; back then, as today, there was more to it than just picking up an indulgence to deposit as credit in the Bank of Grace. The pilgrimage was one of the few opportunities for the average Middle Ager to attain a consciousness and understanding beyond the strict limits of Church dogma.

All the humbuggery over the 'discovery' of the Apostle's relics in the far northwest corner of Spain would never have caught the popular imagination so powerfully had it not been for its

17th-century pilgrim's hat

deep mythopoeic resonances already present; especially for the Celts, the far west was the abode of souls that pass on. It was an ancient Indo-European belief that a star appears in the Milky Way whenever a mortal is born, and shoots towards the west when they die, towards the realm of the dead in, as for example the Celts conceived it, the Castle of the Goddess Arianhrod (the constellation *Corona Borealis*). Similarly, in Plato, the dead go to the celestial west, to the spot where the Milky Way meets the circle of the Zodiac—towards the real 'Compostela' (*campus stelae in finis terrae*), the field of stars at the world's end.

To make the journey to the end of the world while still alive was to come to terms with our ultimate destiny, to vanquish and harrow hell, to understand the mystery in a unique way with both the body and mind. There were certainly plenty of miracles and mysteries for the pilgrims to ponder as they followed the setting sun, both in legends and in the subject matter chosen by the sculptors who decorated the portals and capitals of the churches along the way. Much of their symbolism is enigmatic in the extreme. With the destruction, deterioration and ham-handed restoration of so many pilgrim churches and hospitals, many important clues left by the itinerant guilds of builders were lost, but the remains include Celtic and other pagan symbols, man-eating lions, eagles and snakes, two-headed monsters, jovial eroticism, labyrinths, figures from the zodiac or from the 'labours of the months', and much more, along with a wide range of orthodox and unorthodox depictions of scenes from scripture.

Aymery Picaud's *Codex Calixtinus* divided the *camino francés* into 13 days or stages. Some are rather long hauls, possible only with a fresh horse, others are short and walkable; some of the stages are to famous towns like León and Burgos, others to dusty one-horse nowheres, apparently chosen arbitrarily, which existed on their reputation only as long as the *Codex Calixtinus* was consulted. The number 13 has its own deep resonance, going back to the proto-pilgrimages of ancient Egypt, when a journey down the Nile was a living re-enactment of the journey made by an Egyptian after death. Egypt itself was a metaphor for heavens, while the Nile itself was divided into 12 parts representing the Zodiac, as a lunar year is 12 or 13 months. As if to prove such ideas reached Spain, a curious 9th-century BC Egyptian alabaster burial urn, found at Almuñécar and displayed in the Casa Castril in Granada, has hieroglyphs that suggest such a pilgrimage:

> *I have arrived from my foreign land. I have passed through countries and have heard about your being, you of the primordial state of the two lands, you who has engendered what exists. In you your two eyes shine. Your Word is the way of life that gives breath to all throats. Now I am in the horizon, flooded by the happiness of the harija oases and I speak to it like a friend. In me there is a source of health, of life, beyond your shores.*

III. The Wild Goose Chase

13th-century pilgrim's badge

One theory has it that the Goose Game, a favourite childrens' pastime in Spain and most continental countries, is a playful memory of the pilgrimage, the medieval path of initiation. The Goose Game first became popular at the time of Felipe II, the age when anything faintly outside church dogma was likely to lead to an *auto-da-fé*. In the Goose Game, the board has a path of 63 squares set in a spiral, leading inwards to the goal, with a picture of a goose in the centre, for a total of 64. Twelve of the 63 squares also have pictures of geese, which are invariably good to land on; another nine have obstacles (the bridge, the inn, the dice, the well, the labyrinth, the prison, the dice, death, and the gateway to the goal). Players roll dice to move their markers around the board.

A number of writers on Compostela, beginning with Louis Charpentier's *The Mystery of Compostela* (1973), have remarked on the persistency of the word 'goose' in the place names along the *camino* de Santiago. *Oca* is Spanish for goose, *Ganso* is the Visigothic German, *Anser* the Latin, and a look at the map reveals that northwest Spain has far more than its share of goosey names: El Ganso, the Montes de Oca, Rio Oja, Puerto de la Oca, the river Anso.

Goosiness permeates the other side of the Pyrenees too. In France, *dévider les jars,* 'to spin the ganders', meant to speak in argot, the secret language of the builders' confraternities. The mysterious, now vanished Agotes (or Cagots in French), an outcast race who lived on either side of the Navarrese Pyrenees, were often forced to wear a goose foot around their necks. Basques had a race of lovely but goose-footed fairies, the *laminak,* and Toulouse was the home of the famous Visigothic queen Ranachile, wife of Theodoric II. Better known as *La reine pédauque,* the 'goose foot', her story inspired the legend of goose-footed Berthe, Charlemagne's mum, a rather domestic queen who told children stories by her spinning wheel (French fairy tales customarily begin with 'In the time when good Queen Berthe spun'.) Andrew Lang found the first reference to Mother Goose, *La Mere d'Oye,* in 1650.

So why choose, of all God's creatures, a goose as the key? One guess is that the goose is only a European adaptation of the Egyptian ibis, the bird sacred to Isis that destroyed the eggs of the Nile crocodile and annually battled winged serpents from Arabia (geese are pretty handy with serpents too, as every farmer knows). The figure of Isis distantly haunts the whole *camino,* littered with miraculous, usually dark-faced statues of the Virgin, her Christian equivalent. The Universal Way to Compostela, the Milky Way, the Starry Stairway to heaven, was a path of initiation into the mysteries of life and death and unity of all things. A wild goose chase, for those who understood the cosmic joke. Why else would the figures Master Mateo carved on the cathedral of Santiago laugh so merrily?

To the insufficiently pious, the real revelation of the pilgrimage to Santiago is that when you get to the end, there's simply nothing there—just a corpse that could be a mythical character's or anybody's. In the Goose Game, the square just before the goal is the Tomb, and if you land here you're dead and have to start again from the beginning. To those who see the pilgrimage as containing a secret teaching for a few, that's just the point. Once you have made it to Santiago de Compostela, it would hardly make sense not to go all the way to land's end. It isn't far, and the trail meets the sea at Noia, a place that intriguingly enough was a holy site long before Compostela, with Neolithic dolmens, and a churchyard full of mysterious tombstones from the Middle Ages, carved with signs and motifs that no one has ever explained.

Of Racial Purity and Pork

I. Bloody-minded Ethnic Cleansing, Spanish Style

Spanish history is shot through with tragicomic implosions. One of the most destructive was the mania for *limpieza de sangre* (purity of blood), a doctrine that so undermined the national economy in the 15th–17th centuries that all the loot from the Americas couldn't patch the gaping wound. Purity of blood meant pure Christian ancestry, something probably only a few Asturian and Basque hillbillies could claim with a clear conscience. But as the Reconquista swept south, Castile, more than any of the other kingdoms of the northwest, began to define itself as a nation by religious segregation. Many Jews and Moors tried to conform by converting and, although at first they were accepted without stigma, bigotry raised its ugly head in the 1400s, just as the Christians achieved total control.

The Jews were the first to go. In Spain since the Diaspora, they were an educated and useful minority, many of them doctors and moneylenders (two of the few professions they were allowed to exercise). They were the subject of the first purity of blood law, the 1449 Toledo decree, issued in spite of opposition from the king of Castile and the Pope: 'We declare that the so-called *conversos*, offspring of perverse Jewish ancestors, must be held by law to be infamous and ignominious, unfit and unworthy to hold any public office or benefice within the city of Toledo.' Many cities followed suit. In 1480, Isabel and Fernando re-founded the Inquisition to institutionalize discrimination against *conversos*: any of them suspected of backsliding in the faith—or often anyone merely accused of it— would have their property confiscated by the state, and probably be burned at the stake.

In 1492, Isabel celebrated the conquest of Granada by booting the Jews out of Spain. The kings of Navarra took them under their wing, at least until 1514, when Navarra itself was gobbled up by Fernando. Not satisfied with this, the Inquisition after 1530 began posting in the cathedrals the names of everyone who had any dealings at all with the Holy Office, so that people suspected of 'tainted blood' could always be readily identified—and not hired for any important post. In response, books of family trees were published, to prove one's own purity or to disparage someone else's. *Limpieza de sangre* contributed more than anything to the prevailing atmosphere in 16th-century Spain, which could be described as raging, surreal paranoia. The economic result was more concrete: by bankrupting and expelling the Jews and *conversos*, the perennially broke kings of Spain had to borrow money from Genoese bankers at calamitous rates. The annual silver fleet from the Americas would sail into Sevilla only to be sucked up whole by the Italians.

Muslims who refused to convert were given their walking papers in 1502. Those who did convert, the *moriscos*, were robbed and booted out a century later. The *moriscos* were excellent farmers, experts in irrigation, and willing to perform jobs no pure-blooded Spaniard would touch. Although the usual mafia of aristocrats, especially the Count of Lerma, picked up a tidy bundle from the sale of their confiscated lands, the *moriscos*' departure left many parts of Spain not far from Skid Row. Felipe III, imbecile spawn of many generations of Habsburg family incest, was the king who allowed the *moriscos* to be put out. Felipe, incidentally, died from sitting too close to the fire—so weighty was his concept of his own nobility that he couldn't imagine getting up and moving away from the flames on his own. The blood obsession was becoming increasingly kinky. In Spain, a true aristocrat would bleed 'blue', while his younger brothers, poor *hidalgos* (and Christ himself, profusely, in a thousand horror-show Spanish statues) bled red, and everyone else bled 'plain blood' unless they were Moors, Jews or Lutheran heretics, whose blood was said to be 'black'.

The *hidalgos*, once the backbone of medieval Castile, were by now a mentally deranged caste of haughty layabouts. Located at the bottom of the noble ladder, with neither land nor vassals, they came to be the class most obsessed with blood and honour. It was their sole capital, all that they had from the ancestors who achieved the Reconquista. Many of them went to America as *conquistadores*, but most stayed, impoverished and futile like Don Quixote, guarding the iron-bound coffers where they kept their letters patent, attesting to their arms, rank, and privileges that exempted them from direct taxation and debtors' prison, all the time depriving Spain of productive men and poisoning society with their attitude.

> *My father was afflicted by a disgrace which he passed on to all his sons like original sin. He was a* hidalgo. *This is not unlike being a poet, for there are few* hidalgos *who escape perpetual poverty and continuous hunger. He possessed letters patent of his nobility so ancient that even he was unable to read them, and no one cared to touch them for fear of getting their fingers greasy from the bedraggled knots and ribbons of the tattered parchments. Even the mice took care not to gnaw them lest they were stricken with sterility.*
>
> Estebanillo González (1646)

II. Delights of the Castilian Kitchen

Short of resorting to being bled by barber to see what colour of *sangre* leaked out, there were two sure-fire ways to tell a true Christian Spaniard: he hardly ever washed (monks in particular, never bathed, and called the inevitable result 'the odour of sanctity'), and he ate lots of pork. Bathing was Jewish, Moorish and effeminate: one of the first acts of Isabel and Fernando after the conquest of Granada was to close the baths. If a suspect hadn't bathed recently, the second test was to offer him a bit of pig meat. Now this was perhaps a more honest vetting; Spain has been known for pork since ancient times; and even a serious historian like Diodorus Siculus could rave about Iberian 'hams transcendently superlative' in the 1st century AD.

We can suppose that making the pig into a badge of the True Faith could not happen without some distortion of the national psyche. Pigs and Spanish strangeness went hand in hand, sometimes in the most uncanny ways. Extremadura was long Spain's hog heaven, and the best, most exquisite porkers there were fed on vipers. Like so many *conquistadores*, the great, unspeakable Pizarro came from there; he was suckled by a sow, and started his career as a swineherd. The Spanish national psychosis of the old days, a witches' brew of *limpieza de sangre*, lust for gold, vicious imperialism, hatred and bigotry, found its reflection in the kitchen too, in an obsession with pork that can be disconcerting.

In Castile, not much of the pig gets thrown away. Besides the famous ham, the bacon, chops and such, Castilians take what's left to make endless sausages, smoked sausages, blood sausages, tripes and puddings. Castilians make the somewhat extravagant claim that pork 'spiritualizes the stomach', and the less expensive pig parts are the staple of cooking; big chunks of pig meat get thrown into all the heavy stews and casseroles that Castilians love. The apotheosis of the porker in Spain is *cochinillo asado*, roast sucking-pig, and its capital is Segovia, where top *asadores* wear medals and cover their restaurant walls with parchment certificates that look like Papal bulls, proclaiming their culinary achievements. *Cochinillo* can be a genuine treat, though from here the attractiveness of the cuisine drops off rather sharply. Another favourite is the famous *botillo* of El Bierzo, which can include minced pork, sausages, fat, lips and ears. Wrap all this up in a pig's intestine, hang it in the chimney for two or three months, and there you are.

One of the most unwelcome things you could encounter on a Spanish menu is *sopa castillana*, a glutinous swill made of boiled bread, eggs, machine oil, garlic, lard and soap, with unidentifiable gobbets of pork tossed in for luxury. For most Spaniards, Castilian soup is only a queasy memory, gathering dust under the bed with Franco, but you can still seek it out in certain restaurants in and around Burgos—dark restaurants with heavy dark furniture, and a few old men smoking cigars.

One of the symptoms of pork abuse is a permanent craving for pulses on the side. Red beans, white beans, chickpeas and lentils, the Spaniards' real staple is all those spirit-laden dried delights that Pythagoras and other philosophers warned us against (of course any Pythagoreans in Spain would have been tidied away by the Inquisition long ago). The 'musical fruit' adds much to the, let us say, expansive nature of much traditional cooking, as in the countryman's *olla podrida* , praised by Cervantes, or the 'Maragato stew' with chickpeas, pig's ears and trotters, and a few inches of blood sausage. Pork and beans is wagon cooking, the simple food of pioneers—pig-farming pioneers—and the presence of such a humble cuisine is another of the curious phenomena bobbing in the wake of Spain's curious history. It is the cuisine of the frontier experience.

The Spanish Distemper

I. Home on the Range

If you want to see the best-preserved early medieval frescoes in Spain, you'll have to go to Gaceo, a dusty nowhere off the road from Vitoria to Pamplona. It's an unpromising spot, but if you can find the man with the key, there is a wonderful cartoon vision of heaven and hell—a rare relic from a lost world. So often in Spain, the real treasures are hidden in out-of-the-way places. Gaceo is a somewhat special case—a Roman road, later the Camino Real (now the N1) once ran through it.

Still, it would be only natural to ask why such a huge expenditure, by medieval standards, of money and talent should have been lavished on tiny Gaceo. That question itself is a key to understanding Spain. All over Castile, in scores of cities and even villages, you will sense there were great expectations long ago, and greater disappointments after. A dusty hamlet will sport an arcaded Plaza Mayor that never quite grew into a stone one like Vitoria's or Madrid's. Similarities with provincial American towns are obvious: a half-built air, streets ludicrously too wide for the traffic, laid out anticipating a boom that never came, and a couple of Plateresque palaces, sticking out from the humble tile roofs like the grand Victorian business blocks amidst the car parks of wasted American city centres.

Like America, and unlike any European country save Russia, Spain has a heritage as a frontier society. Nearly every valley and plain south of the Cordillera Cantábrica knows a history of reconquest from the Moors and Christian resettlement. Romans, Vandals, Alans, Suevi, Byzantines, Franks, Visigoths and Arabs had all done their part to make Spain's central plateau into an empty waste. From the 800s, when the Asturians and others began to cross the mountains, to the final victory over the heathen Moor in 1492, the wave of the Reconquista spread gradually southwards; at one time every part of it was the scene of pioneers reclaiming land and founding villages and towns. And as in the American West, the money that fuelled the expansion came largely from livestock—sheep, not cows, though. The biggest ranchers were the *hidalgos,* and they dominated frontier political life by influence and main force; the towns found themselves constantly on the defensive against the *hidalgos'* attempted land grabs and extortions (and sadly the towns usually lost).

Few frontier expansions in history ever came off quite like this one, though. The people that started America's push west arrived logically from behind the frontier; many of Spain's, bizarrely enough, came from *beyond* it. The northwest was hardly overflowing with population at the beginning of the Reconquista, and the numbers were largely supplied by Mozarab Christians from Muslim-ruled Spain, from al-Andalus, looking for free land and a Christian atmosphere. Few facts were ever recorded about this trickling exodus, but it is reasonable to assume that Mozarabs with the gumption to pack up and move into the lonesome *meseta* were also likely to be the most fanatical supporters of Christianity and the new Christian states. And instead of half-naked Indians without towns or technology, the heathen enemy of the new Spanish frontiersmen happened to be probably the most delightful and sophisticated civilization in the western world, led by caliphs whose greatest joys were writing lyrical poetry and planting pleasure gardens with tinkling fountains. Such irony can weigh on a nation's soul.

The pioneer warriors of the north had a secret weapon in their fight against the Moors—utter ruthlessness. Organized in highly mobile raiding parties, they could extort tributes from the Muslim lands simply by threatening to girdle their irreplaceable olive trees. Destroying crops and villages was another key tactic—the same as the Americans did to the Indians, and the Texans to the Mexicans. The Christians expanded their boundaries by making the lands beyond it uninhabitable. It all worked brilliantly, and behind the lines the new Spain gradually took shape.

What happened in the end to all the hard work and hopes of the frontiersmen can be read in Spain's sad history. The boom did come, fitfully and unequally, but nearly every village and town of Castile enjoyed at least a few decades of dizzying prosperity, enough to at least begin some grandiose projects. The woebegone church at Villalcázar de Sirga comes to mind. Santa María looks to have been planned to match the size of Burgos cathedral; thrown up in a hurry, and sadly, it never got more than a third finished, and the dust blows around it today. As always, after the boom came the bust, and what a bust it was. Castile has been busted ever since.

II. El Cid Campeador

In the Spanish pantheon El Cid Campeador comes in a close second to Santiago himself, but unlike Arthur, Siegfried, Roland and other heroes of national medieval epics, the Cid, Rodrigo Díaz de Vivar (1043–99) was entirely flesh and blood. Born in Vivar near Burgos, his unique title is derived from the Arabic *sayyidi* ('my lord'). Campeador means 'Battler', and his fame spread widely among both Moors and Christians (in his career he served both Alfonso VI of Castile and the Emir of Zaragoza); even before his death ballads celebrated his prowess. The greatest achievement of his life, the capture of Valencia from the Moors in 1095, took place when he was already 52 years old.

Through modern eyes, Rodrigo was little better than a gangster, but for the warrior class of the Reconquista, he served as a model of virtue—fearless, with an exaggerated sense of honour, devoutly Catholic yet wholly pragmatic, a generous conqueror, devoted to his family, who paid his debts and always kept his word. The Cid was the perfect man for his time, living in the frontier society among Christians, Moors and Jews, where a king's powers were limited, and the main issues of the day were the simple pleasures of turf and booty.

For all that, 'O Born in a Happy Hour'—Rodrigo's other nickname—would not have had such a long shelf life, inspiring such diverse spirits as Corneille and Hollywood (where he was played, inevitably, by Charlton Heston) if there wasn't something more to his character. This comes through in the epic *Poem of the Cid,* composed around 1140, less than half a century after his death. For 500 years the actual poem was lost, until 1779, when the royal librarian, through some literary detective work, located a copy from 1307, appropriately enough in Vivar, the Cid's hometown. Not a single ounce of the magic or marvellous touches the text; the Rodrigo Díaz that emerges lies and cheats, but has a rustic sense of humour and a certain generous charm, always ready to praise another, happy to have his wife and daughters present to watch him 'earn his bread' fighting the Moors. You can't help liking the guy. His saga, though somewhat repetitive to read, is also the first known example of the Spanish gift for realism that would reach its climax in *Don Quixote.* Actually, even more realism would have been in order, for life on the frontier was not always the stuff of poetry.

III. Reconquista Man

Here he comes. Slouching in a rough woollen tunic, García Gómez is riding out of the sorrowful wilderness of the Cantabrian mountains and into history. García Gómez may look the Arkansawyer redneck of the American frontier, the sort that proverbially 'never had nothin', never learned nothin', and don't wan't nothin', but he is a man on the make. He's got himself an iron sword, while his daddy had to get by with a big stick that he cut himself, like Little John; he carried it around, and anyone that gave him any lip was likely to get a taste of it—with iron, such encounters are fewer but a little more dangerous. Of course being a Castilian, he is a *hidalgo*, really *hijo de algo*, a 'son of somebody'; we're all *muy noble y muy leal*, ain't we boys? At least as much as the big shot who owns the castle—he just came and nicked it from the former proprietor. Nicked his wife too.

The first thing to do is clear some land. And as you can see from the Castilian landscape today, there was something in García Gómez that didn't love a tree. They used to say that a squirrel could go from Portugal to the Pyrenees, if he wanted, without touching ground. Juan José and his sons will do their best to blot out the offending forests, and the *coup de grâce* will be administered by the Habsburgs, who as we remember were always building Armadas, and also creaming the profits off the timber trade for themselves and sending them home to Germany. Next thing to do is wrestle all the stones out of the fields, and build a dry-stone house. Piece of cake. In a generation or two, with a lot of luck and an eye constantly on the main chance, the family will be able to afford a little showplace—one of the hundreds of rude hilltop castles that gave Castile its name.

Unlike the settlers of the American west, García Gómez did not come over the mountains with his Bible in his hand. He couldn't really read it, and anyhow the Church doesn't exactly hand them out—a little later, when Fernando and Isabel bring in the Inquisition, a man could get himself incinerated just for reading one in Spanish. It might give him ideas. But García Gomez is content to let the learned clerics tell him what to believe. The mysteries of faith, all conducted in Latin of course, are too subtle for him, and the church supplies the insistent, shrill propaganda that shapes his life: the triumph of the only faith over the godless Moors and Jews. Every now and then fire-eating preachers like St Peter Martyr do the circuit, rousing the fools in the towns against the heathens, and our man will ride into town for the show; afterwards the good townspeople usually let off some steam, and any resident heathens are happy to escape with their lives. The towns are mostly of the one-horse variety (León, the biggest, counted a thousand souls at most in the early 11th century, maybe ten times that while they were building their extravagant cathedral) and they are not there to show a Gómez a good time. They're full of suspicious merchants, officials and monks, and though they'd usually let him through the gate when he and the town weren't feuding, García Gómez hardly ever has reason to go.

Status in this neck of the woods is a horse. Being able to afford one of these most prized commodities ensures García Gómez's position as one of the mounted warriors in the local count's retinue, ready to form an army for the king or a springtime expedition south to fight the Moors and grab some booty. A horse was the most significant investment the average man could have, but the men of the Reconquista knew how to make it pay. Then as now, Arabian blood was prized most of all—it was mainly through Spain that Arabian horses first came into Europe. The profits to buy the beast came from sheep. Gómez has a nice little spread, and a village of malodorous tenant farmers to kick in a little rent. They pay taxes and tithes, as do the townspeople. Gómez, being a *hidalgo*, does not.

Keep your eye on this boy, for he is blessed by the gods. Tucked away on a peninsula at the extremity of Europe, the *hidalgo* has nobody to bang away against except the hapless Moors, and eventually he will have all their land and goods. By 1500, flushed with ill-gotten wealth, he will be troubling the peace of Europe, and soon after he and his sword will be tramping around the Andes, up into Kansas and down the Amazon. And finally, before he rides off into the sunset he will burn himself out completely, tilting at windmills on the plains of La Mancha.

The Saving Grace

For all the sound and fury of the Reconquista, all the waste and futility, was anything left that would last? There are people capable of conjuring up beauty and delight in any age, and at the beginning of the Middle Ages, Europe had the cash to do it in stone for the first time since the late Roman Empire. 'So it was,' wrote an 11th-century chronicler, 'as though the world had shaken herself and cast off her old age, and were clothing herself everywhere in a white garment of churches.' Spain shared fully in this flowering of Romanesque architecture and art; indeed the little Christian kingdoms of the north were the unlikely vanguard of the movement.

Where did the Romanesque come from? Unlike most parts of western Europe, northern Spain had very few Roman buildings left to serve as models. But from scattered examples around Europe and the Middle East, it is easy to see a continuous progression everywhere from late Roman architecture through the Dark Ages. The real homeland of Romanesque seems to be Syria, where Greek Christians built elegant basilican churches with plenty of rounded arches, windows and blind arcading up until the 7th-century Muslim conquest. Syrian monks, including most likely the architects and painters, spread across Christendom after that as refugees, taking the style with them. In this age buildings of any kind are few, and records almost non-existent, and while early Romanesque works in Armenia, northern Italy and Asturias may show some striking similarities, it is impossible to say too much about how they got that way.

Europe's first Romanesque churches appeared in the hills of Asturias in the 9th century, practically the only important architecture anywhere in Europe from that dark time. These showed classical elements, pediments, columns and arches, as well as considerable borrowings from the Muslim south: notably delicate double windows called *ajimeces,* divided by a column, and horseshoe arches, a native Spanish style that the Moors had adapted from the Visigoths. In the sudden, explosive burst of energy and economic expansion after the magic year 1000, the impulse to build and create spread across Europe; in Spain, as elsewhere, the Romanesque churches were the symbol of the new civilization that had emerged from the chrysalis of the Dark Ages.

One of the oldest Asturian buildings, San Miguel de Lillo at Oviedo, has carvings of what seems to be a circus scene, setting the tone for the wild imaginative freedom that characterizes all Romanesque art. The greatest charms of most churches are the carved portals, capitals and cloisters, on which you will see not only scriptural scenes, but legions of fantastical monsters, legendary heroes from Hercules to Roland, mermaids, farting monks, droll-looking insects, intricate floral designs and arabesques, demons, house cats, camels and leopards (the way medieval Europeans imagined they might look from travellers' descriptions), spirals, labyrinths, hunting scenes, whales—everything in God's good creation, along with many things God never thought of, boiling up from the depths of the medieval unconscious. Unlike every age of religious art that followed, the Romanesque was never constrained by any narrow Church dogma; perhaps the most striking example is the number of frankly erotic scenes, as on the portal of the country church at Cervatos in Cantabria. Anything at all that could be experienced, or imagined, was a fit subject to decorate the House of God.

Expressive freedom in the Romanesque was hardly limited to stone carving. The buildings themselves show a wide variety of ideas. Every province of Europe had its own distinct style and, within each, builders were often free to follow their fancy; eccentricities in northern Spain range from the octagonal churches at Eunate and Torres del Rio in Navarra, modelled after the Holy Sepulchre in Jerusalem (these were either built or inspired by the Templars), to the outlandish Santa María del Sar at Santiago, built with the columns and walls of the nave tilted precariously outwards, or the Basque church of San Miguel de Arratxinaga in Markina, built over a huge dolmen—many early churches, most perhaps, replaced pre-Christian holy sites. What ties all the disparate Romanesque works together is a simple theory of proportions. Instead of the classical 'orders', medieval builders employed a new system of sacred architecture based on constructive geometry. Anyone with a mathematical bent will enjoy looking over the buildings, seeing how every point in them can be proved with a compass and straightedge, just as their builders designed them.

Later ages of religious building may be more showy, more technically sophisticated, but none has the same hold over the imagination. The Romanesque is the art of springtime, of a new world where rules were few and fancy could wander where it liked. The pilgrimage trail to Santiago is also a pilgrimage through some of medieval Europe's finest creations, from rustic one-aisled village churches to the great basilica of Santiago de Compostela, the biggest and most ambitious Romanesque work in Spain. Some of the other major attractions include Santo Domingo de Silos, south of Burgos, with the most beautiful Romanesque cloister in Spain; Estella, with a wealth of Romanesque buildings; San Martín at Frómista, west of Burgos; and the remote area called the 'Románico Palatino', north of Frómista, with the biggest concentration of Romanesque country churches in Europe.

Estella

Navarra and La Rioja

Europe's traditional front door to Spain, Navarra is also a good introduction to the Spanish plurals, the 'Spains' combining a sizeable,
often nationalistic Basque minority up in the misty western
Pyrenees and a conservative, non-Basque Navarrese majority
tending the sunny vineyards and gardens of the Ebro valley
flatlands to the south. The combination (in Spain both
sides are known as tough cookies lacking polish)
hasn't always been comfortable, and only now that
much of the population has abandoned the countryside have tensions between the two groups
loosened up. As everyone must know by now,
much of this 'loosening up' is concentrated in
Pamplona, the capital both groups share, into an
ecstatic week-long bacchanalia of inebriated
recklessness, bull-running and partying
known as 'Los Sanfermines'.

Leiza

Betelu

Sierra de Aralar

Lekunberri

Sanctuario de
S. Miguel in Excelsis

Altsasu

Huarte

N240

Monasterio de
Iranzu

Estella/Lizarra

Monasterio de
Irache

Miranda de
Ebro

A1

A68 E804

Briñas

Sorlada

Los Arcos

Sajazarra

Haro

San Vicente de la Sonsierra

Viana

Torres del Río

Casalarreina

Briones

San Asensio

LOGROÑO

N A V A R R A

Granón

Bañares

N120

Río Najerilla

Lodosa

Santo Domingo
de la Calzada

Cañas

Nájera

Navarrete

Alberite

N111

Río Ebro

N232

Sorzano

Clavijo

Ezacaray

San Millán
de la Cogolla

Viguera

Calahorra

Río Oja

Monasterio de
Valvanera

Anguiano

Río Iregua

L A   R I O J A

Valdezcaray

Torrecilla
de Cameros

Arnedillo

Arnedo

N232

La Demanda

Sierra de Cameros

Munilla

Préjano

Canales

Mansilla

Villanueva de Cameros

Enciso

Cornago

Aguilar del
Río Alhama

Contrebia
Leukade

Cervera d
Río Alham

68

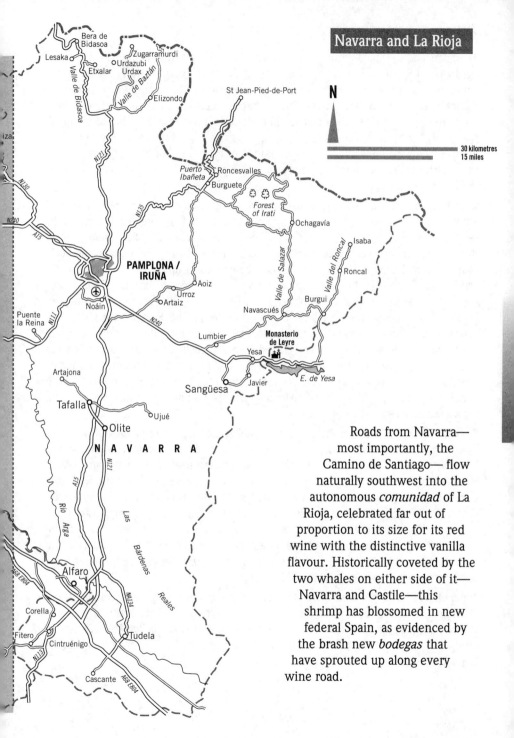

Bera de
Bidasoa

Lesaka

Valle de Bidasoa

Zugarramurdi
Urdazubi
Etxalar Urdax

Valle de Baztán

Elizondo

St Jean-Pied-de-Port

N

30 kilometres
15 miles

N121

N130

N240

A15

Puerto
Ibañeta   Roncesvalles

Burguete

Forest
of Irati

Ochagavía

N135

Isaba

Valle del Roncal

Roncal

Valle de Salazar

PAMPLONA /
IRUÑA

Aoiz

Urroz
Artaiz

Navascués

Burgui

Noáin

N240

Puente
la Reina

N111

Lumbier

Monasterio
de Leyre

Yesa

E. de Yesa

Artajona

Javier

Sangüesa

Tafalla

Ujué

Olite

N A V A R R A

N121

A15

Río Arga

Las Bardenas

Reales

Alfaro

N68 E804

Corella

Fitero

Cintruénigo

Tudela

NA134

N113

Cascante

A68 E804

Roads from Navarra—
most importantly, the
Camino de Santiago— flow
naturally southwest into the
autonomous *comunidad* of La
Rioja, celebrated far out of
proportion to its size for its red
wine with the distinctive vanilla
flavour. Historically coveted by the
two whales on either side of it—
Navarra and Castile—this
shrimp has blossomed in new
federal Spain, as evidenced by
the brash new *bodegas* that
have sprouted up along every
wine road.

Navarra: A Potted History

To understand the stand-offish, weird, James Dean rôle Navarra traditionally plays, you need a bit of Spanish history, which is full of the phrase 'except Navarra'. Even in 'the nation of nations' the region has stood apart ever since 605, when the Franks tried to harness it as part of the Duchy of Vasconia, a huge untenable territory that extended from the Garonne to the Ebro. Charlemagne himself came down in 778, either to discipline the unruly duchy or to force it to join his fight against the Moors, and after razing the walls of Pamplona he went stumping back to France—except for his rear guard, which the furious Basques of Pamplona ambushed in 778 at the pass of Roncesvalles ('Valley of the Thorntrees').

Charlemagne taught the Navarrese that owing nothing to nobody was the way to go, and within a few years of his passing they created the independent kingdom of Navarra. Its most talented king, Sancho III the Great (1004–34) firmly established the *camino francés* through Navarra and controlled much of French Basque country and Galicia, and pocketed Castile and León after the death of its last count, setting up his son Fernando I as the first to take the title of 'King of the Spains'. The centre was too precocious to hold, and by the time of Sancho IV (1054–76) Navarra was once again a fierce rival of Castile, but avoided entanglements—marital or martial—by playing the French card. 'The Flea between Two Monkeys', as it became known, was ruled by three different French dynasties between 1234 and 1512, when Fernando the Catholic slyly demanded that Navarra let his armies march through to France. His demand, as he anticipated, was refused and he used the refusal as an excuse to grab Navarra south of the Pyrenees. France was left with only Basse Navarre, a thimble-sized realm but one that gave her a long line of kings, with the accession of Henri IV (1589–1610).

Fernando kept the Navarrese happy by maintaining their *fueros* (or privileges), which in practice gave the region an independence enjoyed by no other in Spain; it was ruled by a Viceroy, minted its own coins and had its own government. Napoleonic and Liberal attempts to do away with the *fueros* in the cause of central unity turned the Navarrese into fierce reactionaries and the most ardent of Carlists (supporters of the pretender, Carlos III). In the 1930s Navarra rejected the Republic's offer of autonomy; instead, the Navarrese Carlist *requetés* in their distinctive red berets became among Franco's best troops, fighting for their old privileges and Catholicism—just as the Basques were, only on the Republican side. Franco rewarded Navarra by leaving the *fueros* intact, making it the only autonomous region in Spain until his death.

Note: Of late Navarra has made an effort to improve reasonably priced accommodation. Traditional houses have been restored as *casas rurales*, or bed and breakfasts: write to the Pamplona tourist office for their *Guía de Alojamientos de Turismo Rural.* Also, a central reservation office © (948) 22 93 28 or 22 07 41, will book beds for pilgrims along the Camino de Santiago.

Approaches from France: Down the Valleys of the Pyrenees

The Navarrese Pyrenees don't win many altitude records, but they're green, wooded and shot through with legends, many lingering in the mists around Roncesvalles, for centuries the pass most favoured by French pilgrims. Much of Navarra's Basque population is concentrated in the three valleys of Roncal, Salazar, and Baztán where seemingly every house in every hamlet is emblazoned with a coat-of-arms—for the Basques have traditionally considered themselves all equal and therefore all noble.

Getting Around

By bus: no trains here; and in most cases the buses from Pamplona go only once a day. La Tafallesa, *✆* 22 28 86, and La Roncalesa, *✆* 30 02 57, both serve the Valle del Roncal; they stop at Yesa, near the lake, and 4km from the monastery of Leyre (*see* below). For the Valle de Salazar, Río Irati has one bus daily to Ochagavía, *✆* 22 14 70. For Roncesvalles, you can go as far as Burguete and walk 3.2km (La Montañesa, *✆* 21 15 84). La Baztanesa, *✆* 22 67 12, serves the Valle de Baztán.

Tourist Information

Roncal: Ayuntamiento, *✆* (948) 47 51 36

The Eastern Valleys: Valle del Roncal and Valle de Salazar

Like many Pyrenean valleys, the Roncal was so remote for centuries that the central authorities were content to let it run its own show. Time has changed a few things: timber logged on its thickly forested slopes now travels by truck instead of careering down the Esca River, and the valley's renowned sheep's cheese, *queso de Roncal*, is now made in a factory (but according to farm traditions). Mist often envelops **Isaba**, the Valle del Roncal's biggest town, gathered under its fortress church of **San Cipriano** (1540). Every 13 July since 1375, at stone frontier marker no. 262, the mayor of Isaba and his colleagues don traditional costume and march up to meet their counterparts from the Valle de Baretous in France and ask them three times for the 'Tribute of the Three Cows', in exchange for the right to graze their herds in the Valle del Roncal in August—something both sides used to kill for before the annual tribute was agreed on. Isaba provides an excellent base for exploring the magnificent mountain scenery: hike up Navarra's highest peaks, **Pic d'Anie** (2504m) and **Mesa de los Tres Reyes** (2431m), or make the most beautiful walk of all, into the Parque Natural Pirenáico to the **refugio de Belagua**, set in a stunning glacial amphitheatre.

Roncal, once the capital of the valley, is a pretty village surrounded by pine forests.The great, amiable Basque tenor Julián Gayarre (1844–90) was born here and lies buried in a suitably high operatic tomb just outside town; the **Casa-Museo Julián Gayarre** (*open Tues–Sun 10–1.30 and 5–7, 4–6 in winter, adm*) contains costumes and photos from his glory days. **Burgui**, south, has a Roman bridge, and two roads that cut over to the Valle de Salazar: an easy one westward to Navascués and a narrow one northward by way of the remote village of Vidángoz.

The sparsely populated **Valle de Salazar** is much less visited but just as lovely, abubble with trout streams, beech forests, and old white stone Basque chalet-like *caserónes* with their pompous coats-of-arms. The best line the riverfront and cobbled lanes in **Ochagavía**, the local metropolis and another good base for walks; an easy one is up to the 13th-century chapel of **Santa María de Muskilda**, topped by an unusual square tower with a round roof: its *romería* on 8 September is celebrated with some of Navarra's most ancient dances. A more strenuous hike north on the GR 11 leads into the vast beech and ancient yew **Forest of Irati**, the largest primeval forest in the Pyrenees, with majestic Mt Orhi (2017m) as a backdrop. Besides the usual Basque fairy folk, the forest is haunted by a rather unexpected ghost: that of Jeanne d'Albret, queen of Navarra and mother of Henri IV, a nasty, diehard Protestant fanatic. Poisoned in 1572, Jeanne tours her old domain on windy nights with an escort of Basque *lamias* or nymphs, with whom she never would have been caught dead while still alive. Near Orbaitzeta a dolmen called **Azpegi I** is surrounded by a circle of 123 stones.

To the south, the spectacular 1000ft sheer-sided limestone gorge, the **Foz de Arbayún** extends for six miles below the road, home to Spain's largest colonies of rare griffon vultures (*buitres*) with their 2.5m wingspan and an assortment of smaller eagles; you can nearly always spot them floating majestically around the roadside belvedere between Navascués and Lumbier. Manmade wonders, Leyre and Sangüesa, are just south (*see* pp.86–88).

Where to Stay and Eating Out

Valle del Roncal

In Isaba, the new, luxurious ★★★**Isaba**, © 89 30 00, 🖹 89 30 31 (*moderate*), has the most modern rooms in the valley, as well as a sauna and gym. ★**Hs Lola**, at Mendigatxa 17, © 89 30 12 (*moderate*), has good rooms and a good restaurant; **Pensión Txiki**, © 89 31 18 (*moderate*), offers reasonable half board rates, as does the even cheaper **Pensión Txabalkua**, © 89 30 83. At the mountain refuge **Venta de Juan Pito**, Puerta de Belagua, © 89 30 80, you can try inexpensive local dishes such as *migas pastor* (fried bread) and Roncal cheese. In Roncal itself choose between the ★**Hs Zaltua**, Castillo 23, © 47 50 08 (*moderate/inexpensive*), and **Pensión Begoña**, © 47 50 56 (*inexpensive*).

Ochagavía

Most accommodation in the Salazar valley is in *casas rurales* or there's the 12-room ★**Hs Ori-Alde**, © 89 00 27, featuring Basque cooking in the kitchen (open July–Oct); the ★**Hs Laspalas**, © 89 00 15, is open all year (*both moderate*). The restaurant **Auñamendi**, © 89 01 89 (*moderate*), has some inexpensive rooms and serves a good asparagus and prawn pudding and trout with ham. In Oronz, just south of Ochagavía, the new ★★**Hs Salazar**, © 89 00 53 (*moderate*), has a pool and pretty views.

Of all the passes over the Pyrenees, introverted Roncesvalles was the most renowned in the Middle Ages. French pilgrims would mumble verses from the *Chanson de Roland* as they paid their respects to the sites associated with Charlemagne and his nephew Roland, then say their first prayer to another gallant knight, Santiago. From Roncesvalles' Colegiata it's 781km to Compostela, a distance the fittest pilgrims could cover in 20 days. The Colegiata had a sad, has-been look back in the 1970s, when the medieval floods of pilgrims had dried to a trickle of eccentrics. No one predicted that in the 1990s the number of pilgrims who stopped to have their documents stamped would grow by the thousands each year, especially in the last Holy Year, 1993.

Tourist Information

Roncesvalles: Antiguo Molino, ✆ (948) 76 01 93.

Roland the Rotter

All over the Pyrenees, you'll find memories of Roland—the *Brèche de Roland* in the High Pyrenees, hewn with a mighty stroke of his sword Durandal to a menhir on Mt Aralar that he tossed like Obelix. From here, his fame spread across Europe, remembered in everything from Ariosto's Renaissance epic *Orlando Furioso* to the ancient, mysterious statue of 'Roland the Giant' that stands in front of Bremen city hall. But who is this Roland really?

Outside of the *Chanson de Roland*, information is scarce. The chronicler Eginhardt, writing *c.*830, mentions a certain Roland, Duke of the Marches of Brittany, who perished in the famous ambush in the Pyrenees in 778, without according him any particular importance. Two hundred years later, this obscure incident had blossomed into one of the great epics of medieval Europe. Here is the mighty hero, with his wise friend and companion-in-arms Oliver. Here is the most puissant knight in the army of his uncle Charlemagne, come down from the north to crusade against the heathen Muslims of Spain. Charlemagne swept all before him, occupying many lands south of the Pyrenees and burning Pamplona to the ground before coming to grief at an unsuccessful siege of Zaragoza. On their return, Roland and Oliver and the peers of the rearguard are trapped at the pass of Roncesvalles, thanks to a tip from Roland's jealous stepfather Ganelon. Numberless hordes of paynims overwhelm the French; though outnumbered, they cut down Saracens by the thousands, like General Custer or John Wayne against the savage Injuns. Finally Roland, cut with a thousand wounds, smites his sword Durandal against the rock, meaning to keep it from the hands of the infidels (although in the *Chanson* he ends up heaving it in the air, where it finally ends up stuck in the cliff at Rocamadour, a major site on the pilgrims' road in southwest France). He then sounds his horn Oliphant to warn Charlemagne, alas too far away to rescue them, puffing so hard that he blows his brains out, as Michael and Gabriel appear to escort his soul to heaven.

History says it wasn't a Muslim horde at all, but rather the Navarros who did Roland in. And why shouldn't they get their revenge on these uncouth Franks who were devastating their land, trying to force this democratic nation to kneel before some crowned foreign thug who called himself their king? We might excuse a people who did not even have a word in their language for 'king' if they were not much impressed with Charlemagne. How this affair metamorphosed into an epic at the turn of the millennium or how the caterpillar Roland of history re-emerged as the mythological butterfly in the *Chanson* is murky, but as with most epics it involved a modicum of propaganda. The immediate source of the *Chanson* is said to have been a famous vision of Roland given to an 11th-century archbishop of Pamplona, which transformed Basque farmers into infidel knights (just in time for the Crusades). For the French there was another bonus: glorification of Carolingian imperialism provided poetic justification for the expansionist dreams of the Capetian kings.

The three main pilgrims' routes from France converged at Saint-Jean-Pied-de-Port then continued up to the busy frontier town of **Valcarlos**, the 'carlos' in its name referring to Charlemagne, who was camped here when he heard the dying Roland's horn blast. From here the road winds up through lush greenery to Roncesvalles, where the 12th-century church of **Sancti Spiritus** (the 'Silo de Charlemagne') is said to have been first built as Roland's tomb; according to legend, by the time the emperor arrived not only were Roland and the peers dead, but so were all the Saracens, so he couldn't tell who was who (poor Charlemagne! His legends always make him seem as thick as a pudding) so he asked heaven for a sign to make sure he gave all the Franks a Christian burial, and all at once the Christian corpses looked up to heaven, with red roses sprouting from their lips. Equally unlucky pilgrims were laid in the 7th-century **ossuary** underneath; according to Aymeric Picaud, author of the first guide to the Camino de Santiago, many of these were done in by 'false pilgrims', most of them Navarrese 'expert in all deeds of violence, fierce and savage, dishonest and false, imperious and rude, cruel and quarrelsome' and worse. Adjacent, a 13th-century church of **Santiago** is neglected and nearly always locked.

Set back from the road, the **Colegiata de Roncesvalles** is a French-style Gothic church consecrated in 1219, replacing the first Colegiata, built up at Puerto Ibañeta in 1127; after five ghastly winters the frostbitten monks moved down to the foot of the pass. What was originally the front of the church caved in under the snow in 1600 (hence the incongruous corrugated zinc roof on the rest) and was replaced by a **cloister**, from where you can pop into the 14th-century chapterhouse to see the stained glass (1960) showing a scene from the 1212 battle of Las Navas de Tolosa, where Sancho VII the Strong led the Navarrese to their greatest victory over the Moors. The chains in the chapel are among those that bound 10,000 slaves at the ankle and wrist, forming a human shield around the emir's tent, a scurvy tactic that failed to prevent the Christians from leaping over and carrying off the tent as booty. The chapterhouse holds the **tomb of Sancho the Strong**. Apparently in life the king was exactly as tall as his 7ft 4in effigy: pilgrims used to think that his battle maces, now in the museum, belonged to Roland.

Sancho financed the Colegiata, which over time has been stripped of its costly gifts, with the exception of a much revered 13th-century image of the Virgin under her baldachin. Its jumbled, anachronistic, pious legend goes that after the battle at the pass, Charlemagne founded a monastery up at Ibañeta. When the Moors poured though to attack France in 732, the monks hid the statue, and it remained hidden until 1130 when the hiding place was revealed to a Basque shepherd by a red stag with a star shimmering between its antlers.

The fascinating **museum** (*open summer and weekends 11–1.30 and 4–6, adm, or by appointment,* © 76 00 00) contains such rarefied medieval treasures as the emerald which fell from the Emir's turban when giant King Sancho burst into his tent at Las Navas de Tolosa (surely it was a sight enough to scare the emerald off anybody), an 11th-century *pyx,* or golden box used to hold the Host, a reliquary of gold and enamel called 'Charlemagne's chessboard' (*c.* 1350) for its 32 little cases, each designed to hold a saintly fingertip or tooth. Among the paintings there's an excellent 15th-century Flemish triptych and a *Holy Family* by Morales, and two books on Confucianism, purchased in India in the time of St Francis Xavier.

An easy and beautiful path from the monastery leads up in half-hour to the **Puerto Ibañeta** (1057m) where the Basques, hidden on Mounts Astobizkar and Orzanzurieta, dropped boulders on the heads of the Franks. A modern chapel replaces the monastery of San Salvador, where the monks would toll a bell to guide pilgrims through the mists and snow storms. Heading south, the pretty villages of **Burguete/Auritz** and **Espinal/Auritzberri** were the pilgrim's next stops and are still good places to stay. *Tour de France* fans should keep an eye peeled for Miguel Induraín, the Pamplonan with the magic thighs, who trains in the area.

© *(948–)*   *Where to Stay and Eating Out*

Roncesvalles

If you want to stay in comfort **★★Hs La Posada,** © 76 02 25 (*moderate*), has 11 spacious rooms in the Colegiata, with a fine restaurant located in the medieval inn that formerly served the pilgrims. **★Hs Casa Sabina,** © 76 00 12 (*moderate*), next to the monastery gate, has six pleasant rooms, and good Navarrese cooking. In Burguete, 3km away, **★★Hs Loizu,** © 76 00 08, offers plenty of atmosphere for its moderate rates, or try one of several *casas rurales* or restaurants with rooms.

Western Valleys: Valle de Baztán and Valle de Bidasoa

Frequent rains off the Atlantic make the valleys west of Roncesvalles so lush that they're called the 'Switzerland of Navarra'. Both are dotted with well-preserved, unspoiled white Basque villages, trout streams, and quietly beautiful scenery. The **Valle de Baztán** once had Spain's largest *agote* population (*see* p.87) and perhaps not entirely coincidentally a legendary colony of witches in the early 17th century, who based their activities in **Zugarramurdi**, a pretty place just in from the French frontier. Just outside the village, carved out of the mountain by the Infernuko Erreka (Hell's Stream), the vast **Cuevas de Zugarramurdi** were the scene of black sabbaths, or *akelarres*, in which the participants smeared themselves with an unguent made of human brains and bones, mixed with belladonna, toads, salamanders and snakes—at least according to the 31 people imprisoned and 'put to the question' by the Logroño inquisition in 1609; of those condemned, 13 died under torture and six survived to be burned alive at an *auto da fé*. On the summer solstice the locals still gather in the caves for a feast and a dance. Even older magic was built into the **cromlechs of Mairuillarrieta**, dedicated to the Basque goddess Mairu or Mari, reached by a path from the village. There are other caves, the lovely stalactite **Cuevas de Urdax** just south at Urdazubi/Urdax, where Basque nymphs or *lamias* once frolicked in the stream; guided tours run roughly every 20 minutes in the summer.

Elizondo, the chief village in the Baztán valley, has an informal tourist office in C/ Jaime Urrutia where you can pick up a map that pinpoints the historic houses: those along the river are especially impressive. **Arizcun**, 7km west, has the fortified stone house of one of Spain's busiest conquistadores, Pedro de Ursúa, leader of the search for El Dorado up the Amazon in 1560. The parish church has a striking Baroque façade. Further south a road turns east to France by way of the spectacular **Izpegui pass** (summer only).

Navarra's westernmost Pyrenean valley, the **Valle de Bidasoa**, embraces streams filled with salmon and trout and more prosaically, the main San Sebastián–Pamplona road. Buses between the two offer a chance to visit charming old Basque villages such **Vera (Bera) de Bidasoa**, only a couple miles from the French frontier, where the former home of the anarchistic Basque novelist Pío Baroja (1872–1956; author of *Memorias de un hombre de acción*) is now an ethnographic museum (© 63 00 20 for an appointment). **Lesaka**, equally pretty, claims one of the best preserved fortified feudal houses in Navarra. Tiny **Etxalar/Echalar**, a hamlet that time forgot, is on a tiny stream on the pretty, seldom-used road to Zugarramurdi—seldom used except in October, during the annual wild pigeon and woodcock holocaust. The church at Etxalar is surrounded by 100 Basque funerary steles with their distinctive star discs.

Further south, the **Parque Natural del Señoro de Bértiz**, a former private estate, has foot, bicycle and riding paths through thousands of acres of oak, beech and chestnut forests; the gardens near the manor boast over 120 species of exotic trees (*garden open 9–2 and 4–6, until 8 in summer, park open during lunch*). Note the coat-of-arms of the lord of Bértiz, showing a mermaid holding a mirror and comb; Carlos III ordered her placed there in 1421 in honour of the persuasive powers of his ambassador, Micheto de Bértiz. Two villages just west of here, **Zubieta** and **Ituren**, are famous for a carnival ritual that could have been invented by Dr Seuss: men called the *Ioaldun* dress up in striped dunce's caps and lacey smocks, and tie a pair of noise-making *polunpak* (giant bells) to their backs, nestled in furry sashes. Thus arrayed, the *Ioaldun* make a *zanpantzar*, or march from village to village, their *polunpak* smacking and jangling as they walk.

Urdazubi/Urdax

Sitting out on the terrace at **Menta**, on the Dantxarinea road, © 59 90 20 (*moderate*), you can feast on a superb mix of French and Navarrese dishes, with game dishes in season; good wine list, too (closed Mon eve and Tues).

Elizondo

The modern ★★★**Baztán**, on the main road, © 58 00 50, ◉ 45 23 23, has panoramic views, a pool and a garden (closed Dec–Mar). ★★**Hs Saskaitz**, M. Azphilikueta 10, © 58 04 88, ◉ 58 09 92 (*expensive*), is cosy enough in the centre of town; for something cheaper, try **Pensión Eskisaroi**, © 58 00 13 (*moderate*), which also does inexpensive dinners. Elizondo is famous for its *txuritabeltz*, a stew of lamb's tripe, served most days at **Galarza**, C/ Santiago 1, © 58 01 01 (*inexpensive*), a haven of traditional Baztanian cuisine and cheese, a rival to Roncal (closed Tues). Livestock still baa and moo on the ground floor of the **Casa Rural Urruska**, 10km away in Barrio de Bearzún, © 45 21 06; the simple but solid homecooking attracts hungry clients from all down the valley.

Pamplona/Iruña

Whether you call it Pamplona, the town founded by Pompey in 75 BC, or by its older name Iruña, which means simply 'the city' in Basque, the capital of autonomous Navarra sits on a strategic 450m pimple on the beautiful fertile plain, its existence as inevitable as its nickname, the 'Gateway of Spain'. For a few years in the 730s, Abd al Rahman used it in reverse, as the gateway to France, until Arab dreams of Europe were hammered at Poitiers. Over the next decades the Vascones regained control of Pamplona, clobbered Charlemagne after he burnt their walls, and set up their own king. In 918, the Moors came back and razed Pamplona to the ground again. To encourage rebuilding, Sancho III the Great invited his subjects in French Navarre to come and start trades in what became the two new districts of Pamplona, San Cernín and San Nicolás. The fact that the three districts of the city were practically independent and had their own privileges led to violent rivalry, so much so that in 1521 the French Navarrese unsuccessfully besieged Pamplona in an effort to regain San Cernín and San Nicolás. Wounded while fighting for Castile was a certain Captain Íñigo López de Recalde, who convalesced in Pamplona, got religion in a militant way and founded the Jesuits.

Pamplona seems to have been naturally conducive to that sort of thing, with a reputation for being crazily austere, brooding and puritanical. For anyone who knows the city only for throwing the wildest party in Europe, this comes as a shock of *desfase* or maladjustment, a word that means (and gleefully celebrates) the unresolved contradictions that co-exist in post-Franco Spain. Stern catholicism is part of the city's fabric. 'From the top to the bottom of Pamplonese society, I have found the whole place poisoned by clerical alkaloid,' grumped Basque philosopher Unamuno. 'It oozed out of every corner...one drop in the eye is enough to infect you forever.' In the 1950s, the secretive Opus Dei, Christianity's ultra-conservative fifth column, chose Pamplona to build their Universidad de Navarra. In the 1960s, the city's new tennis club still built separate swimming pools for men and women. Thirty years later, a new Pamplona prides itself for setting up Spain's first shelter for battered women, the first city workshops for training disadvantaged youth and the first urban rubbish recycling programme. 'Pamplona is a city that gives much more than it promises,' said Victor Hugo. It certainly will if you come the second week of July for the Sanfermines, but expect it to take as well: your money, your watch, your sleep and a lifetime supply of adrenalin.

Getting Around

By air: Pamplona's airport is 9km south of the city, ✆ (948) 31 75 12, with connections to Madrid, Barcelona and Santander. The cheapest way to get to the airport is to take a Beriainesa bus from the bus station (every half-hour) to Noaín, which drops you a few hundred yards from the airport.

By train: Pamplona's train station is 2km out of town on Avda. San Jorge. Bus no. 9 makes connections from the centre every 10 minutes, ✆ (948) 13 02 02; tickets and information can also be had at the railway office in town at C/ Estella 8, ✆ (948) 22 72 82.

By bus: the bus station is in town, near the citadel, at C/ Conde Oliveto 8; information ✆ 22 38 54. Besides provincial connections, there are three buses to Vitoria, four to Bilbao, three to San Sebastián, four to Zaragoza, and two to Huesca and Jaca.

Tourist Information

C/ Duque de Ahumada 3, just off Plaza del Castillo, ✆ (948) 22 07 41, 🖅 21 20 59.

There is a **market** every morning except Sundays at the Mercado de Santo Domingo, Plaza de los Burgos.

A Walk through the Casco Viejo

Pamplona was squeezed in a tight girdle of walls until the early 1900s, when the city spread in all directions and accumulated around 185,000 inhabitants in the process. But for all its 20th-century flab, the vital organs in the historic Casco Viejo remain intact, beginning with the city's heart, **Plaza del Castillo**, shaded by the knitted boughs of the plane trees, circled by too many cars, framed by arcades sheltering stylish cafés. Off the southwest corner extends the **Paseo de Sarasate**, populated by stone kings and queens and the overwrought **Monumento a los Fueros**, erected by popular subscription after Madrid tried to mess with Navarra's privileges back in 1893. The bronze allegory of Navarra holds a copy of the *Ley Foral*, or Fueros' Law, surrounded by the broken chains from the battle of Las Navas de Tolosa, symbolizing freedom; these also feature on Navarra's coat of arms. Historical frescoes decorate the neo-classical **Palacio de Navarra**,

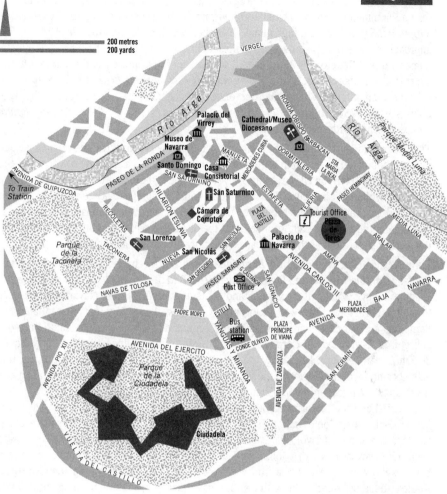

N

200 metres
200 yards

VERGEL

Río Arga

Palacio del Virrey

Cathedral/Museo Diocesano

RONDA OBISPO BARBAZAN

Río Arga

Parque Media Luna

Museo de Navarra

MANUETA

MERCADERES CURIA

DORMITALERIA

STA MARIA LA REAL

PASEO DE LA RONDA

AVENIDA DE GUIPUZCOA

To Train Station

Santo Domingo

Casa Consistorial

SAN SATURNINO

San Saturnino

ESTAFETA

TEJERIA

PASEO HEMINGWAY

RECOLETAS

HILARION ESLAVA

Cámara de Comptos

PLAZA DEL CASTILLO

Tourist Office

MEDIA LUNA

Plaza de Toros

San Lorenzo

TACONERA

NUEVA

San Nicolás

SAN NICOLAS

Palacio de Navarra

ARALAR

Parque de la Taconera

NAVAS DE TOLOSA

SAN GREGORIO

PASEO SARASATE

G CASTAÑON

SAN IGNACIO

AMAYA

AVENIDA CARLOS III

NAVARRA

PADRE MORET

Post Office

ESTELLA

PLAZA MERINDADES

BAJA

AVENIDA

YANGUAS Y MIRANDA

Bus station

PLAZA PRINCIPE DE VIANA

AVENIDA DEL EJERCITO

CONDE OLIVETO

AVENIDA DE ZARAGOZA

SAN FERMIN

AVENIDA PIO XII

Parque de la Ciudadela

Ciudadela

VUELTA DEL CASTILLO

also in the Paseo; the archives contain one of the best caches of medieval documents in Spain and the garden boasts a massive sequoia.

Off the east end of Plaza del Castillo, the narrow streets jammed with shops and bars were once the *Judería*, where Pamplona's Jews, 'a gentle and reasonable race' according to the King of Navarra, lived unmolested until Navarra was gobbled up by the Castile of Fernando and Isabel. Behind these, tucked up near the ramparts, the gracious 14th–15th-century Gothic **Cathedral** hides behind a dull-witted, neoclassical façade, slapped on in the 18th century by a misguided do-gooder; a shame because the original front, according to travellers' descriptions, was as lusty as the one at Cervatos (*see* p.176). When completed, it was the second largest cathedral in Spain after León's, and suitable shelter for the beautiful alabaster tombs of the cathedral's sponsors, big-nosed Carlos III 'the Noble' and his big-nosed queen Leonora de Trastámara, sculpted in the 15th century by Jean de Lomme of Tournai. The kings of Navarra were crowned before the Romanesque *Virgen del Sagrario* on the high altar. The delicacy of the Gothic **cloister** (1280–1472) approaches gossamer in stone and reaches a climax of decorative bravura in the justly named **Puerta Preciosa** (1325), carved with a superb Dormition of the Virgin. Off the cloister, the **Museo Diocesano** (*open mid-May to mid-Oct, 9–2; adm*) occupies the refectory and kitchen where pilgrims once dined and contains two remarkable reliquaries—the 1258 *Relicario del Santo Sepulcro* and the 1401 *Relicario del Lignum Crucis*, adorned with precious stones.

The narrow old lanes around the Cathedral belong to the **Navarrería**, the original Basque quarter, populated in the Middle Ages by cathedral builders and farmers who tilled the Bishop's lands. Here on the promontory you'll find the most impressive segment of the surviving **walls** built by Felipe II, with a reputation for impregnability so powerful that no one tried to challenge their reputation until the French tried to hole up here against Wellington; the views stretch for miles over the plain. Just west, the 13th-century **Palacio del Virrey** started out as the royal palace and now houses the local military government.

Through the attractive **Portal de Zumalacárregui** (16th-century, but renamed after the Carlist hero), the **Museo de Navarra** (*open 10–2 and 5–7, Sun 11–2, closed Mon; adm*) occupies a huge 16th-century hospital and contains everything from Navarrese prehistory to contemporary art, with Roman mosaics, Gothic wall paintings, carved capitals from Pamplona's original Romanesque cathedral (minus any of the naughty bits), an ivory coffret from Leyre made in Córdoba in the 11th century and a fine portrait of the Marqués de San Adrián by Goya. Just below the museum, wooden barricades remind you that this is the beginning of the *encierro*; the bulls leave their corral near Plaza Santo Domingo and head up C/ Mercaderes and Estafeta. Follow their route and you'll come to Plaza Consistorial and the colourful Baroque **Casa Consistorial**, topped with jaunty allegorical figures. Pamplona's nobles built their finest escutcheoned palaces just off this square, along C/ Zapatería and C/ Mayor. Plazas de Consejo and San Francisco, set diagonally opposite each other, are also worth a look, the latter with a *modernista* hotel converted into a bank. Nearby in C/ Ansoleaza, the well-preserved Gothic **Cámara de los Comptos Reales**, the kings' mint in the 12th century, has a magnificent porch opening onto a vault and patio with some original decorations intact.

The not always tremendously popular *francos* (Gascons, mostly), invited to Pamplona by Sancho the Great, lived just to the south in their two rival quarters named after, and defended by, 13th-century churches that doubled as fortresses when their fellow citizens went on the war path: these are **San Saturnino** (or San Cernín) in C/ San Saturnino and **San Nicolás** in lively, bar-lined C/ San Nicolás; a plaque by the former marks the site where the first Pamplonans were converted by San Saturnino. Further west, **San Lorenzo** is best known for its chapel dedicated to San Fermín, built by the city in 1717, where his bust reliquary quietly resides 51 weeks of the year, presiding over weddings; so many Pamplonese want to be married under his protective eye that there's a two-year waiting list.

Pamplona is well endowed with parks, which especially come in handy for naps during the fiesta. The oldest, the French-style **Parque de la Taconera** closes out the west end of the Casco Viejo near San Lorenzo and has one of the city's nicest cafés, the **Vienés**, in a charming old kiosk. Just south, the star-shaped **Ciudadela**, built on the orders of Felipe II, is now a green park, inside and outside the steep walls—where the Pamplonese tune up their rock climbing skills. The prettiest garden, **Parque Media Luna**, lines the river east of the city and has a path ending at the medieval bridge used by the pilgrims. The park in front of the **Plaza de Toros**—the third largest in the world—was renamed Paseo Hemingway and has a grizzled bust of the writer whose *The Sun Also Rises* (1926) made Pamplona a household word.

Pamplona's Annual Meltdown: *Los Sanfermines*

Before Hemingway, there was Fermín, son of a Roman senator and first bishop of Pamplona. His family had been converted by San Saturnino (or Sernin, or Cernín) of Toulouse who was martyred by being dragged about by a bull. Fermín, for his part, travelled as a missionary to the Gauls and was beheaded in Amiens for his trouble. Some time between then and 1324, when Pamplona held its first fiesta, Fermín decided to take bullfighters under his saintly cape; by 1591 his festival had found its current dates and form. Although it's the insanely dangerous running of the bulls that has made *los Sanfermines* world-famous, it's only a tiny portion of the nine days of non-stop revelling when 'Pamplona becomes the world capital of happiness', a state of hyper-bliss fuelled by three million litres of alcohol. A year.

There is some order to the madness. The Sanfermines officially open at noon on 6 July, when thousands of Navarrese in their festival attire (white shirts and white trousers or skirts, red sashes and red bandanas) gather in front of the town hall to hold their bandanas aloft as a rocket called *El Chupinazo* is fired off the balcony and a city councillor cries in Spanish and Basque: 'People of Pamplona! Long live San Fermín!' The city explodes with a mighty roar, while popping tens of thousands of champagne corks (and smashing the bottles on the pavement, usually causing the first casualties). In the afternoon the giants and big heads (*gigantes y cabezudos*)—as essential to the fiesta as the bulls—leave their 'home' in the bus station. The eight 13ft plaster giants supported by dancers date from 1860 and represent kings and queens, who whirl and swirl the minuet, their sweeping skirts flowing in the air. They are accompanied by the *cabezudos* and *kilikis*, big-headed figures in tricorn hats with names like Napoleon and Patata who wallop children on the head with foam rubber balls tied to bats. This is also the prerogative of the *zaldikos,* the colourfully dressed men wearing cardboard horses around their waists; all are accompanied by dancers and *txistularis* (Basque flutes) and *gaiteros*. At 4 o'clock a massive scrum, the *Riau Riau,* begins when members of the Corporación de San Fermín dressed in all their finery try to proceed 400m down the Calle Mayor to the chapel of San Fermín at San Lorenzo's for vespers, but everyone else tries to prevent them in a gung-ho defiance of authority, to the extent that it's often late at night before the Corporación achieves its goal. The mayor of Pamplona has tried for several years to ban the chaotic *Riau Riau*, but it seems to be unbannable.

After a first night of carousing and dancing in the streets, the dawn of 7 July and every following day is welcomed with the *dianas*, a citywide wake-up call performed on screeching pipes. The *encierro*, or running of the bulls, begins daily at 8am, but if you want a good place to watch, wedge yourself into a spot along the route—Cuesta de San Domingo, Mercaderes and Estafeta—at least an hour earlier. Before running, the locals sing a hymn to Fermín and arm themselves with a rolled-up newspaper to distract the bull's attention, since the animals—1200lbs of muscle and fury—charge at the nearest moving object, ideally at a flung newspaper instead of a falling runner. A rocket goes up as the first bull leaves the corral; a second rocket means that all are released; and a third signals that all have made it to the bullring—on a good run the whole *encierro* only lasts three minutes. The most dangerous moments are when the runners and bulls have to squeeze into the runway of the bullring, or when a bull gets loose from his fellows and panics. People (and not all of them tourists) get trampled and gored every year; if you run you can hedge your bets by running on weekdays, when it's less crowded, and by avoiding the *toros* of the Salvador Guardiola ranch, which have the most bloodstained record. The spirit of abandon is so infectious that, even if you come determined not to run, you may find yourself joining in on a self-destructive spur of the moment. Women do defy the authorities and run, although the police try to pull them out.

During the *encierro* the lower seats of the bullring are free (again, arrive early), except on Sunday; from here you can watch the bulls and runners pile in, and afterwards, more fun and games as heifers with padded horns are released on the crowd in the ring. The traditional breakfast is huge (bull stews, lamb's sweet-breads, ham and eggs in tomato sauce, washed down with gallons of chilled rosé and *pacharán)*. The bullfights themselves take place daily at 6.30 in the after-noon—tickets sell out with the speed of lightning and are usually only available from scalpers. The *sombra* seats are for serious aficionados, while members of the 16 *peñas* (clubs devoted to making noise and in general being as obnoxious as possible) fill up the *sol* seats and create a parallel fiesta if the action in the ring isn't up to snuff or create pandemonium if it is. Afternoons also see other bull sports that are bloodless (for the bull, at any rate): the dodging, swerving *concurso de recortadores* or leaping *corrida vasca-landesa.*

In between the bull fights there are concerts, *jotas* and Basque dances, processions of the relics of San Fermín and various other religious services, parades, special activities for young children and senior citizens. At night fireworks burst over the citadel and the *toro de fuego* or 'fire bull' carried by a runner and spitting fireworks chases children down the route of the *encierro*. Then there's the midnight *El Estruendo de Irún*, led by an enormous drum called the *bomba* in which hundreds of people—just about anyone who can lay their hands on anything that makes a sound—gathers around and lets loose in an ear-bashing sonic disorder. At midnight on 14 July Pamplona winds down to an exhausted, nostalgic finale, a ceremony known as the *Pobre de mí;* everyone gathers in front of the town hall (or in the Plaza del Castillo for the livelier, unofficial ceremony), with a candle and sings 'Poor me, poor me, another San Fermín has come to an end'. As the clock strikes 12 everyone removes their red scarves and agrees, like Hemingway, that it was 'a damned fine show' and promises to do better and worse next year. Die-hards party on until 8am the next day, and perform one last feat, the *encierro de la villavesa*: the bulls are all dead so they run in front of a bus.

Pamplona ℗ (948–)–   **Where to Stay**

During San Fermín, hotel prices double and often triple, supplemented by scores of overpriced rooms in *casas particulares*, advertised weeks ahead in the local newspapers, *Navarra Hoy* or *Diario de Navarra*. The tourist office has a list of these as well; prices range around 5000 pts a night. If you end up sleeping outside, any of the gardens along the walls or river are preferable to the noisy, filthy, vomit-filled citadel. Keep a close eye on your belongings (petty criminals, unfortunately, go into overdrive along with everyone else during the fiesta) and check in what you don't need at the bus station's *consigna*; everyone else does, too, so get there early. Two free campsites are set up along the road to France, but again, don't leave anything there you might really miss. If you stay outside Pamplona and drive into town, beware that breaking into cars is epidemic but discerning: thieves took our toothbrushes, Tampax and travel iron but left everything else.

luxury

Conveniently located a short walk from the old town, ★★★★**Los Tres Reyes**, Jardines de la Taconera, ✆ 22 66 00, ☎ 22 29 30, pampers its well-heeled guests with every possible convenience and an indoor, heated pool and tennis.

expensive

★★★**Maisonnave**, C/ Nueva 20 (next to Pza. San Francisco) ✆ 22 26 00, ☎ 22 01 66, offers comfort and prestige and a peaceful garden in the back. Another good choice in the centre, ★★★**Europa**, just off Pza. Castillo on C/ Espoz y Mina 11, ✆ 22 18 00, ☎ 22 92 35, is one of Pamplona's prettiest choices, with its flower-bedecked balconies, some overlooking the *encierro* action in Estafeta; the restaurant, one of the city's finest, is run by the same management as the Alhambra's (*see* below). In the centre, the family-run ★★★**Yoldi**, Avda. San Ignacio 11, ✆ 22 48 00, ☎ 21 20 45, has long been the favourite of *toreros* and aficionados in general. The small, quiet, cozy ★★**Eslava**, Pza. Virgen de la O, ✆ 22 22 70, ☎ 22 51 57, is run by a friendly family and has views over the walls of Pamplona.

At Berrioplano, 5km from Pamplona on the Guipúzcoa road, ★★★**El Toro**, ✆ 30 22 11, ☎ 30 20 85, has quiet rooms in a traditional-style mansion, overlooking a statue group of the *encierro*.

moderate

There's not a lot in this range: Hemingway always stayed at Pamplona's oldest hotel, ★**La Perla**, Pza. Castillo, ✆ 22 77 06, ☎ 21 15 66, at least as long as room 217 was available; the others, recently renovated, still have their high ceilings and plaster mouldings from 1880. ★**Hs Bearán**, San Nicolás 25, ✆ 22 34 28, ☎ 22 34 28, is one of the few decent *hostales*, where doubles come with baths. A pair of sisters run ★★**Hs Príncipe de Viana I and II**, in the same building on Avda. Zaragoza 4, ✆ 24 91 47 or 24 91 46, some rooms with, some without baths.

inexpensive

Cheaper *hostales* and *fondas* are mostly on C/ San Gregorio and C/ San Nicolás. The least inexpensive hostal, **Hs Casa García**, C/ San Gregorio 12, ✆ 22 38 93, offers 10 double rooms without bath, and an adequate *menú del día* in its restaurant. Located in an 18th-century palace, **Casa Santa Cecilia**, C/ Navarrería 17, ✆ 22 22 30, is one of the nicest cheap sleeps under lofty ceilings in huge rooms. **Otano**, San Nicolás 5, ✆ 22 50 95, has been popular for years for its nice rooms with baths, and a good inexpensive restaurant-bar. The nearest campsite, **Excaba**, is 7km north, ✆ 33 03 15.

Pamplona's classic, **Josetxo**, C/ Príncipe de Viana 1, ℗ 22 20 97 (*expensive*), has been a local gourmet institution for 40 years. Try to book one of the small Belle Epoque dining-rooms upstairs, and chose between delicacies such as *ajoarriero con langosta* (seafood casserole with lobster) or the chef's prize *solomillo a la broche con salsa de trufa* (steak filet on a spit with truffle sauce); closed Sun and Aug). The excellent **Hartza**, C/ Juan de Labrit 19, ℗ 22 45 68 (*expensive*), is famous for its *bonito encebollado* (tuna with onions), hake dishes and good home-made desserts (closed Sun eve, Mon, and mid July–early Aug). At the fashionable **Alhambra**, C/ Bergamín 7, ℗ 24 50 07 (*expensive*) look for more imaginative dishes: potatoes stuffed with truffles and scampi and home-made desserts; good *menú degustación* at 4400 pts (closed Sun). At the family-run **Rodero**, C/ E. Arrieta 3, ℗ 22 80 35 (*expensive*), delicious dishes based on Navarrese, Basque and French recipes are prepared with the finest seasonal ingredients (closed Sun and Aug). On weekends half of Pamplona drives 11km out towards Irún to dine on the imaginative home-cooking at **Sarasate**, ℗ 33 08 20 (*moderate*) in a traditional *caserío* with a fireplace for winter dining and a terrace in the summer. Near Parque Media Luna, the **Chalet de Izu**, Avda. Baja Navarra 47, ℗ 22 60 93 (*moderate*), has plenty of swish atmosphere and good *menús*. For a big grilled meat and wine feast, try **Asador Olaverri**, C/ Santa Marta 4, ℗ 23 50 63 (*moderate*); for Navarrese-style seafood, try **Erburu**, C/ San Lorenzo 19, ℗ 22 51 69 (moderate; inexpensive lunch *menú*). **Casa Sixto**, C/ Estafeta 81, ℗ 22 51 27, is well known for its succulent home-cooked game dishes (closed Oct). The chef at **La Campana**, C/ Campana 12, ℗ 22 00 08 (*inexpensive*), takes special pride in preparing unusual recipes such as chicken in champagne. Other inexpensive choices include **Casa Paco**, C/ Lindatxikía (behind San Nicolás church) ℗ 22 51 05, a favourite for lunch since the 1920s; **Urricelqui**, C/ Jarauta 30, ℗ 22 21 46, even older, a good bet for liver or mushroom dishes, and another **Sarasate**, C/ San Nicolás 19, ℗ 22 57 27, for the best vegetarian meals in Pamplona (closed Sun and evenings, except Fri and Sat).

cafés and bars

At the last count Pamplona had some 700 bars, or one for every 280 inhabitants, many of whom seem to be always in them, day and night. There are elegant cafés, most famously the 1888 *modernista* **Café Iruña**, a fixture on the Plaza del Castillo, where you can also tuck into inexpensive light meals until 2.30am. The **Mesón del Caballo Blanco**, near the cathedral in Redín, is an atmospheric old stone house with a terrace, a delightful place to linger; in winter sandwiches are served around the fireplace. **Roch**, C/ Comedias, is small, lively and usually packed at the start of *la marcha*, thanks in part to their superb *fritos de pimiento* tapas. Favourite late night bar crawling zones in the Casco Viejo are C/ San Nicolás and San Gregorio, San Lorenzo and Jarauta, and Navarrería, the latter still popular with the Basques and alternative Pamplonese. **El Cordovilla**, one of the bars here, claims to make the biggest *pinchos* (kebabs) in the world.

East of Pamplona: Sangüesa, Leyre and Javier

Pilgrims from Mediterranean lands would cross the Pyrenees at Somport in Aragón and enter Navarra at Sangüesa, home of one of the very best Romanesque churches and one of the craziest palaces in all Spain, but these days, if the wind's wrong, the pong of the nearby papermill hurries visitors along; note that if you go by bus from Pamplona (La Veloz Sangüesina, © 22 69 95) there are only three a day and you'll be stuck with the stink longer than you might like. If you're driving, there's enough interest in the area to make a day's excursion.

Tourist Information

Aoiz: C/ Nueva 2, Edificio del Ayuntamiento, © (748) 33 60 05

Sangüesa: C/ Alfonso el Batallador 20, © (748) 87 03 29.

Aoiz (Agoitz)

The region due east of Pamplona, crossed by the Río Irati, gets few tourists but, if you're driving, the undulating landscapes and nearly deserted villages make an interesting alternative to the more direct N 240 to Sangüesa. Aoiz itself has fine old houses, a medieval bridge and the 15th-century church of **San Miguel Arcángel**, worth a look for its excellent *retablo mayor* (1580) by Basque master Juan de Achieta and its unusual 12th-century painted stone font. Romanesque connoisseurs should go out of their way to **Artaiz**, a tiny blip to the southwest (due south of Urroz), where the church of **San Martín** has the finest sculpture in rural Navarra, including some not too scary monsters.

Sangüesa

Sangüesa was a direct product of the pilgrimage, purposely moved from its original hilltop location in the 11th century to the spot where the road crosses the River Aragón. In 1122 Alfonso el Batallador, king of neighbouring Aragón, sent down a colony of *francos* to augment Sangüesa's population, and ten years after that ordered the Knights of St John to build a church well worth stopping for: **Santa María la Real**. This possesses one of the most intriguing and extraordinary portals on the whole Camino (unfortunately the street in front is quite busy, so you have to look at it between the cars), so strange that some writers believe that its symbols (knotted labyrinths, mermaids, two-headed beasts symbolizing duality, etc.) were sculpted by *agotes* or by a brotherhood of artists on to something deeper than orthodox Catholicism; even the damned are laughing in the *Last Judgement* on the tympanum, presided over by a Christ in Majesty with a secret smile and vigorous Evangelists almost dancing around the throne. Below, the elongated figures on the jambs show stylistic similarities to Chartres cathedral, although again the subjects are unusual: on the left the three Marys (the Virgin, Mary Magdalene and Mary Solomé, mother of St James), on the right Peter, Paul and Judas, hanged, with the inscription *Judas Mercator*. The upper half of the portal is by another hand altogether, crossed by two tiers of Apostles of near-Egyptian rigidity and another Christ in Majesty surrounded by symbols of the four evangelists. If the church is open, ask the sacristan to show you the capitals in the apse, hidden behind the Flemish Renaissance *retablo*. Note the well in the corner: not something you find every day inside a church. Walk around to see the beautiful carved corbels on the apse and the octagonal tower.

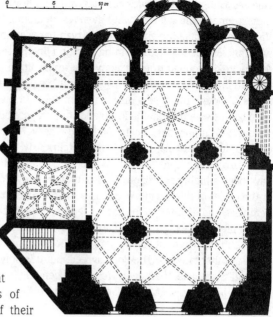

Santa María la Real

When Aragón and Navarra went their separate ways, the kings of Navarra made Sangüesa one of their several residences. Sangüesa's arcaded Rua Mayor is lined with palaces, including the **Casa Consistorial**, built over the old royal patio of arms, today a charming leafy square; behind this is the austere 12th-century, twin-towered Palacio del Príncipe de Viana. The 12th-century church of **Santiago** has a huge battlemented tower and carved capitals and conserves a large stone statue of St James, discovered buried under the floor in 1965. The slightly later, Gothic **San Salvador** has a pentagonal tower and a huge porch, sheltering a carved portal; its Plateresque choir stalls come from Leyre. Just around the corner in C/ Alfonso el Batallador, the brick **Palacio Vallesantoro** catches the eye with its corkscrew Baroque portal and the widest, most extraordinary wooden eaves in Spain, carved with a phantasmagorical menagerie that makes the creatures on Santa María look tame.

Europe's Untouchables: The *Agotes*

Some of Europe's best-known outcasts, the *agotes* (*cagots* in French) lived in the valleys of Navarra and especially across the Pyrenees in Basse Navarre and Gascony. Apartheid laws forced them to live apart and only marry other *agotes*; to enter church only by a certain door and hear Mass in a special corner; to dress differently, with a goose foot sewn on to the backs of their coats; to play castanets at all crossroads and other public places to warn passers-by of their presence. Trades were forbidden them—except as builders and carpenters, a craft they excelled at to the extent that they were often called 'the Master Carpenters' instead of *agotes*.

Guesses as to who the *agotes* actually were and how they came to be pariahs varies in the extreme: some say they were dwarves, or albinos covered with a blond down, or Visigoths who failed to give up their Aryan heresies and took refuge in the mountains when the Moors invaded. A strong tradition linking the *agotes* to leprosy suggests that they were descended from a colony sent to live up in the remote valleys; but leprosy is not hereditary, and the *agotes* who lived in Sangüesa and other towns were not lepers, although the stigma may have remained. In the Middle Ages, their ranks may have been swollen by all the loose ends of Europe who landed up along the road to Santiago. Or it may have been that the *agotes* were only symbolic lepers, kept at a distance for the stigma of their heresies (curiously, they were also *Crestias*, or Christians, as if emphasizing that they were still, really, in the fold). This heresy may have been a highly contagious kind of universal mysticism practised by the Templars or the Order of the Knights of St Lazarus, an Order founded in the East before the Templars, and devoted to the care of lepers, using Lazarus as their symbol of death within life. Whatever the real reason for their pariah status, it was forgotten by the 16th century, when the fed-up *agotes* petitioned the Pope to give them the same rights as other citizens. The Pope agreed, but it is only in this century, after a long civil rights struggle, that the *agotes* have been fully integrated into society, intermarrying with non-*agotes* and vanishing without trace.

Javier and Leyre

Sangüesa is the base for visiting two of Navarra's holy sites. **Javier**, 13km away, is topped by a picturesque if over-restored battlemented castle, the birthplace in 1506 of St Francisco de Javier (Xavier), Jesuit apostle of the Indies and Japan. Though the castle is now a Jesuit college, you can take the tour (*open 10–1 and 4–7; adm*) and learn a lot, both about St Francis Xavier and castles—this one dates back to the 11th century, was wrecked in 1516 by Cardinal Cisneros' troops, and restored after 1952. Perhaps most fascinating is the fresco of the *Dance of Death*, a grim reminder that the Pyrenees were especially hard hit by the plague.

Just north of Javier, at **Yesa** the Río Aragón has been dammed to form the vast **Yesa Reservoir**. A road from Yesa leads up into the beautiful Sierra de Leyre and the **Monasterio de San Salvador de Leyre** (*open 8am–9pm*). Its foundation predates the Moors, and in the 8th century its most famous abbot San Virila so constantly prayed to heaven for a peek into infinity that he was granted his wish, by the lovely warbling of a bird. To the abbot, the vision was a sublime moment, but when he went down to tell his monks about it he found that all had changed—his eternal second had lasted 300 years.

Leyre essentially dates from the 11th century when Sancho the Great declared it 'the centre and heart of my realm'. The first kings of Navarra were buried there, and the abbot of Leyre served as the bishop of Pamplona. Abandoned in the 19th century, the monastery was reoccupied in 1950 by the Benedictines, who began a restoration programme that unfortunately obscures much of the older building. Visits begin in the 11th-century pre-Romanesque **crypt**, where the first impression is that the church is sinking into the ground; the columns are runty little stubs of unequal height weighed down by heavy block capitals, carved with simple geometric designs that stand at about chest level. Above, the church, harmonious, light and austere, provides the perfect setting for the Benedictines' beautiful Gregorian matins and vespers. The bones of the first ten kings of Navarra lie in a simple wooden casket behind a fine grill; the 13th-century statue of the Virgin of Leyre sits on the altar. The west portal, the **Porta Speciosa**, is finely carved with a mix of saints and monsters. If Rip Van Winkle legends don't faze you, it's a 10-minute walk up to the **Fountain of San Virila** for the magnificent view of the artificial lake and Navarrese country-side that the abbot contemplated during his prayers, although the warbling birds have been replaced by hang-gliding Spaniards.

Nature is a main attraction in eastern Navarra. The Sierra de Leyre divides the Roncal and Salazar valleys (*see* p.71), but there are two splendid gorges quite close at hand: the **Foz de Lumbier**, formed by the Irati river, and the even more spectacular, sheer-sided, 6km **Foz de Arbayún** (*see* p.72) along the Salazar; both are accessible from Lumbier.

© (948–) | *Where to Stay and Eating Out*

Aoiz/Agoitz

★Hs Beti Jai, Santa Agueda 4, © 33 60 52 (*inexpensive*), has a few rooms and an excellent restaurant (*moderate*), a soul-satisfying, good-value mix of the best regional traditions with the most modern techniques; the hake in langoustine sauce is especially good (closed Mon).

Sangüesa

The cosiest places to stay are **★★Yamaguchi** on the road to Javier, © 87 01 27 (*moderate*), with a pool and nice restaurant, and the cheaper **★★Hs Las Navas**, C/ Alfonso El Batallador 7, © 87 00 77 (*inexpensive*). The Basque **Asador Mediavilla** on the same street, © 87 02 12 (*moderate*) serves delicious charcoal-grilled fish and meat with excellent local wine (closed Sun eve and Tues); on Friday, Saturday and Sunday nights everyone heads to **La Solana**, © 87 10 43, to feast on an enormous variety of dishes to live music (*moderate*).

Javier/Leyre

You can stay and eat next to the castle in the antique **★★★Xavier**, © 88 40 06, ✆ 88 40 78, or do the same rather more basically at **★El Mesón**, ©88 40 35, ✆ 88 42 26 (*both moderate*). At Leyre, the former pilgrim's hostel is now the charming **★★Hospedería de Leyre**, © 88 41 00, ✆ 88 41 37 (*inexpensive*), the perfect antidote to stress; its restaurant specializes in traditional Navarrese cuisine (open Mar–Nov).

South of Pamplona to Tudela

The green valleys of the Pyrenees are a distant memory south of Pamplona; here the skies are bright and clear, the land arid and toasted golden brown after the last winter rains, except for the green swathes of vineyards of La Ribera, cradle of Navarra's finest freshest rosés.

By train: most trains between Pamplona and the main junction of Alsasua stop at Huarte-Araquil; trains linking Pamplona and Zaragoza call at Tafalla, Olite and Tudela. Conda (✆ 21 10 08) stops at Tafalla, Olite and Tudela on the way to Zaragoza.

Olite: Galerías/Plaza de Carlos III el Noble, ✆ (948) 74 00 35
Tudela: Gaztambide, Esq. Carrera 11, ✆ (948) 82 15 39.

There are **markets** in Tafalla on Plaza Navarra on Fridays; in Olite in Paseo del Portal on Wednesdays; in Fitero in Plaza San Raimundo on Tuesdays and Fridays.

Tafalla and Olite

In the 17th century, a Dutchman named E. Cock described Tafalla and Olite as the 'flowers of Navarra' and both have determinedly crowed Cock's sweet nicknames ever since. Old **Tafalla** has wilted a bit over the centuries and grass grows between the cobbles, but it still has an impressive Plaza Mayor and claims one of the finest and biggest *retablos* in the north: a masterpiece by Basque artist Juan de Ancheta tucked away in the austere church of **Santa María**. West of Tafalla, **Artajona** has the air of an abandoned stage set: majestic medieval walls with startlingly intact crenellated towers defend little more than the 13th-century fortress church of **San Saturnino**. This has a tympanum showing the saint exorcising a woman, watched by Juana de Navarra and Philip the Fair of France, while the lintel shows Saturnino's martyrdom with the bull. The Hispano-Flemish *retablo mayor* dates from 1515. This is the second church on the site; Artajona's walls, re-done in the 1300s, were first built between 1085 and 1103 by the Templars and canons of Saint-Sernin (San Saturnino) of Toulouse, at a time when the Counts of Toulouse were among the chief players in Europe, leading the First Crusade and fighting side by side with the Cid. Near Artajona, the **Ermita de la Virgen** shelters a lovely bronze and enamel 13th-century Virgin holding a bouquet of roses and has two mega-lithic gallery tombs nearby.

Olite, south of Tafalla, is dwarfed by its huge battlemented, lofty-towered **Castle of Carlos III**, built for the king of Navarra in 1407 (*open Mon–Sat 10–2 and 6–8, winter 4–5, Sun 10–2; adm*). Each of its 15 towers and turrets has its own character, and restorers have made the whole thing seem startlingly new. Inside, the décor is *mudéjar*; hanging gardens were suspended from the great arches of the terraces, and there was a 'leonera' or lion pit, and a very busy set of dungeons; the Navarrese royal families led messy, frustrated lives. At night the whole complex is illuminated with a golden light, creating a striking backdrop to performances in the summer Festival of Navarra. The castle's Gothic chapel, **Santa María la Real** (*open 9.30–12 and 5–8*) has a gorgeous 13th-century façade and the Romanesque church of **San Pedro** (*same hours*) has an octagonal tower and portal adorned with two large stone eagles, one devouring the hare it has captured (symbolizing force) and the other, more friendly, representing gentleness.

East of Tafalla and Olite, **San Martín de Unx** has a superb crypt under its 12th-century church. From here a by-road branches south for the striking medieval village of **Ujué**, set on a hill corrugated with terraces, where a shepherd, directed by a dove (*ujué*), found the statue of the black Virgin now housed in the powerful 13th-century Romanesque-Gothic church of **Santa María**. The doorway has finely carved scenes of the Last Supper and the Magi and the altar preserves the heart of King Carlos II of Navarra. Every year since 1043, on the first Sunday after St Mark's day (25 April), the Virgin has been the object of a solemn pilgrimage that departs from Tafalla at 2am.

Tudela

Founded by the Moors, Tudela, the second city of Navarra and capital of La Ribera region, was the last town in Navarra to submit to Fernando the Catholic, and it did so most unwillingly; before the big bigot, Tudela had always made a point of welcoming Jews, Moors and heretics expelled from Castile or persecuted by the Inquisition, and it was no accident that its tolerant environment nurtured three of Spain's top medieval writers: Benjamin of Tudela, the great traveller and chronicler (1127–73), the poet Judah Ha-Levi of the same period, and doctor Miguel Servet (1511–53), one of the first to write on the circulation of the blood.

Don't be disheartened by Tudela's protective coating of dusty, gritty sprawl, but head straight for its picturesque, labyrinthine Moorish-Jewish kernel, around the elegant 17th-century **Plaza de los Fueros**; the decorations on the façades recall its use as a bull ring in the 18th and 19th centuries. The Gothic **Cathedral** (*open 8.30–1 and 4.30–8*) was built over the Great Mosque in the 12th century and topped with a pretty 17th-century tower. It has three decorated doorways: the north and south portals have capitals with New Testament scenes, while the west portal, the **Portada del Juicio Final**, is devoted to the Last Judgement, depicted in 114 different scenes in eight soaring bands. The delightful choir, behind its Renaissance grille, is considered the finest Flamboyant Gothic work in Navarra, carved with geometric flora, fauna and fantasy motifs; note, under the main chair, the figures of two crows picking out the eyes of a man—the dean who commissioned the work but refused to pay the sculptors the agreed price. The main altar has a beautiful Hispano-Flemish *retablo* painted by Pedro Díaz de Oviedo and yet more chains from Las Navas de Tolosa; there's an ornate Gothic *retablo* of Santa Caterina and a chapel of Santa Ana, patroness of Tudela, with a cupola that approaches Baroque orgasm. The 13th-century cloister, with twin and triple columns, has capitals on the life of Jesus and other New Testament stories, while the *Escuela de Cristo*, off the east end of the cloister, has *mudéjar* paintings and decorations.

Among the best palaces are the **Casa del Almirante** near the cathedral and, in the C/ de Magallón, the lovely Renaissance **Palace of the Marqués de San Adrián**. An irregular, 17-arched, 13th-century bridge spanning the Ebro still takes much of Tudela's traffic, with help from a new ultra-modern suspension bridge.

Around Tudela

Just east of Tudela is a striking, desert region straight out of the American Far West known as the **Bárdenas Reales**, where erosion has sculpted steep tabletops, weird wrinkled hills and rocks balanced on pyramids. The best way to see it (and not get lost) is by the GR 13 walking path, crossing its northern extent from the Hermitage of the Virgen del Yugo. South of Tudela, **Cascante** is known for its wines and church of the Virgen del Romero (Our Lady of the Rosemary Bush), built in the 17th century and reached by way of an arcaded walkway from the village below. The small spa town of **Fitero** (the waters are used in treating tuberculosis) grew up around the 11th-century Cistercian **Monastery of Santa María la Real**, whose abbot, San Raimundo, founded the famous Order of the Knights of Calatrava in 1158. Don't miss the Romanesque Sala Capitular, a monumental *retablo* from the 1500s, the ornate 18th-century chapel of the Virgen de la Barda, and among the treasures a 10th-century ivory coffer from the workshop of the Caliph of Córdoba. **Cintruénigo** and **Corella** just north are important producers of D.O. Navarra wine, with a good dozen *bodegas* in the environs.

✆ (948–) | *Where to Stay and Eating Out*

Tafalla

★★Hs Tafalla, on the Zaragoza road, ✆ 70 03 00, ✉ 70 30 52 (*moderate*), has nice rooms and food, especially when the dishes involve asparagus, lamb and hake (restaurant closed Fri). Atxen Jiménez, the chef at **Tubal**, Plaza de Navarra 2, ✆ 70 08 52 (*moderate–expensive*) draws in diners from Pamplona and beyond with her delicious variations on classic Navarrese themes—*menestra de verduras* and innovations such as crèpes filled with celery in almond sauce (closed Sun eve, Mon and late Aug).

Olite

Next to the Castle of Carlos III is the 13th-century Castillo de los Teobaldos, now converted into the **★★★Parador Príncipe de Viana**, ✆ 74 00 00, ✉ 74 02 01 (*expensive*). A garden, air conditioning and beautiful furnishings make castle-dwelling a delight, as do delicious Navarrese gourmet treats in the dining-room (*expensive*). Little **★★Casa Zanito**, Rúa Revillas, ✆ 74 00 02 (*moderate*), offers simple, cheerful rooms and excellent meals, based on market availability, topped off with good homemade desserts. **Gambarte**, Rúa del Seco 13, ✆ 74 01 39 (*inexpensive*), is pleasant and also serves the most reasonably priced food in town.

Ujué

The place to dine has long been the terrace of **Mesón las Torres**, ✆ 73 81 05 (*moderate*), serving Navarrese taste treats and Ujué's special candied almonds.

Tudela

Unfortunately there aren't any places to stay in the old town, and elsewhere prices are high: **★★Hs Remigio**, C/ Gaztambide 4, ✆ 82 08 50, and **★Hs Nueva Parrilla**, Carlos III el Noble 6, ✆ 82 24 00, ✉ 82 25 45 (*both moderate*), are the only two that don't ask an arm and a leg. Tudela is the chief producer of the ingredients of Navarra's famous *menestra de verduras*: delicious asparagus, artichokes, peas, celery and lettuces. Book a table at **Casa Ignacio**, Cortaderos 9, © 82 10 21 (*moderate*), to taste them at their freshest (closed Tues and 15 Aug–15 Sept), or try **Choko**, Pza. de los Fueros, © 82 10 19 (*moderate*), with pretty views (closed Mon). **La Estrella**, C/ Carnicerías 14, © 82 10 39 (*inexpensive*), has good home-cooking based on garden vegetables.

Cintruénigo

The most seductive reason to stop in the village is to dine *chez* **Maher**, C/ La Ribera 19, © 81 11 50, for delicious Navarrese dishes with an imaginative nouvelle cuisine touch: traditional *menú* 2800 pts, or for a splurge opt for a *menú degustación*.

West of Pamplona: Aralar and San Miguel in Excelsis

Navarra's magic mountain, **Aralar**, is a favourite spot for a picnic or Sunday hike, grace-fully wooded with beech, rowan, and hawthorn groves. It has been sacred to the Basques since Neolithic times, when they erected 30 dolmens and menhirs in the yew groves around Putxerri, the biggest concentration of neolithic monuments in all Spain. On top is Navarra's holy of holies, the **Sanctuary of San Miguel in Excelsis** (*open 9–2 and 4 to sunset*), on a panoramic north–south road that climbs over Aralar between Huarte-Arakil and Lekunberri.

The Knight, the Dragon and the Archangel

 In the 9th century, Count Teodosio de Goñi went off to fight the Saracens with his Visigothic overlord King Witiza and was returning home when he met a hermit (the devil in disguise) who warned him that his wife was unfaithful. Seething with rage, the knight stormed into his castle, saw two forms lying in his bed and without hesitation slew them both. When he ran out he met his wife returning from Mass, who told him, to his horror, that she had given his own aged parents the bed. Horrified, Teodosio went to Rome to ask the Pope what penance he could possibly do, and after three nights the Pope had a dream that he should wear heavy chains in solitude until God showed his forgiveness by breaking them. Binding himself in chains, Teodosio went up to the top of Mt Aralar and lived as a hermit for years, when one day, when he was sitting next to a cave a scaly green dragon emerged, smoke billowing from its nostrils. Teodosio implored the aid of St Michael, who suddenly appeared with his sword in hand, and spoke to the dragon in perfect Basque: '*Nor Jaunggoitkoa bezaka?*' ('Who is stronger than God?'). The dragon slunk back into its cave, and the archangel struck off the knight's chains and left a statue of himself—an angelic figure with a large cross on its head and an empty glass case where the face ought to be. Every year between March and August the figure goes on a fertility blessing tour through a hundred Navarra villages; on Corpus Christi pilgrims walk or cycle up to the chapel to pay their respects.

Aralar is hardly the only mountain in Europe dedicated to heaven's Generalísimo: there's Mont-Saint-Michel in France, St Michael's Mount in England, Monte Sant'Angelo in Italy to name a few. In art Michael is often shown with a spear, not slaying as much as *transfixing* dragons to the earth: these are sources of underground water. And sure enough, the Sierra de Aralar is so karstic as to be practically hollow; under the sanctuary there's an immense subterranean river that makes moaning dragonish sounds, feeding an icy lake under a domed cavern.

The gloomy stone chapel, built by the Count of Goñi, was consecrated in 1098. Traditionally guarded by mastiffs (we didn't see any), the chapel has had an empty air ever since French Basques plundered it in 1797, when they knocked off St Michael's head (or so say apologists who find the crystal head too weird); the hands of the desecrators were chopped off before they were put to death and nailed over the chapel door. You can see the chains worn by Teodosio de Goñi and the hole through which the dragon appeared; pilgrims still stick their heads into it, although no one remembers why. A high-tech alarm system protects the recently stolen, but recently rediscovered, enamelled Byzantine *retablo*, showing the Virgin on a rainbow in a mandorla with the Christ Child; the only comparable work in Europe is the great altarpiece in St Mark's in Venice. Tentatively dated 1028, it was probably originally stolen in Constantinople by a Crusader and sold to Sancho the Great, who donated it to the chapel.

Around Aralar

Of the villages under the mountain, **Lekunberri** is the most orientated to tourism, but **Leiza**, just north, is a prettier choice, besides being the home of Basque legend Iñaki Perurena, the *arrejazotzale*, or champion heavy stone weightlifter. Along the road to Tolosa, **Betelu** not only bottles Navarra's mineral water, but has a fun little roadside swimming hole with slides where the stream has been dammed. **Zudaire**, south of Aralar, is the head town in a broken terrain called **Las Améscoas**, the refuge of the Carlists and delight of speleologists: most of the caves are located above Zudaire around Baquedano with its craggy ravine and streams.

Aralar ℗ (948–)   ***Where to Stay and Eating Out***

The pilgrims' hostel next to the church of **San Miguel de Aralar**, ℗ 56 10 66, is rugged and comfortable enough but isn't famous for its food. In Lekunberri, **★★Hs Ayestarán II**, C/ San Juan 64, ℗ 50 41 27 (*moderate*), has a pleasant old atmosphere, tennis, children's recreational facilities, a pool and garden; menus feature home-cooked stews, stuffed peppers and codfish with almonds. Just west, between Betelu and Azpirotz the **Asador Betelu** attracts hordes of hungry diners. Right in the centre of Leiza, you can sleep and eat reasonably at **★Hs Basa Kabl**, ℗ 51 0 1 25 (*moderate*); the lively **Taverna Oilade** functions as the town beanery, bar, mess hall and gambling den; good fish soup and other filling dishes (*inexpensive*).

West of Pamplona: The Camino de Santiago

Few places in Europe can boast such a concentration of medieval curiosities as this stretch of the road, where the mystic syncretism of the Jews, Templars, pagans and pilgrims was expressed in monuments with secret messages that tease and mystify today.

Getting Around

By bus: La Estellesa buses, ✆ (948) 21 32 25, from Pamplona stop at Puente le Reina and Estella (with a fancy neo-Moorish station) en route to Logroño five times a day.

Tourist Information

Estella: Palacio de los Reyes de Navarra, C/ San Nicolás 1, ✆ (948) 55 40 11. There is a market every Thursday in Plaza de San Juan.

From Pamplona to Estella

A short turn off the N 111 (about 15km from Pamplona) leads to the old village of **Obanos**, and 1.6km beyond that village to a lonely field and **Santa María de Eunate** (*open 10–1 and 4.30–7, closed Mon*), a striking 12th-century church built by the Templars. The Templars often built their chapels as octagons, but this one was purposely made irregular, and is surrounded by a unique 33-arched octagonal cloister—hence its name 'Eunate' (the Hundred Doors). Many knights were buried here, and it's likely that its peculiar

Santa María de Eunate

95

structure had deep significance in the Templars' initiatory rites. There are only a few carved capitals—some little monsters, and pomegranates on the portal, which oddly faces north. During its restoration, scallop shells were discovered along with the tombs—the church served as a mortuary chapel for pilgrims. The lack of a central key stone supporting the eight ribs inside hints that Arab architects were involved in the building; the Romanesque Virgin by the alabaster window is a copy of the one stolen in 1974.

The *camino francés* from Roncesvalles and the *camino aragonés* converged at the 11th-century bridge in **Puente la Reina**, which hasn't changed much since the day when pilgrims marched down the sombre Rúa Mayor, where many houses preserve their coats-of-arms. The pilgrims traditionally entered Puente la Reina through the arch of another Templar foundation, **El Crucifijo**, a church with scallops and Celtic interlaced designs on the portal and two naves. The smaller was one added to house a powerful 14th-century German crucifix left by a pilgrim, where the Christ is nailed not to a cross but the trunk and branches of a Y-shaped tree. Towards the bridge, the church of **Santiago** has a weathered Moorish-style lobed portal and inside, two excellent polychrome 14th-century statues. From Puente la Reina, the path (although not the road) continues up to atmospheric old **Cirauqui** propped on its hill, where the church of San Román has another multi-foiled portal framed in archivolts with geometric designs. The ancient road to the west of Cirauqui, paved with Roman stones, predates even the pilgrims.

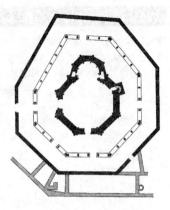

Santa María de Eunate
Solid black: existing structure
Shading: uncovered foundations

Estella/Lizarra: the Town of the Star

Estella, known as Estella la Bella for its beauty, was a much anticipated stop along the pilgrimage route. It owes its foundation in 1090 to a convenient miracle: nightly showers of shooting stars that always fell on the same place on a hill intrigued some shepherds, who investigated and found a cave hidden by thorns, sheltering a statue of the Virgin. Returning from the siege of Toledo the same year, King Sancho I founded Estella on the opposite bank of Río Ega from the old settlement of Lizarra (coincidentally the Basque word for 'star') and populated it with *francos*, or freemen: artisans, merchants and others who owed allegiance to no feudal lord (although confusingly, most of these *francos* were Franks from Gascony, who fought in the Reconquista for pay or piety's sake). Thanks to them, Estella has numerous fine medieval buildings; if many have been cropped, thank the Grand Inquisitor of Castile, Cardinal Cisneros, whose troops literally cut Navarra down to size in 1512. The most exciting time to visit Estella is the Friday before the first Sunday in August, when it holds the only *encierro* where women are welcome, even if the bulls are really heifers with padded horns.

The arcaded main square, **Plaza de Santiago**, is on the newer, Estella side of town, where for pious pilgrims the most important monument is the **Basílica de Nuestra Señora de Puy**, built on the overlook where the stars fell on Navarra that night. The Virgin is still there, but the old basilica was replaced in 1951 with a concrete and glass star-shaped church. South of Plaza de Santiago, the highlight for art pilgrims is 12th-century **San Miguel**, the parish church of the *francos*, set on a craggy rock atop its original set of steps. Don't hesitate: march right up them for the magnificent portal, where Christ in majesty holds pride of place among angels, Evangelists and the Elders of the Apocalypse. On the left St Michael pins the dragon and weighs souls; on the right an angel shows the empty tomb to the three Marys. The top, sadly, fell to the Cardinal's tower-bashing squad, but the brackets are good, especially the man-eating wolf.

Near San Miguel you'll find Estella's medieval bridge, which pilgrims crossed to the Lizarra side to visit the 12th-century **San Sepolcro**, with a fascinating façade added in 1328 but again truncated by Cisneros. The tympanum has an animated Last Supper, Crucifixion, Resurrection and what looks to be the harrowing of hell; statues of the twelve apostles flank the door; one of them appears to be holding a stack of pancakes. To the right of the bridge is the piquant centre of old Lizarra, with churches and palaces bearing proud coats-of-arms, most now occupied by antique shops, along Calle de la Rúa ('street of the street'). The finest palace is the Plateresque brick **Casa Fray Diego**, now used as the Casa de Cultura. Off to the left was the Judería, or ghetto, its 12th-century synagogue converted into **Santa María de Jus del Castillo**, where the apse is decorated with a rich assortment of Romanesque modillions. The church is dwarfed by the adjacent 13th-century monastery of **Santo Domingo**, recently converted into a retirement home. Further up, near the new bridge, a 16th-century fountain under a canopy of linden trees in **Plaza de San Martín** makes a delightful place to linger.

A curving flight of the stairs leads up to the 12th-century **San Pedro de la Rúa** (*open in summer 10.30–1.30, and at 4.30, 5.30 and 6.30; adm*), defended by a skyscraper bell-tower. The Moorish-inspired foiled arch of the portal is crowned by a relief of St James in a boat with stars, blessed by a giant hand emerging from the water. Inside, the church has its share of curiosities: a unique column made of three interlaced 'serpents' and the black Virgin de la O, a cult figure of the masons, who left their marks all over the church. The Baroque chapel to the left houses St Andrew's shoulder-blade; the story goes that the Bishop of Patras took it with him for good luck while making the pilgrimage in 1270. Luck failed him in Estella, where he died and was buried in San Pedro's cloister, along with his relic. The apostle's shoulder-blade wasn't going to have any of this, and made itself known by a curious light that appeared over the tomb; in 1626, the day when Andrew was proclaimed patron of Estella, a burning vision of his X-shaped cross hovered over the church. Of the cloister, only two galleries survive, reconstructed after the castle above was blown up in 1572 and crashed down on top of it. The capitals are especially good, carved with the lives of the saints and the Apocalypse: the twisted column is a copy of the one in Santo Domingo de Silos in Burgos.

Over the years Estella became a favourite residence of the kings, whose 12th-century **Palacio de los Reyes de Navarra,** opposite San Pedro, is one of the best preserved civic buildings from the period. Prominent at street level a capital bears the oldest known depiction of Roland, clad in scaly armour, fighting the equally scaly giant Ferragut; further up, another capital shows a scene of devils and animal musicians, including a donkey playing a harp. The palace now houses the **Museo Gustavo de Maeztú** (*open Tues–Sat 11–1 and 5–7, Sun 11–1, closed Mon; adm*), devoted to works by Estella's best-known painter (1887–1947). In the tourist office next door, take a look at the model showing the evolution of Estella between 1090 and 1990.

Around Estella

Estella is an important producer of D.O. Navarra wine, and the most interesting *bodega* to visit just happens to be the Benedictine **Monasterio de Irache,** 2km west at Ayegui (*open 10–2 and 5–7, Sat and Sun 9–2 and 4–7, closed Mon*). First recorded in 958, it later received a generous endowment from Sancho the Great, who helped finance one of the very first pilgrims' hospitals here. In 1569, Felipe II moved Sahagún's university of theology here, where it remained, enjoying the same privileges as Salamanca until it closed down with the expropriation of monasteries in 1824. The complex is a handsome mix behind an eclectic façade. The entrance is through an elegant Plateresque door, and leads into an austerely beautiful Romanesque church with three apses under a Renaissance dome, stripped of centuries' encrustation of altarpieces: the original Romanesque north door is decorated with hunting scenes. The sumptuous Plateresque cloister has grotesque and religious capitals. The small wine museum preserves Irache's 1000-year-old custom of offering free drinks to pilgrims.

Twelve km up the San Sebastián road, the **Monastery de Iranzu** (*open 9–2 and 4–8.30*) was founded in the 11th century by Cistercians, who chose to live in a dramatic ravine true to their preference for remote settings in the wilds. It was recently restored by the government of Navarra and given to the Theatine order. The monks will show you around their medieval kitchen, and Romanesque-Gothic cloister with a hexagonal fountain and church. South of Estella on the Ebro, **Lodosa** is famous for its *appellation contrôlée* red peppers, *pimientas del piquillo*, that are dried in long garlands over the white façades of the houses; its church San Miguel has an immense rococo *retablo*.

Los Arcos and Sorlada

After Estella, the pilgrims walked to **Los Arcos**, where, tucked off the N 111, is an arcaded plaza and a 16th-century church, Santa María, with a pretty cathedral-size Gothic cloister, carved choirstalls and frantic Baroque *retablos*. Seven km north of Los Arcos at **Sorlada**, a grand 18th-century Baroque basilica belongs to **San Gregorio Ostiense**, a once immensely popular saint who lost much of his influence to modern fertilizers. His story is told in the basilica's naive paintings: back in 1039 locusts plagued the region so badly that a group of farmers walked to Rome and asked the pope for help. The pope had a dream that Cardinal Gregory of Ostia was the man for the job, and off he went to Navarra, where he preached and dispersed the locusts, an exertion that killed him after five years. He was buried at Sorlada and forgotten, until a light redirected farmers to his tomb. Remembering his good juju against the locusts (and their ancestral Celtic head cult) they would cart his skull reliquary around their fields, pouring water through the hole which made it into 'holy Gregory water'. Felipe II had gallons of it sent down to water the orchards of the Escorial.

West of Los Arcos, **Torres del Río** has a striking tall octagonal church, **Santo Sepolcro**, built by the Knights of the Holy Sepulchre; like Santa María Eunate, it may have been a mortuary chapel for pilgrims. The cross-ribbed vaulting is exactly like the ones built in Córdoba under the Caliphs; if restoration work has been completed, don't miss the shadowy interior.

Viana: Where Cesare Borgia Bit the Dust

Just before La Rioja, **Viana** fits a lot of monumentality into a small space. Founded by King Sancho VII the Strong in 1219 to defend his frontier with Castile, it became the hereditary principality of the heir to the throne of Navarra in 1423. Although its once proud castle fell to Cardinal Cisneros' demolition programme, nobles and courtly hangers-on stayed on and built themselves splendid mansions with big coats-of-arms and the elegant 17th-century **Casa Consistorial**, crowned with an escutcheon the size of an asteroid, and the 13th–14th-century church of **Santa María**, hidden by a magnificent concave Renaissance façade, based on a triumphant arch with a coffered ceiling designed and carved by Juan de Goyaz (1549). Inside, the Gothic interior is quite airy and lovely, culminating in an intricate gilded Baroque retable. The façade could be considered the tombstone of Cesare Borgia (1475–1507), whose memorial, or all that remains of his desecrated remains, lie buried under the marker in front of the church. Now how did Pope Alexander VI's son and Machiavelli's hero end up in Viana? With the papacy and central Italy in his pocket by 1502, married to Charlotte, sister of the King of Navarre, and supported by France, Cesare had just embarked on a brilliant career as a ruthless Renaissance prince-assassin when his father pulled the rug out from under him by dying suddenly in 1503, when Cesare himself was too ill to get to the Vatican and influence the conclave to elect a Borgia candidate; according to Machiavelli's *Prince*, it was the only political mistake he ever made. It proved to be fatal. Once Julius II, arch-enemy of the Borgias, was elected in late 1503, Cesare's conquests in Italy were frittered away in anarchy, the French turned against him, and he went from being on top of the world to a man whose life was in danger. He fled to Aragón, the cradle of the Borgias, only to be imprisoned by Fernando. Navarra proved to be his only refuge, and he died in a skirmish in Viana, fighting Castilian rebels.

Puente la Reina

The stone and timber **Mesón del Peregrino**, on the Pamplona road, © 34 00 75, ✆ 34 11 90 (*moderate*), isn't as old as it looks, but it has cosy, air-conditioned rooms and a pool, and serves up excellent meals with a French gourmet touch in a split-level dining room (closed Mon). ★**Hs Puente**, in the centre, © 34 01 46 (*moderate*), has some cheaper rooms without bath: **Fonda Lorca** in the main plaza is the cheapest of all.

Estella

The largest and most comfortable, the ★★★**Irache**, is 3km away on the Logroño road in Ayegui, © 55 11 50, ✆ 55 47 54 (*expensive*), set in a 1970s *urbanización* (air conditioning, pool). ★**Hs Cristina**, C/ Baja Navarra 1, © 55 07 72 (*moderate*), is run by a kindly woman; for something less try ★**Pensión San Andrés**, C/ Mayor 1, © 55 04 48 (*inexpensive*). Cheapest of all are the doubles at the **Fonda Izarra**, C/ Caldería, © 55 06 78. **La Cepa**, Pza. Fueros 8, © 55 00 32 (*moderate*), specializes in Basque and Navarrese cuisine, with *menús degustación* at 3000 and 4000 pts (closed all day Mon and most evenings except Fri and Sat). The medieval **La Navarra**, Gustavo de Maeztú 16, © 55 10 69 (*moderate-expensive*), is another good bet, perhaps more for its atmosphere than food, which is good if a bit pricey.

Los Arcos

A pair of choices here: ★★**Hotel Monaco**, Pza. del Coso 22, © 64 00 00 (*moderate*), with doubles with bath, and the slightly dearer ★★**Hs Ezequiel**, La Serna 14, © 64 02 96 (*moderate*), with singles as well as doubles and where pilgrims get a 10% discount.

Viana

The avant-garde decor of **Borgia**, Serapio Urra, © 64 57 81 (*moderate–expensive*), is Aurora Cariñanos' temple of personal, imaginative cuisine, where you can dine delectably on dishes such as *pochas con caracoles al tomillo* (fresh haricot beans with snails and thyme), accompanied by an excellent cellar (closed Sun and Aug). In the centre, **La Granja**, Navarro Villoslada 19, © 64 50 78 (*moderate–inexpensive*), has rooms with bath and average cooking.

La Rioja

La Rioja may be named after the river Oja, one of its seven tributaries of the Ebro, but to most people it means wine, wine and more wine. The banks of the Ebro are frilly with vineyards and pinstriped with rows of garden vegetables on the flat, tremendously fertile plains of Rioja Baja around Calahorra. In the Sierra de la Demanda in the southwest, mountains are high enough to ski down; in the gullies of Rioja Baja, dinosaurs once made the earth tremble, or at least left their curious tracks in the squodge of a prehistoric bog, which hardened and petrified for posterity.

Wedged up against the Ebro, between Navarra and Castile who once so hotly contested its fields and vineyards, the *comunidad* of La Rioja is now the smallest autonomous region in Spain (5000 sq km)—not that there is any distinctive Riojan language or race, although in the 11th century a king, one of the four sons of Sancho the Great of Navarra, sat in Nájera. This was a brief but marked period of independence, when Riojans began the history of Castilian Spanish as a written and poetic language and contributed to the invention of Santiago, with a first sighting of the battling Son of Thunder at Calvijo and more than one miracle and saint along its stretch of the pilgrimage road.

Logroño

Half of all the 250,000 Riojans live in Logroño, their shiny, up-to-date capital famous not only for wine but coffee caramels. It began under the Visigoths as *Gronio*, the 'ford', but really bloomed only with the advent of the pilgrimage, when a stone bridge was built over the Ebro by San Juan de Ortega, one of La Rioja's two building saints. Unfortunately, in its haste to become a modern agricultural market, the medieval part of town has run to seed.

Getting Around

By train: several trains a day link Haro, Logroño, and Calahorra on the Bilbao-Zaragoza route.

By bus: several buses a day run to Burgos (via the towns on the pilgrims' route), Zaragoza, Vitoria, Pamplona and Rioja's villages. In Logroño the bus station is at Avda. de España 1, ℂ (941) 24 35 72, and the train station (with a left luggage) is nearby in Pza. de Europa, ℂ (941) 23 17 37.

Tourist Information

Miguel Villanueva 10, ℂ (941) 29 11 60, ✆ 29 13 88. If you get stuck somewhere, La Rioja has a freephone tourist information service: ℂ (901) 300 600 (for outside the region) or ℂ (901) 300 615 while you're there. There is a market for country produce and products at Mercado del Campo, Marqués de la Enseñada 52 (open Tues and Fri 8–2).

A Walk Around Logroño

Logroño is a big long sausage of a town, but the interesting bits are concentrated in a small area near the Ebro. Barely an arch survives of San Juan's first bridge, which was replaced in the 1800s by the **Puente de Hierro**, or iron bridge. Just off this the pilgrims would pass in front of the 16th-century fountain and lofty Gothic **Santiago**, the oldest church in town. This was rebuilt in 1500, with a single nave a startling 16m (53ft) wide and still standing in spite of the fact that its architect had no confidence in his handiwork and left town as soon as it was completed. It has a Renaissance *retablo*, and at the front a mighty 18th-century statue of Santiago Matamoros ('St James Moor-killer') rides a steed with *cojones* as big as beach balls. The sculptor of the equestrian statue of General Espartero (in Logroño's central park, the **Espolón**) took them into consideration and equipped the mortal general's mortal horse a few degrees less generously.

The skyline of Logroño is stabbed by church towers, including two slender 18th-century Churrigueresque towers by Martín de Beratúa that frame the magnificent Baroque façade of the cathedral, **Santa María de la Redonda** in Plaza del Mercado, a front that belies the Gothic-inspired gloom inside (*open 8–11 and 6–8*); the rotundity of its name (the first Romanesque church was octagonal) is recalled in an exuberant round rococo altar. Near here, in a high security strong box, is the *Tabla de Calvario*, supposedly painted by Michaelangelo for his friend and muse Vittoria Colonna. Logroño's most distinctive landmark is its nubby pyramidal 'Needle' , the 149ft 13th-century spire atop the lantern of **Santa María de Palacio**, in C/ Marqués de San Nicolás, a church said to have been founded by no less than Emperor Constantine. If it's open, pop in to see the Renaissance choir stalls, the 13th-century *Nuestra Señora de la Antigua*, and what remains of the Gothic cloister. Another tower, brick 11th-century *mudéjar* this time, looks over **San Bartolomé** with a ruggedly carved, time-blackened 14th-century Gothic façade; the smooth white interior, recently restored, has lovely shallow choir vaults.

The 17th-century Palacio del General Espartero in Plaza San Agustín now holds the **Museo Provincial de La Rioja** (*open 10–2 and 3–9, Sun and hols 11.30–2, closed Mon*), full of art from disappeared churches (14th-century painting from San Millán and *San Francisco with Brother Lion* by El Greco), Flemish coffers and orphaned academic 19th-century paintings from the Prado's storerooms. There are a number of wine cellars in the area, including **Bodegas Marqués de Murrieta**, at Ygay, Ctra. de Zaragoza, km 403, ✆ 25 81 00, founded in 1872 and famous for its 35–40-year-old *Gran Reservas* .

Logroño ✆ (941–)   **Where to Stay**

Logroño has a surprising number of spanking new hotels and the antique ★★★★**Carlton Rioja**, which offers a taste of old world charm at Gran Vía del Rey Juan Carlos I 5, ✆ 24 21 00, 🖃 24 35 02 (*expensive*). The ★★★**Ciudad de Logroño**, Menéndez Pelayo 7, ✆ 25 02 44, 🖃 25 43 90 (*moderate*), is central, modern and comfortable, with views on a park. ★★**Paris**, Avda. de La Rioja 8, ✆ 22 87 50 (*moderate*), is small, central and welcoming. Near the cathedral, the handsome ★★★**Hs Marqués de Vallejo**, Marqués de Vallejo 8, ✆ 24 83 33 (*moderate*), has recently been restored and offers reasonable half-board rates. Cheaper choices include ★★**Hs Niza**, C/ Capitán Gallarza 13, ✆ 20 60 44 (*moderate*), and ★**Hs Sebastián**, C/ San Juan 21, ✆ 24 28 00 (*inexpensive*).

Eating Out

Logroño's (and La Rioja's) best restaurant is **La Merced**, Marqués de San Nicolás 109, ✆ 22 11 66 (*expensive*), exquisitely set in an elegant 18th-century palace, with superb food and a vast *bodega* containing 40,000 bottles of the finest Rioja. The *rabo estofado* *al vino Rioja* is excellent and the 6500-pts *menú degustación* is a delight (closed Sun eve and 1–20 Aug). The original, lovingly restored Merced *bodega* just opposite is now the **Mesón Lorenzo**, ✆ 20 91 30 (*moderate*), with good food and wine. For a delicious *menestra*, go where the locals go: **El Cachetero** on C/ Laurel 3, ✆ 22 84 63 (*moderate*): arrive early because it fills up fast (closed 15 July–15 Aug). **Las Cubanas**, C/ San Agustín 17, ✆ 22 00 50 (*inexpensive*), owes its popularity to excellent regional cuisine, its friendly atmosphere, and good value (closed Sat eve and Sun). **Zubillaga**, C/ San Agustín 3, ✆ 22 00 76, offers succulent roast meats and fish, and treats like leek and gambas *pastel* (closed Wed and 1–25 July). For tapas, try C/ Laurel and C/ San Juan.

Calahorra and the Rioja Baja

Down the Ebro, east of Logroño, La Rioja Baja is flat, fertile, well watered and endowed with a sunny Mediterranean climate. Olive oil and wine are the two mainstays of the economy, with the kind of peppers the Spanish devour by the kilo coming in a close third. Few tourists pass through here, and those who do are mostly dinosaur fanciers: it's one thing to see a pile of dusty old bones in a museum, but quite another to walk along and find their splayed footprints at your feet.

Tourist Information

Calahorra: C/ Mayor, ✆ (941) 14 72 06.
Arnedo: Palacio de la Baronesa, ✆ (941) 38 31 64.

There are **markets** in Calahorra on Pza. del Raso on Thursdays; in Alfaro on Fridays; in Cervera de Río Alhama on Fridays, and in Arnedo on Mondays and Tuesdays.

Calahorra

Calahorra owes its quiet contented look to its rich *vega*, planted with orchards and vegetables, and has been inhabited for so long (since palaeolithic times) that St Jerome speculated that it was founded by Tubal, grandson of Noah. It first makes history as Kalauria, an important Celtiberian fortress-town under Carthaginian sway that, thanks to the Ebro, traded with the Greek colonies on the Mediterranean coast. In 187 BC the town was grabbed by Rome, then in a dispute between Pompey and Sertorius in AD 72 it held out against Pompey until all the defenders were dead through starvation, a fanaticism that gave rise to the expression 'Calagurritan hungers'. The Romans rebuilt it, and Calahorra returned the favour by giving Rome Marcus Fabius Quintilian (42–118), the first salaried professor of rhetoric in Rome and author of *Institutio Oratoria*, the Empire's textbook on the fine art of talk. In the Middle Ages, Calahorra was a prize craved by both Aragón and Castile, and in a famous incident in the romance *Las Mocedades del Cid* (and in the film with Charlton Heston), the Cid fought one to one for the city against Aragón's champion, vowing to lose not only the town but his head if he were defeated, but gaining both Calahorra and the hand of his beloved Jimena if he won. Which of course he did.

Calahorra has been an episcopal see since the 5th century, but the **Cathedral** has been fussed with frequently. Behind a fruity, floral neoclassical façade pasted on in 1700, the nave with graceful star vaulting is a product of 1485. The furnishings are equally eclectic: the Gothic *Cristo de la Pelota*, 'Christ of the ball', is part of a Deposition from the Cross, the alabaster statues of the saints are 17th century, and there are paintings attributed to Titian and Zurbarán. The Plateresque cloister houses the **Museo Diocesano** (*open 12–2 Sun and hols only*) with a 12th-century Bible and 15th-century Custodia called *El Ciprés*, made of gold and silver, donated to the cathedral by Henri IV. Just over the Río Cidacos note the unusual 13-spout fountain.

Near the cathedral, the church of **Santiago** and its *retablo* of St James is considered the finest neoclassical work in La Rioja. Nearby, the rarely open **Museo Municipal**'s archaeological collection stars the serene Roman bust of the *Dama Calagurritana*. Just north of this, the church of **San Andrés** has a Gothic portal illustrating the triumph over paganism and the arch **Arco del Planillo** is the only gateway surviving from the Roman walls of Calagurris; other Roman bits are further up, along panoramic Camino Bellavista.

East of Calahorra: the Alhama Valley

Down the Ebro holding down the east end of La Rioja, **Alfaro** was known as Ilurcis in the 5th century BC but kept its Arab name even after the Reconquista. Its chief monument is the enormous twin-towered **Colegiata de San Miguel**, built in the 16th and 17th centuries and reminiscent of colonial churches in South America. The Colegiata's chief claim to fame, however, are its lodgers: it has more stork nests on its generous roof than any other in Spain, a colony of some 250 birds.

Further south, **Cervera del Río Alhama** long had an Arab majority and still has a Moorish feel to it: villagers speak *cerverano*, with hundreds of words that are a last relic of the lost language of the Mozarabs, or Christians living in Moorish Spain. Between **Aguilar del Río Alhama** and **Inestrillas**, the Celtiberians, fleeing after the conquest by Mantis Acidinus (181 BC), holed up from the Romans for a hundred years at **Contrebia Leucada**, built on terraces, defended on one side by the river and the others by a vast ditch. It is a rare surviving example of Celtiberian town planning and water system, and is currently being excavated.

La Rioja's Dinosaurs

South of Calahorra, **Arnedo** is a shoe-making town where every 27 September its patron saints Cosme and Damián are honoured in the usual Spanish effigy procession, only here the parade is combined with a scrum: villagers from Navarra come in to attack the procession and make three bold attempts to make off with the saints' statues, claiming that the Riojans stole them centuries ago. South of Arnedo, **Arnedillo** has been La Rioja's most important spa since 1847, with hot salty water good for rheumatic arthritis and stress.

This is all recent history compared to the main attraction in these parts. 'When there is no trace of Spielberg left,' reads the tourist brochure, 'The dinosaur tracks will still be here.' Take that, Hollywood! La Rioja Baja has 5000 footprints—Europe's largest concentration of dinosaur tracks, or ichnites as they're called—dating back 120 million years when La

Rioja was lush, warm and wet and the denizens of the Cretaceous (post-Jurassic) stomped through the marshes. Somehow conditions for preserving their prints in these broken hills were better than most places: a different kind of mud filled in the tracks, preserving the impression after the mud was turned to stone. In the Middle Ages, the ichnites were said to be the hoofmarks of Santiago's horse or prints left by giant chickens that lived in the time of the Moors. The best places to find them are in **Préjano** just east of Arnedillo and the Los Cayos gully at **Cornago**. **Enciso** has the largest number, especially at the Valdecevillo bed; other are just north in **Munilla** in a gully called Peñaportillo. **Igea** has more tracks and petrified plants, including a tree trunk.

✆ (941–)　　　　　　　　　　　　　　　　　*Where to Stay and Eating Out*

Calahorra

The modern ★★★**Parador Marco Fabio Quintiliano**, Parque Era Alta, ✆ 13 03 58, 🖂 13 51 39 (*expensive*), is near the scanty Roman ruins of Calagurris, with good views, comfortable rooms and air conditioning; like all *paradores*, it has a good restaurant serving regional and international cuisine. ★★**Chef Nino**, C/ Padre Lucas 2, ✆ 13 20 29, 🖂 13 25 16 (*moderate*), is new and central and airconditioned; the restaurant serves an excellent Basque-Riojan 2000-pts *menú*. For something cheaper, try ★**Teresa**, C/ Santo Domingo 2, ✆ 13 03 32 (*inexpensive*). Calahorra's best known restaurant, **La Taberna de la Cuarta Esquina**, Cuatro Esquinas 16, ✆ 13 43 55 (*moderate*), is justly renowned for its well-prepared fish, game and vegetable dishes and reasonably priced wines (closed 6–31 July). **Casa Mateo**, Pza. del Raso 15, ✆ 13 00 09, serves a tasty *menestra* and other dishes at the lowest prices in town.

Arnedo

Just out of the centre ★★★**Victoria**, Pso. de la Constitución 103, ✆ 38 01 00 (*moderate*), is recent and comfortable, and offers good value with a pool and tennis court. Closer to town, ★★**Virrey**, Pso. de la Constitución 27, ✆ 38 01 50, 🖂 38 30 17 (*moderate*), is welcoming, one of the few hotels in the *comunidad* with disabled facilities. Arnedo is famous for its *fardelejos,* almond-filled pastries which appear on the menus of the town's two fine, inexpensive, restaurants: little **Picabea**, C/ Virrey Lezana 1, ✆ 38 13 58, with good seafood (closed Sun and Mon eve), and the long-established **Sopitas**, C/ Carrera 4, ✆ 38 02 66, set in an old *bodega*, serving traditional favourites (closed Sun).

Enciso

In a little red 19th-century house, the **Posada de Santa Rita**, Ctra. de Soria 7, ✆ 39 60 66 (*inexpensive*), is a cosy place to stay, with a small library devoted to dinosaurs. If it's a weekend or holiday, **La Fábrica**, Ctra. de Soria , ✆ 39 60 51 (*inexpensive*), serves delicious meals based on game dishes, served in the atmosphere of an old flour mill.

South of Logroño: into the Sierra

Dry history and misty legend are often one and the same in three-digit years in northwest Spain. Although the western bit of La Rioja was reconquered by Alfonso I of Asturias back in the 8th century, the Christians' hold on the land was tenuous and often lost for long periods to the Moors, whose Caliph made the Christians pay a tribute of a hundred maidens into their harem in return for the right to worship. This humiliating loss of young womanhood was the source of the legendary Battle of **Clavijo**, where Santiago Matamoros made his famous debut on his white horse to lead Ramiro and the Christians to victory. In gratitude, Ramiro decided to donate to Santiago a measure of wine and wheat for every *yugada* of land he reconquered, in a document known as the *Voto de Santiago* dated May 844—a 13th-century forgery by the monks of guess where. The hamlet of Clavijo is on a dead end road south of Logroño under a rocky outcrop and a ruined castle, with crenellations that look like a witch's teeth.

The end of the tribute is celebrated on the third Sunday in May in the village of **Sorzano**, just west of the N 111, when a hundred girls dressed in white carrying holly and flowers make a pilgrimage to the hermitage del Roble.

The N 111 ascends through the forested **Valley of Iregua**, which narrows between the sheer cliffs and buttes of the Sierra de Cameros, dotted with old, now partly abandoned villages of shepherds, who still follow the old transhumance paths to Extremadura in the winter. There are especially lovely views of the square-cut natural gorge, the Peñas de Islallana, and the Vega del Iregua below it from the heights of **Viguera**.

Two km away, in Castañares de las Cuevas, the 12th-century hermitage of **San Estéban** has frescoes of the Apocalypse and more good views. **Torrecilla en Cameros** has an attractive old centre and another church with frescoes, the 16th-century Nuestra Señora de Tómalos (guardian ✆ 46 01 08).

Along the Pilgrim Route: West of Logroño

Beyond Logroño, the segment of the Camino de Santiago that crosses La Rioja is short but choice and full of interest, even though only a fraction of the monuments a 12th century pilgrim would have known remain intact. A nearly obligatory detour remains: the famous pair of monasteries at San Millán de la Cogolla.

Tourist Information

Nájera: C/ Carmen, ✆ (941) 36 16 25.

San Millán: ✆ (941) 37 30 49.

Santo Domingo: C/ Zumalacárregui, ✆ (941) 34 16 25.

Ezcaray: Avda. de Navarra, ✆ (941) 35 40 59.

There is a **market** in Nájera in Pso. de San Fernando on Thursdays.

Navarrete

Eleven km west of Logroño, **Navarrete** makes ceramics and rosé wine, and in the Middle Ages it would make pilgrims comfortable in its hospital of San Juan de Arce. Of this, only the gate survives, doing duty as the entrance to the cemetery. It has lively capitals—of St Michael and the dragon, a pair of picnicking pilgrims, and Roland grappling with the giant Ferragut; a pile of rocks, known as the *Poyo de Roldán*, marks the spot where Charlemagne's nephew floored the big bully with a boulder. The older houses in Navarrete look narrow and pokey but are actually quite spacious (due to a tax on façade sizes). The 16th-century church of the **Asunción**, sometimes attributed to Felipe II's architect Juan de Herrera, contains an elaborate Churrigueresque *retablo* and a triptych (in the sacristy) by Rembrandt's student Adrian Ysenbrandt.

Nájera: the Residence of Kings

Arabic *Náxara*, or 'between two hills', Nájera is a bustling furniture-making town with an illustrious pedigree. It straddles both banks of the trout-filled Najerilla, where the Moorish giant Ferragut was defending the bridge like Troll in Three Billy Goats Gruff when Charlemagne's knights tried to cross it. Ferragut picked them up by the armour and gathered them under his arm—at least until Roland arrived on the scene and gave him what for.

After the Moors flattened Pamplona in 918, the kings of Navarra chose to live in Nájera, mainly to keep an eye on the ambitious upstart kingdom of Castile. The first *Rex Hispaniorum*, Sancho III the Great (1004–35) held his court in both Nájera and Pamplona; in 1020 he diverted the Camino de Santiago to pass through Nájera's centre, assuring it of a good income. When he divided his kingdom between his sons, one took Pamplona and another, García III, made Nájera his capital and reconquered Rioja Baja, creating a buffer between Castile and Aragón. His grandsons were squeezed by these two medieval powerhouses, and in 1076 Nájera was snatched by Alfonso VI of Castile and the Cid. The Cid's daughter, Doña Elvira, made a happy second marriage with the son of the last king of Nájera and their son, García V, became King of Navarra in 1134.

In 1052, García III was hunting on the banks of the Najerilla when he saw a dove fly past over the thick woods on a hill. He sent his falcon after it and followed the birds through the trees into a cave, from which a bright light emanated; inside he found the dove and falcon cooing side by side and a statue of Virgin and Child, a jar of fresh lilies, a lamp and a bell. To celebrate the miracle, García founded an order of knights, the Caballeros de la Terraza (the Knights of the Jar—a mystic receptical like the Holy Grail) and the church, which was rebuilt in the 15th century as the monastery of **Santa María la Real** (*tours 9.30–11.30 and 4–7.30; adm*) and restored after 1895 by the Franciscans.

The entrance is through a beautiful Flamboyant Gothic door, the **Portal of Charles V**, crowned with the Emperor's coat-of-arms. Through here waits the serene and lovely Gothic-Plateresque **Claustro de los Caballeros**, with 24 arches half veiled by intricate sculpted screens, carved to imitate lace: no two are alike. Cloister chapels hold the elegant effigy tomb of a 13th-century Queen of Portugal. From here a Plateresque walnut door leads into the solemn 15th-century **church**. The original Flemish *retablo mayor* was sold for a piece of bread when the monastery was dissolved in 1835, but the 17th-century wowser in its place still holds the miraculous 11th-century statue of Santa María la Real. Originally she wore a large ruby. This was pinched by Pedro the Cruel in 1367 to pay the Black Prince and the English for whipping the French-supported army of his brother Enrique de Trastámara in a battle near Nájera. The ruby now glows on the State Crown of England, but it cost the Black Prince his life—from a Spanish fever.

Near the high altar are the tombs of the Dukes of Nájera, King Fernando of Aragón's right-hand men, who gave Ignatius of Loyola his first job as a soldier. At the entrance of the holy cave are 16th-century tombs of the 10th–12th-century dynasties of Pamplona and Nájera, among them the original **sarcophagus** of Sancho III's 21-year-old wife Blanca. This is the finest Romanesque Spanish tomb to come down to us, with a Christ in Majesty, the Massacre of the Innocents (note, unusually, how everyone seems to be smiling), the death of the queen and mourning of the king. Behind the kings is the holy cave; up the spiral stair is the remarkable Isabelline Gothic **choir** (1493–95), believed to have been carved by Jewish *conversos* (note the Hebrew letters on chair 23), a masterpiece of grace, detail and fantasy. The armour-clad King García figures on the main chair and Gothic paintings of kings and queens around the top create a charming *trompe l'oeil* effect.

Just outside Nájera, hilltop **Tricio** was an important Roman town known as *Tritium Megalon*. Its small mortuary temple was converted wholesale in 1181 into the **Ermita de Los Arcos** to house a miraculous dark-skinned statue of the Virgin; mellow Roman columns support Visigothic arches covered with Baroque stuccoes that at first glance look made of white icing. Traces of Romanesque paintings (the only ones found so far in La Rioja) remain on the walls: scenes of the Last Supper, Passion and Jerusalem.

San Millán de la Cogolla: Yuso and Suso

From Nájera it's a 17km detour south into the Sierra de la Demanda and **San Millán de la Cogolla**, a village that grew up around two ancient monasteries, Yuso ('the lower' in old Castilian) and Suso ('the upper'); *Cogolla* was a nickname for the monks' habit. San Millán (473–574) spent much of his 101 years living in the caves on the hill, his sanctity attracting numerous male and female anchorites. In the 7th century the anchorites built the first monastery at **Suso**, signposted up a 2km narrow road (*open 10.30–1.15 and 4–7.15*), and soon became known for their literary efforts, when the 7th-century monk San Baudelio wrote the *Life of San Millán*. Carved out of a wooded hill, the shadowy little church has a cloister at the entrance, containing the tombs of three queens of Navarra and those of the Seven Infantes de Lara and their tutor Nuño Salido, who met a tragic end after a game played at their uncle's wedding went all wrong and a member of the bride's family was accidentally killed (*see* p.236). Poet Gonzalo de Berceo, the first to write in Spanish, loved to sit and write in the Visigothic portico. The church was heavily damaged by Al Mansour in the Reconquista and had to be rebuilt in the 10th and 11th centuries, with Romanesque arches on one end and Mozarabic and Visigothic down the second aisle. Because of the lack of security, Suso's treasures—especially its golden Flemish diptych—have been removed.

Even the 11th-century tomb with its recumbent alabaster effigy of San Millán is empty, not due to any 20th-century security precautions, but rather because in 1053 King García III decided that Millán's relics belonged in Nájera. The bones were loaded onto a cart, but the oxen, once they reached the bottom of the hill, refused to budge another inch. Realizing that 'the saint didn't want to leave his lands', García built a new more splendid monastery on the spot where the oxen stopped. This is **Yuso** (*rather long guided tours by the monks from 10.30–1.30 and 4–6.30, closed Mon*), known as the 'Escorial of La Rioja' after it was rebuilt on a grand scale in the 16th century, its main entrance crowned by an equestrian relief of San Millán in the guise of Santiago Matamoros. In the Middle Ages Yuso continued Suso's reputation as a literary centre, and what the monastery is proudest of is its one anonymous monk who, in the 10th century, was writing a commentary in the margins of his Latin text, or to be precise, on folio 72 of the *Emilian 60 Codex*, when for 43 words he lapsed into the vernacular—the first known use of Castilian: it's engraved on stone along with other exhibits (mostly portraits of kings) in the **Salón de Reyes**. Interestingly enough, Yuso also has the first known example of written Basque; under the Kings of Navarra, both languages were current in medieval La Rioja.

The Cradle of Spanish

 When the Arabs invaded Iberia, the Christians who fled into the mountainous regions of the north were isolated for several centuries. Latin speakers and a sprinkling of Visigoths found themselves among half-pagan speakers of Iberia's pre-Roman languages, and cut off from the Moors and from each other, several languages developed in addition to the Stone Age tongue of the Basques: Catalan, Gallego, Babel (in Asturias), Aragonese, and several minor Pyrenean languages. From Babel, the first language of the Reconquista, evolved the tongue that would dominate: Castilian, or *Castellano*, or what most people know simply as Spanish.

The predominance of Castilian, however, owes as much to Castile's conquering rôle in history as to the fact that the language is one of the most efficient means of communication ever devised. The Visigoths endowed it with aspirates and a stricter framework than any other Romance language, 'a dry, harsh, stone-cracking tongue,' according to V. S. Pritchett. 'A sort of desert Latin chipped off at the edges by its lipped consonants and dry-throated gutturals…and each word is as distinct and hard as a pebble.' It was the first modern language to have a grammar written for it. When a copy was presented to Queen Isabella in 1492, she quite understandably asked what it was for. 'Your majesty,' replied a perceptive bishop. 'Language is the perfect instrument of empire.' In the centuries to come, this concise, flexible and expressive language would prove just that, an instrument that would contribute more to Spanish unity than any laws or institutions, while spreading itself effortlessly over much of the New World.

In 1870, the aforementioned Emilian gloss long held in Yuso was carted off to the Royal Academy of History in Madrid, and La Rioja wants it back. But Yuso has another feather in its cap: Gonzalo de Berceo, the shepherd-priest who took

Castilian out of the margins and made it into poetry. Born in the nearby village of Berceo in 1198 and educated as a choir boy at San Millán, Gonzalo's verses on the lives of local saints have a simple, sweet quality, and as a good Riojan, were inspired by a draught of wine. His *Vida de San Millán* ends:

> *Quiero fer una prosa en román paladino,*
> *en cual suele el pueblo fablar con su vecino,*
> *ca non so tan letrado por fer otro latino;*
> *bien valdrá, como creo, un vaso de bon vino.*

> (I want to make a verse in the clear Romance
> used by the people to speak with their neighbours,
> those who aren't so lettered in real Latin,
> it's well worth, I think, a cup of good wine).

The Renaissance church has weighty ogival vaulting and a 16th-century *retablo* on the life of San Millán; you can learn more about him in the paintings along the upper cloister, built in 1572. The library has hundreds of old codices and manuscripts, if not the precious Emilian gloss, while the small **museum** contains Yuso's prizes: the ornate reliquary chests of San Millán and San Felices de Bilibio, commissioned in 1063. Made of wood, covered with ivory plates, gold and precious jewels, they were stripped of their gold and jewels by Napoleon's troops, who fortunately had no eye for medieval ivories.

There are yet two other important religious houses in the vicinity. Just north of San Millán and Berceo, **Santa María de Cañas** was founded in 1169 and has a fine tall Gothic church with two floors of windows filling the nave with light. Off the cloister, the chapter-house has the superb 14th-century tomb of the abbess-daughter of the founder, Doña Urraca López de Haro, decorated with nuns, ladies, bishops and abbots, as well as a benevolent 13th-century statue of St Anne, holding her daughter Mary and grandson Jesus on her lap. The nuns have long been famous for their engraved ceramic work. South of San Millán, 5km from Anguiano in the verdant foothills of the Sierra de la Demanda, the 12th century Benedictine **Monasterio de Valvanera** (*open continuously, 10–7*), was built to shelter its much venerated Virgin, the Patroness of La Rioja, discoved in a hollow tree by a thief named Nuño who became a saint. On her knee baby Jesus, in regal robes, is turned to the left, to avert his gaze, they say, ever since a couple fornicated in the church, a sin that led the monks to erect a circle of white crosses around the church, which no woman was allowed to cross. The monastery's other works of art were pillaged by the French or lost when the monks abandoned the monastery in 1839. They returned in 1885 and have been distilling their herbal Valvanera liqueur ever since, carefully plucking the herbs according to the phases of the moon.

Further south, on the C 113, **Mansilla** has an artificial lake and the impressive ruins of an 12th-century church dedicated to St Catherine, while the hamlet of **Canales de la Sierra** is overlooked by the curious church of San Esteban, with strange composite monsters on its capitals.

Santo Domingo de la Calzada and Its Chickens

As they made their way across La Rioja, pilgrims especially looked forward to Santo Domingo de la Calzada, a delightful walled village that owes its name and existence to the first road saint. Born a shepherd, Domingo (1019–1109) applied for a monkish career at Valvanera and San Millán, and when he was rejected he devoted his life to building bridges and *hostales* and generally making the pilgrims' way easier, clearing paths with a magic sickle just like a druid, making him the patron saint of engineers and public works, hence *de la Calzada* ('of the causeway'). His village grew up by a whole complex of his works: a long stone bridge over the Río Oja, a hospital (now a *refugio*), a guest house (now a *parador)* and a church. The local people call him their *abuelito*, or little grandfather.

His church, now the **Cathedral** of La Rioja *(open 10–2 and 3.30–7)* was founded on land donated in 1098 by King Alfonso VI, a pilgrimage booster who came in person to lay the first stone. Reconstruction began in 1158 and took centuries to finish: the first tower was destroyed by lightning in 1450, the second one, completed in 1750, began to sag menacingly, and was torn down in 1760; the third, 243ft- (69m)-high, freestanding and neoclassical to match the façade, was built by Basque tower-master Martín de Beratúa in 1762 on boggy ground, shored up with sand, lime, stone and a ton of cow horns.

The Gothic interior is simple but lavishly decorated, but what everyone remembers best are the rooster and hen, cackling in their own late Gothic **henhouse**. Their presence recalls the miracle that took place in Santo Domingo's *hostal*: a handsome 18-year-old German pilgrim named Hugonell, travelling with his parents, refused the advances of the maid, who avenged herself by planting a silver goblet in his pack and accusing him of theft. Hugonell was summarily hanged by the judge while his parents sadly continued to Compostela. On the way back, they passed the gallows and were amazed to find their son still alive and glad to see them, telling them it was a miracle of Santo Domingo. They hurried to the judge and told him; the judge, about to dig into a pair of roast fowl, laughed and said their son was as alive as the birds on his table, upon which both came to life and flew away. Since then, a white hen and cock have been kept in the church, and are replaced every month; pilgrims would take one of their feathers and stick it in their hats for good luck. Under the window you can even see a piece of the gallows.

Opposite the henhouse is the magnificent tomb of Santo Domingo, designed by Felipe de Vigarni (1517–29); the saint's recumbent statue suggests he could be a starter in heaven's basketball league. On the high altar, the huge Plateresque *retablo* (1540) is the last and best work of Damián Forment, one of Spain's finest Renaissance painters. The carved choir is another excellent, detailed Plateresque work (1530s), decorated with painted scenes on the life of St Domingo, while the chapels are equally beautiful and ornate, especially the screen of the **Capilla de la Magdalena**. The Gothic-*mudéjar* cloister is now used as a museum *(open Mon–Sat 11–7)*.

Outside the cathedral, take a look at its ornate Romanesque apse, at the nearby walls, erected by Pedro the Cruel, and at the handsome if preternaturally quiet arcaded plaza, with a stately 16th-century **Casa Consistorial**. On the west end of town, the

Renaissance **Convento de San Francisco** was built to the designs of Felipe II's favourite architect, Juan de Herrera, to house the elaborate tomb of the king's confessor, Fray Bernardo de Fresneda.

South of Santo Domingo, the most dramatic of La Rioja's seven valleys, the Oja, slices through the lofty Sierra de la Demanda up to the handsome stone village of **Ezcaray.** Ezcaray made its fortune on merino wool, but now serves as a centre for mountain excursions, with the ski resort of **Valdezcaray** on Mt San Lorenzo (2262m), and paths and picnic tables in the beech and pine forests. Don't miss a trip up to the **Ermita de la Virgen de Allende**, site of recent archaeological digs and where some delightful paintings by a well-meaning artist show St Michael dressed up like an 18th-century generalísimo, his avenging sword replaced by a harquebus.

ℭ *(941–)*   *Where to Stay and Eating Out*

Nájera

★★★★**Hostería Monasterio de San Millán**, ℭ 37 32 77, ✆ 37 32 66, is situated in the monastery itself, with a good restaurant. On the Najerilla river, ★★**San Fernando**, Pso. San Julián 1, ℭ 36 37 00, ✆ 36 33 99 (*moderate*), is centrally located, or try the serene ★**Hs Hispano**, Duques de Nájera, ℭ 36 29 57. In the old town, **Pensión El Moro**, C/ Mártires 21, ℭ 36 00 52, is the cheapest. **El Mono**, C/Mayor 43, ℭ 36 30 28 (*moderate*), is Nájera's favourite for monkfish stuffed with lobster. A few doors down, family-run **Los Parrales**, ℭ 36 37 35 (*moderate*), is another fine choice, and has a summer terrace. To the south the **Abadía de Valvanera** (*see* above) has simple rooms, ℭ 37 70 44; peace and quiet guaranteed.

Santo Domingo

Grim on the outside but lovely within, the ★★★★**Parador de Santo Domingo de la Calzada**, Pza. del Santo 3, ℭ 34 03 00, ✆ 34 03 25 (*expensive*), occupies the pilgrim's *hostal* built by Santo Domingo; the restaurant serves a delicious 3700-pts *menú.* ★★**Hs Santa Teresita**, C/ Pinar 2, ℭ 34 07 00 (*moderate/ inexpensive*), is a pleasant guesthouse run by Cistercian nuns or, for something cheaper, try ★**Hs Río**, Echegoyen 2, ℭ 34 00 85 (*inexpensive*). There is a pair of good restaurants specializing in regional cuisine: the well-known **El Rincón de Emilio**, Pza. de Bonifacio Gil 7, ℭ 34 09 90, with a 1500-pts *menú* and **El Peregrino**,with a garden at Avda. Calahorra 19, ℭ 34 02 02, which has similar prices (closed Mon).

Ezcaray

Since the beginning of the century, the recently renovated ★★★**Echaurren**, Héroes del Alcázar, ℭ 35 40 47, ✆ 42 71 33 (*moderate*), has been the place to sleep and eat (closed Nov); in summer, in ski seasons, or weekends, it's essential to book a table at the hotel's restaurant, known far and wide for its stylish food at reasonable prices (*menú* 1900 pts). Quiet ★★**Iguareña**, C/ Lamberto Felipe Muñoz 14, ℭ 35 41 44, ✆ 35 45 76 (*moderate*), is a good second choice, with a moderately priced Basque restaurant.

To the north along the Ebro lies the Rioja Alta, a lush region of abrupt natural features rising above rolling hills, carpeted with vineyards and roads lined with brash spanking new wine *bodegas* that speak of La Rioja's rising reputation, and just might lose their sharp kitsch edge over the next 200 years.

Tourist Information

Haro: Plaza Hermanos F. Rodríguez, ℂ 312 726. There is a market on Tuesdays and Saturdays on Arco de Santa Bárbara.

Haro

Built at the confluence on the Ebro and Tirón, Haro is a bustling working wine town built around a large arcaded square. Its chief monuments are a handful of noble houses, the attractive **Casa Consistorial** (1775) and the 16th-century church of **Santo Tomás** up in Plaza Iglesia, bearing a handsome, recently restored Plateresque façade with sculpture and reliefs in several registers, paid for by the Condestables de Castilla. Since 1892, Haro's **Estación Enológica**, C/ Bretón de los Herreros 4 (just behind the bus station) has tested new winemaking techniques and varieties; its **Wine Museum** (*open Tues–Sun 10–2 and Sat 4–7*) offers detailed explanations of the latest high-tech processes used in La Rioja.

For a far less serious initiation, or rather baptism, in Rioja, come on 29 July when San Felices is celebrated with a *Batalla del Vino*. Everyone dresses in white, and after the mass, fortified with *zurracapote* (Rioja *sangría*, made with red wine, citrus fruit and cinnamon) and armed with every conceivable squirter, splasher and sprayer, opposing groups douse one another with 100,000 litres of wine. This Dionysian free-for-all takes place 3km from Haro at the **Peña de Bilibio**, below the striking rock formation and pass of the Conchas de Haro, 'the Shells of Haro', where Felices, a hermit-follower of San Millán, lived in a cave. Archaeologists have recently discovered a 10th-century church and the ruins of a Roman town Castrum Bilibium, or Haro la Vieja, just under the rocks.

Rioja in the Bottle

Spain's only DOC (AOC) classified wine, La Rioja tastes like no other: soft, warm, mellow, full-bodied, with a distinct vanilla bouquet. The Phoenicians introduced the first vines, which after the various invasions were replanted under the auspices of the Church; the first law concerning wine was decreed by Bishop Abilio in the 9th century. The arrival of masses of thirsty pilgrims proved a big boost to business, much as mass tourism would do in the 1960s and '70s.

Despite a long pedigree, the Rioja we drink today dates from the 1860s, when growers from Bordeaux, their own vineyards wiped out by phylloxera, brought their techniques south of the border and wrought immense improvements on the native varieties. By the time the plague reached La Rioja in 1899, the owners were prepared for it with disease-resistant stock. During the First World War, when the vineyards of the Champagne were badly damaged, the French returned to buy up *bodegas*, sticking French labels on the bottles and trucking them over the Pyrenees. Rioja finally received the respect it deserved after Franco passed on to the great fascist parade ground in the sky. In the last 20 years, *bodegas* have attracted buyers from around the world and prices have skyrocketed: in 1993, Italian investor Mario Benedetti set a record, paying 3,500,000,000 pts for Bodegas Berberana.

La Rioja's growing area covers 48,000 hectares and is divided into three sub-zones: Rioja Alta, home of the best red and white wines, followed by Rioja Alavesa (on the left bank of the Ebro in Alava province) known for its lighter, perfumed wines, and the decidedly more arid Rioja Baja, where the wines are coarse and mostly used for blending—a common practice in La Rioja. The varieties used for the reds are mostly spicy, fruity Tempranillo (covering some 24,000 hectares alone), followed by Garnacha Tinta (a third of the red production, a good alcohol booster) with smaller portions of Graciano (for the bouquet) and high-tannin Mazuela (for acidity and tone). Traditional Rioja whites are relatively unknown but are excellent, golden and vanilly like the reds: Viura grapes are the dominate grape, with smaller doses of Malvasía, and Garnacha Blanca. Unlike French wines, Riojas are never sold until they're ready to drink (although of course you can keep the better wines even longer). DOC rules specify that La Rioja's *Gran Reserva*, which accounts for only 3% of the production, spends a minimum of two years maturing in American oak barrels (six months for whites and rosés) then four more in the *bodega* before it's sold—all the vintages were good (except for '84) in the last 15 years : the special ones to look out for are '62, '64, '68, '70, '75, '78, '81, '82, '87 and '91). *Reservas* (6% of the production) spend at least one year in oak and three in the *bodega*. *Crianzas* (30% of the production) spends at least a year in the barrel and another in the bottle. The other 61% of La Rioja is *sin crianza* and labelled CVC (*conjunto de varias cosechas,* combination of various vintages): this includes the new young white wines and light reds (*claretes)* fermented at cool temperatures in stainless steel vats, skipping the oak barrels altogether and losing most of the vanilla tones.

Haro is the growing and marketing centre for the wines of Rioja Alta, with a clutch of *bodegas* near the train station. While most *bodegas* welcome visitors, they usually require advance notice. An exception is **Bodegas Bilbaínas**, C/ Estación 3, ℂ 31 01 47, with a pretty façade in *azulejos*, usually open mornings and late afternoons. In the same area along Costa del Vino, you'll find the celebrated cellars of the **CUNE** (or CVNE, ℂ 31 06 50) home of a fine bubbly; Chilean-owned **López de Heredia**, ℂ 31 01 27, makers of one of the best Riojas, *Viña Tondonia*; and the vast, French-founded **Rioja Alta**, Avda. Vizcaya, ℂ 31 03 46, with 25,000 barrels. The even larger **Federico Paternina**, ℂ 31 05 50, founded in 1896 by the Plaza de Toros, houses 4 million bottles, and welcomes visitors daily except for Monday. Another, **Martínez Lacuesta Hnos**, C/ Ventilla 71, ℂ 31 00 50, is in the old gas company that became obsolete back in 1891, when Haro became the first city in Spain to have public electric street lighting—hence the slogan *Ya se ven las luces,* *ya estamos en Haro*. Among the shops, **Selección Vinos de Rioja**, Pza. Paz 5, ✆ 30 30 17, offers tastings and a wide variety of different Riojas.

Around Haro: the Sonsierra

There aren't any five-, four- or even three-star landmarks around Haro, but a handful of villages are worth a look if you're trawling about looking for that perfect bottle. A good place to start is the Sonsierra, a pocket of La Rioja on the Left Bank of the Ebro. **Briñas**, just north of Haro, has a number of noble escutcheoned manors left over from the days when it was the playground of the Haro nobility. These days wine is the be-all and end-all; there's even a *bodega* under the church. Don't confuse Briñas with **Briones** to the east, with a nubbly church tower as its landmark and the bridge to **San Vicente de la Sonsierra**, a village best known in La Rioja since 1499 for its Guild of Flagellants, *Los Picaos*, headquartered at **Ermita de Vera Cruz**. During Holy Week, clad in anonymous hoods , the *Picaos* whip themselves across the shoulders, then pique the bruises with wax balls full of crystal splinters until the blood runs. Just outside San Vicente, the curious 12th-century Romanesque church **Santa María de la Piscina** was founded by Ramiro Sanchez, son-in-law of the Cid, who allegedly brought back a piece of the True Cross from the Crusades, where he fought side by side with Godefroi de Bouillon. In front of the church there's a stone well and over the door a shield carved with mysterious numbers and symbols. Paintings inside represent the *piscina probática* (waters of the flock) of Jerusalem and representations of the Grail. Just east, **Abalos** has one of the oldest cellars in Spain, the **Bodegón Real Divisa**, ✆ 25 81 33, owned by descendants of the Cid, and a 16th-century church, San Esteban Protomártir, decorated with dragons.

Back on the south bank of the Ebro, **Cenicero**, in spite of jokes about its name (it means 'ashtray'—apparently shepherds once came here to gather around huge bonfires) is another important wine town which proudly bears the sobriquet the 'Humanitarian' since the 1920s, when the inhabitants went out of their way to care for victims of a train wreck. It has some of Rioja's grandest *bodegas*: ultra-modern **Berberana**, ✆ 45 41 00, and **Amérzola de la Mora**, ✆ 45 45 32, on the San Asensio road, a fine example of old *bodega* achitecture, ideal for its *crianzas* and *reservas*.

West of Haro, **Sajazarra** boasts a well-preserved 13th-century castle, and **Cellórigo**, 'the Pulpit of La Rioja' has views as far as Logroño and a 11th-century castle under the sharp pointed crags of Peña Lengua. **Casalarreina** is a little Renaissance hamlet around the Renaissance convent of La Piedad (1508); 2km east in **Cihuri** the Río Tirón is crossed by a pretty Roman bridge.

Where to Stay and Eating Out

Haro (✆ 941–)

Superbly restored and centrally located, ★★★★**Los Agustinos**, C/ San Agustín 2, ✆ 31 13 08, 🖷 30 31 48 (*expensive*), occupies a former Augustinian monastery that later served as a prison: note the graffiti carved in the columns of the garden cloister. Rooms are quiet, air-conditioned and equipped with satellite TV. Along the highway, overlooking Haro, modern ★★★Iturrimurri, Ctra. 232, ✆ 31 12 13, 🕮 31 17 21 (*expensive/moderate*), is plain, comfortable and has a pool. The very basic ★Hs Aragón, La Vega 9, ✆ 31 00 04, is probably your only bet for a cheap sleep. At La Kika, C/ Santo Tomás 9, ✆ 31 11 81 (*moderate*), the kitchen changes its repertoire daily, so there's no menu—rely on the waiters' suggestions for fine Rioja cuisine; reservations are a must. Since 1867, Terete, C/ Lucrecia Arana 17, ✆ 31 00 23 (*moderate*), has filled the centre of Haro with the divine aroma of its famous roast lamb and huge choice of other dishes; good 1500-pts *menú* (closed Sun eve, Mon and Oct). Traditional mushroom, fish and vegetable dishes are the prizes at the three dining rooms of Beethoven I, II y III, C/ Santo Tomás and Pza. de la Iglesia 8, ✆ 31 11 81 (*all moderate*; the one in Plaza de la Iglesia is the prettiest); closed Mon eve, Tues and 1–15 July.

Briñas (✆ 741–)

★El Portal de La Rioja, ✆ 31 14 80, has, in addition to just barely moderate rooms with bath, an excellent restaurant (*moderate*) serving chops grilled on vine cuttings (*chuletas al sarmiento*), a craft shop and a wine museum with century-old bottles.

Tolosa

The Basque Lands/Euskadi

The Basque
lands, known in
the Basque
language as
Euskadi
('collection of
Basques')
contain, according
to the autonomy
agreement of 1981, the
three provinces of
Vizcaya, Guipúzcoa and
Álava. To the Basques themselves, however, Euskadi
means all lands inhabited by
Basques–the 'Seven
Provinces' that include Labourd,
Haute-Navarre and the Soule in France
and the northern part of Navarra. When it isn't
raining, Euskadi is one of the most charming
corners of Spain—rural for the most part, lush and
green, criss-crossed by a network of mountain

Cabo Higuer
Fuenterrabía
Bay of Biscay

SAN SEBASTIÁN / DONOSTIA

Lekeitio
Mendexo
Ondarroa
Costa Vasca
San Pedro
Irún
Pasai-Donibane
Motrico
Zumaya
Getaria
Deba
Zarautz
Orio
Errenteria
Hernani
I Z C A Y A
Markina
Lasarte
Bolívar

Sanctuary of
St Ignatius of
Loiola
Azpeitia
Villabona
Azkoitia
Régil
Eibar
Tolosa

Elorrio
Bergara
GUIPÚZCOA
Urretxu
Zumarraga
Arrasate/
Mondragon
Río Oria
Río Oria

Euskadi

xandio
Oñati
Beasain
Segura
Idiazabal

Sanctuary of
Aránzazu
Embalse de
Ullivarri

Zalduendo

Argomaniz
Gaceo
Eguilaz
Salvatierra
Sorginetxe
Alaiza

Arrala Maeztu/
Maestu

streams that
meander every which
way through steep, narrow
valleys in their search for the
sea. Great stone country houses
resembling Swiss chalets dot the
hillsides and riverbanks—though
the next valley over may have a grotty
little town gathered about a mill. Spain's
industrial revolution began in Euskadi,
and even today the three Basque
provinces are among the most industrial-
ized and wealthy in the country. But in
most of Euskadi, industry and finance seem
remote. Basque nationalism, on the other
hand, is ever present; every bridge, underpass, and
pelota court has been painted with the Basque flag
and slogans of the *Euskadi Ta Askatasuna*, 'Freedom
for Basques'—the notorious ETA—the small but
violent minority that has given this ancient people a
bad press (as they've had for most of their history).

Laguardia
Elciego
Oyón
La Puebla

*Nomansland, the territory of the Basques, in a region called
Cornucopia, where the vines are tied up with sausages. And in those
parts there was a mountain made entirely of grated Parmesan
cheese on whose slopes there were people who spent their whole
time making macaroni and ravioli.*

The Decameron, VIII

Wild stories like Boccaccio's have often been told about the Basques and their inscrutable ways, but the conclusions reached by many scholars from many different fields are almost as hard to believe. It seems likely that the Basques are no less than the aborigines of Europe, having survived in their secluded valleys during the great Indo-European migrations of peoples from the east thousands of years ago; recent discoveries in Euskadi's caves suggest that they may even be descendants of Cro-Magnon man. Tests have shown that the Basques have an extraordinarily high proportion of type A 'European' blood; an even more extraordinarily high proportion—the highest in the world—have blood with a negative Rh factor, characteristic of the indigenous prehistoric European race. Basques have slight but telling physical differences from their neighbours. Not only are they bigger and stronger, but the distinct shape of their skulls is matched only by those of their ancestors, buried under dolmens in 2000 BC.

One doesn't visit the Basque country to see the sights, which are few and far between. The real attraction is the Basques themselves, a taciturn though likeable lot, and their distinctive culture and way of life. The setting also helps to make the trip worthwhile, emerald landscapes that have been well tended by the same people for millennia (and well they should be emerald; the Basque country gets as much rain as the west of Ireland).

History

'The Basques are like good women; they have no history.' So runs the old saying, but traces of habitation in the Basque lands go back at least 100,000 years, and somebody was painting on the walls of mountain caves as early as 35,000 BC. Where did the Basques come in? Another of their jokes is that, when God created the first man, he got the bones from a Basque graveyard. Some theories have them present as far back as 20,000 BC, but a more likely premise would be that they are the descendants of the Neolithic culture that once occupied much of western Europe, and arrived in these parts *c.* 4000 BC. Practically every word for common tools in Basque comes from the ancient root *haiz*, meaning stone, even *haiztur*, scissors. The possibility of a relationship between the Basques and the Iberians, the most ancient known inhabitants of Spain, is an open question. About 800 BC, Celtic peoples started moving through the region, probably often co-existing and intermarrying with the original peoples. Still, when the Romans came, they found a nation they called *Vascones* occupying most of the land between the rivers Ebro and Garonne, including almost all of the Pyrenees.

The Romans never really exercized much control over the Basques' mountain fastnesses, and the Visigoths and Franks who followed found the Basques a permanent headache. Charlemagne pacified the inhabitants of the plains by 781, but the mountain Basques held out, and taught the aggressive emperor a costly lesson in the legendary battle of Roncesvalles (see p.73). As the medieval states that claimed Basque property—Navarra, Asturias/Castilla, England, Béarn and France—grew in wealth and power, there was increasingly little chance that an event like Roncesvalles could be repeated. This was a world dominated by a feudal aristocracy, one made up of foreigners, the descendants of Germanic invaders and Roman landowners, and with such bossy neighbours it is not surprising that the Basques never coalesced into a nation. The Basques in this period are practically invisible, their language merely the *patois* of countrymen, and nobody paid much mind to them. All through the Middle Ages, in fact, the Basque boundaries shrank gradually but inexorably, as the natives were either pushed out or assimilated by Spaniards, Gascons and Catalans. Many place names, especially in the eastern Pyrenees, give clues of a Basque origin, but by the 1300s the Basque lands had contracted roughly to the boundaries they retain today.

Despite the decline, the Basques survived as a nation throughout. When they finally did agree to recognize the suzerainty of Castilla it was on their own terms, retaining *fueros* (privileges) and ancient laws, one of which was that every king upon being crowned should come to Gernika and swear under the sacred oak tree to uphold their laws. Since then, Basques have always played an important role in Spanish affairs, far out of proportion to their numbers. They were great sailors and explorers, shipbuilders and whalers, conquistadores and pirates, and nowadays they run most of Spain's banks. The Basques organized the first whale fishery, in the Middle Ages. At first they only nabbed whales which came too close to the shore, but as the whales got wise the Basques began chasing them ever farther out to sea. Without much evidence, the Basques say they landed in the Americas long before Columbus (who took a Basque pilot along); Basque sailors helped the English conquer Wales, built the Spanish Armada, and founded a number of Spanish colonies, including the Philippines, as well as cities like Buenos Aires. The conquistadores Lope de Aguirre (so well portrayed by Klaus Kinski in Herzog's film *Aguirre, the Wrath of God*) and Pedro de Ursúa were Basques; the Basque captain Sebastián Elcano became the first man to sail around the world. Two of Spain's most important saints, St Ignatius pf Loyola and St Francis Xavier, were also Basque.

In the 19th century, the Basque lands suffered as much as any other part of France or Spain from rural poverty and depopulation. Young Basques from the mountain uplands found their way in great numbers to the Americas, especially to Argentina and the United States, where the Basque connection goes back to the 1500 sailors, many of them veterans of the corsairs, who came to join Lafayette and fight for American independence. Simón Bolívar, liberator of Venezuela and Colombia, was of Basque descent. In the bayous of Louisiana and east Texas, as well as on the Argentine pampas, Basques became some of the New World's first cowboys in the 1840s, setting the model and contributing much to the image (lariat, among other cowboy terms, is a Basque word, and exotic cinema locales such as Durango, Colorado and Laredo, Texas were named after Basque villages. Later in the century they moved on further west, taking lonely jobs as shepherds in the Rockies. There are still large Basque communities in Idaho, Utah, California and other states.

Throughout history, the Basques have wanted only to be left alone, and they always support any sort of politics that would promise to uphold their ancient rights and liberties. In modern times, this has meant adventures with both the far right and the far left. In the 19th century, when progress meant doing away with quaint relics like Basque culture and *fueros*, the Basques remembered their pious nature and took the side of Fernando VII's reactionary brother Don Carlos in the second Carlist war (1876), and lost the *fueros* as a result. At the same time Euskadi with its iron deposits and port towns began to industrialize, and while many prospered, the majority of workers, seeing their traditional society threatened on all sides, flocked to the banner of Basque Nationalism.

Nationalism is hardly a recent phenomenon. It started in the 18th century, with a community of liberal bourgeois in Bilbao and the other outward-looking port cities; these supported Enlightenment thinkers such as Manuel de Larramendi, who developed a concept of Basque nationhood based on language and tradition. Throughout the 19th century, nationalist thought and the development of Basque culture proceeded apace in Spain, while at least on the political side it ran into a stone wall in the much more repressive climate of France. French Euskadi thus became a side show to main events, while in Spain, the PNV, the first Basque nationalist party, controlled a majority of the region's parliamentary seats from 1917 on.

In 1931, when supporters of a republic offered the Basques autonomy in exchange for their support, they jumped at the chance, despite reservations about the new Second Republic's secularism. When the Civil War broke out, they remained loyal to the Republic and even the priests fought side-by-side with the 'Reds'. To break their spirit, the German Condor Legion practised the world's first saturation bombing of a civilian target at Gernika. Franco later took special pains to single out the Basques for reprisals of all kinds, outlawing their language and running the region as a police state, so that even the thousands of Castilians who immigrated to Euskadi to work in the factories felt oppressed enough to sympathize with Basque Nationalist goals.

Franco's rule was a catastrophe for the Basques: over 100,000 prisoners and 200,000 exiles after the Civil War, including the entire intelligentsia and political leadership. Resistance groups did not start forming until 1952, and the grim atmosphere of Francoist repression determined the equally poisonous nature of the antidote. The ETA (*Euskadi Ta Askatasuna*, or Basque Homeland and Liberty), was founded in 1959. Its bombing campaign near the end of Franco's reign was singularly effective—notably when they blew the car carrying Franco's anointed successor, Admiral Carrero Blanco, over the roof of a Madrid church. In the new Spain the Basques got all they wanted: full autonomy and the right to their language and culture, along with their own police and schools; this left the ETA out in the cold as a band of die-hards demanding total independence. That did not keep them from continuing their terror tactics up until the present day, with help and safe havens among the Basques over the border in France.

The autonomy agreement was an excellent bargain, and the large majority of Basques vote their aspirations through the moderate PNV (*Partido Nacional Vasco*) rather than the political wing of the ETA, *Herri Batasuna*, and on the whole they are progressive—left on most issues (strongly anti-nuclear and anti-NATO). Herri Batasuna, the Basque Sinn Fein, are everywhere; their garish posters cover any and every spare bit of wall. Terrorist ETA has gone steadily downhill since its failure to make an impression during Spain's year of celebrations in 1992. Widespread disgust with terror tactics has made the ETA fall out of favour, though support for a totally independent Euskadi remains considerable; most people, however, are in no hurry for it, and would rather see independence brought about as part of a peaceful and evolutionary process.

Language

Want to impress your hosts with a few words of Basque? Go ahead and try it! The Basques point out with great pride that their language is not only Europe's oldest, but by far the most difficult; the only language ever found to have any kind of similarity to it is Berber. There are four distinct dialects, and in each the grammar is Kafkaesque, to put it mildly. Verbs, for example, can vary according to the gender of the person you are addressing. The vast number of grammatical tenses includes not only a subjunctive, but two different potentials, an eventual, and a hypothetical. But grammatical complexity permits beauty and economy; you can express anything in Basque in far fewer words than in most other languages.

Basque is maddeningly, spectacularly indirect. For example, to say 'I am spinning', comes out *Iruten ari nuzu* , or literally, 'In the act of spinning doing you have me!' Or try out this proverb: *Izan gabe eman dezakegun gauza bakarra da zoriona* . Having without, give (*Izan gabe eman*), we can (*dezakegun*), one thing only is (*gauza bakarra da*), happiness (*zoriona*)—'happiness is the only thing we can give without having'. Pronunciation, thank God, is not such a problem; it's phonetic, and there are only a few letters you need to know: **e** as long a; **u** as oo; **j** as ee; **s** as something halfway between s and sh; **tz** or **z**, as s; and **x** as sh. Pronounce all the vowels, and don't make any soft consonant sounds; practise on the village of Azcoitia (ahs-ko-IT-ee-ah).

Peculiarities of the language include the habit of doubling words for effect, unknown to any European tongue but common among the Polynesians, and some entertaining onomatopoeia. In Basque, something very hot is *bero-bero*, and when a Basque walks on all fours this is called *hitipiti-hatapata.*. Looking at a menu in a Basque restaurant (they have the best cuisine in Spain, so you'll want to do this often) you may well be *keko-meko* (undecided); if you choose *birristi-barrasta* (carelessly), you might get *ttattu* (little cat), a supposed speciality in Bilbao in the 19th century. Basques can put it away; other Spaniards accuse them of *mauka-mauka* (gluttony). Like eskimos, who know no generic word for 'ice', the Basques have no word for 'tree' or 'animal'. And being the democratic folk they are, there's no word for 'king' either—they had to borrow one from the French and Spanish potentates they were forced to pay taxes to.

Here are some important Basque words and phrases you will never need on your trip:

ongi-etorri	welcome
kontuz, lanak	danger, road works
hondartza	beach
zuzen	straight ahead
turismo bulegoa	tourist office
itxita	closed
tren geltokia	train station
atzerapena	delay
kaixo, zer moduz?	hello, how are you?
zuritoa	a small beer
garagardoa	a large beer
sardinak, mesedez	some sardines, please
gizonak	men's
emakumiak	ladies'
zer da hau?	What is this?
xipiroiak	squids
bai	yes
ez	no
nik ez dut ulurtzen	I don't understand
gero arte	see you later

Have fun. In all the Basque lands, though, on average only a third of the inhabitants still speak their language. Due to the severe cultural oppression in Spain under Franco, the percentages are much higher on the French side: 72 per cent in Basse-Navarre and 60 per cent in the Soule, as opposed to 40 per cent in Guipúzcoa, 16 per cent in Vizcaya and only 4 per cent in Álava (those are the Spanish names: *Gipuzkoa, Bizkaya* and *Alaba* in Basque). But following the example of the Catalans, Basques on both sides of the border have begun actively to promote their own language in the schools, with some success. It's important to remember that Basque is a living literary language, the centrepiece of a living culture. The plays known as *pastorales*, possibly descended from medieval mystery plays, are still written and produced at festival times, and Basques pay great reverence to the *bertsulari*, poets who have memorized a vast repertoire of traditional pieces and who are also skilled at improvization.

Note that both the Spanish and Basque names for towns and provinces are official, and used together on road signs: San Sebastián/Donostia, Bilbao/Bilbo, Vitoria/Gasteiz, Fuenterrabía/Hondarribia, etc.

The Basque Cuisine

Basques know how to eat. Go into a village restaurant at 9 in the morning on a market day, and watch the boys tuck into their three-course breakfasts—soup, tons of meat, fish and potatoes, with a gallon or so of wine for each. Fortunately for them, the Basques also know how to cook. Their distinctive cuisine will be one of the delights of your visit to the Basque country. Like the Greeks, the well-travelled Basques took their culinary skill with them everywhere. Basque restaurants turn up in unlikely places all over France, and it isn't unusual to drive through a dusty, one-horse town out in the American west where the only restaurant serves up good Basque home cooking.

Not surprisingly, Basque cooks exert most of their talents on seafood. Marseille has its *bouillabaisse*, among a score of other exotic and treasured fish stews of southern Europe, but the Basques stoutly maintain their version, called *ttoro* (pronounced tioro), is the king of them all; naturally there is a solemn *confrérie* of the finest *ttoro* chefs. A proper one requires a pound of mussels and a mess of crayfish and congers, as well as the head of a codfish and three different kinds of other fish. Basque cuisine relishes imaginative sauces; another seafood delight is fresh tuna cooked with tomatoes, garlic, aubergine and spices and *chipirones* (squid)—reputedly the only one in the world that's all black, and better than it sounds. Each Basque chef knows how to work wonders with elvers and cod, salmon and the famous *txangurro*—spider crab; most famous of all is a dish called *cocochas* (or *kokotchas*, in Basque), the 'cheek' of the common *merluza* (hake) with garlic and parsley. Around San Sebastián they throw in clams and red peppers.

These peppers are another icon of the Basque kitchen; housewives still hang strings of them on the walls of their houses for drying (and for decoration). Peppers turn up everywhere: in omelettes, in sauces for seafood, or in the common stewed chicken. Basques like to wash it down with *txakoli*, a tangy green wine produced on the coast with just a modicum of sunlight. Southern Álava produces an excellent Rioja (*see* p.113), and you can top off your meal with a tipple of deadly Basque hooch, *pacharán* (sloe brandy). The Basques are also fond of good hard cider. They claim to have taught the more famous cider makers of Normandy and Asturias their secrets long ago, and back in the 1500s Basque fishermen used to trade the stuff to the American Indians for furs.

Folklore

The Basques are not alone. In fact, their long intimacy with their land has forced them to share it with an unreasonably large number of gods, demons, spirits and fairies, creatures of one of the richest mythologies of Europe. Many tales are connected to the dolmens and other Neolithic monuments that grow so thickly on the mountains here; often their names connect them to Mari, the ancient Basque great goddess. The dolmens were built by the *jentillak*, the race of giants that once lived side by side with the Basques. The *jentillak*, often a great help to their neighbours, invented metallurgy and the saw, and introduced the growing of wheat. One day a strange storm cloud appeared from the east, and the wisest of the *jentillak* recognized it as an omen and interpreted it as the end of their age. The giants marched off into the earth, under a dolmen still visible in the Arratzaran valley in Navarra. One was left behind, named Olentzero, and he explained to the Basques: 'Kixmi [Jesus] is born and this means the end of our race.' Olentzero lives on today, as the jolly fat doll or straw figure prominent in the Basques' celebrations of Christmas and New Year's Day, the leader of all the processions. Often bearing an unusual resemblance to the Michelin man, you will find Olentzero in Basque homes and even in the churches; he'll probably be surrounded by food because, being one of the *jentillak*, Olentzero likes to eat all day.

Other familiar creatures include the *laminak*, originally small female fairies with a capacity to help or harm, now a sort of leprechaun, which get blamed for everything that goes wrong. And where mythology fades off into nursery-lore, we have the 'man with the sack' who comes to carry off naughty children, and a large bestiary with jokes like the elusive *dahu*, a kind of izard with legs shorter on one side—the better to walk the mountain slopes. Along with the myths goes a remarkable body of pre-Christian religious survivals, including rituals that lasted well into the 20th century; many old Basques in isolated villages can remember festivals with midsummer bonfires in their childhood, and in some villages the custom is coming back, just as it is in the Catalan Pyrenees (any excuse for a party).

16th-century Basque costume

Basques are passionately fond of music, whether it's choral music at mass (which they do extremely well), Basque rock (rare, fortunately), or traditional tunes played by village bands. Dozens of traditional dances are still current, and small groups in many villages keep them up; you'll have a chance to see them at any village fête—and especially in Guipúzcoa, you can tour the villages on a Sunday morning and usually find at least one or two have traditional dances going on in the square. Traditional Basque instruments include the *txistu*, a three-holed flute played with one hand, while the other hand beats out the rhythm on the tambour; another is the *dultzaina*, a primitive bagpipe. When they're in the mood, the Basques dance some of the most furiously athletic dances in the world, especially the *Bolant Dantza* (the 'flying dance') or *La Espata Dantza* ('sword dance').

The real monument of Euskadi is the *etxe*, a word that means much more to a Basque than just 'house'. In the old days, it was the heads of households who met to make laws at the assemblies, and it is common to find families that have constantly kept their home on the same site for over a thousand years. The cemeteries have been around even longer. Basques have their own distinctive 'discoidal' or round-headed tombstone. Archaeologists have dug up some models 4500 years old, and they've been using the same style ever since. The earliest ones often had human figures, sun symbols or other symbols carved on them; since the coming of Christianity the stones usually show crosses. You will see them in any churchyard, usually turned south so that the sun shines on the carved face all day.

Basque Diversions

The real national sport, of course, is smuggling sheep over the border. But the Basques love to play, and over the millennia they have evolved a number of outlandish games that are unique in the world. Many of these are based on pure brute strength, a major element of the national mystique. Even today, especially strong, tall people are said to be descendents of the *jentillak*. One can imagine them, back in the mists of time, impressing each other by carrying around boulders—because that's what they do today, in a number of events generally called the *harri altxatzea*, literally 'stone lifting'. In one, contestants see how many times they can lift a 500lb stone in five minutes; in others, they roll boulders around their shoulders. Related to this is the *untziketariak*, in which we see how fast a Basque can run with 100lb weights in each hand. They're fond of the tug-of-war too; they probably invented it. Besides these you will see them at the village festivals pulling loaded wagons, racing with 200lb sacks on their shoulders, or chopping huge tree trunks against the clock. Don't fool with these people.

The miracle is that at the same time they could develop a sport like pelota, the fastest ball game in the world. Few sports in the world can offer an image as beautiful and memorable as the *pelotari* in his traditional loose, pure white costume, chasing down the ball with a long, curving *chistera*. Pelota takes a wide variety of forms, but the basic element is always the ball: a hard core, wrapped tightly with string and covered with hide—like a baseball, only smaller and with much more bounce; in a serious match this ball can reach speeds of 150 mph. The oldest form of the game is *rebot*, played without a wall. This is done bare-handed; other versions, played in an outdoor *frontón*, may be bare-handed, with a leather glove (*pasaka* or *joko garbi*), or with the *chistera*, made of leather and osier, which enables a player to scoop up the ball and fling it back in the same motion. Whatever the game, it usually requires teams of two players each. The ground in front of the wall is marked off in *cuadros* every 4m from it; to be in, a ball bounced off the wall must usually hit between the 4th and 7th *cuadros*, if it is not returned on the fly. Games are usually to 35 points.

Every Basque village has a *frontón*, usually right in the centre. On some village churches from as far back as the 1600s you can see how the architects left one smooth, blank wall to accommodate the game. Besides the *frontón*, the game may be played in a covered court, or one with another wall on the left side, a *jaï-alaï*, in which case the game is called *cesta punta*, the fastest and most furious form of pelota (thanks to Basque immigrants this has become a popular sport around the Caribbean).

Along the Coast: France to San Sebastián

Getting Around

It's only 20 minutes by bus from San Sebastián to Irún or Fuenterrabía on the frontier; connections are frequent by bus and train and not a few people watching their pesetas stay in Irún (or in France) rather than in the more pricey capital. If you're not in a hurry, take the narrow-gauge 'El Topo' for a leisurely ride through some fine scenery.

Tourist Information

Irún: Puente de Santiago (Puente de Behobia), ✆ (943) 43 62 26 27, and in the train station.

Fuenterrabía (Hondarribia): Javier Ugarte 6, ✆ (943) 43 64 54 58

If you are driving in from France, there is a choice of routes: either the A 8 motorway which is expensive though occasionally dramatic, or the old routes through Hendaye and **Fuenterrabía** (Hondarribia), built up around the sandy ford of the Río Bidasoa that has endowed it with a spacious protected sandy beach. Fuenterrabía gets overlooked with all the border confusion, but this is one of the most agreeable destinations on the coast; the village glows with colour—in its brightly painted houses, especially along Calle San Nicolás, or Calle Pampinot, in its balconies loaded with flowers, and in its fishing-fleet that has not been afraid to take on France in the EU's battles over fishing rights. The town has had its share of sieges—you can still see the ancient walls and a **castle of Charles V**, now a *parador*—and every summer sees an invasion of French tourists (the local defensive measure of raising prices has had little effect in repelling them). In the evening, head out towards the lighthouse on Cabo Higuer—the northeasternmost corner of Spain—for views of the sunset over the bay.

A Border Anomaly

In the Río Bidasoa between Hendaye and Fuenterrabía there is a small island called the Isla de la Conferencia, or Ile des Faisans. This was a traditional meeting place for French and Spanish diplomats since the 1400s. In 1659 the Treaty of the Pyrenees was signed here, ending the long wars between France and Spain; the following year representatives of both sides returned to plan the marriage of Louis XIV and the Spanish infanta. A special pavilion was erected for the occasion, and the King of Spain sent his court painter, Velázquez, to decorate it. Unfortunately the artist caught a bad cold here that eventually killed him.

The last big meeting in the area was the one in 1940 between Hitler and Franco (not on the island, but in the Führer's private rail car in Hendaye station). Even today the island is owned jointly by both countries, and there is a solemn agreement in a cabinet somewhere that details how the Spanish police shall look after it from April to October, and the French for the other six months. But really, there isn't anything at all to watch over; the island at present is uninhabited and completely empty.

Irún, known to all as the grim border stop of endless, pointless waits, is further up the Bidasoa, with only plenty of cheap accommodation to recommend it. This sad state comes courtesy of Franco and

Pasajes de San Juan

his German friends, who bombed it to smithereens in the Civil War. Inland you can climb **Monte San Marcial** for a memorable view over the Bay of Biscay (there is an auto road to the top), or else flee the bustling coast for the serene Valley of Oyarzun, one of Euskadi's rural beauty spots, with the pretty villages of Oyarzun, Lesaca and Vera de Bidasoa. There are plenty of Neolithic monuments all through this region, on both sides of the border; the place where the Pyrenees meet the sea seems to have been a particularly holy spot. A site called Oianleku, off the main road near Oyarzun, includes some small stone circles among the dolmens.

If you're driving you can take the coastal road from Fuenterrabía along **Monte Jáizkibel** offering superb views over the Bay of Biscay, the French coast and the Pyrenees. Just east of San Sebastián, the long ribbon town of **Pasajes de San Juan** (Pasai Donibane) lines the east bank of an estuary, with more picturesque old houses. Victor Hugo lived in one for a while, and the Marquis de Lafayette lodged in another before sailing off to aid Britain's American colonists in their revolution. Philip built part of the Invincible Armada here, although now all such business affairs are handled by San Juan's ugly step-sister across the estuary, **Pasajes de San Pedro**.

© (943–) **Where to Stay and Eating Out**

Fuenterrabía

The castle that housed so many kings and dukes on French business over the centuries has been converted into the ★★★**Parador El Emperador**, Pza. de Armas 4, © 64 55 00, ◙ 64 21 53, and is prettily situated, with only 16 rooms. Smaller, but just as noble, the ★★★**Pampinot**, C/ Mayor 3, © 64 06 00, has eight rooms in a restored 15th-century mansion in the heart of the old quarter (*expensive*). In the moderate and inexpensive ranges there are few choices (actually, rooms are a better bargain across the border in Hendaye, though Fuenterrabía would make a more pleasant stay). The ★★**San Nicolás** has attractive, functional rooms right on Pza. de Armas 6, © 64 42 78. Of the small number of *hostales*, a dependable and relatively cheap one is the **Hs Txoko Goxoa**, C/ Murallas, © 64 46 58.

Ramón Roteta, C/ Irún, © 64 16 93 (*expensive*), offers gracious dining in a lovely villa with a garden, grand cuisine and superb desserts (closed Sun eve and Thurs). Next to the sea, the **Arraunlauri**, Pso. Butrón 6, © 64 15 81, is the best bet, offering scrumptious seafood (*moderate*).

Irún

Near the train station, the ★★**Lizaso**, Aduana 5-7, © 61 16 00, is a good bargain. The **Hs Irún**, at Zubiaurre 5, © 61 16 37, has decent rooms with or without bath at the cheapest rates in town. The **Romantxo** on Pza. de Urdanibia, © 62 09 71, has good home cooking (*moderate*). A number of places nearby are cheaper.

San Sebastián/Donostia

Here at the end of the 20th century, it is difficult to imagine that a place like San Sebastián (*Donostia* in Basque) could ever exist. The Belle Epoque may be a hundred years away, but in San Sebastián the buildings are still made of ice-cream, with florid brass streetlights and trim in Impressionist colours; many people still dress up instinctively for the evening *paseo* around the Playa de la Concha. It's a movie set when the sun's shining, which is most of the time.

San Sebastián has probably been around as long as the Basques, but the oldest mention of it is as a Roman port called *Easo*. The town resurfaces in the Middle Ages; in the 12th century when the Navarrese controlled this part of the coast they built the first fortress on Monte Urgull, one that has been rebuilt and reinforced many times since. The first recorded tourist came rather against his will: François I, King of France, who was locked up in the fortress for a time by Charles V after he captured him at the battle of Pavia in 1527. But long before there were any 'costas', wealthy Spaniards were coming to spend their summers bathing at San Sebastián. In the 1850s it was blessed by the presence of Queen Isabel II, who brought the government and the court with her in summer (*see* p.168); also in her reign San Sebastián was made capital of the province, and the Paris–Madrid railroad was completed, making the city convenient to holidaymakers from both capitals.

Queen Regent María Cristina again made San Sebastián the rage in 1886—following the example of Empress Eugénie of France, who had popularized nearby Biarritz. Despite being the sister city of Reno, Nevada, it's been a classy place to go ever since, a lovely, relaxed, seaside resort in a spectacular setting, built around one of the peninsula's most enchanting bays, the oyster-shaped **Bahía de La Concha**, protected from bad moods of the Atlantic by a wooded islet, the **Isla de Santa Clara,** and by **Monte Urgull**, the hump-backed sentinel on the easternmost tip of the bay.

Getting Around

By air: San Sebastián's airport to the east, near Fuenterrabía, ✆ (943) 64 22 40, has connections to Madrid and Barcelona. The bus to the airport, Fuenterrabía and Irún departs from C/ Oquendo 16, ✆ 42 03 83, every 12 minutes—note that this is really the bus for Fuenterrabía, and lets you off across the road from the airport.

By train: RENFE trains depart from the Paseo de Francia, in Gros, from Estación del Norte, ✆ 28 35 99. There are frequent connections with Irún and Hendaye, Paris, Burgos and Madrid; less frequent trains to Barcelona, Pamplona, Salamanca, Vitoria, Zaragoza and León. *Talgos* whizz all the way to Madrid, Málaga, Córdoba, Algeciras, Valencia, Alicante, Oviedo and Gijón.

The two narrow-gauge lines have neighbouring stations on the C/ de Easo: Topo trains, ✆ 47 08 15, depart from the Estación del Tranvía for Hendaye at 28 and 58 minutes past every hour, going by way of Oyarzun. Eusko Trenbideak-Ferrocarriles Vascos, ✆ 45 01 31, depart from the Estación de Amara less frequently for Bilbao, stopping everywhere on the way.

By bus: a bewildering number of small bus companies leave from the station on Pza. de Pio XII on the southern end of town, a block from the river. The ticket office is nearby on C/ Sancho el Sabio 33, though some lines have their offices on Paseo de Vizcaya. There are 19 bus lines in San Sebastián itself (✆ 28 71 00); no.16 goes to Igueldo and the funicular (daily in summer 10am–10pm, every 15 minutes).

Motor **boats** make excursions out to the Isla de Santa Clara every half hour from the port, where you can also rent a rowing boat to do the same yourself.

Tourist Information

Municipal: on the river, C/ Reina Regente, ✆ (943) 48 11 66.
Basque Government: Pso. de los Fueros 1, ✆ (943) 42 62 82.

Playa de la Concha and the Comb of the Winds

Sheltered within the bay is the magnificent golden crescent of the **Playa de La Concha**, San Sebastián's centrepiece and its largest beach; on its western end stands a promontory topped by the mock-Tudor **Palace of Miramar** of María Cristina, now owned by the city and used for receptions and special exhibitions. A tunnel under the Miramar leads to the **Playa de Ondarreta**, a traditional society retreat. Ondarreta itself meets a deadend at seaside **Monte Igueldo**, crowned by a **Parque de Atracciones**. You can get to the top by road or by the delightful, rickety old *funicular* from the end of the beach, and the reward is a spectacular view over San Sebastián, the Bay of Biscay (*Bizkaiko Golkoa* in Basque) and the Cantabrian mountains. Back on the shore, beyond the beach and the funicular stands one of the most talked-about monuments of modern Spanish sculpture, Eduardo Chillida's **Peine de los Vientos**, the 'Comb of the Winds'. The work is a series of terraces, built into the rocks that guard the entrance to the bay, decorated with cast iron constructions, the 'teeth' of the comb that smooths the winds coming from the sea towards the city. Chillida is a native of San Sebastián (he was once goalie for the local football side), and his house is on the cliffs above the monument.

Nearly all the city behind these beaches dates from the 19th century; San Sebastián is an ancient place, but it has been burnt to the ground 12 times in its history, lastly by Wellington's drunken soldiery, who celebrated the conquest of the town with their accustomed murder and mayhem. The city was rebuilt and even expanded soon after, in a neat neoclassical grid with the **Catedral del Buen Pastor**, completed in the 1880s, at its centre.

A promenade-lined river, the **Urumea**, divides 19th-century Sanse (as the city is affectionately known) from the newer quarter of **Gros**, the workingmen-student-bohemian enclave, a lively place full of cheap bars and endowed with its own beach, the **Playa de Gros**, which is always less crowded but lies outside the sheltered bay, subject to the wind, waves and filthy debris. Of the three charming bridges that span the Urumea, the one named after María Cristina (near the station) most resembles a cream pastry.

La Parte Vieja and Monte Urgull

Most of the action in town takes place beneath Monte Urgull in the narrow streets of **La Parte Vieja**, or old town. From La Concha beach, its entrance is guarded by a beautiful

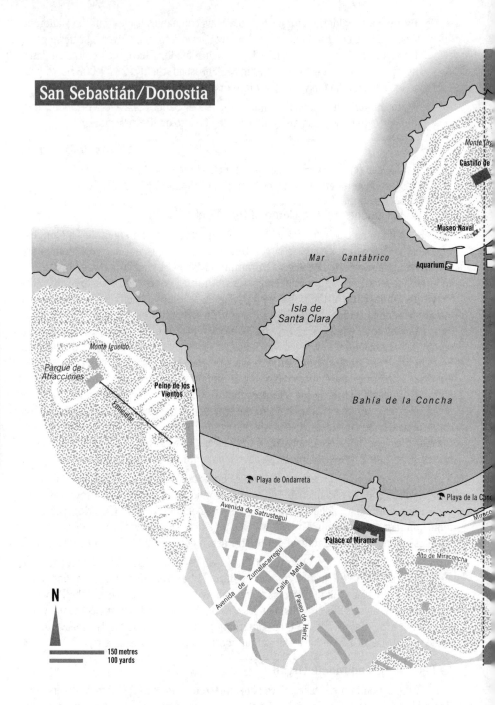

San Sebastián/Donostia

Monte *Urg*

Castillo de

Museo Naval

Mar   Cantábrico

Aquarium

Isla de
Santa Clara

Monte Igueldo

Parque de
Atracciones

Peine de los
Vientos

Funicular

Bahía de la Concha

Playa de Ondarreta

Playa de la Conc

Avenida de Satrustegui

Miraco

Palace of Miramar

Alto de Miraconcha

Avenida de Zumalacarregui

Calle Matia

Paseo de Heriz

N

150 metres
100 yards

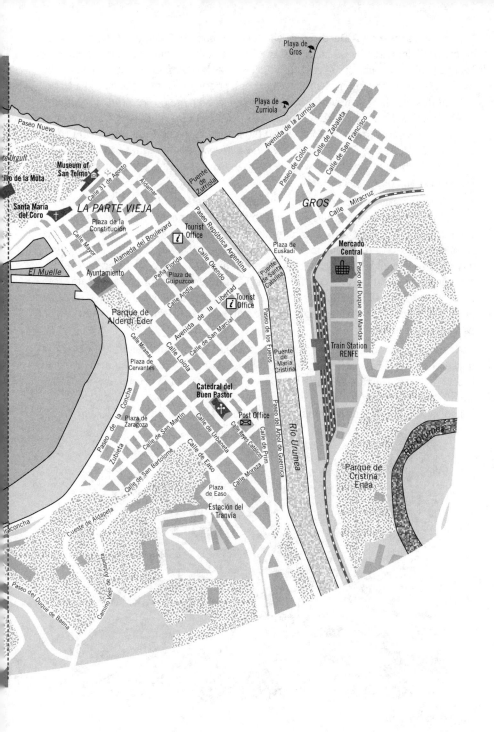

square, the **Parque de Alderdi Eder**, and the enormous 19th-century **Ayuntamiento**, or town hall, formerly the Casino that María Cristina built (the new one is in the Hotel de Londres). What remains of the city's fishing-fleet may be seen in the harbour behind the Ayuntamiento, an area rimmed by souvenir shops, pricey tourist restaurants, and a pair of salty museums: the recently-refurbished **Museo Naval** *(daily exc Mon, in summer, Tues–Sat 10–1.30 and 4–7.30, otherwise 10–1.30, 5–8.30; Sun all year 11–2)*, devoted to the Basques' proud naval history, and at the far end of the port, the **Aquarium** *(daily exc Mon 10–1.30 and 3.30–7.30, til 8pm July and Aug)*, stuffed with ships' models, the skeleton of a Basque whale that went belly-up in San Sebastián's port, and downstairs, tanks of fish and other sea creatures from around the world.

From here you can stroll along the outer edge of **Monte Urgull** on the Paseo Nuevo, a splendid little walk between turf and surf. In the late afternoon, when the light is best, stroll up one of the numerous paths to the summit of the rock; Monte Urgull is really the city's park, closed to traffic and including surprises along the way such as a British cemetery from Wellington's campaign, and some of the old bastions and ancient cannon of the city's defences. Up at the top is the half-ruined **Castillo de Santa Cruz de la Mota** (16th century), with a small museum of arms inside. Nearby an ungainly kitsch statue of Christ (from the Franco era) called the **Sagrado Corazón** keeps an eye on the holiday-makers on La Concha beach below.

The centre of La Parte Vieja is the arcaded **Plaza de la Constitución**; within a few blocks of this local centre of Basque nationalism stand San Sebastián's three best monuments—the hyper-ornate façade of **Santa María del Coro** (18th century) on Vía Coro, the fine Gothic church of **San Vicente** on San Vicente and, nearby, the old Dominican monastery of San Telmo, now the fascinating **Museum of San Telmo** *(daily exc Mon 9.30–1.30 and 4–7, in*

San Sebastián harbour

summer until 8pm, Sun 10–2; adm). The monastery's church is adorned with golden murals by the Catalan artist Josep Sert (1930) on the history of the Basque people. Old Basque tombstones, with round heads adorned with geometric patterns, are lined up in the cloister; upstairs the museum contains three El Grecos, two bear skeletons, Basque lucky charms and amulets, Basque sports paraphernalia, the interior of a Basque cottage and more.

The main attraction of La Parte Vieja is its countless bars, where the evening crowds hasten to devour delectable seafood tapas and Basque goodies. Eating is the city's greatest obsession, and there are societies (for some reason, all male) devoted to the preparation and devouring of enormous Basque meals. A fun excursion is to gather some good food and row it out to **Isla de Santa Clara** for a picnic (in summer there is a regular **ferry** to the island from El Muelle, the dock behind the Ayuntamiento; boats run from 10 to 8.30).

San Sebastián © (943–)   **Where to Stay**

San Sebastián is not the place to look for bargains, and many of the cheaper *hostales* and *fondas* are packed full of university students most of the year. In general, the farther back you are from the sea, the less expensive the accommodation will be.

expensive

For a touch of Belle Epoque elegance, one of Spain's best hotels is the old grande dame, ★★★★★**María Cristina**, Pso. República Argentina 4, © 42 49 00, @ 42 39 14, looking onto the Río Urumea's promenade, a short walk from La Concha. The city's other most luxurious address, the ★★★★**Hotel Londres y Inglaterra**, on La Concha beach at Zubieta 2, © 42 69 89, @ 42 00 31, has splendid views, first-class service, and plenty of charm, as well as one of the city's best restaurants (meals around 3500 pts). Quiet, small, comfortable, and located halfway up Monte Igueldo, the ★★★**Gudamendi**, Barrio de Igueldo, © 21 41 11, @ 21 40 00, has superb views.

moderate

San Sebastián being the posh resort it is, most *hostales* here fall into the moderate price category, and there are plenty of chances of a simple double room for 5000 pts. One well-run place right in the centre is the ★**Hs Eder II**, on the Alameda del Boulevard at the edge of the Parte Vieja, © 42 64 49. Another nearby, the ★★**Ozcariz**, Fuenterrabía 8, © 42 53 06, is in a noisy location but very welcoming.

inexpensive

The best you'll find will be at the higher end of the inexpensive range, and there are a fair number of them both in the Parte Vieja and in the centre. In the old town, the **Hs Kaia**, at C/ Puerto 12, © 43 13 42, has little going for it but the price; rooms with bath or without. Slightly more comfortable, and with friendly owners, is the **Hs San Jerónimo**, around the corner on C/ San Jerónimo, © 42 55 26. Places in the centre seem much the same, without the atmosphere. Good bargain choices include the **Hs Easo**, C/ San Bartolomé, © 46 68 92, and the old-fashioned **Hs La Perla**, C/ Loiola, © 42 81 23.

The best camping option is up on Monte Igueldo, the **Camping de Igueldo**, Paseo Orkelaga, ℰ 21 45 02, though it's quite expensive. At the end of Ondarrena beach, at the foot of the road up Monte Igueldo, there is a youth hostel, **La Sirena**, ℰ 45 29 70; it's the cheapest place in town.

Eating Out

As eating is the municipal obsession, it's not surprising that the city can claim three of Spain's most renowned, award-winning restaurants, the cathedrals of Basque cuisine: **Arzak**, Alto de Miracruz 21, ℰ 27 84 65, offers a constantly changing menu of delights (its 8500-pts *menú de degustación* may be the best choice in this book for a big splurge). **Akelare**, in the Barrio de Igueldo, ℰ 21 20 52, combines exquisite meals with a beautiful setting and views over the sea (5500-pts menu). The third culinary shrine, **Nicolasa** on Aldamar 4, ℰ 42 07 55, specializes in classic Basque cookery and offers a large choice of dishes (6500 pts); all three close Sun eve and Mon, as do most restaurants in the city. Other good, and slightly less expensive, restaurants are **Urepel**, Pso. de Salamanca 3, ℰ 42 40 40, and **Salduba** at Pescadería 6, ℰ 42 56 27, both again serving fine Basque food at moderate prices. Another superb choice, specializing in grilled fish and meat and with a huge wine cellar, the **Rekondo**, Pso. de Igueldo 57, ℰ 21 29 07, offers elegant dining for around 4500 pts.

Cachon, San Marcial 40, ℰ 42 75 07, fills up fast with diners in search of a wide variety of reasonably priced seafood and other dishes on the 900-pts menu. The **Oquendo Café**, C/ Oquendo 6, near the theatre, has a bistro atmosphere and some more unusual dishes (and lots of striped tuna) on its 1200-pts menu. Good seafood at reasonable prices is served at the **Bar Igueldo** near the fishing harbour on C/ Pasealekua for around 1500 pts (occasional live music); for something cheaper, follow the crowds through the tapas bars of the Parte Vieja.

Entertainment and Nightlife

The centre of the serious party action is C/ Reyes Católicos (nicknamed Reyes Alcohólicos), and the surrounding streets south of the cathedral, where the cars are shut out on weekends and everyone does it in the road. Bars with live music are mostly in the Parte Vieja, including the **Etxekalte**, on C/ Mari (jazz sometimes), **Erniope**, C/ San Juan, with traditional Basque music, **Lanbroa**, on Plaza de la Constitución, and the aforementioned Oquendo Café. Late-night bars and discos are found around the end of Ondarreta beach, including **La Piscina**, in a pretty outdoor setting, and **Tenís**, a salsa disco; up on Monte Igualdo nearby is **Ku**, the original of the more famous place of that name on Ibiza.

Inland from San Sebastián

Tourist Information

Tolosa: Bajos del Ayuntamiento, ℰ (943) 43 65 04 14
Oñati: Foru Enparatza 11, ℰ (943) 43 78 30 69

There is a **market** in Tolosa on Saturdays in Plaza del Tinglado.

Tolosa

Guipúzcoa, San Sebastián's province, is the most densely populated rural part of the Basque Country, where plenty of fat villages bear unpronounceable, unimaginable names. There being only one fast route through the area, from San Sebastián to Tolosa, you'll have to invest a lot of time on some lovely, lazy back roads if you want to see any of them. Despair will probably set in at a corner with signs pointing you to Aizarnazabal, Azpeitia, Azkoitia, Azkarate, or Araiz-Matximenta; you'll begin to think the Basques are doing this just for you.

One of the first Basque towns to join the industrial revolution, **Tolosa** (named after Toulouse) is the largest town on the river Oria, thriving on paper mills, which explain the aroma, along with the manufacture of wicker *cestas* for pelote, and sweets, especially *tejas* (almond biscuits) and *delicias*. You can learn all about them in the **Museo de Confitería** at Lechuga 3, next to the Plaza del Ayuntamiento, or taste them in Tolosa's *pastelería* of renown: **Gorrochategui**, in C/ Arbol de Gernika. Dining out is the other main reason to stop (*see* below).

Oñati

Southwest of Tolosa on the N 1, there's the pretty mountain village of **Segura**, its main street lined with the palaces of a locally powerful family, the Guevaras, and other nobles. Segura lay on the original pilgrim route. Up in the mountains beyond Zegama bits of the original Roman road to Vitoria are still visible, but today there's no road at all, and this valley has become something of a dead end.

Before Segura at Beasain, the main route branches westwards for **Oñati**, capital of the Pretender Don Carlos in the Carlist wars. This was one of the few towns in Euskadi to be ruled by a noble, and it retained a sort of independence until 1845. For many years the town had the only Basque **university**, founded in 1540; its building, Oñati's landmark, has a beautiful Plateresque façade and a plain but distinguished arcaded courtyard. Oñati is known also for its number of well-preserved medieval palaces, one of which saw the birth of conquistador Lope de Aguirre, the deranged 'Wrath of God' in the film by Werner Herzog. The parish church **San Miguel** (15th century) contains a number of treasures, including the alabaster tomb of the university's founder, Bishop Zuázola de Ávila, attributed to Diego de Siloé, and an attractive Plateresque cloister. Other noteworthy buildings include the **Ayuntamiento** and the Franciscan **Convento de Bidaurreta**, but perhaps the greatest charm is the town's setting in a rich, rolling valley, dominated in the distance by the bluish pointed peaks of Mount Amboto and Udalaitz.

A scenic road up from Oñati climbs in 9km to the **sanctuary of Aránzazu**. Here, in 1469, a shepherd found an icon of the Virgin by a thorn bush and a cow bell; the Virgin of Aránzazu became the patron saint of Guipúzcoa. The church that houses it has been rebuilt innumerable times since, lastly in 1950. Usually filled with tour buses and pilgrims, this is a curious temple of Basque modernism in a lonely and rugged setting, its two towers covered with a distinctive skin of pyramidal concrete nubs, creating a waffle-iron effect—a reference to an eccentric Renaissance conceit popular in Spain, seen in many buildings from Salamanca to Naples. The main doors are the work of Eduardo Chillida.

The only town of any size in the region has two names: Basques call it **Arrasate**, Spaniards Mondragón. Though a nondescript industrial town these days, Arrasate used to be a spa—a Spanish prime minister, Antonio Cánovas del Castillo, was murdered here by an anarchist in 1897 while taking a cure. Arrasate still has some of its medieval walls and gates, along with the 14th-century Gothic church of San Juan. Farther north, the pretty village of **Bergara** has a number of palaces, churches and other monuments from the 16th and 17th centuries; note the Palacio Arrese, with its cut-out corner window in the best Spanish Renaissance style. If not for Bergara you would be reading this by candlelight. A professor at the former Real Seminario Patriótico Bascongado here, in the 18th century, discovered tungsten, the element used in the filaments of light bulbs.

Loiola: St Ignatius's Home Town

Just south of Tolosa the twisting GI 2634 branches westwards into the mountains, passing first **Régil**, a pretty mountain town with beautiful views from the Col de Régil, the 'Balcón de Guipúzcoa'. This picturesque road continues to the ancient village of **Azpeitia** and the nearby hamlet of **Loiola** (Loyola), home of the **Sanctuary of St Ignatius**. Ignatius, or Íñigo López de Loyola, was born here in 1491, the last of 13 children of a noble family who became the founder of those intellectual stormtroopers of Christ, the Jesuits. The actual house, built by the saint's grandfather after a four-year exile among the Moors, is a fortress-like *mudéjar* structure, redesigned inside as a museum with solemn chapels and over-the-top gilded ceilings. Next to it stands the **basilica**, one of the outstanding Baroque works in all Spain. Carlo Fontana, a student of Bernini who had worked on many of the great Baroque building projects in Rome, was the main architect, and the costs were paid by a Habsburg queen of Austria; her family's coat of arms in stone hangs over the main door. Begun in 1689, this circular temple with its 211ft-high dome took almost 50 years to complete. To give an Italian building the proper Spanish touch, the ornate church rotunda is flanked by two plain, broad wings of monastery buildings, making a façade almost 500ft wide—creating the sharp contrast of vast, austere surfaces and patches of exuberant decoration that marks so many of the best Spanish buildings.

At the entrance, a monumental stairway guarded by very stylized lions leads up to a porch under three arches; in it are five niches with statues of early Jesuit heroes, including St Francis Xavier, another Basque who met martyrdom, proselytizing the Japanese. Nothing on the exterior, though, prepares you for the overwrought stonecarving that covers every part of the dome inside, designed by a group of masters that included Joaquín de Churriguerra, one of the three brothers whose taste for ornament gave Spanish architecture the word *churrigueresque*. As in most Jesuit monuments, no expense was spared, from the fine Carrara marble frieze around the rotunda to the elaborate pavement in coloured stone. Over the main altar, a life-size statue of St Ignatius is covered with silver contributed by the Basques of Caracas, Venezuela.

Tolosa

★Urrutitxo, Kondeko Aldapa 7, © 67 38 22, 🐾 67 34 28, offers 10
rooms in a pretty villa in the centre of Tolosa (*moderate*). Simple,
cheap rooms equipped with a sink are available at the **Hs
Oyarbide** in Plaza Gorriti, © 67 00 17. Tolosa's oldest restaurant, **Casa Julián**, Santa Clara 6, © 67 14 17 is still one of the
best, specializing in grilled steaks, *pimientos del piquillo* and *tejas de
Tolosa*, with a good list of Rioja wines (*moderate*; closed Sun). In the same price
range, **Nicolás**, Zumalacárregui 6, © 65 47 59, does delicious things with fresh
and dried cod, as well as charcoal grilled steaks (*moderate*; closed Sun and Aug).
For a drink and a snack, join the crowd at the pretty but nameless Art Deco bar at
San Francisco/Ibiltokia 4; there's also a 1100-pts menu (© 65 29 41). **Basarri** in
Plaza Euskalherria is a bar with tasty red pepper *pinchos*; in the same square,
Astelena has a good 1000-pts *menú del día*.

Azpeitia

The upmarket **★Izarra**, near the basilica on Av. de Loyola 25, © 81 07 50, has a
swimming-pool (*moderate*). Azpeitia also has the modest **★Hs Uranga**, B. de
Loyola, © 81 25 43, with bathless rooms (*inexpensive*, also a restaurant with inexpensive meals). In Zumárraga on the main road to Azpeitia, the **Etxeberri** is
extremely cosy and welcoming, specializing in Basque game dishes, © 72 12 11
(*inexpensive/moderate*; closed Sun eve).

Oñati

You couldn't find a nicer spot to stay in this part of Guipúzcoa; there is only a
single 10-room *hostal*, though, the pleasant **★Etxeberria**, R.M. Zuazola 14, © 78
04 60, in the middle of town. A good restaurant in Oñati, the **Txopekua**, on the
road to Aránzazu, is located in a Basque homestead at Barrio Uribarri, © 78 05 71
(2500 pts). At the Sanctuary of Aránzazu itself there's the large **Hospedería de
Aránzazu** for pilgrims, © 78 13 13, with simple, clean doubles with bath (*cheap*).

Along the Coast: San Sebastián to Bilbao

Getting Around

The coast is served by frequent buses from San Sebastián and Bilbao; the narrow
gauge Eusko Trenbideak line stops four or five times a day at Zarautz, Getaria,
Zumaya, Deva and Durango; another branch runs out of Bilbao to Bermeo via
Gernika.

Tourist Information

Zarautz: Nafarroa Kalea, © (943) 83 09 90
Getaria (summer only): © (943) 14 01 03

Zumaya (summer only): ✆ (943) 86 10 56
Lekeitio: Arranegiko Zabala 10, ✆ (94) 624 33 65
Gernika: C/ Artekale 8, ✆ (94) 625 58 92

West of San Sebastián, the coastal cliffs keep all roads inland as far as **Orio**, a venerable fishing village that looks like an industrial town, at the mouth of the Río Orio, one of the most polluted rivers in Spain. Although the beach by Orio's very popular campground is clean enough, rough seas can bring out the no swimming flags. If you're planning a picnic, drive up to the lush hilltop **Parque de Pagoeta**, signposted along the N 634.

These same waves and a mile and a half of sand draw surfers to nearby **Zarautz**. Whaling and shipbuilding in the Middle Ages put Zarautz on the map, while more summering royalty—this time Belgium's King Baudouin and Queen Fabiola—inaugurated its international reputation as a resort. Now the second biggest resort in Euskadi after San Sebastían, Zarautz is especially popular among well-to-do Basque nationalists—hence summer courses in Basque language and folklore events, to go with the golf course, riding stables, and good food (with some harder-to-swallow prices).

In the historic centre of Zarautz, look for its trio of tower houses, especially the **Torre Luzea** in Calle Mayor and the one incorporated into the 16th-century **Palacio de Narros**. The most important church, **Santa María la Real**, has a half Plateresque, half Renaissance *retablo*; the *campanile* was added atop yet another medieval tower house in the 18th century.

Getaria/Guetaria

Zarautz's shipbuilders built the *Vitoria*, the first ship to circumnavigate the globe, while the next fishing town to the east, **Getaria**, produced the man who captained it, Juan Sebastían Elcano: approaching from the east, a massive stone monument in his honour will be your introduction to this petite and utterly charming resort.

The First Man to Sail around the World

In the great age of discovery, no Spanish or Portuguese captain worth his salt would set out without a Basque pilot, the heirs of centuries of experience in whaling boats off Europe's westernmost shores—they may have actually found the American coast in medieval times, and kept the knowledge a closely guarded secret. Columbus took a Basque pilot, and Elcano had the post of second-in-command to Magellan. In 1519, Charles V backed the Portuguese navigator Ferdinand Magellan's attempt to find a quick western route to the Indies by sailing southwest around the newly discovered continent of America to the Molucca islands, then cutting back to Spain around the Cape of Good Hope. Charles gave Magellan five ships, and in August they set forth from Seville. One ship turned back before attempting the Straits that took Magellan's name (October 1520). If already dismayed by the distances involved just crossing the Atlantic, Magellan must have been appalled at the extent of the Pacific. Even worse, by the time his little fleet made it to the Moluccas in 1521 a civil war had just broken out, which through tragic accident numbered Magellan among its victims. Elcano took over the helm of the expedition and sailed halfway around the world to Seville in the only surviving ship. He arrived in October 1522, the holds stuffed to the brim with spices.

In spite of his singular feat, Elcano was destined to remain forever in Magellan's shadow— except of course in the eyes of his fellow Getarianos. Besides the aforementioned monument, they erected a statue of Elcano just outside the gate of the old town, and stage a historical re-enactment of his homecoming every four years. Below the monument lies Getaria's port, sheltered by a peninsula and an islet known for its shape as **El Ratón**, the mouse.

From the coastal road, you wouldn't think there was much to Getaria at all. Only pass through the old gate next to the monument, and you will find one of the loveliest villages of Euskadi, hugging the steep slope down to the harbour. Whenever the Getarianos go to mass in the church of **San Salvador**, in the centre of the old town, they step on his grave, located just inside the door. Elcano was lost in the Pacific in 1526, so there probably isn't much of him in there anyway.

Once beyond Elcano's tomb, this church has other surprises up its sleeve. Founded in the 13th century, it was rebuilt in 1429 in a curious off-kilter fashion: the wooden floor lilts as if on rough seas, and the choir vaulting is just as tilted. No one knows why. Along the right wall, near the suspended ex-voto of a ship, is something you rarely see in a church: a menorah. A double flight of stairs rises in the back, and the crypt and another chapel lie along the alley descending to the port. The crypt contains the remains of the ancestors of the same Queen Fabiola who made nearby Zarautz a resort. Getaria doesn't mind; although it has two small beaches of its own, it picked up all of Zarautz's fishing business. From the port, with its brightly painted boats and seafood restaurants, a path leads up to the top of Mouse Island.

Zumaya

West of Getaria the N 634 rises dramatically over the sea before descending to Zumaya, a pleasant town set at the mouth of the river Urola. A kilometre before Zumaya itself, keep an eye peeled for the town's chief attraction, the **Museo Zuloaga**, a cosy villa set in a small park of ancient trees, surrounded by a wall (*open Jan–Sept, Sun only 10–2; adm*). This was the home of the Basque painter Ignacio Zuloaga (1870–1945), and it holds not only a selection of his own works, but the masterpieces he collected over the years: several El Grecos, Goyas, Moraleses, two saints by Zurbarán and an excellent collection of medieval statues and *retablos*. Adjacent, the little 12th-century church and cloister of **Santiago Etxea** was a stop for pilgrims taking the coastal route to Compostela. Below stretches the pine-rimmed beach named after the painter, **Playa Zuloaga**.

There's more art in the middle of Zumaya, in the 15th-century church of **San Pedro**: two triptychs on either side of the altar, the one on the right Flemish, and a dark, Gothic St Christopher on the back wall. There's another beach to the west at **San Telmo**, a dramatic swathe of sand under steep red cliffs, known for the strength of its pounding surf.

Orio

Orio is known for its bream, safely nabbed far from its dirty river; at **Arrillaga**, Areizaga 4, © 83 21 48, you can share one with a friend, along with a salad and bottle of wine (*moderate*). For something less expensive, continue east of Orio on the N 634 to the **Oliden**, where 800 pts gets you a wide choice of dishes from the set menu.

Zarautz

Zarautz can be as pricey as San Sebastián. ★★★★**Karlos Arguiñano**, Mendilauta 13, © 13 00 00, is a formidably expensive modern hotel, but its restaurant is one of the best dining places along this stretch of coast, with sophisticated seafood dishes and a warm, welcoming atmosphere (5500 pts). As for accomodation, the more reasonable ★**Sol y Mar**, Avda. de Navarra, © 83 23 19, ✆ 83 04 53, is a trim modern building with in-room TV (*moderate*). An inexpensive and quiet campsite, the **Camping Talai-Mendi**, is near the beach at Monte Talai-Mendi, © 83 00 42.

Getaria

In Getaria you can lodge near the beach at the ★★**Hs San Prudencia**, © 83 24 11, a good bargain for the area; inexpensive rooms without bath. Getaria is not only a good town for seafood, but for drinking *txakolí* wine, grown in the nearby hills. You can taste it at any of the restaurants that crowd the harbour, including the **Kaia**, upstairs at Gral. Arnao 10, © 83 24 14, along with good Basque seafood (*moderate*); downstairs you can eat roast meats at the less expensive **Asador Kai-Pe**.

Zumaya

Jesuskoa in Zumaya's Barrio de Oikina, © 86 17 39, has good grilled fish meals (1500-pts menu). No hotels here, but some of the bars in the main square have inexpensive rooms.

Zumaya to Gernika

After Zumaya the main road dives inland, but you can continue along the old winding coastal road to **Deva**, a sweet village with a fine beach, so far not much exploited by tourism, and **Motrico**. Motrico is set back on a narrow inlet 3 km from the quiet beach of **Saturrarán**. Crossing from here into Vizcaya province at **Ondárroa** used to mean paying duty at the provincial customs house near the medieval stone **Puente Vieja**. The village is another pretty fishing-port, but most people press on west to **Lekeitio** (Lequeitio), with its better beaches, **Isuntza** and **Carraspio** further out. Lekeitio still catches more fish than tourists, despite its gorgeous situation under the Cantabrian hills; it's a town that never bothered to attract any before, so it's still fun.

Gernika/Guernica

The ancient, sacred city of the Basques is mostly rebuilt now, and most of the inhabitants are too young to remember the horror that occurred one market day in 1937. But beyond the beautiful setting in the Mundaka valley near the sea, and the oak tree by the old Basque parliament building (**Las Casas Juntas**), there's not much to see. The **Tree of Gernika**, the seedling of an ancient oak, is the symbol of Basque democracy; under it the people of Vizcaya met in assembly from the earliest times, and here the laws were proclaimed. Later, Spanish kings would come here to swear to uphold Basque liberties. Remnants of its 600-year-old trunk can be seen under a nearby pavilion. Though the tree was destroyed in the bombing, its descendant serves as a potent symbol of freedom and hope, not only for the Basques, but for everyone—Gernika shocked the world because it was the first time modern technology was used as a tool of terror, a prelude to our own greatest nightmares.

The First Victim of Saturation Bombing

Gernika in 1937 became the kind of symbol for its times that Sarajevo is for the '90s, a civilized little place that some thugs had chosen to flatten. Almost as soon as it happened, the Nationalist propaganda machine began sending out stories that the Communists had really destroyed the town by placing bombs in the sewers. It may have been the only time in his life that Francisco Franco was actually embarrassed. Just how much responsibility the Generalísimo had for Gernika will probably never be known, but there is nothing in his long shabby career that suggests he was capable of such a stunt—Franco could massacre prisoners and fill prisons with priests and professors, but Gernika was evil on a Nazi scale.

Hitler had sent his 'Condor Legion' to Spain not only to give Franco a hand, but to test the new Luftwaffe's theories of terror bombing, and his commanders coldly determined Gernika to be the site of the first lesson (on a market day too). Though the town had no military significance whatsoever, as a symbol of Basque nationhood it was the perfect spot for a bombing designed especially to destroy the enemy's morale—by breaking their hearts, perhaps. While Gernika had little effect on the war—the isolated Basque pocket was bound to fall anyhow—the Nazis were pleased enough with the results and the notoriety they gained from them to make such bombing the centre of their strategy; after Gernika came Warsaw, Rotterdam and Coventry among many others.

Picasso's great painting, resting safely in New York during the Franco years, did as much as the bombing itself to catch the world's attention. Since 1981 it has been proudly displayed in the Prado in Madrid, perhaps the ultimate exorcism of the War and the General. The *Guernica* that seemed so mysterious and revolutionary in its time now seems quite familiar and eloquent to us, so much have our ways of seeing changed since that distant age. The black and white gives it the immediacy of a newspaper photo. Picasso's preliminary sketches show that the central figure in the painting, the fallen horse and rider, was in his mind from the beginning. We can see in them the image of Gernika's destroyers: the eternal bully on horseback, the caudillo, the conqueror. In a way *Guernica* may have been Picasso's prophecy—with such an atrocity as this, the man on horseback may finally have gone too far.

Gernika was rebuilt in the Franco era, though neither the planning nor the architecture won any prizes. There are two modern memorials to commemorate the bombing: **Gure Aitaren Etxea**, 'our father's house', is an eloquent contribution by Chillida, dedicated to peace and sighted on the Tree. Behind it is an amorphous work of Henry Moore, 'Large Figure in a Shelter'.

North of Gernika extends a pretty, pine-forested estuary, the Ría de Gernika, with a number of small, sandy beaches—at **Laida** and **Laga** near the mouth of the Ría, and **Pedernales** and **Mundaka** on the western shore. About 5km east of Gernika, the **Cueva de Santimamiñe** has Euskadi's best Palaeolithic art: two rooms with engravings of bison, horses, arrows, a bear and a deer, and geometric designs; they are rather faint, as only some of the black paint of the outlines has survived (*open for free guided tours Mon–Fri, 10, 11.15, 12.30, 4.30, 5.30—note that due to the fragility of the art, only 15 people at a time are allowed in. As it's something of a climb up, get there early and stand right by the gate to be assured of a place*).

Along the Coast to Bilbao: the Castle of Butrón

Bermeo, near Mundaka, is Euskadi's largest fishing-port, a colourful, working town that makes few concessions to tourism, although it has a fine collection of seafood restaurants. Just to the west, off the shore of **Baquio** the hermitage-topped islet of **San Juan de Gaztelugatxa** is linked to the mainland by an artificial bridge. In the old days it supported a castle; the best one remaining in the vicinity is the 11th-century **Castillo de Butrón**, rebuilt in fairy-tale style in the 19th century and located in the wooded hills (take the C/ 6313 west of Gatika). Butrón really deserves a visit (*open daily exc Mon, 10–8, Sun 11–6.30; adm*); it's the Disneyland castle on a bad trip, an incredible pile of towers and corbelled ramparts in a gloomy dark stone, done in a style that other countries in the Victorian era generally saved for prisons and asylums. If you aren't careful you may end up on a guided tour; the place is kitted out with props and dummies in costume to better evoke the fantasy medieval atmosphere.

© (94–) | *Where to Stay and Eating Out*

Lekeitio

For accommodation Lekeitio has the fine little **Piñupe**, Avda. P. Abaroa 10, © 684 29 84 (*moderate*), or the more expensive ★★**Beitia**, Avda. Abroa 25, © 684 01 11 (*moderate*). Good, abundant and cheap fish dinners are served at **Zapiraia**, Igualdegui 3 (*inexpensive*).

Gernika

Near Gernika's Santimamiñe caves there's the **Lezika**, a fine restaurant located in an 18th-century Basque chalet in a charming woody grove (*moderate*); and in town itself **El Faisán de Oro**, Adolfo Urioste 4, Ⓣ 685 10 01, is smart and elegant, serving food to match (*expensive*). Accommodation is limited to the simple ★★**Gernika**, Carlos Gangoiti 11, Ⓣ 625 03 50, and the very similar **Boliña**, C/ Barrenkalle 3, Ⓣ 625 03 00 (*both moderate*).

Mundaka

This little resort at the edge of the Ría near Bermeo has one of the loveliest hotels in the region: the ★★**Atalaya**, Pso. de Txorrokopunta 2, Ⓣ 617 70 00, ✆ 687 68 99. Located right on the river, this is one of those glorious Basque buildings of a century ago with glass galleries all around. Small but lavishly appointed rooms, with satellite TV and minibars (*expensive*).

Inland: San Sebastián to Bilbao

Along the coast, the narrow twisting roads will take you nearly a day. The more common route west is the A 8 motorway, with its exorbitant tolls, and the slower, parallel N 634, both of which cut inland near Deba and follow some of the more somnolescent landscapes of Euskadi. If you avoid the tolls and follow the latter you'll get an object lesson in the life of the average Basque, passing through tidy, grey little industrial splotches like Eligobar and **Eibar**, a typically peculiar Basque factory town stuffed in a narrow valley, with plenty of tall apartment blocks around Spain's biggest sewing machine plant. Ermua, the next village up the road, is much the same.

Further south, on the BI 632, **Elorrio** is an attractive village of grand palaces and impressive little squares, adorned with a set of unique **crucifixes** from the 15–16th centuries. The façade of the Ayuntamiento bears a curious verse from Matthew 12: 36: 'I tell you, on the day of judgment men will render account for every careless word they utter'. From the centre it's a lovely walk out to the hermitage of **San Adrián de Argiñeta**, where you can see the 9th- and 10th-century **tombs of Argiñeta**, carved out of rock, some adorned with pinwheel-like stars or Latin inscriptions. Nobody knows to whom these sarcophagi belong; some speculate they are the tombs of some leftover Visigoths.

It's another 6km to the biggest town in the area, **Durango**, a name that conjures up cowboys and Westerns in the New World (besides the Durango in Colorado, there is another in Mexico, which in colonial times was capital of the province of 'Nueva Vizcaya': there must have been a lot of Basques about). The original has nothing to detain you long, though there is an attractive Baroque centre behind its **Portal de Santa Ana**, an ornate survival from the old walls. In the centre, note the brightly painted Ayuntamiento, and the stone mosaic maze under the portico of **Santa María de Uribarri.** The most unusual single monument is the 19th-century **Kurutziaga Cross**, just outside the centre in a neighbourhood of the same name.

North of Durango, in the heartland of old Basque traditions, is the minute village and valley of **Bolívar**, from whence came the family of the great Liberator of South America, Simón de Bolívar. His Art Deco monument dwarfs the village square, and down the village's one lane, the site of his ancestral house has been fixed up as a **Museo Bolívar** *(open Tues–Fri 10–1, Sat and Sun 12–2, July and Aug also 5–7, closed Mon)*. Near the old parish church of **Santo Tomás** you can see the 'cattle trial yards' and the huge stone weights hauled by oxen at festivals.

Markina (Marquina), further north, is nicknamed the 'University of *Pelota*'; its historic *frontón* has produced champions who have made their mark around the world. In Markina, on the right bank of the Río Artibay, stands the uncanny, hexagonal church of **San Miguel de Arretxinaga**, built around an enormous altar constructed by the giant *jentillak* (or, according to some, fallen from heaven) that consists of three massive rocks propped against one another. Probably a work of Neolithic times, it now shelters a statue of St Michael. There is another 'cattle trial yard' next to the church.

Ⓒ *(94–)*   **Where to Stay and Eating Out**

Unlike the coast, this is definitely not tourist country, and you'll find only simple accommodation anywhere near the A 8.

Durango

Though it's the biggest town in the area, don't count on workaday Durango either for a place to stay or a meal. It has one mid-range *hostal*, the **★★Hs Juego de Bolos**, San Agustinalde 2, Ⓒ 681 10 99. On C/ San Antonio in Berriz, just outside Durango, **Josu Mendizabal**, Ⓒ 622 50 70, runs a very popular restaurant with plenty of fresh seafood (menu 1900 pts).

Markina

Here you can get a good night's sleep at the central **★★Vega**, Abesúa 2, Ⓒ 686 60 15 *(moderate)*. For dinner, there is **Niko**, San Agustín 4, Ⓒ 616 89 59, good cooking on a bargain 800-pts menu.

Bilbao/Bilbo

Tucked into the deep lush folds and clefts of Euskadi's coastal range, where the river Nervión, once a notorious industrial by-product and now almost clean enough to support fish, discharges its last effluents in the flushing tides of the coast's deepest estuary, you'll find Bilbao. The name is *Bilbo* in Basque, but its inhabitants prefer to call it lovingly the *botxo*, Basque for hole, or orifice.

The orifice was originally a scattering of fishing hamlets, huddled on the left bank of the *ría* where the hills offered some protection from the Normans and other pirates. In 1300, when the coast was clear of such dangers, the lord of Vizcaya, Diego López de Haro, founded a new town on the right bank of the Ría de Bilbao. It quickly developed into the Basques' leading port, trading Vizcaya's iron to France and Castile's wool to Flanders. In 1511 the merchants formed a council to govern their affairs, the Consulado de Bilbao, an institution that survived and thrived until 1829.

The 19th century had other treats in store: the indignity of a French sacking in 1808 and the brunt of two Carlist revolts, during one of which the city was besieged by the Carlists. But this century also made Bilbao into a city. Blessed with its iron mines, forests, cheap hydraulic power and excellent port, Bilbao got a double dose of the Industrial Revolution. Steel mills, shipbuilding and other associated industries sprang up, quickly followed by banks and insurance companies. Workers from across the country poured into the tenements, and smoke clogged the air. The resemblance to Pittsburgh was striking; it still is. After being crushingly punished by Franco for its support of the Republicans, Bilbao gradually grew back to its former prominence as the industrial centre of Spain.

Of late, as in Pittsburgh, the machinery has begun to rust—not so much on account of showers (average annual rainfall: four feet) as from the general decline of heavy industry in the West. Meanwhile Greater Bilbao/Bilbo/*botxo*, with its population of over a million, the sixth city of Spain and its greatest port, not to mention the sister city of Boise, Idaho, is not twiddling its thumbs awaiting obsolescence. Thanks to banking, insurance and such less obviously dirty business, the economy is doing pretty well, and the city has embarked on an ambitious redevelopment programme, reclaiming vast areas of the centre formerly devoted to heavy industry. New projects include the Guggenheim museum, a concert hall and a convention centre built on the site of the old shipyards; a metro, with stations designed by Norman Foster, is well underway. Bilbao may be one of the cities of Europe's future; come back in ten years and see.

Getting There

By air: Bilbao's Sondika Airport is the busiest in northwest Spain, with daily flights from London, Brussels, Frankfurt, and Milan, and to most airports in Spain, including Santiago and Vigo (information, © 453 35 00 or 420 66 10). The airport is 9km north and approximately a 1500-pts taxi ride away from the centre; a bus service to the airport (from C/ Sendeja, © 425 82 00) runs roughly every 45 minutes.

By train: Bilbao has several train lines and about a dozen stations, although as a non-suburban commuter you have to be aware of only four of them. The main RENFE station, with connections to France, Madrid and Galicia is known either as Estación de Abando or del Norte, and is located in the heart of town on the Hurtado de Amézaga (© 423 86 33 or 423 8623). Next to Abando at Bailén 2 but facing the river with a colourful tile front is the Estación de Santander, where scenic, narrow-gauge FEVE trains come and go to Santander, Oviedo, and El Ferrol (© 423 22 66). The pretty little Estación Atxuri, at Atxuri 8 in the Casco Viejo, is used by the Basque regional line, Eusko Trenbideak (© 433 95 00 or 433 77 00) for connections to Donostia/San Sebastián, by way of Durango, Gernika, Bermeo, Zarautz and Zumaya. Eusko Trenbideak also offers the easiest way to Bilbao's beaches at Getxo and Plentzia, although from their other station at Plaza San Nicolás, in the Casco Viejo near the Plaza Nueva.

By bus: Someday Bilbao plans to have a central bus terminal, but until then you'll have to seek out each individual bus line; most are fairly central.

From Alameda Rekalde 68, Viacar buses (© 44 4 31 00) travel to Asturias and Galicia as well as London, Paris, Toulouse, and Portugal; Intercar (© 44 21 20 49) go to Santiago, Vigo and Tui; and Turitrans (© 44 21 03 63) go to Santander and Gijón.

From Autonomía 17, ANSA and GETSA buses (✆ 44 44 31 00) go to Reinosa, Santander, Asturias, León and Galicia.

From Hurtado de Amézaga, in the RENFE building, PESA buses (✆ 44 24 88 99) go to Donostia/San Sebastián, Bayonne, Durango, Eibar, Tolosa, Ondarroa, Bergara, Mondragón Arrasate and Oñati; Automóviles Vascongados (✆ 44 23 78 60) to Bermeo, Gernika, Lekeitio, Zornotza and Bakio.

From Henao 29, La Unión (✆ 44 24 08 36) go to Pamplona, Logroño and Vitoria.

From Nicolás Alkorta 1, ✆ 44 10 08 15, GEASA buses to to Pontevedra, Lugo and Ourense.

From Pedro Martínez Artola 4, ENATCAR (✆ 44 44 00 25 or 44 44 17 12) buses go to Burgos and León and SAIA buses (✆ 44 44 17 08) go to London, Amsterdam Hanover and Hamburg.

Getting Around

Bilbao's excruciatingly complex topography of hills and valleys makes it a beast to negotiate by car; miss one turn, and you may have to circle around 40km (no exaggeration!) back and around, only to end up in a field of orange barrels called Asua Crossroads from which few have ever returned. If you ever make it to the centre, parking will prove equally frustrating; you'll find city-run garages at Plaza Nueva, Instituto Correos and Plaza del Ensanche. If the car you parked in the street vanishes, call the Grúa Municipal (towing) ✆ 423 46 41.

Although the city is currently excavating an underground to unclog its central arteries, nearly all of its attractions are within walking distance in the centre; the efficient city bus line (Bilbobus) will take you there if you're elsewhere. For a radio taxi, call ✆ 416 23 00 or 444 88 88.

Tourist Information

Next to the theatre at Plaza Arriaga 1, 48005, ✆ (94) 416 02 88; there is also an airport office, ✆ 453 23 06.

The **post office** is on the Alameda de Urquijo 15; **telephones** are at Buenos Aires 10, both in the Ensanche near the rail station.

The Casco Viejo

The Casco Viejo, the centre of the city from the 15th to the 19th century, is a snug little region on the east bank of the Nervión; tucked out of the way across the Puente del Arenal from the bustling centre, it remains the city's heart. The bridge leaves you in **Plaza de Arriaga**, known familiarly as *El Arenal* from the sand flats that stood here long ago. Fittingly for a Basque city, its monuments are both musical, the opera house, or Teatro Arriaga, and a glorious Art Nouveau pavilion in steel and glass—band concerts every Sunday afternoon. Adjacent to the Arenal is an arcaded, enclosed **Plaza Nueva**, now a bit down-at-heel, but in its day the symbol of Bilbao's growth and prosperity.

Philosopher Miguel de Unamuno was born on nearby Calle La Ronda, not far from the

Basque Archaeological, Ethnographical and Historical Museum on Cruz 4 (*Tues-Sat 10.30–1.30 and 4–7, Sun 10.30–1.30*). Located in an old Jesuit cloister, this offers for your perusal a scale-model of Vizcaya, a reconstruction of the rooms of the Consulate, the old merchants' organization, as well as tools, ship-models and Basque gravestones. In the middle of the cloister, the ancient *Idolo de Mikeldi* is the museum's treasure—it looks like a primitive depiction of the cow that jumped over the moon. Around the back of the museum, the **Catedral de Santiago** sends its graceful spire up over the centre of the Casco Viejo. Begun in the 1200s, most of this understated but elegant grey stone church is 14th–15th-century Gothic (though the façade was added only in the 1880s). It matches its setting perfectly; everything to the south is the calm grey world of the 'Seven Streets', the core of Bilbao when it was still a village. All the colour and animation the neighbourhood has to offer is concentrated in the 1929 **Mercado de la Ribera** on the riverfront, the largest covered market in Spain.

The 'Seven Streets' being closely hemmed in by cliffs, Bilbao's centre migrated over the bridge as the city grew up, while garden suburbs grew up on the cliffs. Behind the large church of San Nicolás, off El Arenal, an elevator ascends to the upper town, from where it's a short walk to the Viscayans' holy shrine, the **Basílica de Begoña** with its unusual spire stuck on an early 16th-century church. Inside a venerated statue of the Virgin holds court with some huge paintings by the slapdash Neapolitan Luca Giordano, probably the most popular painter of his day. There are fine views of the old town below.

The Ensanche

Nobody in the 19th century had a sharper sense of urban design than the Spaniards, and wherever a town had money to do something big, the results were impressive. Like Barcelona, Bilbao in its industrial boom years had to face exponential population growth, and its mayors chose to plan for it instead of just letting things happen. The area across the river from Bilbao, the 'Anteiglesia de Abando', was mostly farmland in the 1870s when the city annexed it. A trio of planners, Severino de Achúcarro, Pablo de Alzola and Ernest Hoffmeyer, got the job of laying out the streets for what came to be known as the *Ensanche*, or 'extension', and they came up with an simple-looking but really rather ingenious plan, with diagonal boulevards dividing up the broad loop of the river like orange sections.

The Ensanche begins across from El Arenal; just over the bridge from the old town, a statue of Bilbao's founder, Diego López de Haro, looks benignly over the massive banks and circling traffic in the **Plaza de España**. This has become the business centre of the city, with the big grey skyscraper of the **Banco Bilbao Vizcaya**, built in the '60s, to remind us who is the leading force in the city's destiny today. The RENFE station occupies one corner of the square; you'll have to walk around behind it on the riverfront to see one of the city's industrial age landmarks: the tiny **Bilbao-Santander rail station**, a charming Art Nouveau work with a wrought iron and tile façade, designed by Severino de Achúcarro. The vast desolation of tracks and sidings behind these two stations, wasted space at the heart of the city, is about to be reclaimed as the centrepiece of Bilbao's ambitious facelift—the **Intermodal**, a huge commercial project to be built on air rights over the tracks. Included is to be a new station, under an elliptical glass dome.

From Plaza de España, the main boulevard of the Ensanche extends westwards: the **Gran Vía de Don Diego López de Haro**. A block to the north, the façade of the **Corte Inglés** department store is one vast high relief mural evoking the industry and history of Bilbao. The centre of the Ensanche scheme is Plaza de Federico Moyúa, better known as **La Elíptica**. The Hotel Carlton here, still one of the city's posh establishments, served as the seat of the Basque government under the Republic and during the Civil War. From La Elíptica, C/ Elcano takes you to the **Museo de Bellas Artes**, on the edge of the large and beautiful **Parque de Doña Casilda Iturriza**, between the Gran Vía and the tourist office (*10.30–1.30 and 4–7.30*). It contains a worthy collection ranging from Flemish paintings (Metsys' *The Money Changers* is one of the best) to Spanish masters like Velázquez, El Greco, Zurbarán and Goya, to modern art by Picasso, Gauguin, Léger and the American Impressionist Mary Cassatt, and efforts by 19th- and 20th-century Basques. The park itself

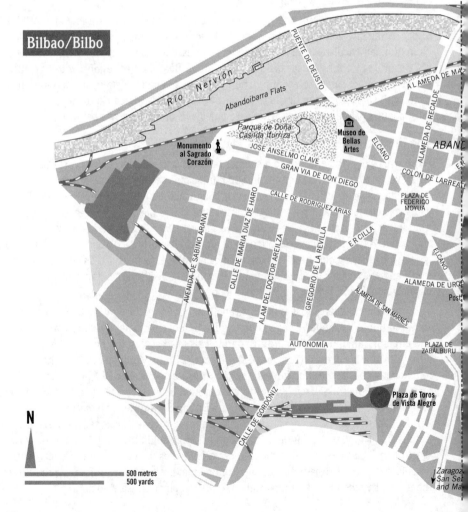

is an agreeable place to spend an hour or two, with exotic trees carefully labelled, a lagoon, and a new light-and-colour bauble called the 'Cybernetic Fountain'.

Just behind the park is the **Abandoibarra flats**, site of the old Euskalduna Shipyards, once the city's biggest employer. Now abandoned and barren indeed, it is slated to become Bilbao's biggest riverfront redevelopment, bookended by the **Museo Guggenheim**, a showcase for contemporary art, and the **Palacio de la Música y de Congresos Euskalduna**. The Guggenheim is a coup for Bilbao; soon the city will be sharing the collection and special exhibitions now limited to New York and Venice. Its building is being designed by the noted American architect Frank Gehry; from the models it looks to be a very bold, flowing structure, built around the approaches to the busy Deusto bridge and almost enveloping them.

Only a third of Bilbao's million-odd souls live within the city itself. Bilbao is the heart of a sprawling conurbation that lines the Nervión for 20 miles, with factories and tower blocks squeezing in wherever the terrain permits, for miles on every side. The fancier suburbs are found near the seacoast, where there are dramatic cliffs and a number of beaches. Of these the biggest is **Getxo**, a combination suburb and beach resort full of lovely villas. On the way from Bilbao, you'll pass a rather remarkable industrial landmark, the 1880s iron **Puente Colgado**, the 'hanging bridge'.

Funicular de Archanda

CASTAÑOS

Río Nervión

Palacio de Ibaigane

NDO

RCILLA

Ayuntamiento

San Vicente Mártir

BUENOS AIRES

DE HARO
Diputación

PLAZA DE ESPAÑA

PUENTE DEL ARENAL

Estación de Abando (RENFE)

Estación de Santander (FEVE)

Tourist Office

Teatro Arriaga

San Nicolás

AVENIDA DE ZUMALACÁRREGUI

Basílica de Begoña

Office

HORTADO DE AMÉZAGA

CALLE DE BAILEN

CALLE DE LA RIBERA

JARDINES VICTOR

PLAZA NUEVA

CALLE DEL PERRO

CASCO VIEJO

San Sebastián

Catedral de Santiago

Basque Archaeological, Ethnographical and Historical Museum

SOLOKOETXE

CAR VIEJA

ARTECALLE

SAN FRANCISCO

Mercado de la Ribera

Estación de Achuri

Monte de Mira-villa

goza,
Sebastián
Madrid

The beaches continue eastwards along the coast. Though they're jam-packed with Bilbaínos on weekends they can be fun; both the beaches and the water are surprisingly clean. Two of the most popular are at **Sopelanas** and **Plentzia**. And if you are spending much time in Bilbao, we might recommend (though not for the faint-hearted) a ride around the mountains that hem the city in. On **Monte Artxandamendia**, or in the hills above Erandio or Portugalete you will see incredible landscapes of steel mills perched on mountaintops, grazing sheep, Victorian castles, shantytowns and roads on stilts, scenes from some surrealist comic book.

Bilbao ✆ *(94–)*

Where to Stay

expensive

Bilbao has quite a few luxury hotels, catering for the businessmen who pass through. Many stay at the ★★★★★**Villa de Bilbao**, Gran Vía 87, ✆ 441 60 00, with every luxury that 22,000 pts will buy.

moderate

The average visitor would probably prefer to stay in the Casco Viejo—there are several choices on C/ Bidebarrieta, including the ★★**Hs Hostal Arana** at no. 2, ✆ 415 64 11, with comfortable modern rooms. The ★**Arriaga**, off Plaza Arriaga at C/ Ribera 3, ✆ 479 00 01, is similar in qualtity though a bit more expensive. Both these hotels have parking, an important consideration in this crowded town.

inexpensive

Most of the inexpensive rooms will be found in the Casco Viejo. ★★**Hs Gurea** Bidebarrieta 14, ✆ 416 32 99, has nice simple rooms (with bath), and just around the corner by the cathedral at Lotería 2, ✆ 415 07 55, there's the friendly ★★**Roquefer**, in an old building with high ceilings and nice showers down the hall. Another good choice on this street is the very inexpensive ★**Ladero**, ✆ 415 09 32.

Eating Out

This city may not get as wild about cuisine as San Sebastián, but eating is still a pleasure in Bilbao—you can splurge at the city's finest, the traditional and sumptuous **Bermeo**, C/ Ercilla 37, ✆ 410 20 00; if it's on the menu, this is the place to try one of the ultimate Basque treats, *cocochas*—the 'cheek and throat' of a hake in a garlic and parsley sauce (menu 5400 pts). For the purest Basque cuisine, look for the strangest names: **Zortziko**, Alameda de Mazzarredo 17, near Plaza de España, ✆ 423 97 43, with innovative dishes with a wide variety of Rioja wines (menu 4800 pts). **Guría**, Gran Vía 66, ✆ 441 05 43, is another old favourite, though quite expensive (menu 7800 pts)

You can eat very well for less at **Aitxar**, C/ María Muñoz in the Casco Viejo, with good seafood and typical dishes for about 1000 pts, or **La Granja**, an attractive old place on Plaza de España (*moderate*). **Amboto**, C/ Jardines, is a seafood place off Plaza Arriaga that specializes in *merluza* (hake) in a delicious sauce made from crabs (1500–2000 pts). For snacks, sandwiches and *platos combinados* until late, there is **Café Gargantua**, on C/ Barrenkale (*inexpensive*).

Nightlife

Fans of Bertolt Brecht and Kurt Weill will be disappointed to learn that 'Bill's Ballhaus in Bilbao' was only a figment of their imagination. Nightlife is generally limited to weekends, in the streets of the Casco Viejo. C/ Barrenkale is a busy place with a number of clubs; in the Ensanche, there are more on C/ Pérez Galdós. The big techno-disco in town is called Distrito 9, on C/ Ajuriagerra.

Vitoria/Gasteiz

Vitoria has style. It also has the air of a little Ruritanian capital—because it is one. The seat of the inland province of Álava, and since 1980 the capital of autonomous Euskadi, Vitoria has grown to be one of Spain's modern industrial centres, a phenomenon that has so far done little harm to one of the most surprisingly urbane cities in the nation. Although Wellington soundly defeated the forces of Joseph Bonaparte here in 1813, Vitoria's name has nothing to do with victory, but recalls the height (*Beturia* in Basque) on which the city was built. In the Middle Ages this was a hot border region between the kingdoms of Navarra and Castile. Navarrese King Alfonso VI founded a fortress and town here in 1181, but the Castilians managed to snatch it away from them soon after. Like everything else in medieval Castile, Vitoria boomed, and extended itself logically in concentric rings of streets—oddly enough, a plan exactly like Amsterdam's, without the canals. Hard hit by the wars and plagues of the 1300s, Vitoria stagnated for centuries, and began its recovery only with the industrial boom of the 1890s. It has preserved itself beautifully throughout, probably an important factor in getting Vitoria named the Basque capital in the autonomy agreement of 1981.

The important thing to know about Vitoria is the *Fiesta de la Virgen Blanca*, on the 4th of August. It's a typically berserk six-day Spanish blowout, with champagne everywhere, lots of high-powered fireworks, and parties 'til dawn, but the image of it that sticks in the mind is **Celedón**, a dummy in a beret and workman's clothes. Celedón holds an umbrella aloft, which is attached to a wire from the top of the cathedral tower; from this he descends as gracefully as Mary Poppins, gliding across the Plaza to start the festival. On the morning of the 10th he glides up the wire and pops magically back into the bell tower, and it's all over for another year.

Getting Around

Foronda airport, 7km west of Vitoria, has connections with Madrid and Barcelona (℡ (945) 27 33 00). Trains between San Sebastián and Madrid pass through Vitoria, and Salvatierra is a stop along RENFE's Vitoria–Pamplona run. Otherwise you'll have to take the bus, or hitchhike. Generally the more remote the area, the more likely you are to get a ride—friendly locals will often stop and ask you if you want a lift. Vitoria's stylish train station is at the head of C/ Eduardo Dato, six blocks from the old town (℡ 23 20 30). The bus station is at C/ Francia 34 (℡ 25 84 00/25 84

11), a short walk east of the old town. There are regular services to San Sebastián, Bilbao and Logroño, as well as to the provincial villages, and because of the city's position on the main route north from Madrid, you can get nearly anywhere from here—buses to Bordeaux, Paris, Germany and even London.

Though small, Vitoria can be a puzzle if you are driving. Most of the centre is a closed-off pedestrian zone, and parking is hard to find.

Tourist Information

Parque de la Florida, ✆ (945) 13 13 21.

There is a **market** on Thursdays, in Plaza de Abastos; also a flea market on Sundays in Plaza Nueva, and a clothes market Wednesdays and Thursdays in C/ Arana.

La Parte Vieja

The old city, with its old core of neat, concentric streets, begins with **Plaza de la Virgen Blanca**, a delightful example of asymmetrical medieval town design. Adjacent to it, the enclosed and studiously symmetrical **Plaza de España**, or Plaza Nueva, provides a perfect contrast; this grand neoclassical confection was built at the height of Spain's flirtation with the Enlightenment, in the 1780s, and now houses mostly city offices. Plaza de la Virgen Blanca is the centre of Vitoria's big party on 4 August, and it takes its name from the statue in the niche over the door of **San Miguel**, the 14th-century church that turns a graceful portico towards the top of the square. An 18th-century arcade called **Los Arcillos**, reached by a stair, runs under some graceful old glass-front buildings to connect Plaza de la Virgen Blanca to yet a third connected square on the slope of the hill: **Plaza del Machete**, named after the axe over which city officials would swear their oaths of office.

Behind San Miguel, Calle Fray Zacarías leads into the medieval streets; this was the high status street for palaces, as evidenced by two 16th-century Plateresque beauties, the **Palacio Episcopal**, and the **Palacio Escoriaza-Esquivel**, built by a local boy who became physician to Charles V; this one has a refined Renaissance courtyard with a marble loggia. Take a left at C/ La Soledad for the old cathedral, **Catedral Santa María**, also from the 14th century, with a beautifully carved western doorway and impressive central nave, the aisles lined with the tombs of Vitoria's notables from medieval times.

Just behind the cathedral on C/ del Herrería, the **Torre de Doña Otxanta** is a defensive tower of the 15th–16th centuries. Italian early Renaissance cities, with their skylines of skyscraper-fortresses, set a fashion that found its way to other countries—fortresses like these were private castles in town, and city officials had to fight hard to keep their owners from acting like rustic barons on their manors, bossing everyone around and generally disturbing the peace of the neighbourhood. Now fully restored, the tower is home to the province's **Natural Science Museum** (*open weekdays 10–2, 4–6.30, Sat 10–2, Sun 11–2, closed Mon; adm*). Another conspicuous tower nearby, the **Torre Hurtados de Anda**, lurks just to the north on C/ Correría: this is a blank-walled fort with a half-timbered house planted on top—a proper urban castle.

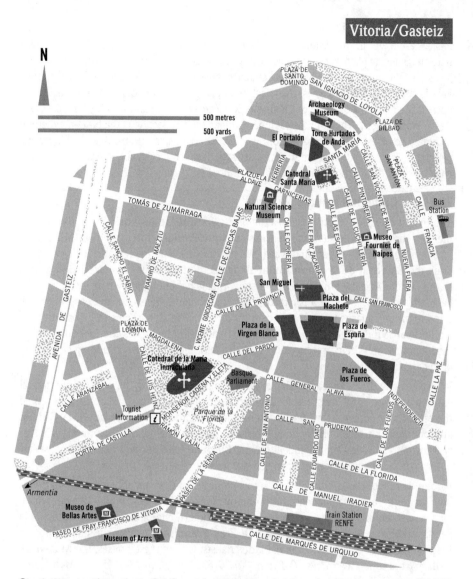

Continuing northwards to C/ Correría, a rambling brick and timber structure called **El Portalón**, built in the early 1500s, is one of the oldest buildings in town, and it gives an idea of what most of Vitoria must have looked like at the time. Just across the street at Correría 116, the **Archaeology Museum** occupies a lovely half-timbered house (*same hours as the Natural Science Museum*) containing Roman finds and Basque 'star' tombstones, as well as some fascinating medieval finds, such as the exceedingly strange 'Relief of Marquinez.' There are over a hundred artificial caves in the province of Álava, and exhibits recount the story of the religious hermits who occupied many of them a thousand years ago.

The House of Cards

Palaces are fewer in the eastern quarter of old Vitoria, across C/ Las Escuelas; the houses here are generally plainer, though older, especially those in the former **Judería**, the medieval Jewish neighbourhood that covered much of this area. On C/ Cuchillería, in the Plateresque Palacio Bendaña, Spain's biggest manufacture of playing cards (an old Vitoria speciality) has opened the **Museo Fournier del Naipe** (*open Tues–Fri 10–2 and 4–6.30, Sat 10–2, Sun 11–2, closed Mon*). The Fournier Company thinks their collection is the best anywhere; it includes the oldest surviving card (from the 1300s), as well as card-making machinery and paintings. The collection includes plenty of Tarot decks too; originally there was no difference between the cards for fortune telling and those for playing games.

The New Cathedral and the Museum

The tourist information office shares the pretty **Parque de la Florida**, Vitoria's monumental centre, with the stern, no-nonsense **Basque Parliament** building (© 24 78 00, if you want to sit in the gallery and watch them deliberate) and the remarkable 'new cathedral', the **Catedral de la María Inmaculada**. Here, the Basques showed their devotion to the Middle Ages by building a completely 'medieval' building, by medieval methods, beginning in 1907. Most of it is already finished, though there is enough decorative work undone inside to last them another century or two. The style seems to be part English Gothic, part Viollet-le-Duc, though the most endearing feature is the rows of comical modillions around the cornices—lots of satirical and monster faces, including caricatures of the architects and masons.

Vitoria is a city of unexpected delights; one example, completing the park's monumental ensemble, is one of the most resplendent Art Deco petrol stations in all Spain, just behind the cathedral. Another, a few blocks east on Calle Eduardo Dato, is the fantastical **RENFE station**, done in a kind of Hollywood Moorish style with brightly coloured tiles. The city is also currently finishing a new embellishment: **Plaza de los Fueros**, a new square just east of Plaza de la Virgen Blanca designed and decorated by Eduardo Chillida.

Parque de la Florida, laid out in 1855, retains much of the Romantic spirit of its times, with grand promenades, hidden bowers and overlooks. It was the centre of the city's fashionable district, and a shady walkway from the southern end of the park, the Paseo de la Senda, takes you to the elegant **Paseo de Fray Francisco de Vitoria**, lined with the Hispano-Victorian mansions of the old industrialists. One of these houses, the **Museo de Bellas Artes** (*open weekdays 10–2 and 4–6.30, Sat 10–2, Sun 11–2, closed Mon; adm*), features a well displayed collection ranging from early paintings to Picasso and Miró, with a handful of great Spanish masters in between, all in a beautifully restored space with original features such as a Tiffany-style stained glass skylight.

Some of the finest works are of the type museums here call 'Escuela Hispanoflamenca', paintings from the early 16th century, at a time when the influence from the Low Countries was strong here; most are anonymous, and it is impossible to tell which country the artist was from. One of the finest works, a *triptych of the Passion* by the 'Master of the Legend of Santa Godelina', shows the same sort of conscious stylization as an Uccello; the longer you look at it, the stranger it seems. Medieval painted carved wood figures are well represented, and there are no fewer than three paintings by Ribera, including a *Crucifixion*. As in all Basque museums, Basque painters are more than well represented; here you'll find some surprises: a great early 20th-century landscapist named Fernando de Anarica, or his contemporary Ramon Zubiaurre, whose *Autoridades de mi Aldea* shares the not-quite-naive sensibility of Rousseau or Grant Wood. The façade of a 13th-century hermitage has been reconstructed in the museum's garden. Up the Paseo at no. 3, the **Museum of Arms** (*open weekdays 10–2 and 4–6.30, Sat 10–2, Sun 11–2, closed Mon; adm*) houses suits of armour, medieval weapons, and dioramas and displays on Wellington's victory at the Battle of Vitoria.

Seeing the last of Vitoria's little secrets means a pleasant 20-minute walk to the southwest (from the Paseo de Fray Francisco, take Paseo de Cervantes and Avenida de San Prudencio; this is part of the *camino francés*, one of the Santiago pilgrimage routes), to the **Basílica of San Prudencio**, in Armentia, a village swallowed up by the city's suburbs. The church was built at the end of the 12th century, with a fine doorway and curious reliefs and capitals carved inside.

West of Vitoria, you can visit Roman ruins including a long, 13-arched bridge at **Trespuentes**, near the remains of a town, the oppidum of **Iruna** (*open daily exc Mon 11–2 and 4–8, Sat 11–3, Sun 11–2; in winter daily exc Mon 11–3, Sun 10–3; adm*). Two km away at Mendoza, near the airport on the A 3302, a 13th-century defensive tower with great views over the countryside has been restored to house the **Museo de Heráldica**, Spain's only museum dedicated to the origins and graphic styles of heraldic escutcheons; the exhibits give special attention to the histories of the great families of the Basque country (*open daily exc Mon, 11–3; May–Oct, 11–2 and 4–8 pm, Sun 11–2; adm*).

Vitoria ℂ (945–) **Where to Stay**

expensive

 In Vitoria, the best value among the several large hotels in the new part of town is the ★★★**General Álava**, Avda. Gastéiz 79, ℂ 22 22 00, ✆ 24 83 95, with modern, comfortable rooms with TV.

moderate

Vitoria offers a wide range of choices for about 6000 pts, mostly catering to businessmen. One well-equipped one is the ★**Achuri**, C/ Rioja 11, ℂ 25 58 00, ✆ 26 40 74. Near the rail station, ★★**Dato 28**, C/ Dato 28, ℂ 14 72 30, ✆ 24 23 22, is convenient, modern and imaginatively furnished; cheaper than the others, it's a good bargain too.

inexpensive

Quite a few of these too, mostly in the Casco Viejo: the ★**La Riojana**, C/ Cuchillería, ℂ 26 87 95, is one of the cheapest. The **Garay**, Portal del Rey 22, ℂ 25 651 6, and the **Gamarra**, Portal del Rey 17, ℂ 25 40 90, are two neighbouring establishments, clean and cheerful old-fashioned '*casas de huéspedes*' (just another fancy word for a cheap hotel), with very low rates, just east of Plaza del Machete. By the bus station on C/ Verdástegui, the **Balzola**, ✆ 25 62 79, also offers a good deal.

Eating Out

Most of the good bars and restaurants in Vitoria are in the old town— especially good is **El Portalón**, Correría 151, ✆ 14 27 55, with tables on three floors of a 16th-century building and traditional Basque food (*expensive*). Other, less expensive places to look out for, all serving excellent Basque cuisine for around 3000 pts, are **Mesa**, Chile 1, ✆ 22 84 94 (closed Wed); **Naroki**, Florida 24, ✆ 23 15 40; and **Poliki**, Fueros 29, ✆ 25 04 58 (closed Tue eve and Wed). The best and most popular pizzeria in town is run by a former cycling champ named Galdós: **Dolomiti**, C/ Ramón y Cajal, also does Italian dinners (1500 pts for pizza).

Nightlife

Vitoria has its share of nightlife, mostly in the Parte Vieja, though C/ Dato near the station can also be noisy after hours. Some of the clubs, like **El Cadillac** on C/ San Prudencio, stay open until six or seven in the morning. For grown-ups, there is the **Café Caruso**, a coffee house on C/ Enrique de Eguren 9, which has occasional concerts and exhibitions. Currently the most popular discos are **Dato Sur** across from the rail station, and **El Elefante Blanco**, Plaza San Antón; for salsa, the place is **Salsumba**, C/ Tomás de Zumárraga. Alternative music of all sorts can be found at **Gaztetxe**, C/ Fray Zacarías.

Álava Province

Just because the Basque capital is located here, you might think that Álava (*Araba* in Basque) is the Euskadi heartland. In fact speakers of Basque make up precisely 4 per cent of the population here, by far the lowest in the 'seven Basque provinces'. Having lost ground to the Spaniards for centuries during their long economic decline, one senses that the Basques purposely planted their Parliament here as part of a careful plan to reclaim the soil. Araba is home to the historical oddity of the County of Treviño, an enclave of Castilian Spaniards smack in the middle of the province. They are quite happy being part of Castile, just as they were in the Middle Ages, leaving Álava the only province in Spain, maybe in the world, that is shaped like a doughnut.

Tourist Information

Antoñana: Cuesta de Lavadero, ✆ (941) 41 02 26
Laguardia: ✆ (941) 10 08 45

There is a **market** in Laguardia on Sundays

Gaceo and Alaiza

There aren't a lot of sights here, but for anyone interested in things medieval the province offers something truly outstanding—and almost totally unknown outside the area. The miniscule village of **Gaceo,** on the N 1 east of Vitoria, offers nothing less than one of the finest ensembles of Gothic fresco painting anywhere in Europe. These are in the simple church of San Martín de Tours (address of the keyholder is posted on the church door); covered in plaster, they were not rediscovered until 1966.

Research places these works sometime between about 1325 and 1450. The style, a bit archaic with its Romanesque attention to flowing draperies, is distinctive enough for scholars to speculate about an obscure 'Basque-Navarrese' school of artists, perhaps centred in Vitoria; Byzantine influence is also strongly present, though details like the gnarled rugged cross are uniquely Spanish (such a cross was the symbol of the 19th-century Carlist rebels). Thanks to the plaster most of the paintings are well-preserved though oddly enough many of the faces have vanished, as in the *Trinity*, with a grand figure of God enthroned, supporting Jesus on the cross, painted on the apse over the altar. True fresco work requires that the plaster underneath the paintings, applied fresh each morning for an artist's day's work, be absolutely right in composition and application. The secrets were just being rediscovered in the 14th century in Italy; artists elsewhere hadn't got it quite right.

The figures around the Trinity on the apse seem to be arranged to represent the commemoration of All Saints' Day: various scenes of *Los Bienaventurados*, the Blessed—apostles, martyrs, confessors, virgins and more, all arranged neatly by category. On the right, note the conspicuous figures of *St Michael*, weighing souls at the Judgement Day, and *Abraham*, gathering the fortunate to his bosom. The choir vault too is entirely covered in frescoes, stock images of the *Life of Christ* divided by charming borders of *trompe l'oeil* designs and fantasy architecture. At the bottom right is something no medieval mural picture-book could be without: the souls of the damned getting variously swallowed up in the mouth of hell or cooked in a big pot.

Gaceo is not such an illogical spot for art as it seems. The modern N 1 that connects Vitoria to Burgos and Pamplona roughly follows the course of the main Roman road into the north. Enough of this survived in medieval times to keep it an important route, heavily used by pilgrims on their way to Compostela. Perhaps no one ever imagined Gaceo growing into a metropolis, but it may well have been that the village was a popular pilgrim stop, and some pious gentleman or lady paid for the paintings to edify the soujourners' spirits, and give them something to think about as they made their way westwards.

While you're out in Gaceo you might as well carry on a little further and see some quite different paintings at another tiny hamlet, **Alaiza** (from the N 1, take the A 3100 south from Salvatierra). The Iglesia de la Asunción here is a barn-like 13th-century building; it too has a painted apse and choir, but the contrast with Gaceo's is like day with night. Instead of flowing Gothic draperies, Alaiza has one-colour cartoons so weird and primitive they might have been done by a Palaeolithic cave artist on a bad day. The central work, on the apse, shows soldiers besieging a castle, while on the choir vault and walls bizarre hooded figures joust, murder, or indulge in bodily functions not often seen on church walls. There is a contrastingly precise inscription underneath in Gothic letters, but no one has ever managed to decipher it. The best guess the Spaniards can come up with for this singular work is that these scenes were done *c.* 1367, while Alaiza was under the control of some rough English mercenary soldiers; one of them might have done it.

The closest village of any size in this region, **Salvatierra** is a pleasant old village of warm stone within striking distance of two of Euskadi's best dolmens—**Aizkomendi** at Eguilaz, visible in a little roadside park off the N 1, and **Sorginetxe** in Arizala.

North of the city, the biggest features on the landscape are the big dams and lakes of **Urrunaga** and **Ullivarri**. The lakes have become popular spots for fishing and water sports; Ullavarri even has a nudist beach. Further north, on the road to Durango, **Otxandio** was the original Basque iron town, a fact commemorated by a statue of the god Vulcan in the main square.

South of Vitoria: the Ebro Valley

Some of the best Rioja vines actually come from the province of Álava, a region known as **La Rioja Alavesa**, along the Ebro river facing the real La Rioja across the way. Perched high over the river, the key wine town here is walled, medieval **Laguardia** (Biasteri) where you can learn all about local wines and their production at **La Casa del Vino**, and visit more bodegas. Don't miss the 14th-century apostles carved in the portal of Laguardia's Gothic **Santa María de los Reyes**. Near Laguardia, an excavated Iron Age village is open to the public: the **Poblado de la Hoya** (*open daily 11–2 and 4.30–7.30 May–Oct, rest of the year mornings only*).

As for the **County of Treviño**, though this forgotten fief looks strangely compelling on the map, in reality there's plenty of oak woods and good farmland, but unhappily no greater attractions. There is one village, Treviño, which has the County's only petrol pump.

Where to Stay and Eating Out

Argómaniz (℘ (945–)

This village, east of Vitoria near the paintings of Gaceo, is home to the ★★★**Parador de Argómaniz**, located on the N 1, ℘ 29 32 00, ✉ 29 32 87. It's one of the smaller and simpler *paradores*, with some rooms set in the original building, a 17th-century mansion with iron balconies (*expensive*).

Laguardia (℘ 941–)

Definitely the place to stop over if you are passing through La Rioja Alavesa: the choice is between two fine establishments. First, ★**Pachico Martinez**, C/ Sancho Abarca, ℘ 10 00 09, which has been in the same family since 1806 (!) and is still doing fine (*moderate*); the ★★**Posada Mayor de Migueloa**, C/ Mayor de Migueloa 20, ℘ 12 11 75, seems even older; it is installed in a 17th-century mansion with antique furnishings (*expensive*); they also have an excellent but expensive restaurant. For cheaper dining, there is ★**Marixa**, C/ Sancho Abarca 8, ℘ 10 01 65, with moderate-range rooms and meals; menu 1800 pts. You might try an unlikely local favourite—*acelga rellena* (stuffed Swiss chard)—that is better than it sounds.

Picos de Europa

Cantabria

Spain's steep emerald-green dairy-land, Cantabria is wedged between the extraordinary Picos de Europa, the Cordillera Cantábrica and a coastline of scenic beaches. Santander, the capital and only large city, is a major summer resort, and while there are a handful of other tourist spots (Laredo, Comillas, and the medieval Santillana del Mar) much of Cantabria is serenely rural, claiming to have the highest density of cows in Europe. The majority of the bovine population lives indoors, and in the evening the most common Cantabrian sight is the farmer or his wife, often wearing wooden clogs, driving home an ox-cart laden with grass which

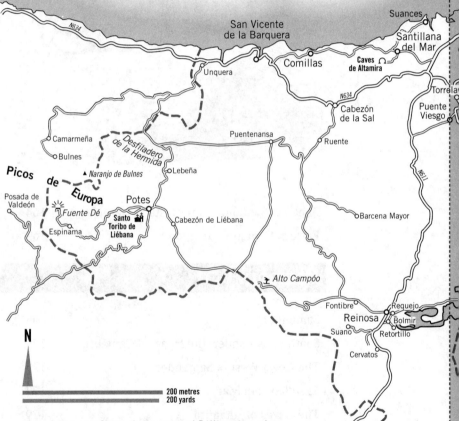

they have cut from their several Lilliputian plots of land scattered over the hills. On rainy winter evenings in remote areas they gather to hear the strains of the *rabel*, a three-stringed instrument from the Moors, made only of wood cut by the light of a full moon.

Humanity has found Cantabria to its liking literally since its first cows, or prehistoric aurochs, came home some 38,000 years ago. It has Spain's greatest concentration of Upper Palaeolithic cave art, from indecipherable scratches to the masterpieces in Altamira. Back in the Iron Age, just before the arrival of the Romans, the Cantabrians carved star reliefs on large stone discs that still mystify everybody: were they part of a Celtic

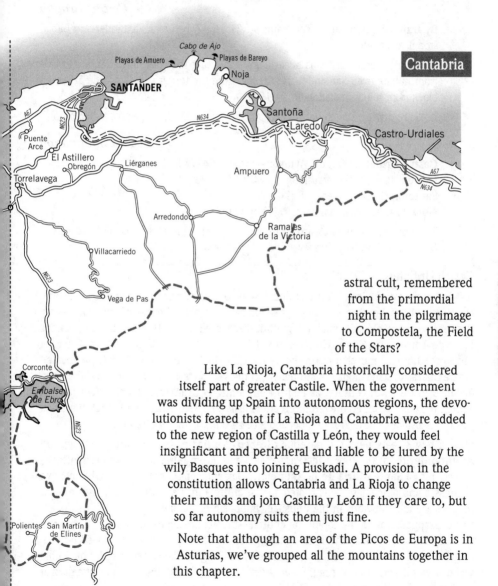

Cantabria

astral cult, remembered from the primordial night in the pilgrimage to Compostela, the Field of the Stars?

Like La Rioja, Cantabria historically considered itself part of greater Castile. When the government was dividing up Spain into autonomous regions, the devolutionists feared that if La Rioja and Cantabria were added to the new region of Castilla y León, they would feel insignificant and peripheral and liable to be lured by the wily Basques into joining Euskadi. A provision in the constitution allows Cantabria and La Rioja to change their minds and join Castilla y León if they care to, but so far autonomy suits them just fine.

Note that although an area of the Picos de Europa is in Asturias, we've grouped all the mountains together in this chapter.

Bilbao to Santander: the Costa Esmeralda

If this eastern stretch of coast is all you see of Cantabria, you may think what you have just read about rural serenity is pure fiction. This seems to be the busiest coast in all northern Spain in the summer and especially at the weekend, when half of Bilbao is out here looking for a bit of beach and seems to end up on the endless sweep of sand at Laredo.

Getting Around

By train: the two daily FEVE trains, ✆ 21 16 87, between Santander and Bilbao stop near Laredo.

By bus: Several Turytrans buses a day run along the coast from Santander and from Bilbao; from Santander they depart from the terminal at Navas de Tolosa, a block from the train station, ✆ 21 19 95.

If you're driving, watch out for jams on the coastal E 70; roadworks are common.

Tourist Information

Castro Urdiales: Pza. del Ayuntamiento, ✆ (942) 81 82 51
Laredo: Pza. del Generalísimo, ✆ (942) 61 10 96
Santoña: C/ Santander 5, ✆ (942) 66 00 66
Noja: Pza. del Ayuntamiento, ✆ (942) 63 00 38

There are **markets** in Castro Urdiales on Thursdays; in Laredo at the Mercado Municipal, daily exc. Sundays.

Castro Urdiales

Just an hour west of Bilbao, Castro Urdiales is one of Cantabria's most scenic fishing-ports, endowed with a beach and seafood restaurants that draw hordes of *bilbaínos* every summer weekend. Magdalenian-era graffiti, discovered in the 1960s in a cave near the Plaza de Toros, date Castro Urdiales' first inhabitants back to 12,000 BC. In historical times, the Romans muscled in on the native Cantabrians to found *Flavióbriga*, located where the castle stands today. A stronghold of the Templars in the Middle Ages, the town declined in the 14th century, as Pedro I and Enrique II de Trastámara fought for this stretch of coast. It suffered even more grievously in 1813, when the French punished Castro's resistance in the War of Independence by burning most of it to the ground.

Only a few streets near the harbour escaped the flames, beyond the 18th-century **Ayuntamiento**, at the top of the Paseo Marítimo. From here, walk up to the fortress-like church of **Santa María de la Asunción**, a magnificent Gothic temple with massive buttresses and pinnacles. Constructed almost entirely in the 13th century, its Templar touches are most obvious in the unusual symbolism of the figures carved in the lovely frieze wrapped around the top of the church—rabbits kissing oxen, dragons devouring serpents devouring birds and more, although to see them properly you'll need binoculars. Inside there's a 13th-century sculpture of the *Virgen Blanca* and a series of Gothic woodcarvings. You can also see the *Santa Cruz*, or 'holy cross', the Christian standard at the battle of Las Navas de Tolosa (1212).

A Roman milestone remains in place in front of the church, while over the striking Roman/medieval bridge, most of the walls of Castro's pentagonal **Templar castle** have survived and now shelter a lighthouse.

Castro Urdiales' beach, **Playa Brazomar**, is at the other end of town; if you're feeling like peeling, there's also a naturist beach just outside town at **El Pocillo**. The best beach, however, is 8km west up to **Islares**, a small village with a magnificent strand of sand under the cliffs, interspersed with shallow lagoons that are ideal for young children. Just west of Islares there's another beach and campsite at **Oriñón**.

Laredo

Cantabria's biggest resort has little in common with its namesake on the Río Grande. The scenery in fact isn't too different, but on its streets there is hardly a cowboy live or dead to be seen. This Laredo does have an old town, hidden somewhere among the *urbanizaciones*, but you'll remember it mostly as a somewhat brash and totally modern holiday playground, a bit of the Costa somehow dropped on Cantabria by mistake. People from Bilbao and Madrid and France love it, and it does have its charms.

Laredo was the Roman *Portus Luliobrigensium*, the place where the Romans finally subdued the last die-hard Celtiberians in a great sea battle. The medieval Puebla Vieja over the harbour was walled in by Alfonso VIII of Castile to safeguard the region from pirates; its 13th-century church **Santa María de la Asunción** has five naves (rare for the period) and curiously carved capitals. In the sacristy note the two eagle-shaped lecterns, donated by Charles V, who landed here on his way to his retirement at Yuste. The late Renaissance **Ayuntamiento** in Plaza Cachupín is said to mark the location of the harbour quay the megalomaniac Emperor actually stepped on; behind it is the attractive tiled market building erected in 1902. Not really glossy or chic, Laredo especially attracts families, who cover its splendid beach and fill the scores of cafés, bars, and discothèques in the Puebla Vieja. *Urbanizaciones* have marched nearly to the tip of Laredo's wide, sheltered pride and joy: **Playa de Salvé**, a gentle three-mile-long crescent of sand.

From Laredo to Santander

West of Laredo the parade of beaches continues: **Santoña** is another fishing-port resort and hometown of Juan de la Cosa (b.1460), the cartographer who accompanied Columbus on his second voyage to America (1493) and is remembered with a suitably large monument. Santoña also claims that its shipbuilders made the *Santa María* for Columbus. Another lovely area, **Noja**, has another stretch of fine, sandy beaches and a considerable villa and apartment *urbanización* along the shore. According to local legend the village takes its name from Noah; the Ark washed up on one of the mountains nearby. The rest of the way to Santander there are plenty of unexploited beaches, reachable on back roads off the main coastal route: the **Playas de Arnuero**, near the lighthouse at Cape Ajo, and the **Playas de Barayo**, west of Ajo.

Castro Urdiales

If you're just looking for a place to stay over or hang out for a day or two, Castro will prove much more interesting than Laredo, though inexpensive places are hard to find. There are two plum choices by the town beach (*both expensive*): the luxurious and tranquil ★★★**Las Rocas**, Avda. de la Playa, ✆ 86 04 00, ✍ 86 13 82, near the beaches, and the stylish ★★**Miramar**, Avda. de la Playa, ✆ 86 02 00, ✍ 87 09 42, which offers comfortable rooms, garden and attentive service, but only from March–Oct. The antique ★★**El Cordobés**, C/ Ardigales 15, ✆ 86 00 89, is prettily located in the Mediavilla. ★**Hs Alberto**, near the town park on Avda. de la República Argentina 2, ✆ 86 27 57, has cheap and cheerful bathless doubles.

The well-known **Mesón El Marinero**, in the historic Casa de los Chelines next to the fishing port at La Correría 23, ✆ 86 00 05, is the place to go for heaping plates of delicious, fresh seafood at reasonable prices—for less than the typical 4000-pts meal, feast on a wide selection of tapas at the bar. For roast sucking pig or a seafood grill (15,000 pts for two) make your way to Castro's second culinary shrine, **El Segoviano**, La Correría 19, ✆ 86 18 59 (5000 pts average). Bar and nightlife in Castro is concentrated along C/ de la Rúa and the Paseo Marítimo.

Islares

There's a large comfortable campsite by the beach, the **Camping Playa Arenillas**, and one pleasant little *hostal*, the ★★**Hs Arenillas**, ✆ 86 07 66, quiet and near the beach (*moderate*).

Laredo

Hotels in Laredo are small and fairly dear, and reservations are essential in the summer. Newest is the modern, mid-size ★★★**Miramar**, Alto de Laredos, ✆ 61 03 67, ✍ 61 16 92, with huge windows to take in the huge sea views (*moderate, expensive in high season*). ★★★**Risco**, C/ La Arenosa 2, ✆ 60 50 30, ✍ 60 50 55, has commodious rooms enjoying superb views of the protected bay and beach and a restaurant generally rated as Laredo's top seafood palace, featuring elaborate creations such as a *capricho* of lobster, chicken breasts and figs (*moderate*). ★**Montecristo**, C/ Calvo Sotelo 2, ✆ 60 57 00, is one of the better beach hotels in town (*moderate*; open mid-April to mid-Sept). Near Playa de Salvé, **Squash**, Avda. Reina Victoria s/n, ✆ 60 40 69, has nothing to do with the game, but instead offers both modern hotel rooms near the beach and furnished apartments for five persons (20,000 pts in high season). ★★**Hs Ramona**, C/ General Mola 4, ✆ 60 53 36, is another reasonable moderate choice. In the centre, you won't find a better deal than the ★**Hs Salomón**, C/ Menéndez Pelayo 11, ✆ 60 50 81, with immaculate rooms and wooden floors. For anything under 4000 pts, ask at a bar.

Some of the best seafood you'll find in the coastal towns are informal outdoor places on the docks, often run by fishermen's families. At the far end of Laredo's fishing port, there's the popular **El Rincón del Puerto**, a few long tables under an awning next to a grill, where you can feast on fresh sardines, prawns, striped tuna, *paella*, fish soup and other delicacies, and happily spend anything from 1500 to 5000 pts. Another good place for simple seafood gratification is the **Bar Mariscal** on C/ Garelly (1500-pts menu, and a wide choice of seafood plates for 1000 pts or less).

Eastern Cantabria: Inland

This corner of the *comunidad* can offer absolutely nothing but scenery, but it is some of the sweetest and greenest cow country you'll ever see. Villages are tiny and the roads little more than paved mule tracks, meandering exasperatingly up and down the mountains, in and out of the eternal fog and mists. Almost all of the houses are the lovely traditional Cantabrian type, with carved and painted wooden balconies on the front.

Tourist Information

Liérganes: Pso. del Hombre Pez, ✆ (942) 52 83 46

There is a **market** in Solares on Wednesdays.

Small Nowheres and Secret Caves

South of Laredo, the N 629 for Burgos heads into the rugged and empty valley of the Soba. Near Ampuero you can visit one of the major sanctuaries of Cantabria, **Nuestra Señora de la Bien Aparecida**, a 17th-century chapel commemorating a miraculous appearance of the Virgin. Near **Ramales de la Victoria**, on the borders of Euskadi, there are a number of Palaeolithic painted caves—not officially open, but ask at the Ramales Ayuntamiento if they're letting anyone in.

The area directly south of Santander is an odd region. Once one of the biggest mining areas in the north, it is currently letting the landscape recuperate; there are mineral springs everywhere, and a small, modern spa resort, **Liérganes**, is also the biggest village in the area. South of Liérganes, there are more Palaeolithic paintings at the **Cueva del Salitre** near Miera; again, ask at the Liérganes tourist office if it is yet open to the public.

El Hombre Pez

 In Liérganes, you might note the unusual name of the main street, the Paseo del Hombre Pez, which commemorates a wonderfully strange story from the 1700s. The 'fish man' was a native of this village named Francisco de la Vega Casar, who went off to Bilbao to work as a carpenter. One day he went out for a bath in the river and never returned; his friends and family assumed he'd drowned. Nine years later, some fishermen trawling in the Bay of Cádiz, way down in Andalucía, pulled up their nets and found an odd sort of fish inside, a damp and chilly man with a kind of scales covering most of his body. When they brought him back to Cádiz, a Cantabrian who had known him recognized him by a birthmark. The fishman had lost the power of speech, but he understood enough to agree that he was in fact Francisco de la Vega Casar of Liérganes. He lived on land for nine more years, and it seems that he was exploited as a kind of curiosity. De la Vega stayed chilly and damp until the end, and never accepted any food but raw fish. Needless to say, the people who were looking after him never let him get anywhere near the water. One day he simply slipped away, and was never seen again.

Now, all this happened in the middle of the Age of Enlightenment, and Spain was full of learned sceptics, including the famous writer Fray Benito Feijóo, who couldn't let a chance like this slip by without looking into the common belief in the miraculous. The Hombre Pez's career was thoroughly investigated, and plenty of witnesses confirmed all the details of the case. So did it really happen, or was it simply one of the most successful carnival tricks of all time?

✆ (942–)   *Where to Stay and Eating Out*

Liérganes

Liérganes is a thermal spa, and consequently the most dependable place to look for a hotel in these little-touristed parts. One place that stands out is the ★★★**Posada del Sauce**, C/ Cdr. José Antonio, ✆ 52 80 23, 📧 52 81 17 (*moderate*), a century-old stone inn with attractively decorated rooms, a pool and a very good restaurant. Other choices range from the modern and luxurious ★★**Cantábrico**, Pso. del Hombre Pez, ✆ 52 80 48, 📧 52 83 58 (*expensive*), to the inexpensive ★Hs **Continental**, La Costera, ✆ 52 80 46. For an even cheaper option, ask for one of the three guest rooms at the Cistercian monastery of **Nuestra Señora del Rio**, Los Prados 8, ✆ 52 81 50; tranquillity assured.

Ramales de la Victoria

This village is the unlikely setting for one of Cantabria's best restaurants: the ★★**Río Asón**, Barón de Adanzata 17, ✆ 64 61 57 (*inexpensive*), which also has nine rooms. The restaurant's 2000-pts menu is an excellent bargain, with game dishes, grilled meats with *cèpes* and a rarity—real salmon from the nearby Asón.

Santander

The capital of Cantabria, Santander has a lot in common with San Sebastián—a large city beautifully situated on a protected bay, popularized by royalty as a summer resort. The story has it that Queen Isabel II first came down in the 1860s, in the hope that the sea air would help with a bad dose of the clap (which she probably got from General O'Donnell, the Prime Minister, or another up and coming politician). Again, after the First World War, it was *the* fashionable place to go for Madrileños, especially with the founding of an international summer university (named after Menéndez Pelayo, Santander's favourite son and Spain's greatest antiquarian), offering holiday-makers high-brow culture to complement its wide beaches. Still, despite this and its widely acclaimed International Music Festival in August, Santander lacks the excitement and *joie de vivre* of San Sebastián.

On the other hand, Santander has been a great town for disasters. Two of the most recent were the explosion of a ship full of dynamite in 1893, killing 500 and clearing most of the harbour area, and the fire of 1941, which started in the Archbishop's Palace and destroyed most of the old centre. No city in northern Spain shows a more striking split personality. At the centre, it's a gritty, workaday town rather like Bilbao without the smokestacks, but stray a few streets to the other side of the peninsula and you'll be in what seems to be a Belle Epoque dream resort, casino and all. The Santander of the festivals shows a bright and modern face to the world, but the real atmosphere of the place is still best represented by the pigeon-spattered statue of Franco in the centre and the grey streets still named after Nationalist hoodlums of the Civil War.

Getting There

By air: Santander's airport is 7km away at Maliaño (no buses) with daily connections to Barcelona and Madrid. Iberia's office is at Pso. de Pereda 18, © 22 97 00; Aviaco's is at the airport, © 22 32 00.

By ferry: from Santander, Brittany Ferries sails to Plymouth twice-weekly from mid-March to mid-December, once weekly in January and February. For information in Santander, call © 21 45 58, or visit the ticket office at the Estación Marítima.

By train: the train stations are both on C/ Rodríguez, in the city centre. RENFE, © 21 02 88, has connections with Madrid, Palencia, Reinosa, Segovia and Valladolid; tickets are available as well at the travel office at Pso. de Pereda 25, © 21 23 87. The narrow-gauge FEVE, © 21 16 87, has trains to Bilbao, Oviedo, Torrelavega and Unquera; unfortunately they miss the coast east of Santander, which is instead served by buses.

By bus: the central bus station is conveniently opposite the train stations on Navas de Tolosa, © 21 19 95. Connections include: Continental Auto to Burgos, Madrid and Ontaneda-Vejores (© 22 53 18); Turytrans to nearly all the coastal towns and resorts, and to Bilbao, Zarauz, San Sebastián, Llanes, Oviedo, Gijón, Vitoria and Pamplona (© 22 16 85 or 22 65 08); Intercar to Galicia, Asturias and Euskadi (© 22 16 85 or 22 65 08); Fernández to León (© 987–22 62 00) and Autocares de Cantabria to Logroño (© 36 16 14). The main line up to the Picos de Europa is Palomera, with runs to Potes and Fuente Dé.

Within Santander itself, there are frequent buses and trolleys (nos. 1, 2 and 7) that run from the centre to El Sardinero 20 minutes away. Lanchas Reginas runs the **boat service** to the beaches across the bay, with departures every 15 minutes from 10.30am to 8.30pm from the Muelle de Ferrys, two blocks from the cathedral. Radio Taxi: © 33 33 33 or 23 23 23. Every 15 minutes Lanchas Reginas, © 21 67 53, depart for Pedreña, Somo, and Playa del Puntal. They also offer tours of the bay and excursions around the Río Cubas.

N

```
1 kilometre
1/2 mile
```

Tourist Information

Pza. de Velarde 1, ℂ (942) 31 07 08 or 21 14 17, at the centre of the beach strip, and at the Jardines de Pereda, in the city centre facing the port, ℂ (942) 21 61 20 or 36 20 54.

Markets: in Plaza de la Esperanza behind the Ayuntamiento: Tuesdays, Wednesdays, Fridays and Saturdays for food, Mondays and Thursdays for clothes. Plaza de México: Mondays, Wednesdays, Fridays and Saturdays for food, Tuesdays and Fridays for clothes (by the bull ring at the end of Calle de San Fernando).

The Cathedral and Museums

In the centre, Santander's much-altered and rebuilt **Cathedral** is interesting mostly for its early Gothic crypt; this now forms the separate church of **Santísimo Cristo**, where a glass

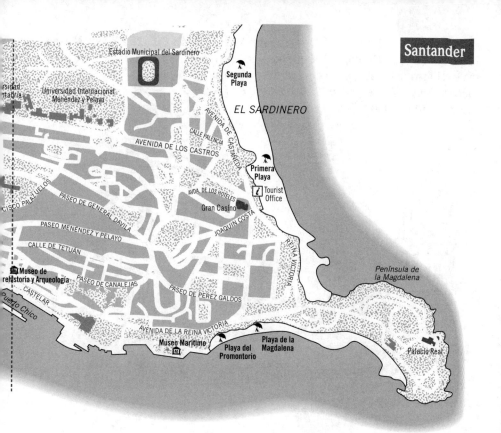

floor has been installed over the remains of a Roman building. The **Museo de Prehistoria y Arqueología**, next to the Provincial Council on C/ Juan de la Cosa (*open Mon–Sat, 9–1 and 4–7, Sun 11–2; adm*) has exhibits devoted to Cantabria's prehistoric cave-dwellers, including tools, reproductions of their art and two disc-shaped star tombstones the size of tractor tyres made just before the Roman conquest, discovered in the valley of the Buelna.

The best parts of old Santander lie to the north, across the main Avda. Calvo Sotelo. Near the Ayuntamiento, the **Museo de Bellas Artes** (*open daily 10.30–1 and 5.30–9, Sun 11–1; adm*) has, besides a contemporary art collection of dubious merit, a Zurbarán and several Goyas, including a portrait of Ferdinand VII, which the city commissioned to flatter the king. Nearby, the **Casa Museo de Menéndez Pelayo** (*open weekdays only 9–1; guided tours every half hour*) has an extensive collection of books, many of them by great Catalan writers, donated to the city by the scholar himself. Behind the Ayuntamiento, the iron and glass **market** is definitely the most colourful sight Santander has to offer, especially the pride of the town, the glorious fish market.

On the way out to the beaches, Avenida Reina Victoria passes Santander's new **Museo Marítimo del Cantábrico**, with ship models and exhibits in the local maritime tradition, and (soon to be opened) an aquarium (*open daily exc Mon 11–1 and 4–7, Sun 11–1; in winter 10–1 and 4–6, Sun 11–2; adm*).

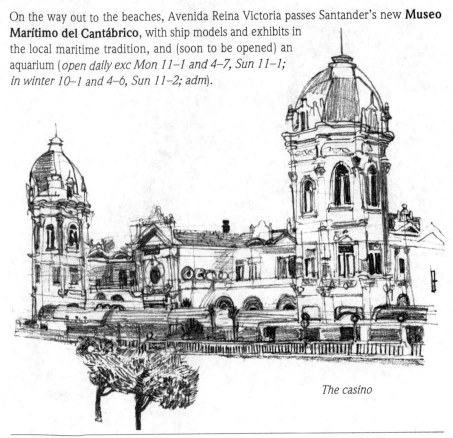

The casino

El Sardinero

The 1941 fire destroyed most of Santander's character, but it spared the suburb of **El Sardinero**, with its fine twin beaches, imaginatively named **Primera** (First) and **Segunda** (Second), backed by the enormous Belle Epoque **casino**, recently refurbished in an effort to revive some of the city's lost panache. El Sardinero is separated from the working end of the city by the beautiful **Peninsula de la Magdalena**, a city park fringed by two more splendid beaches, the **Playa de la Magdalena** and the **Playa del Promontorio**. The Tudor-style **Palacio de la Magdalena** at the end of the peninsula was a gift from the city to Alfonso XIII; when the king accepted it, Santander's return to fashion as a summer resort was guaranteed. Today it is part of the International University.

Besides the beaches in the city, there are several miles of golden dunes across the bay at **Somo**, **El Puntal**, and **Pedrena**, linked every 15 minutes by boat from the centre of town; **Playa las Atenas** nearby is a naturist beach. Just west of Santander at Liencres, there is another fine and very popular beach, **Valdearenas**, a huge expanse of sand bordered by pine woods. And if you have children in tow you will probably be visiting the **Parque de la Naturaleza de Cabárceno**, 10km south of the city at Obregón, where a *menú del día* for 800 pts; at either you can also just order a plate of whatever delicacy has come home with the fishermen for 600–1600 pts.

Around the beaches, restaurants tend to be more elaborate in every way. The fashionable **La Sardina**, C/ Dr Fleming 3 in El Sardinero, ✆ 27 10 35 (*expensive*) offers imaginative renderings of traditional dishes such as *bacalao* with red peppers, in a very pretty setting. Less formal dining can be found at **Bodega del Riojano**, Río de la Pila 5 (north of the Jardines de Pereda), ✆ 21 67 50 (*moderate*) one of Santander's typical *bodegas* in the old quarter, also serving tapas. Specialities are *rabo de buey* (ox tail), *morcillo estofado* (a blood sausage stew), and stuffed peppers (closed Sun eve). Near the Ayuntamiento, **La Casona**, C/ Cuesta 6, ✆ 21 26 88 (*moderate*) is an old favourite that over five decades has accumulated a collection of over a hundred paintings on its walls; grilled meats and seafood are the specialities here. More seafood in sumptuous displays is on offer in numerous eateries in the Puerto Chico, between the centre and the beaches. Especially good are the **Bar del Puerto** on Hernán Cortés 63 (3000 pts) and **Iris**, at Castelar 5 (3500 pts).

Entertainment and Nightlife

Since 1951, the August **Festival Internacional de Santander** has showcased an extraordinary variety of music and dance from around the world: recent bills have featured 7th-century Roman church songs, the Lindsay Kemp Company, the Scholars' Baroque Ensemble, avant-garde selections from the the Laboratorio de Interpretación Musical and the Ballet of the Georgia State Opera performing a homage to Balanchine. Along with all the big league culture, popular Spanish and Latin American song, dance, magic shows and fireworks take place every night in August at the Auditorium and the Finca Altamira. For information contact the Oficina del Festival, Palacio de Festivales de Cantabria, C/ Gamazo s/n, 39004, Santander, ✆ 21 05 08/21 03 45/31 48 19/or 31 48 53, ✉ 31 47 67. Tickets are on sale in advance from the ticket booth at the Palacio de Festivales, from any branch of the Caja Cantabria bank, or from the special Festival booth in the Jardines de Pereda, near the library, ✆ 31 33 42 (*open 11–2 and 5–8*).

Nightlife is concentrated in two places: first a proper *marcha* grounds in the old town, with a vast number of bars and clubs around C/ de la Pila and Plaza de Cañadío. This is the place where you're most likely to find live music and a raucous good time. One old and pleasant bar with good snacks and sometimes live music is **El Conveniente**, C/ Gómez Oreña. This street is also home to some of the flashier discos, including **Blues** and **El Cairo**, which run until dawn. The **Cruz Blanco** on C/ Hernán Cortés is a lively place with some fifty different kinds of beer. For a typical wine *bodega* full of big old barrels, try the **Casa La Montaña** on C/ Vargas, the park boulevard west of Plaza del Generalísimo.

Somewhat more staid entertainment can be had around El Sardinero; the Plaza de talia attracts the older set, while the overdressed young in search of fun head for bit of land wasted by strip mining has been recycled into an attractive and enormous zoo with all the zoo favourites from ape to zebra (*opening hours change regularly; ring ☏ 56 37 36 for information; adm exp*).

Santander ☏ (942–)

July, August and September are the busy months here, especially the first two, when the music festival and International University are in full swing. Prices are as high as in San Sebastián, though again there are plenty of *casas particulares* to preserve your budget. Hang around the bus and train stations and someone will probably lead you to one.

expensive

Santander's most elegant establishments are all on the back side of town by the beaches, starting with the lovely *modernista* ★★★★★**Hotel Real**, Pso. de Pérez Galdós 28, ☏ 27 25 50, ✉ 27 45 73, located near the Playa de la Magdalena and offering marvellous views over the bay, fine rooms and a fine garden. The popular ★★★**Hotel Sardinero**, Pza. de Italia 1, ☏ 27 11 00, ✉ 27 86 53, is conveniently located near the beaches of Sardinero and the casino.

moderate

★★**Roma**, Avda. de los Hoteles 5, ☏ 27 27 00, is an old-fashioned beach hote with old-fashioned fittings and a garden. On Avda. Reina Victoria, the main stre facing the beaches, ★★**Rhin**, ☏ 27 43 00, ✉ 27 86 53, enjoys a smart location hits the expensive range in the summer; ★**Hotel Residencia Carlos III**, ☏ 2 16, is a comfortable place and a good bargain.

inexp

The cheaper hotels have gained a certain notoriety for being either drear offs. A safe one is ★**Hs Gran Antilla**, C/ Isabel II 8, ☏ 21 31 00. At El S inexpensive places are difficult but not impossible to find: try ★**Hs Casti** Joaquin Costa, ☏ 27 22 00, or ★★**Hs Rocamar**, Avda. de los Castros where there are several other choices), ☏ 27 72 68 (open June–Sept is a block back from the beach at C/ Palencia 11, ☏ 27 12 44. T' enormous and well-equipped campgrounds on Avda. del Faro, beaches: the **Bellavista**, ☏ 274 843, and the less expensive **Cabo** 35 66.

Unlike San Sebastián, Santander is hardly known seafood, however, is always good, and the traditior the rather piquant Barrio Pesquero, an area reh behind the train stations. One of the best **José**, C/ Mocejón 2, with a good *men(* Another favourite in the barrio is **La Gaviota**, where the numerous bars and discothèques in Calle Panamá. At the lavish **Gran Casino** you can risk your pesetas from 7pm to 4am (dress up and bring your passport).

South of Santander: the Heart of Cantabria

South of the capital the land gradually rises to the Montañas de Santander, a pretty, hilly region that supports only a handful of villages. There are plenty of wide open spaces along these high roads of the old County of Castile, but there are a few attractions besides the solitude: caves of prehistoric art, untouched forests, the source of the Ebro and one of the sexiest churches in Europe.

Getting Around

By bus: Reinosa's bus station, at the south end of town, is served from Santander by García, ✆ 75 40 67, and Alsa, ✆ 75 40 67; Ansa goes to Bilbao (summer only, ✆ 75 28 13). Donato (✆ 12 20 47) links Reinosa to Espinilla and La Lomba in the Alto Campóo.

Tourist Information

Torrelavega: Ruíz Tagle 6, ✆ (942) 89 29 82
Reinosa: Just a phone, ✆ (942) 75 52 15

There is a **market** in Reinosa on Mondays.

The Caves of Puente Viesgo

If you haven't made an appointment in advance to see the caves of Altamira, you can at least get into Cantabria's second most spectacular set of prehistoric grottoes at **Puente Viesgo**. There are five caves altogether, but the only one open to the public is the Cueva de Castillo (*Tues–Sat 10–2.15 and 3.30–6.30, closed Sun*). Decorated with graceful line drawings of stags, horses and other animals, this ensemble is believed to predate the even more eloquent art at Altamira.

Reinosa, on the rail line, is the main hub in this part of the Cantabrian mountains, with most of the area's hotels and restaurants. The source of northern Spain's longest river, the **Nacimiento del Ebro**, is signposted just to the northwest in **Fontibre** (on the road to Espinilla); you can clamber down in the trees to stick your toes in the stream gurgling out of the ground. The river barely begins, when just on the other side of Reinosa it is dammed to form a massive reservoir, **Embalse del Ebro**, the grass on its jagged shore kept by herds of horses and dairy cows, following the outline of a prehistoric lake. **Corconte**, on the eastern end of the lake, bottles mineral water next to an old spa.

The most beautiful part of the region lies west of Fontibre, in the virgin valleys of the **Saja National Reserve**, where beech, oak and birch forests follow the courses of clear streams. Real explorers can make for **Suano** and the **Población de Suso**, villages that figure on few maps, but can claim a large number of dolmens, a huge cromlech and the ruins of a Templar castle. The region's most important ski installation, **Alto Campóo**, lies to the west in the village of Hermandad Campóo de Suso.

A Trinity of Romanesque Churches

South of Reinosa you'll find good Romanesque churches—in **Bolmir** and more significantly in **Retortillo**. Retortillo is near the scanty remains of the Roman city of **Julióbriga**,
once the most important city of Cantabria. Set amidst the low walls is the church, with a
unique sloping stair leading up to its campanile. Over the door note the carving of two
animals shaking hands.

But the most extraordinary Romanesque church of all is further south in **Cervatos**: the
singular 12th-century **Colegiata**, at the top of a newly cobbled lane. It has a tympanum
with an oriental design, a frieze of lions and, carved onto the corbels and capitals in the
apse, unabashedly erotic figures that a respectable guidebook hesitates to describe. This
unique, medieval tantric temple probably survived clerical prudishness over the centuries
because of its remote location and the explanation that such sexual exhibitionism was
meant to frighten, rather than tempt, parishioners with the horrors of sin.

South of Cervatos, the road to Burgos (S 614) soon meets up again with the Ebro. It's a
lovely road, with lots of trees and local swimming holes by tiny villages. One of the largest
is **Polientes**, with a roadside statue of a spotted dog and one of Cantabria's 'rupestrian
churches' in a cave, although here little old ladies have set up a table by the altar to play
cards. Follow the road and Ebro southeast to an even more remote region and the 12th-
century church at **San Martín de Elines** with a lofty cylindrical tower, keyhole windows,
more fascinating modillons and carvings by the same school as Cervatos but without any
bawdy flashers and sexual contortionists. The kindly caretaker lives in the house nearest
the church and will take you around the cloiser, with a 9th-century wall and tombs excavated from the garden in the centre; the most impressive is the fancy sepulchre of a pilgrim
who died along the route.

If you've made it this far, it would be a shame not to continue towards Orbaneja del
Castillo and the splendid, spectacular **canyons of the Ebro** (see p.223).

© (942–)   ***Where to Stay and Eating Out***

Puente Arce

El Molino, at this village 12km inland from Santander on the road to
Torrelavega, at Ctra. General s/n, © 57 40 52 (*expensive*) is in an old
mill on the river, with valuable oil paintings on the walls, excellent
fish (an *ensalada cantabrica* with seafood and lots of ginger), a
large selection of wines and a monumental 5000-pts gastronomic
menu (closed Sun eve).

Puente Viesgo

If you have come to see the caves, you can stop at the ★★★**Gran Hotel Puente
Viesgo**, Blvd. de la Iglesia, © 59 80 61, ✆ 59 82 61, a sumptuous modern
establishment connected to a spa that's good for your rheumatism and neurolog-
ical troubles; swimming pool, sauna and all the amenities (*luxury*). More
realistically, ★★**Miralpas** at neighbouring Villegar, © 59 42 09, is a simple road-

house along the Santander–Léon road (*moderate*, but so~
without bath). There is a good country restaurant i~
south of Puente Viesgo; the **Méson El Cazador**
pheasant and other game dishes.

Reinosa

★★★**Vejo**, in the newer part on Avda. Cantabria 83, ✆ 75 17 00,
the most comfortable place in town, with a garden, bar and gou
(*moderate*). The more economical ★★**San Cristóbal**, 16 de Agosto 1, &
has simple, bathless rooms (*inexpensive*). If you're driving, a scenic place ᴸ
★**La Casona**, in Nestares, ✆ 75 17 88, an old inn on the Reinosa–Cabezón
Sal highway (*inexpensive*; open all year).

The Coast West of Santander

This lush and lovely seaside stretch has been spared any Laredo toadstools, and what
tourist development there is remains fairly discreet. When the summer hordes have
vanished and the little windy roads belong to you alone, it is haunting and strange in a
fairylike way. Even in the rain.

Getting Around

By train: FEVE trains out of Santander go as far as Torrelavega, with frequent bus
connections to Santillana. Another FEVE station is 3km from San Vicente—a
lovely walk if you're not carrying too much luggage.

By bus: Alternatively, Suances, Santillana, Comillas and San Vicente are linked
around 6 times daily to Santander by La Cantábrica de Comillas or SA Continental
buses from Santander's main bus station.

Tourist Information

Suances: Pso. de la Marina Española, ✆ (942) 81 09 24
Santillana del Mar: Pza. Mayor, ✆ (942) 81 82 51.
Comillas: C/ Maria del Piélago, ✆ (942) 72 07 68.
San Vicente de la Barquera: Avda. Generalísimo 6, ✆ (942) 71 07 97.
Cabezón de la Sal: Pza. de Ricardo Botín, ✆ (942) 70 03 32

There are **markets** in Suances on Tuesdays; Torrelavega on Wednesdays;
Comillas on Thursdays; San Vicente and Cabezón on Saturdays.

Santillana del Mar

Jean-Paul Sartre, who had always wanted to be a guidebook writer but couldn't get a
break, practised on Santillana del Mar, pronouncing it 'the most beautiful village in Spain'.
Sooner or later someone in town will remind you of this, and it's best not to argue. The
tour buses disgorge their hundreds daily upon this tiny village (which despite the 'del Mar'
is not on the sea), and in summer it can be a ghastly tourist inferno, with no place to put

or a mile around. If you come at all, do it out of season, or spend the night after rippers have all gone.

na is at once an evocative medieval town of grand palaces and a country village of farmers, whose pastures lie on the hills just beyond the mellowed stone and half-ered houses that line Santillana's one street. Its past distinctions come from great lth in medieval times, earned from wool and linen. By 1600 nearly every man in town s a noble, or *hidalgo* (from *hijo de algo*, 'son of somebody'), courtesy of easily urchased titles of nobility in the time of Charles V and Felipe II. So of course they stopped doing any work, and Santillana has changed little since. In the 1920s, Juan Antonio Güell López, grandson of the famous Marquis of Comillas (*see* below), became minister for tourism under the dictatorship of Primo de Rivera. He took a special interest in Santillana, and began the restoration of its old churches and palaces.

The village is famous as the birthplace of Spain's favourite fictional rogue, Gil Blas, and home of the real Marqués de Santillana, Íñigo López de Mendoza, the Spanish Sir Philip Sidney, a warrior and poet and courtly lover whose house still stands on the Calle del Cantón. Other houses have equally noble pedigrees; an Archduchess of Austria owned the one across from the **Colegiata**. The latter is a 12th-century masterpiece, dedicated to St Juliana (or Iliana), an Anatolian martyr under Diocletian whose remains have lain here since the 6th century, and who gave her name to the town; the monks who built the cloister for themselves owned most of the town and ran its affairs until the 1400s. The church has a fine weather-beaten façade, rebuilt in the 1700s with bits and pieces of the Romanesque original tacked on; inside, the impressive altar is made of silver from Mexico—plenty of the *hidalgos*' younger sons went off to America to make their fortune, and many of the family mansions in the village are *casas de indianos*. There is a beautiful cloister, with capitals carved with biblical and hunting scenes (*open 9–1 and 4–7.30; adm*).

The ticket to the cloister will also get you into the **Museo Diocesano** (*across town near the parking lot, open 10–1 and 4–7*) installed in the 17th-century **Convento de Regina Coeli**, Gothic in style, displaying an exceptional collection of ecclesiastical artefacts from all over Cantabria, some of Templar origin, and all perfectly restored by the nuns. In the eloquent **Plaza Ramón Pelayo**, the tower house of Don Borja holds one more museum, **Cantabria y la Mar en la Historia**, devoted to the region's seafaring past, and making up in a way for the town's anomalous name 'del Mar' when it's actually two miles from the sea. On the same plaza stands the **Ayuntamiento**, rebuilt in 1770, and from the same century, the Palacio de Barreda-Bracho, now the Parador Gil Blas.

Ten years ago, residents of Santillana still kept cattle on the ground floors of their homes and sold delicious rich milk by the glass and tasty *bizcocho* (cake) by the piece to tourists. You'll see less of that today, but there are still plenty of souvenirs to buy. Fox tails seem to be in fashion. If you're in a hurry to get to the promised Mar, the closest beaches are at **Suances**, just 5km away; it's a fishing village and a small resort, though the sea here isn't the cleanest. Suances began life as *Portus Blendium*, the chief Roman port on on this part of the coast, though there's nothing Roman to be seen.

¡Mira, papa. Bueyes! (Look, papa. Cows!)

María de Sautuola, discoverer of the paintings at Altamira

From Santillana you can walk up to Altamira in 20 minutes, though don't expect to get in unless you've written years in advance (Centro de Investigación de Altamira, Santillana del Mar, Santander 39330) and are one of the 20 chosen ones permitted the 15-minute glimpse at one of the sublime masterpieces of Upper Palaeolithic art. Still, an extraordinary number of people show up at the caves almost with the fervour of pilgrims to pay homage to the genius of the artists of c. 12,000 BC, who covered the undulating ceiling of the cave with stunningly exuberant, vividly coloured paintings of bison, horses, boars and stags. Only at Lascaux, up at the northern end of the Franco-Cantabrian arc of Magdalenian cave painting, will you find such powerful, masterful technique; the movement and strength in the coiled, startled and galloping bisons, the attentive deer, the frisking horses are simply awesome. As they say, 'This is the infancy of art, not an art of infancy'.

The story of the discovery of Altamira, however, is a parable of perceptions. As at Lascaux, an ancient landslide sealed the entrance of the caves and tunnels (and more or less vacuum-packed the paintings) until it was rediscovered by a hunter and his dog in 1868. In 1875, Don Marcelino de Sautuola, an amateur prehistorian, was intrigued by the black drawings on the walls in the outer rooms, and over the years explored them, in 1879 taking his nine-year-old daughter María along. The child wandered a little deeper into the caves, and lifted her eyes to the superb polychrome paintings. Although no one had ever seen the like, the Marquis at once recognized the ceiling for what it was: a ravishing work of genius from the Stone Age. Excited, he published a description of Altamira, but rather than the expected response of awe and wonder from the 'experts' in the field, de Sautuola was mocked, ridiculed, viciously attacked, and even accused of forging the paintings; the scholars simply refused to believe that people who used stone axes were capable of painting, one of the 'civilized arts'. Undaunted, the Marquis held his ground, insisting Altamira was for real and died heartbroken in 1888, vilified and as forgotten as the caves themselves. Fifteen years later, the discovery of a dozen painted caves in the Vézère valley in the Dordogne led to a change of mind, beginning in 1902 with one expert, E. Cartailhac, making a public apology to de Sautuola's memory in his *Mea Culpa d'un Sceptique*.

Although the 'white disease' caused by the moisture in the breath of visitors has restricted admission to the caves, you can do the next best thing at Altamira—see the video and photos in the fascinating **museum** (*open 10–1 and 4–6, closed Sun; adm*) installed on the site. You can also explore a small stalactite cave which is prettily lit to emphasize nature's wonders as compensation for the inaccessibility of the more fragile works of man.

Santillana

At the top of the list there's the wonderfully atmospheric ★★★**Parador Gil Blas** on Pza. Pelayo 11, © 81 80 00, ⊛ 81 89 31 (*expensive*), with medieval rooms; reserve well in advance in season, and request a room on the first or second floor. A good second choice, ★★★**Hotel Altamira**, is installed in another palace nearby on C/ Cantón 1, © 81 80 25 (*moderate/expensive*), with a patio and garden. Both have elegant dining-rooms, especially the *parador*. For something moderate, try ★★**Conde Duque**, © 81 83 36, ⊛ 84 01 70, in a restored medieval building with its own parking. Ask at the tourist office for a list of *casas particulares*, though many of them are in the newer suburbs en route to Altamira; or else, head for C/ Los Hornos or Avda. Le Dorat, which have plenty of rooms. **Camping Santillana**, © 81 82 50, just north of the village, is one of the pricier campgrounds in this area, but it has all the amenities including a pool and tennis courts.

The restaurant of the **Altamira** may be the best in town, with a good bargain 1500-pts menu, and big plates of roast meats (and some seafood). If you happen to be in Santillana at the weekend, you can feast on local and mountain specialities—everything from *fabada* to grilled *langostinos* (crawfish) at **Los Blasones**, Pza. de la Gándara, © 81 80 70, for 1500 or 2500 pts, or at **La Robleda**, C/ Revolgo, © 81 83 36, for a little less; otherwise there are good tapas and reasonably priced meals in the bar nearest the Colegiata.

Suances

Whatever the rating, most rooms in this resort go for about 7500 pts. By far the most interesting ones are in an old mansion by the beaches, the ★**Castillo de Suances**, © 81 03 83, ⊛ 81 03 74, with individually decorated rooms, some with television. There's a good seafood restaurant here, as popular with the locals as the tourists: **Casa Sito**, Pso. de la Marina Española, with a 1500-pts menu and dishes like *paella* with lobster (*paella bogavante*) for a splurge.

Comillas, with a Little *Modernista* Madness

Definitely *the* place to be on this stretch of the coast, the seaside resort of Comillas offers a bit of Catalan quirkiness in a gorgeous setting, framed by two endearing beaches—the **Playa Comillas** just below town and the longer **Playa de Oyambre**, a 20-minute walk away. Comillas' old town, with its rough cobbled streets and arcaded mansions, has been a quiet watering-hole for the Madrid and Barcelona aristocracy for a long time; the latter brought along their favourite architects in the 19th century to add a *modernista* flair.

The Instant Marquis

 The Spain of the Industrial Revolution is a land not very well known, but if the nation's capitalists never could match the mills of the Midlands or Massachusetts in the 19th century, they certainly produced some marvels, and some incredible robber-baron careers. Antonio López was a local boy who went off to Cuba and made a fortune in shipping and slaves (slavery wasn't abolished in Spanish-run Cuba until 1886), and then moved out and made another pile running a monopoly, the Philippine National Tobacco Company. He came back home and purchased the title of Marquis of Comillas. The new Marquis's son married the daughter of Joan Güell, the richest man in Barcelona, who had also started in Cuba and ended up as Spain's biggest textile magnate. If the name is familiar, you're thinking of Antoni Gaudí's famous surreal Güell Park in Barcelona. Like Cosimo de' Medici in old Florence, this robber baron had a talented aesthete to succeed him, whose sponsorship of Gaudí sparked the golden age of *modernista* architecture in Catalunya.

It was the Güell connection that brought Gaudí to Cantabria, where he helped with the López family palace in 1878 and came back to build El Capricho in 1883. The centre of the López interests was Barcelona, where they ran factories, banks, and the Trasatlántica shipping line (which later fell into the grasp of the greatest of all Spanish robber barons, Juan March, and still runs most of the Spanish island ferries). The Lópezes lived on the Ramblas in Barcelona, but they spent their summers here, bringing along their Catalan friends and making Comillas a genteel upper-class resort; locals called them the 'Trasatlánticos'. López's castle-like summer mansion, on the hill overlooking the town, was one of the most spectacular private homes in its day, and the centre of the glittering social season Comillas knew at the turn of the century. But modern capitalist glories never seem to last more than a generation or two, and today López's palace stands as empty and weird and forlorn as *Citizen Kane*'s Xanadu.

The peculiar legacies of the robber barons are up on the hills to the west of the village centre. A walk up a garden path takes you to Gaudí's **El Capricho**, built for a relation of the Marquis', and recently restored and pressed into service as a restaurant (*see* below). If not one of the architect's more ambitious works, it is an utterly delightful house, exciting the envy of the crowd of Spanish tourists usually milling about it. The main feature is an eccentric, perfectly non-functional tower, half lighthouse and half minaret. The decorative theme, held together by lovely ceramic tiles in green and gold and by extravagant wrought-iron balconies and cornices, has a repeated sunflower motif.

Next to El Capricho, you can have a peek through an iron gate at the **summer palace of the Marqués de Comillas,** though a better view can be had from the main coastal road leaving the village. A work of another Catalan, Gaudí's friend Joan Martorell, this ponderous palace in a quirky *modernista* neo-Gothic is protected by an imitation castle wall with oubliettes. The palace has been closed for years awaiting a buyer, though some restoration work is currently underway inside. Next to it, the Marquis's **chapel** adds the perfect touch of discreet surreality to the ensemble. It's bigger than Comillas's parish church, and inside there are furnishings by Gaudí himself and marble sepulchres of the Marquis and his family.

The third member of this singular trio stands on the opposite hill, across the main road through Comillas, but it commands the views for miles around. The **Universidad Pontificia** began in 1883, with a plan by Martorell and some financial help from Antonio López. The Pope's university moved to Madrid in 1964, leaving a huge complex of buildings with no use; still the people of Comillas keep it up and give tours of the sumptuous main building, with decoration by a third major figure of Catalan modernism, Lluis Domènech i Montaner (*open daily 9–3; adm*). There are frescoed rooms and a chapel, but the best features are the delightful figures carved in wood over the main stairway in the form of gargoyles: fearsome monsters share space with among others, a house cat, a chicken and a fly.

If you like Domènech i Montaner, there's a wonderfully florid **Monument to Antonio López** by him near the beach, within sight of Comillas' peculiar **cemetery**, built in a Gothic ruin and topped with a huge marble angel. Domènech i Montaner is responsible for some of the funerary statues inside too, and it isn't difficult to guess which ones.

San Vicente de la Barquera

San Vicente de la Barquera, the next resort to the west, is still as much a fishing port as a holiday retreat, though it's hugely popular with Madrileños in summer—you won't find a place to park your car. Marvellously sited on a hill in the last elbow-bend of the wide and marshy Río Escudo (the best view is arriving on the coastal road from the west), it is linked by a long causeway to the eastern coast, near the town beach. The older, upper town is dominated by the rose-coloured parish church **Nuestra Señora de los Ángeles**, a 13th-century transitional work containing the finely sculpted Renaissance tomb of the Inquisitor Antonio Corro. Below, interwoven branches of plane trees add a French touch to the main plaza. Every quarter hour the bell tower of the church San Vicente booms out a recording of the first phrase of Schubert's *Ave María*, guaranteed to drive you nuts. The locals claim an enemy of their town had it installed—with any luck it will be a bad memory by the time you get there.

If you want to take a dip inland in this western end of Cantabria, the first town south of San Vicente is **Cabézon de la Sal**, a town where the *pozos de sal*—'salt wells'—have been mined since before the Romans came. Cabézon is little more than an industrial centre, but nearby both the landscapes and the area's modest attraction remind you of Cantabria's more rural side: at **Carrejo**, a **Museo de la Naturaleza**, with exhibits of local flora and fauna in an 18th-century farmhouse (*open daily exc Mon and Tues, 11–1*). Beyond that come two rather refined villages, each with a number of fine mansions and other works: **Ruente** and **Bárcena Mayor**. Bárcena especially, up on a back road in the mountains, retains a medieval ambiance, with arcaded streets, wooded balconies, and woodworkers' shops. Legend claims it as one of the first towns of Cantabria, and a stronghold of the *foramontanos*, as they call the mountaineers who resisted the Moors in the Dark Ages; the village has a fountain that goes back to Visigothic times.

Comillas

The ★★★**Casal del Castro**, San Jerónimo, © 72 00 36, 72 00 61 (*moderate/expensive*), is in the centre of town in a fine old building with a pretty garden and rooms (open April to mid-Sept). The ★★**Hs Esmeralda**, C/ Antonio López 7, © 72 00 97 (*moderate*), is a good second choice close to the beach, or try ★**Fuente Real**, C/ Sobrellano 19, © 72 01 55 (*inexpensive*; open all year). The tourist office has a list of *casas particulares* for something cheaper.

Comillas is the only place anywhere you can dine in a building by Gaudí, in **El Capricho de Gaudí**, Barrio de Sobrellano, © 72 03 65 (*expensive*). The interior, if not entirely as the master planned it, has been beautifully restored. The food is a work of art as well, mostly seafood with a *nouvelle cuisine* touch; the 3500-pts menu is a bargain. Ring ahead as it's usually booked solid in season. Just outside the grounds, the **Fuente Real** with its ancient sign and décor of *azulejo* tiles has been a favourite for well over a century, a cheerful seafood place with outside tables (1200-pts menu). **Adolfo**, Pso. Garelli s/n, © 72 20 14, is another good choice with traditional cooking for a bit more.

San Vicente

★★**Luzón**, Ctra. Santander-Oviedo, © 71 00 50 (*moderate*), is a solid, square stone inn smack in the centre of town facing the tidal basin (open all year). ★**La Paz** nearby on C/ del Mercado 2, © 71 01 80 (*inexpensive*), has recently been remodelled and offers stylish, if bathless, rooms. **Camping El Rosal** is conveniently near the beaches, on the main road just outside San Vicente. As for dinner, expect more seafood, notably at a place called **Boga-Boga**, Pza. José Antonio, © 71 01 35 (*expensive*), where the award-winning chef turns out the sort of Cantabrian recipes you've never imagined: red peppers stuffed with *langostinos*, for instance. For a less serious seafood attack, you can do well for 3000 pts at **La Bodega Marinera** on C/ Arenal.

Bárcena Mayor

This village is famed for its mountain cuisine—try it at the **Venta La Franca**, on C/La Franca: stuffed haunch of venison and other game dishes in season. **Río Argoza** is similar; both are good bargains at about 2000 pts.

The Picos de Europa

They are not the highest mountains in Spain, or even in the Cantabrian-Pyrenean *cordillera*, but the Picos de Europa have a certain cachet. So many peaks, packed closely together in a small area, make a memorable landmark for Spain's northern coast. No one knows where the name came from, though it may have been that these mountains, visible

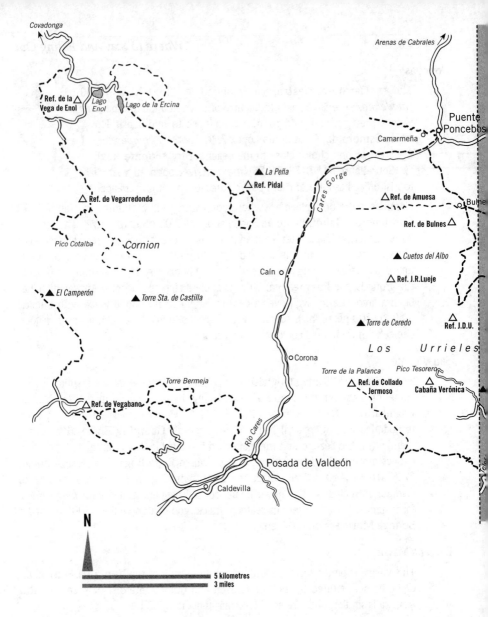

far out to sea, were the first sight of the continent for Atlantic sailors. To the Asturians they are known as the Urrieles.

Thank Asturian ecologists for their efforts in keeping Spain's most beautiful mountains enchanting and unspoiled: what development there is (ski resorts, hotels) is in western Cantabria and northern León. The Picos are divided by rivers into three tremendous massifs—**Andara**, mostly in Cantabria, **Urrieles** in the middle, and **Cornión** to the west.

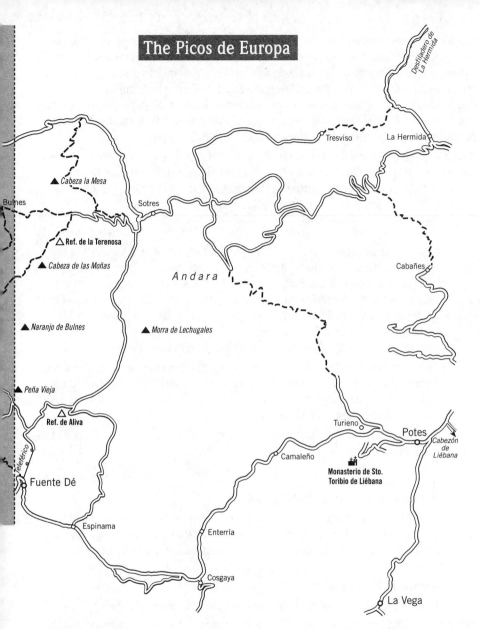

The Picos de Europa

Desfiladero de La Hermida

Tresviso   La Hermida

▲ *Cabeza la Mesa*

Bulnes   Sotres

△ **Ref. de la Terenosa**

▲ *Cabeza de las Moñas*   Cabañes

A n d a r a

▲ *Naranjo de Bulnes*   ▲ *Morra de Lechugales*

▲ *Peña Vieja*

△ **Ref. de Aliva**

Turieno   Potes

Cabezón de Liébana

Camaleño

Teleférico   **Monasterio de Sto. Toribio de Liébana**

Fuente Dé

Espinama

Enterría

Cosgaya

La Vega

The highest peak, Torre de Cerredo, stands 8606ft—not all that much as mountains go. But for sheer beauty and rugged grandeur, for the contrast of tiny rural villages in fertile green valleys against a backdrop of sheer, twisted stone peaks crested with snow the year round, the Picos de Europa are hard to beat.

The range seems to have been dropped from heaven, especially for hikers; there are trails for Sunday walkers and sheer cliffs for serious alpinists. Hiking boots, however, are universally recommended because of frequent patches of loose shale on the trails and slopes. If you're going for an extended holiday in the Picos, get the detailed maps published by the Federación Española de Montañismo, generally available at Potes, the main base for visiting the mountains. The guide *Picos de Europa* by Robin Collomb (West Col, Reading) is a great help, and up-to-date detailed information on guides, itineraries and mountain *refugios* (free overnight shelters) is available from the **Federación Asturiana de Montañismo**, C/ Melquiades Álvarez 16, Oviedo, ✆ 21 10 99.

Hiking in the Picos is practical only from the end of May to October, but even then you may get a soaking—the Picos are only 32km from the rainy Atlantic seaboard. Bring warm clothes and a lightweight plastic poncho, a sleeping bag and food for nights in the refuges, and a pair of binoculars to take in the wonderful array of wildlife and birds.

Getting Around

By bus: There are two buses (one in the winter) daily between Santander and León that stop at Potes and Lebeña; departures are more frequent from Unquera (five buses daily to Potes). From Potes there are three buses from the central square to Fuente Dé and the *teleférico*; jeeps make the link between the upper station of the *teleférico* to the refugio de Aliva if you're not up to the walk. Also, a stable in Turieno next to Potes offers several guided riding excursions in the Picos. If you want to do it yourself, *Viajes Wences* and other firms in Potes rent mountain bikes.

There are daily buses between Arenas and Cangas along the northern rim of the Picos, and a Land Rover connection between Arenas and Poncebos. Cangas itself may be reached once daily by bus from Riaño; there are also a couple of buses daily from Oviedo to Cangas and Covadonga.

Posada de Valdeón is easiest reached from León, via Riaño or Portilla de La Reina (once a day).

Tourist Information

Unquera: C/ Rincón 2, ✆ (942) 71 72 82

Potes: C/ Independencia s/n, ✆ (98) 73 07 87 (for more detailed information and maps try Bustamente's on central Pza. Capitán Palacios, an excellent source for all books on the area—everything from hiking trails to works by Beato de Liébana).

Arenas de Cabrales: Ctra. General, ✆ (98) 584 52 84.

There are **markets** in Unquera on Tuesdays and in Potes on Mondays.

Potes and the Valley of Liébana

The eastern mountains of the Picos are the most visited and the most accessible. The main entrance from the coast begins at **Unquera** (a FEVE stop on the coast to the west of San Vicente de la Barquera); the N 621 from here climbs up through the **Desfiladero de La Hermida**, a dramatic, high, narrow gorge walling in the River Deva and the tiny hamlet of **La Hermida**, famous in sunny Spain for not seeing *el sol* at all from 26 October–28

Santa María de Lebeña

March. The road climbs up from here into the idyllic little valley of the Liébana, more happily fated by geography to have an unusual 'Mediterranean' microclimate. Vines and even olives grow here, though you'll see mostly apple orchards with the vineyards around the first village, **Lebeña**, with its parish church—the 10th-century Mozarabic **Santa María**—signposted south of the village on the N 62.

This is one of the finest pre-Romanesque churches, a little jewel in the middle of nowhere that is the perfect expression of the strange little mountainous state of Asturias and, perhaps, its dreams of future greatness. Built in 925 for a Count Alfonso, Santa María is as impressive a work as any of the more famous churches around Oviedo. Most of the exterior was restored a century ago, but the original roof corbels and other decorated parts of the exterior are carved with real originality, and inside the simple Greek-cross plan—done in horseshoe Visigothic arches with not too much regard for precision—is a delight. A few years ago, the stone step up to the altar was raised and found to be carved with geometric symbols, along with a human figure apparently painted on the stone in blood. The information card the old caretaker hands out claims that the stone is 2000 years old, and carved with Celtic sun symbols; the symbols may be that old, but the stone probably came as the original altar when the church was built. You'll see a photo of a lovely carved wood Virgin, the work of the great Renaissance sculptor Gil de Siloé. Unfortunately the picture is all Lebeña has left; someone nicked the icon in 1993.

Two venerable companions, an olive and yew tree, stand next to the church; they were both planted at the time the church was built—over a thousand years ago.

Potes, the capital of the Valley of Liébana, is the metropolis of the Picos, where you can garner information, catch buses, change travellers' cheques and stock up on supplies. For all the tourist traffic Potes is still a gracious town, with stone arcades to shelter the cafés on the main street and a warren of medieval lanes behind. There are also a number of jeep excursions on offer. The main monument in Potes itself is the 15th-century **Torre del Infantado**, a massive, square defensive-residential work in the centre of town.

The most popular excursions from Potes include the 4km trip up to the **Monasterio de Santo Toribio de Liébana**. Don't miss it, because this is the only place in Cantabria where a visit will earn you an indulgence—time off from purgatory. It is a long-established pilgrimage site, allegedly the home of the world's largest chunk of the True Cross. In the early days of the Kingdom of Asturias the Liébana was a kind of monastic preserve, and this monastery was its centre, founded early in the 8th century. What you see today, though, is mainly Romanesque and Gothic. The 'world's largest sliver of the True Cross' is kept in an ornate Baroque chapel where masses are said daily. In its earliest days the monastery was ruled by the Abbot Beato de Liébana, whose *Commentaries on the Apocalypse* were popular in Spain throughout the Middle Ages. Girona and El Burgo de Osma have beautiful 10th-century illuminated editions of the manuscript, but in the cloister here you can see a full set of copies of one of them, mad and brilliant pictorial prophecies from an age when people were convinced the world would soon be meeting its end.

The nearby **mirador de Santo Toribio** takes in splendid views over the Andara massif. Another, longer, walk south will take you through **Cabezón de Liébana**, where some of the houses have coats-of-arms, and two medieval bridges cross over to the lovely church of **Santa María de Piasca**, built in 1172 with fine Romanesque carvings on the capitals within. The monastery was shared by monks and nuns, which was typical for the mountains but unusual elsewhere.

Beato de Liébana Defends the Faith

Back in the grim 8th century, when the heathen Normans were attacking from the north, the godless Magyars from the east and the infidel Moor from the south, and the Faith was in gravest peril, just what were the Christians up to? Well, they were arguing amongst themselves as usual. Christian Spain in that age may not seem to have been really big enough to generate a proper theological controversy, but somehow it managed. At issue was something called Adoptionism, the doctrine that Jesus the man was only the 'adopted son' of God.

In the far corner, wearing the black trunks, we see Bishop Helipandus of Toledo, then under Muslim rule, who argued for Adoptionism. In the near corner, in the white trunks, stands Beato of Liébana, who isn't about to let anybody say his Saviour does not participate fully in Godhood. Like all such controversies, this brouhaha masked some more mundane conflicts—between the mountaineer Asturians and the more sophisticated Mozarabic Christians of the south, over who was boss in matters of faith and politics. This particular conflict caught the attention of all Western Christianity though, and it found a solution not with the pope in Rome, surprisingly, but at the court of Charlemagne.

In those days, if you were lucky enough to find someone with the necessary wisdom and erudition to decide on such a case, he would probably have been (another surprise) an Englishman. The King of the Franks was fortunate enough to have in his services the greatest doctor of Christendom, Alcuin of York, who was busy trying to reform the Carolingian educational system, and trying with less success to teach Charlemagne how to write his name. In 799 Alcuin pronounced that Adoptionism was just a rehash of the old Nestorian heresy, and awarded a clean decision to Beato, who thereupon retired from the ring of Church politics and went home to write about the End of the World.

From Fuente Dé to Arenas de Cabrales

The classic excursion from Potes is to take the bus west up to the stunning old village of **Espinama** and, 1.6km beyond, to **Fuente Dé**. Here you can catch the *teleférico* for an awesome, vertigo-inducing ride 2568ft up the sheer cliff to the **mirador del Cable** (*the teleférico runs daily, July–Sept, 9am–8 pm; 1200 pts; in peak season, arrive very early or you'll get stuck waiting, maybe for hours*). Once at the top, walk 4km up to the **Refugio de Aliva**, a popular modern version of the old mountain refuge; a path from here leads down to Espinama—a pleasant day's circuit. From Espinama, you can make a longer, more serious hike through the eastern and central massifs north to **Sotres**, a good day's work (jeep excursions also available from Espinama). The landmark near here, in the Central Massif of the Urrieles, is **Naranjo de Bulnes** (Pico Urriello on some maps), a distinct sheer-sided, tower-like pinnacle, loved and hated by daredevil alpinists. From Sotres, a long day's hiking will bring you to **Arenas de Cabrales**, renowned for its stinking mountain cheese, and the most important village in the region, with buses to Cangas and Land Rovers to **Poncebos** (*see* below).

The Divine Gorge

Between Poncebos and Caín, the **Cares Gorge** (better known as simply the 'Garganta Divina') extends north to south across the Picos. It is a spectacular 25.6km walk over sheer drops down to the Río Cares, made relatively easy by a footpath sculpted into the mountainside. The classic approach is from **Caín** in the south, itself linked to civilization (i.e. the fine mountain village of **Posada de Valdeón**) by a regular four-wheel-drive service. Walking south from Poncebos isn't much more strenuous—but you risk either spending the night in Caín, which has no lodgings, or walking the 9km further south to sleep in Posada. Other possible walks from Poncebos are to **Camarmeña** and **Bulnes**, two of the most remote villages in the Picos. Bulnes has a *refugio*; both villages have knockout views of the Naranjo de Bulnes.

The aforementioned Posada de Valdeón is the chief village of the **Valley of Valdeón**, highest in the Picos and a serenely magnificent place to rest up in before or after the Cares Gorge; here tiny farming villages and their rustic granaries, or *hórreos,* built on stilts to protect their contents from moisture and mice, look like mere toys under the loftiest mountains in the Picos. One of the most stupendous views of these is from the **Mirador del Tombo**, 1.6km from Posada, framed by a statue to the chamois goat, an animal occasionally seen in the flesh frisking over the steep slopes. The **Chorco de los Lobos** nearby was used to trap the mountains' most fearsome predator, the now rare wolf.

© (942–)   ***Where to Stay and Eating Out***

It may be paradise for hikers, but there's no need to rough it. Nearly every village in the Picos has at least one *casa particular* or *fonda* or a place to camp, and you can purchase supplies or dine out in a traditional restaurant. Every village has its specialities, and the shops under the arches on the main street of Potes are treasurehouses of the mountains' finest; you can purchase local cheeses (especially *cabrales*) and charcu-terie, honey in various original flavours and especially *orujo*, the clear Cantabrian firewater sold in dangerous-looking little bottles all over town. It's made from grape stems after the wine harvest, like French *marc* or Italian *grappa*.

Potes

Potes has by far the most in the way of accommodation. The top of the line is the **Picos de Valdecoro**, at C/ Roscabado, ✆ 73 00 25, ✉ 73 03 15 (open all year), and the modern, stone-built **Infantado**, on the Oviedo road, ✆ 73 09 39, ✉ 73 05 78 (*both moderate*). The budget choice, **Hs La Serna**, C/ La Serna 9, ✆ 73 09 24, has the only rooms with bath for under 3500 pts in town; **Hs Rubio**, C/ San Roque 17, ✆ 73 00 15, is slightly more expensive, but has rooms in an attrac-tively restored village house. **Camping El Molino**, 9km south of Potes at La Vega, ✆ 73 04 89, offers inexpensive sites in a pleasant setting. For dinner, **Camacho** has an honest 1000-pts menu including *fabada*, trout and other local treats.

Fuente Dé

Since 1965, the magnificently sited ***Parador Río Deva**, ✆ 73 00 01, ✉ 73 02 12 (*moderate/expensive*), has been a part of the Picos experience. A modern building at the end of the *teleférico*, many of its rooms have grand views; the hotel organizes jeep excursions up into the peaks, and its restaurant specializes in moun-tain and Castilian dishes; 2500-pts menu. You could do just as well, immersed in equally stunning mountain scenery, at the modern ***Hotel del Oso**, or the beau-tiful stone original **Del Oso Pardo**, 10km east at Cosgaya: both owned by the Rivas family, ✆ 73 04 18, ✉ 73 01 36 (*both moderate*). A bonus is the superb moun-tain cuisine: try the trout and cheese cake (*tarta de queso*) or the 3000-pts *menú*.

Espinama

In this village, 4km from Fuente Dé, the *Hs Remoña**, ✆ 73 04 95 (*inexpensive*), offers simple rooms with bath, and good, filling, inexpensive meals. About 7.5km up from Espinama, the **Refugio de Aliva**, open 15 June–30 Sept, has a restaurant and comfortable rooms for 70 people, available on a first-come, first-served basis (*inexpensive*). Ring in advance on ✆ 73 09 99. A Land Rover from Espinama will take you up (for other *refugios* in the Picos, ask at the Potes tourist office)

Posada de Valdeón

Posada has several *casas particulares*, some fine *fondas* and the **Hs Abascal**, El Salvador, ✆ (987) 74 05 07, open all year; meals around 2000 pts.

Santa María de Naranco,
Oviedo

Asturias

The Principality of Asturias is the Spanish Wales, a rugged country of mines, stupendous mountains, and a romantically beautiful coastline. The inhabitants have traditionally been a hardy lot, beginning with the Iberian tribe of Astures who gave their name to the province and defied both the Romans and Visigoths. Yet the proudest date in Asturian history is 718, when a band of Visigoths, led by the legendary Pelayo, defeated the Moors in the misty mountain glen of Covadonga, officially beginning the Reconquista and founding the first tiny Christian kingdom in Muslim

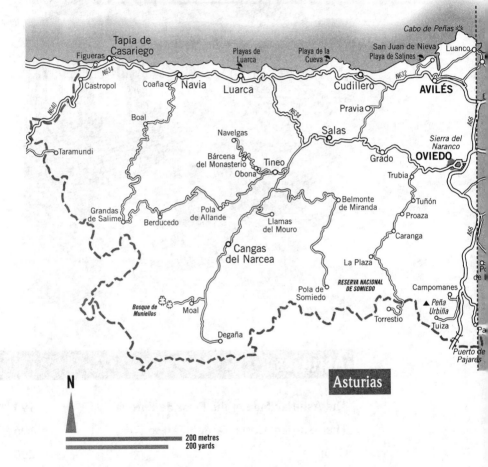

Iberia. Their beautiful churches are Asturias's chief artistic patrimony; the language they spoke, *el Bable*, or 'Babel', survives only as a dialect against the modern dominance of Castilian, its direct descendant.

Since the 14th century, the Spanish heir-apparent has borne the title of 'Prince of Asturias', a practice initiated by John of Gaunt when his daughter married the son of Juan I. Not long after John of Gaunt's day, Asturias fell into an obscurity that lasted centuries. The discovery of iron ore and coal in the 19th century rapidly transformed its traditional agricultural economy into a mining one with radical tendencies. These brought about the second great date in Asturian history: an epic miners' revolt in October 1934 that served as a prelude to the Civil War. Even after the war, resistance to Franco continued in the wild mountains of the province.

The modern autonomous region of Asturias is in its quiet way one of the most progressive in Spain. One of the last areas to be touched by tourism, it is fighting to maintain its

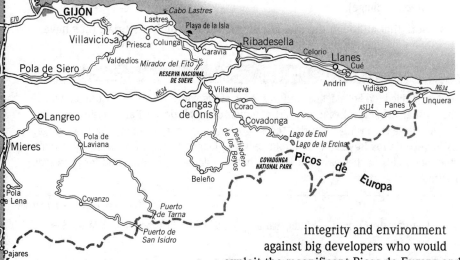

integrity and environment against big developers who would exploit the magnificent Picos de Europa and the coast; instead, Asturias would have you stay in a rural village, to learn something of its culture and architecture. In 1985, the Asturian wildlife protection fund received the European Preservation of Nature (FAPAS) prize for its efforts to preserve the rare Cantabrian bear and the capercaillie from extinction. One of the gentlest ways to get acquainted with the Asturian countryside is to pony trek, especially along the Roman road of Lamesa, between the districts of Somiedo and Teverga (© 98-25 45 57 for information). Cyclists can get advice on the best routes by calling © 98-24 35 96, and the daylight-shy who like peering into caves can call the speleology experts on © 98-89 02 61. Canoeing to suit all standards can be found all over, from the tumbling rapids of the mountains to the gentle streams in the valleys— Asturias has a full national and international programme. Asturias is a

193

fishing paradise; the waters abound in trout, salmon and eel (contact the Asturian Fishing Federation at C/ Uría 10, Oviedo, © 98–21 04 62 for details). If you like your water sports with a flavour of salt, head for the gusty Bay of Biscay for some fun sailing and windsurfing. Divers can contact the Divers' Federation in Gijón (C/ Dindurra 20, © 98–36 99 33). There are two golf courses in the region: at Gijón (© 98–36 99 33) and Siero (© 98–22 49 65).

At least once, visit an old Asturian *chigre* or *sidrería* to taste the local poison *sidra* (cider)—natural but dangerous stuff always poured at arm's length to give it the proper bounce. If you drink enough of it, it even begins to taste good.

The word 'pola' throughout this chapter is the local Asturian word for *pueblo* (village).

Note that although the Picos de Europa are partly in Asturias, they have been grouped together in **Cantabria,** *see* p.183.

The Asturian Side of the Picos de Europa: Cangas and Covadonga

The salmon-filled Río Sella defines the west edge of the western Massif de Cornión, which in its northernmost reaches forms part of **Covadonga National Park**. Easiest reached from Ribadesella on the Asturian coast, or through the stunning narrow gorge, **Desfiladero de los Beyos** (N 625) from León and Riaño, the region lacks the high drama of the mountains further east, but is nonetheless green and tranquil, and for Spaniards constitutes a pilgrimage.

Tourist Information

Cangas de Onís: C/ Emilio Laria 2, © (98) 584 80 05. There is a market on Sundays.

Desperately Seeking Pelayo

Cangas de Onís claims to be the first capital of Christian Spain, where the Asturian kings set up shop right after their victory at nearby Covadonga. The most beautiful things in Cangas de Onís are the high **medieval bridge** (erroneously called 'Roman') with its great arch spanning the Río Sella, and the **Capilla de Santa Cruz**, where the kings worshipped. It was built over a dolmen, and according to legend its founder was Favila, the successor of Pelayo. The original building may really be as early as the 5th century, though it was completely rebuilt in the 15th (get the key at the Ayuntamiento, and they might also let you have the key for the cave of Buxu). On a pillar near the entrance, an old relief shows a cross over a crescent moon, symbolizing the Christians' victories over Islam. As for the dolmen, it is still clearly visible in the chapel's crypt, carved with religious symbols.

From Cangas it's 3km north to **Villanueva**, where Alfonso I founded the **Monasterio de San Pedro** in 746. Now deserted, it has a 12th-century doorway, with capitals carved

Covadonga National Park

with bear hunting scenes. East of Cangas, the AS 114 follows the narrow valley of the Río Güeña, providing the northern part of the circuit around the Picos. In Cardes, the **cave of Buxu** contains rare, very abstract paintings from the Solutrian era (20–15,000 BC).

From here it's 10km to **Covadonga**, dominated by an enormous, kitschy 19th-century basilica. Here Pelayo, supposedly the son-in-law of Roderick, the last Visigothic king, and 300 followers managed to ambush a small Moorish expedition and defeat them, according to legend. The Moors, who didn't much care for the climate to begin with, made the mistake of letting the Christians stay and consolidate their power, preferring to seek richer spoils in France. Next to the basilica is the **cave** where Pelayo fought with his back to the wall and now rests in peace in a sarcophagus next to his wife.

From Covadonga it's a beautiful 20km through the national park to the mountain lakes of **La Ercina** and **Enol**, with the huge Peña Santa mountains as a backdrop. In summer there is a daily bus service from Cangas and Covadonga; otherwise you're on your own. Back on the AS 114, the next village east is **Corao**; nearby at a place called Abamia, the church of Santa Eulalia has parts going back to the 8th century, along with fragments of medieval frescoes.

Ⓒ *(98–)*   ***Where to Stay and Eating Out***

Cangas de Onís

Cangas has pricey hotels and a score of *hostales* where the going rate is about 6000 pts in high season, considerably less the rest of the year; one reliable one is the ***Piloña**, De San Pelayo 19, Ⓒ 584 80 88. Lucky souls can get one of the four rooms at *★**El Sella**, Avda.

Castilla, ✆ 584 80 11 (*inexpensive*), which also offers a decent restaurant with a 1500 pts menu. For something more substantial, *fabada* and other Asturian dishes are to be had at **Casa Juan**, Avda. de Covadonga (*moderate*).

Covadonga

Accommodation is scarce; there's the ★★★**Hotel Pelayo**, ✆ 584 60 61, basic and perhaps a bit overpriced (*expensive in season, otherwise moderate*), and a number of bars and restaurants that hang out *camas* signs along the main road. The restaurant **La Cabaña**, out on the road to Covadonga, ✆ 584 82 84 (*moderate*) is in an old stone house decorated in traditional Asturian style, serving winter warmers such as *cabritu asado*, or roast kid, together with some seafood dishes (closed Thurs). **Hospedería del Peregrino**, 200m below the sanctuary in Covadonga, ✆ 584 60 47 (*moderate*), has a well-deserved name for its *fabada*, seafood and mountain dishes which includes freshly caught salmon.

The Asturian 'Costa Verde': East to West

Although the Picos attract mountaineers and hikers from all over the world, the very attractive coast of Asturias sees relatively few foreigners. There are over fifty sandy beaches, most of them on unmarked roads just off the main coastal N 632; some have spectacular locations, and a few can offer relative peace and quiet even in the middle of August. It's a mountainous and rugged coast for the most part, and the lack of a good road along it (until recently) has kept development to a minimum.

Getting Around

By train and bus: FEVE trains along the coast take in much of the marvellous scenery. Five trains a day run between Santander and Oviedo, with stops at Unquera, Colombres, the beaches at Nueva and Villaharmes and Ribadesella. To continue up the coast from here you'll have to take a Gijón-bound bus. FEVE has frequent connections between Gijón and Avilés, and west to Cudillero, Luarca, Soto de Luiña and Ortigueira. ALSA buses link all these towns as well with Oviedo, while RENFE links Gijón with Oviedo, Madrid, Barcelona and the rest of the peninsula.

By car: turning the old N 632 along the coast into a reasonable route has been the biggest road project in this part of the country for some years. Most of it is already finished, and getting around is no problem—except for the two-lane stretch between Cudillero and Luarca, a nightmare of endless bends and trucks that can take three hours to negotiate. Unfortunately, at the moment there's no other way.

Tourist Information

Llanes: C/ Nemesio Sobrino, ✆ (98) 540 01 64
Ribadesella: Ctra. Piconera, ✆ (98) 586 00 38
Villaviciosa: Parque Vallina, ✆ (98) 589 17 59
Gijón: C/ Marqués de San Esteban 1, ✆ (98) 534 60 46
Avilés: Ruiz Gómez 21, ✆ (98) 554 43 25.

There are **markets** in Llanes on Tuesdays; in Ribadesella and Villaviciosa on Wednesdays; and in Avilés on Mondays.

Llanes

This eastern section of the coast is especially endowed with beaches and quiet coves, especially around Llanes, the first sizeable town. Llanes gets busy in summer—in fact when this agreeably funky old town becomes loaded with *madrileños* it becomes charmingly anarchic. Llanes is so popular because the coast around it contains some of the best beaches in Asturias: El Sablón, a broad and well developed one within walking distance of the town centre, and to the east, two others near two pretty villages. At **Cue**, signs point to the less frenetic Playa de Toro, set among pinnacle-like rock formations; at **Andrín**, 3km further, you can find two good beaches not yet crowded and commercialized: Playa de Andrín and Playa de Ballota. The area's two antiquities lie east of Llanes: near Vidiago and the Playa de France, there's a peculiar Bronze Age monument called **Peña-Tú** or the 'Cabeza del Gentil' (the gentile's head). Even older are the cave drawings in the **Cueva del Pindal** near Colombres (not lighted or attended).

West of Llanes, at **Celorio**, the unspoiled Playa de Borizu faces a small islet you can swim to, and you can find another string of beaches, some ideal for children, around the charming village of **Niembro**, along with the ruins of a 12th-century monastery, San Antolín de Bedo. For more isolation, try the Playa de **Torimbia**, situated in a perfect crescent of cliffs and accessible from a path down the cliffs.

Ribadesella

The next town, Ribadesella, at the mouth of the meandering Río Sella, makes an excellent base for forays along the coast or into the western Picos. Split in two by the river and bridge, with a picture postcard backdrop of mountains, Ribadesella has a handful of old streets, a long protected beach, and plenty of chances for hiking, pony trekking, canoeing and fishing. The beaches lie just across the Sella to the west of town. Just outside town are the stalactitic **Tito Bustillo Caves**, where some 15–20,000 years ago the residents painted the walls with stylish animals and humans in the Altamira fashion, worth a visit although their sienna, purple and black tones have faded (*open 10–1 and 3.30–5.15, sometimes closed weekends*).

Farther west, into what is officially known as the 'Costa Verde', you'll find quiet beaches in the tiny hamlets of **Caravia** (Baja and Alta), and near **Colunga**: **La Isla**, **La Griega** and **Lastres**. Equally renowned for its clams and *sidra*, Lastres's stack of red-tile-roofed houses and noble mansions overlooks one of Asturias' most picturesque fishing harbours. There is a small beach at the village, but a better one just to the west at **Rodiles**, a half-mile of sand lined with eucalyptus trees, very popular in season. Some rare Asturian horses, descendants of the hardy creatures used by the Romans for mountain duty, survive in the **Reserva Nacional de Sueve**, 3km south of Colunga, where you'll also find the **Mirador del Fito** with splendid views of the Picos de Europa and the coast. There is a small pre-Romanesque church, built in 921, in the village of **Priesca**, off the N 632 12km west of Colunga.

Villaviciosa

Apple orchards line the coast around **Villaviciosa**, and as you enter the town you'll pass a sign welcoming you to the 'Apple Capital of Spain'. They grow every sort of apple around here, but most common are the ones that feed the town's dozen cider distilleries. No town makes more of Asturias's favourite sauce, and none seems more devoted to drinking it. Every warm evening the tables go out from *chigres* (cider bars) onto the streets around the market, and the noise goes on half the night. The children run around under the street lamps; cider gets splashed everywhere.

O villa más viciosa, as an old drinking song chides it, is really a quite pleasant place, with a lively centre built around the Parque Vallina, and a small collection of old streets and palaces, including the attractive 13th-century **Santa María de la Oliva**. Not much has changed since 1517, when Villaviciosa became the first town in Spain to see the handsome but all-too-intense face of their new king, Charles V, who was sailing to Santander from his home in Flanders and was blown off course. There is a plaque on the house where the king stayed to mark the biggest surprise in Villaviciosa's history. When it's time for a swim, there are two beaches near Villaviciosa to chose from: long **Rodiles**, facing the sea and the *ría*, and across the *ría*, **Tazones**, a picturesque fishing village on a little cove.

Villaviciosa was a more important town a thousand years ago than it is today, and though nothing from that time survives in the place, its surroundings have a number of early Asturian churches, which can serve as an introduction to the better-known pre-Romanesque churches around Oviedo. One km south of town, signposted off the O 121, the Romanesque **San Juan de Amandi** is noted for its beautiful sculpture: graceful geometric patterns on the portal and the usual vigorous but mystifying scenes on the capitals. The lovely rounded portico was added in 1796. Other churches can be sought out in the nearby villages of Ambás and La Piñeda.

Valdedios was probably an ancient site from the earliest times, and in the days of the Kingdom of Asturias it was the religious centre of the region. Nine km southwest of Villaviciosa, in the pretty Puelles valley, it contains two separate churches. The oldest is the oratory of **San Salvador**, built in 893 by Alfonso III. It's an interesting building, one that shows some of the influences behind Asturian architecture. The top still shows a memory of Roman times with its neat classical pediment, though below this has been amplified into a basilican-style three-aisled church. The windows have stone latticework and *ajimeces* (mullioned windows) derived from al-Andalus. A Cistercian monastery was later built nearby, around the 11th-century basilica of **Santa María** (better known as *El Conventín*); the glorious Romanesque portal and the apse survive from the original building, though most of the interior is much later. The monastery is still in use, and the church interior, usually shut off behind an iron *reja*, glitters like a cave of mystery with its gilt Baroque *retablo* and other furnishings—an effect heightened when the organist monk is practising.

Llanes

Most hotels and restaurants are spread along the beaches, such as
★★★**Montemar**, C/ Jenaro Riestra, ℗ 540 01 00 (*moderate*), with
modern, comfortable rooms with ttelevision and other amenities. At
the same rate, though, you can stay in a 17th-century palace in
Llanes itself: ★★★**Don Paco**, C/ Posada Herrera, ℗ 540 01 50 (*high
moderate*). It's quiet, with a small garden, and the main hall of the mansion is now
an elegant restaurant, serving mostly seafood (3500 pts). Less expensively, there is
another hotel with only four rooms in a pleasant old house: ★★**Hs Los Barquitos**,
C/ La Concepción on the eastern edge of town, ℗ 540 26 12 (*moderate*). Both
Llanes and the villages near the beaches have plenty of inexpensive *hostales*, such as
the good-value ★**Hs Migal**, ℗ 540 12 01, in the pretty village of Cué.

The best places for dinner, as always on the coast, are on the harbour; **Mirentxu**,
a bit classier than the others, does the seafood Basque-style for about 2500 pts; in
season there are also some wonderful instant restaurants, nothing more than a
shelter and a few tables, where you can get anything finned at bargain rates. A few
kilometres outside Llanes is the popular **Casa Moran**, at Puente Nuevo, on the
road from Posada to Robadella, ℗ 540 74 85 (*moderate*) with a traditional menu
featuring items like *fabada asturiana* and roast lamb (closed Tues).

Ribadesella

Ribadesella has more accommodation than most villages around the coast, and you
can choose the posh, air-conditioned, beach-side splendour of the ★★★★**Gran Hotel
del Sella**, La Playa, ℗ 586 01 50 (*moderate/expensive*), with a pool, tennis courts,
and garden—a bit of Costa del Sol luxury on the Atlantic (open April–Sept). Two
moderate-priced *hostales* offer rooms and delicious food: the ★★**Hs Apolo**, by the
beach on C/ Gral. Franco, ℗ 586 04 42, with bathless doubles for 3200 pts (open
all year round) and good inexpensive seafood; and the ★**Hs El Pilar**, near the
bridge, ℗ 586 04 46, with tennis, garden and spiffier rooms; the restaurant features
Asturian home cooking (*both moderate*). The ★★**Boston**, C/ El Pico 7, ℗ 586 09
66, has off-season doubles with bath for 3000 pts.

Possibly Ribadesella's best restaurant, **Bohemia**, Gran Via, ℗ 586 11 50
(*moderate*) offers plenty of seafood but also a chance at something else for a
change, in dishes such as the *entrecôte* with *cabales* cheese. For tapas and cider,
the place to go is the noisy and convivial **Sidrería Corasceo** facing the harbour.

Lastres

This growing resort can still be your best bet for a peaceful place to while away a
few days. There are *casas particulares* and rooms over bars, along with the
★★★**Halcón Palace**, C/ Cofiño Arriondas, ℗ 584 13 12, a new hotel in a restored
18th-century mansion with sea views (*moderate*).

Villaviciosa

It may be a way from the beaches, but Villaviciosa can provide an agreeable night's stay, especially at **La Casona de Amandi**, out in the country at Amandi, © 598 01 30 (*expensive*), a *casa de indiano* (a house built by a returned emigrant to the Americas); today it is a thoroughly charming eight-room hotel in a lovely formal garden. The owners were antique dealers, and the rooms are decorated with their finds (*expensive*). Good if modest choices in town included the ★**Carlos I**, Pza. Carlos I, © 589 01 21, and the ★**Manquín**, Pza. Santa Carla, © 589 05 06 (*both moderate*). The latter has quiet rooms and a restaurant that occupies a pretty square with a fountain; seafood and properly poured cider for 2500 pts. The **Sol**, C/ Sol, © 589 11 30, has plenty of soul indeed, provided by an ancient proprietor, a former guitarist, who stands at his bar and plays '30s jazz records all day (he can talk about them all day too); very nice rooms at bargain rates.

Gijón

With some 250,000 people, Gijón is the largest city in Asturias and a major industrial centre and port, a salty, slightly gritty town with no sights to see but plenty of personality. When coal began to boom it grew into one of Spain's biggest ports. Built on a convenient rock projecting from the sea called the *Cimadevilla*, Gijón goes back to the Romans and possibly the Phoenicians—Cimadevilla is often referred to as the 'Atalaya'. It was the home of the Enlightenment reformer Jovellanos. Parts of Gijón had to be almost totally rebuilt after the Nationalists devastated it in the Civil War. Lately, local regionalists have painted over all the road signs to remind us that the city's proper name, in the Asturian spelling, is *Xixón*.

What sets Xixón apart are the excellent beaches that stretch eastwards from the Cimadevilla. Lined with the slick *urbanizaciones* of the newer town, they give the industrial city a carnival air every day in the warm months—hordes of locals, mostly red as lobsters, decorate the beaches in a way reminiscent of Reginald Marsh's famous caricatures of Coney Island. Cimadevilla, with its dour, quiet streets, suffered the most in the Civil War and has little to see. The *atalaya*, also called the hill of Santa Catalina, is taken up with a sprawling cigar facory where *farias,* the most noxious of Spanish smokes, are made. The centre of town occupies the isthmus leading to the newer quarters; there you will find the enclosed and arcaded **Plaza Mayor,** surrounded with cafés and restaurants. Behind it are the recently discovered **termas romanas**, some ruins including part of a 2nd-century baths complex, notable for its under-floor hypocaustal central heating. This is the start of the main beach, the **Playa de San Lorenzo.**

In the new town, in the newly established Puebla de Asturias on the far side of the Río del Piles, the **Museo del Pueblo de Asturias** displays a host of bagpipes from Celtic northwestern Spain and around the world, as well as a workshop (*open daily 10–8; adm*). Adjacent is a **Museo Etnográfico** (*same hours*) where you can learn how to make cider in the traditional way, and what *horreos* (raised granaries) are used for.

Up to Cabo Peñas and Down Again

Between the industrial centres of Gijón and Avilés, the Asturian coast juts northwards for a bit; the coastal road from Gijón may take hours to find, but eventually it will take you out beyond the new port district to **Candás**, an old tuna-fishing vilage famous for its *corridas marineras*— bullfights in a flooded ring that are unique in Spain. **Luanco**, just up the coast, had similar beginnings, but has now become much more of a resort; acres of holiday cottages surround the tidy, small centre. Luanco is famous for lace and embroideries, which you will see in shops and even in the tourist office. There is a small **Museo Marítimo** in Calle Gijón, with ship models and old maps. Luanco has two beaches close to the centre, but there are quieter ones around the tip of the peninsula, at **Cabo Peñas**: the prettiest, Playa de Ferrero and Playa de Llumere, are found on either side of the cape.

At the opposite side of the peninsula is **Avilés,** another large and friendly industrial town with disheartening sprawl that includes a dilapidated steel mill covered in red dust, right across the *ría*. But unlike Gijón, Avilés has an well-preserved historic centre worth exploring: this medieval town still has a copy of its *fueros*, its charter of rights, kept proudly in the Ayuntamiento. Look especially for the arcaded **Plaza de España**, and the expressively sculpted 16th-century fountain, **Caños de San Francisco**, in little Plaza San Nicolás, next to the 13th-century church of **San Nicolás de Bari**. Inside, among the tombs, note the one to favourite son Pedro Menéndez de Avilés, who founded St Augustine, Florida, the oldest city in the U. S. Avilés can be a pretty lively place at night, especially in the *chigres* and clubs around Calle Galiana, on the western side of the lovely town park, the **Parque de Ferrera**. This was the garden of the Marqués de Ferrera, whose refined 17th-century palace still stands at the edge, across from the Ayuntamiento. Just north of Avilés, an old lighthouse guards the entrance to the *ría*, at **San Juan de Nieva**, and a long, gorgeous beach at **Salinas**.

✆ (98–)   *Where to Stay and Eating Out*

Gijón

Most people don't stay in Gijón, though for an overnight stop there's no shortage of choice. The ★★★★**Parador Molino Viejo**, Avda. T. Fernández Miranda, in the pretty Parque Isabel La Católica, ✆ 537 05 11, @ 537 02 23 (*expensive*), has the best rooms in town with all the usual facilities (except a pool, but the beach is a 10-minute walk) and serves Asturian suppers in its restaurant. A good place in the centre is the ★**Asturias**, located on the quiet, enclosed Plaza Mayor, ✆ 535 06 00 (*moderate*). The cheapest *hostal* in Gijón is the ★**Hs Narcea**, ✆ 539 32 87,with seven basic, bathless rooms for 2200 pts.

Touristically Gijón may have little going for it, but at least it has some of the best restaurants in Asturias. **La Pondala** on Avda. Dionisio Cifuentes 27, in the suburb of Somió, ✆ 536 11 60 (*expensive*) has been going for nearly a hundred years. Specialities are the rice and seafood dishes—try the *arroz con almejas* and the delicious *merluza rellena de mariscos* (hake filled with shellfish), or, for more conservative palates, straightforward dishes like roast beef with potatoes, washed down with some vintage wines. You have a choice of three smart dining rooms, and in summer, dining on the garden terrace (closed Thurs). Also in Somió you'll find **Las Delicias**, Barrio Fuejo by the Evaristo Valle museum, *©* 536 02 27 (*expensive*), another long-established upmarket eaterie which mixes surf and turf—*lubina al horno* (sea-bass from the oven), *medallones de solomillo, escalopines de ternera a la sidra*—and very good service (closed Tues). For something kinder on the pocket but just as interesting to the taste buds, go to **Torremar**, C/ Ezcurdia 120 (one block back from the beach), *©* 533 01 73 (*moderate*) serving seafood and Asturian dishes including *fabes con almejas*—broad beans with clams(!). For a less ambitious dinner the area around the Plaza Mayor is definitely the place to go; try the convivial **Sidrería Plaza Mayor** on C/ Recoletas; 1500 pts for fish and cider, and the very similar **Casa Fernando** next door; the *cazuela*'s nice here, and they do *bacalao* most days too.

Avilés

This unlikely destination has a few good restaurants—**San Félix**, Avda. de los Telares 48, *©* 556 51 46, an old *sidrería* that is now a restaurant in classic Spanish style, serving classic seafood (sea-bass in champagne, no less) for around 5000 pts. At least stop for a drink at the **Café Colón**, C/ de la Muralla, the town's gathering spot where Avilés's history is spelled out in modern murals.

Oviedo

The modern capital of Asturias, Oviedo is a working town though one with little of Gijón's gritty charm. It does have a fine cathedral, a university almost 400 years old, and two of Europe's most exquisite pre-Romanesque churches, built when the rest of the continent was still living in the Dark Ages. Founded by Fruela I in 757, as a fortress guarding the key road over the mountains to the coast, Oviedo became the capital of Christian Spain when Alfonso II 'el Casto' (the Chaste) built himself a palace in 810, and stayed capital until the Asturian kings conquered León in 1002.

The city suffered terribly in the insurrection of 1934 and during the Civil War. It used to earn a living from the surrounding coal and iron mines, but today Oviedo definitely has the look of a place where people stamp papers for a living. It continues to take up a variety of causes—walls are covered with graffiti encouraging the revival of *el Bable*; a helter-skelter mix of pro-abortion, 'Viva la Virgen' and 'Europa Blanca' rally posters are pasted side-by-side on the walls of the numerous *chigres*.

Getting Around

By train: Oviedo has three train stations, all near the centre of town. The RENFE station, with frequent connections to Gijón and less frequent links to León, Barcelona, Burgos, Zaragoza, Pamplona (talgos/high-speed trains), and to Madrid, Valladolid and Palencia, is at the head of the main street C/ Uría, *©* 524 33 64. FEVE trains to Santander depart from the neighbouring station on C/ Económicas,

℀ 528 01 50; trains for Pravia and the western coast to El Ferrol leave from the other FEVE station, on C/ de la Gascona near the cathedral, ℀ 521 90 26.

By bus: Most buses, including those of ALSA, the biggest company, with services throughout Asturias and to Madrid, Sevilla, Barcelona, Valladolid and Valencia as well as Paris, Geneva, Zürich and Brussels, set off from Pza. Primo de Rivera, at the end of C/ de Fray Ceferino near the train station; ℀ 528 12 00. Buses to nearby villages in Asturias depart from the FEVE station for Santander.

By car: Parking can be a pain in Oviedo, as can getting around in general. Almost all of the old centre is closed to traffic; as a last resort there is a parking garage underneath the Campo de San Francisco.

Tourist Information

Pza. de Alfonso II El Casto 6, just by the cathedral, ℀ (98) 521 33 85.

The **post office** is on C/ Alonso Quintanilla; **telephones** at C/ Foncalada.

There is a **market** on Thursdays, and a flea market on Sundays, both in Plaza del Fontan.

The Cathedral

The middle of Oviedo (take C/ Uría from the station) is occupied by the tranquil, shady **Campo de San Francisco**; a typically lavish Spanish city park with fervent memorials to past litterati, grand promenades, exotic trees carefully labelled, ducks to feed, and children getting ice cream all over their best clothes. From here C/ San Francisco leads to the oldest part of the city, and the asymmetrical **Cathedral**, an attractive Gothic temple from the 14th century, its lovely tower with its delicate stone latticework Oviedo's landmark. King Fruela began the first church on this site when he founded the city, and Alfonso el Casto enlarged it in turn, but the current incarnation is a high Gothic work begun in 1388. In the Capilla Mayor look for an enormous florid 16th-century *retablo* of the Life of Christ sculpted by Giralte of Brussels.

Best of all, a door in the right transept leads to the original church of Alfonso el Casto, now known as the **Cámara Santa** (*open daily except Sun, 10–1 and 4–7; adm, free Mon*), strange and semi-barbaric, with fine carvings of the Apostles on the capitals of the outer chamber and disembodied heads on the walls. The upper chamber, the Capilla de San Miguel, was built by Alfonso el Casto in 802 to house the relics of Visigothic Toledo rescued after its capture by the Moors, and largely rebuilt in the 12th century. Today it contains the cathedral's precious treasures: the *Cruz de la Victoria*, supposedly borne by Pelayo at Covadonga, and pictured today on Asturias's coat of arms; the *Cruz de los Angeles* (808), a golden cross embedded with huge rubies and carved gems, reputedly made by the angels themselves and donated by Alfonso II; and a beautiful, silver-plated reliquary chest of 1073. Oviedo cathedral was always famous for its collection of relics—a phial of the Virgin Mary's milk and one of Judas' thirty pieces of silver; most of these are kept here too.

Behind the cathedral the old convent of San Vicente houses the **Museo Arqueológico** (*open 10–1.30 and 4–6, closed Mon and Sun; adm*), featuring finds from the Palaeolithic era to the days of the Asturian kingdom. There are a few attractive old streets to the south of the cathedral around the **Plaza del Fontan**, an enclosed square that was starting to fall down before restoration works were started.

The Asturian Pre-Romanesque Churches

Oviedo has the finest of Asturias's post-Visigothic pre-Romanesque churches. Enjoying the patronage of its kings, this little capital can claim the beginnings of medieval architecture, a sophisticated art that seems to have come out of nowhere in a time when most of Christian Europe was still scratching its carrot rows with a short stick. The two most important of these churches were built on Mount Naranco as part of the palace that Alfonso el Casto built for himself and Ramiro I (842–850) expanded, and it's fascinating to think of these pocket potentates throwing up a summer pleasure-dome in the hills in imitation of the great sultans of al-Andalus.

Some scholars have found a Carolingian influence in their structures, although this is hard to see. The major influence clearly comes from North Africa or the Middle East, via Christian refugees from those newly Islamicized countries. The classical pediment common atop Asturian churches was also common there; it goes back to the origins of Christian building, to the basilicas of Constantine and Theodosius in the Greek east. Hints of later Byzantine elements can be seen in many of the details, but this is all—Byzantium was 3000 miles away. The only building anywhere that has anything in common with Santa María de Naranco and its unusual plan is a unique, mysterious little chapel in central Italy called the Tempio del Clitunno, built a century earlier. Even with these influences, much in these provocative prototypes that never made it to the assembly line is original and beautiful. In 1985 UNESCO declared them the best architecture produced in 9th-century Christian Europe, to be protected as part of the 'Patrimony of Humanity'.

Alfonso el Casto built the oldest of these, **San Julián de Los Prados** (also called *Santullano*), northeast of the centre; C/ de Martínez Vigil will take you there from the back of the cathedral (*open daily exc Mon, 11–1 and 4.30–7; Nov–April, 12–1 only*). This is a simple, solid building with three square apses, a secret compartment in the wall, and interesting murals by an artist who learned his craft from studying monuments left by the Romans.

However, if you're pressed for time, head in the opposite direction up the Cuesta de Naranco, a hill overlooking the town (facing the RENFE station, turn left to the sign at the bridge over the tracks and continue 3km; city bus no. 6 makes cameo appearances as well, starting from C/ Gil de Jaz, between the station and the Campo San Francisco). The two churches here, **Santa María de Naranco** and **San Miguel de Lillo**, can be found halfway up the mountain with a view over Oviedo (*open in summer 9.30–1 and 3–7, winter (mid-Oct–April),10–1 and 3–5, closed Sun; adm*). You may get to see the interiors if the notoriously unpleasant women who guard the site are in a good mood. Both of these churches were built by Alfonso el Casto's successor, Ramiro I; incredibly, the perfectly proportioned Santa María is believed to have been part of the king's summer palace. Built of a fair golden stone and set in a small clearing, it is an enchanting building, supported by unusual flat buttresses and flanked by two porches. The lower level is believed to have served as a waiting chamber and bath; the upper, with a rough hewn altar on the porch, was the main hall. Inside are blind arches of subtly decreasing height, topped by round medallions.

Just up the road, San Miguel is a more traditional cruciform church, although of stunted proportions after an ancient amputation removed two thirds of the original length. Its round windows are adorned with beautiful stone traceries, and what the guides claim is a circus scene is carved on the door jamb, along with some Visigothic arabesques.

Oviedo ℂ (98–)   **Where to Stay**

expensive

 A couple of blocks from the Parque de San Francisco, a lovely 17th-century palace has been converted into the ★★★★★**Hotel de la Reconquista**, C/ Gil de Jaz 16, ℂ 524 11 00, @ 84 32 80, a plush luxury hotel of the highest order, and highest prices; all rooms with satellite TV and air conditioning. **Gran Hotel España**, C/ Jovellanos 2, ℂ 522 05 96, is elegant and conveniently situated downtown. For half as much ★★★**La Gruta**, on the west end of town at Alto de Buenavista, ℂ 523 24 50, @ 525 31 41, is snazzy, immaculate and offers the best views in town.

moderate

Best options in this category include ★**Favila**, near the cathedral at C/ Uría 37, ℂ 525 38 77, ★★**México**, on the same street at no. 25, ℂ 524 04 04, and **La Ovetense**, C/ San Juan 6, ℂ 522 08 40.

inexpensive

These cluster on and around C/ Uría, near the RENFE station. One of the best is the family-run ★**Hs Belmonte**, C/ Uría 3, ℂ 524 10 20. If they're full, try ★★**Hs Alteza**, ℂ 524 04 04, down the street at no. 25. ★**Hs Aramo**, at C/ Independencia 24, ℂ 524 10 04, is acceptable and the cheapest in town. It would be more fun to stay in the old centre, notably at the ★★**Hs Arcos**, ℂ 521 47 73 (*cheap*), just off the Plaza Mayor on C/ Magdalena; some rooms with bath.

Eating Out

There are plenty of restaurants and tapas bars in Oviedo, but the oldest and best is **Casa Fermín** near the park at San Francisco 8, ℂ 521 64 52 (*expensive*), offering classic Asturian cuisine, and seasonal Spanish regional dishes, in a refined atmosphere, (2900-pts *menú*). If it's full the more recent **Trascorrales**, Pza. de Trascorrales 19, ℂ 522 24 41, in a charming building (in a tiny square hidden behind the Ayuntamiento), offers the same with a flair to delight gourmets—try the *lubina a la sidra*, sea-bass in a cider-based sauce; for a splurge there is a 5000-pts *menú gastronómico* with a little bit of everything (closed Sun). In the same plaza, **El Raitán**, ✆ 521 42 18, specializes in grilled meats—a dozen different kinds, on the special 3400-pts *menú de carnes* in the evening.

Hearty Asturian stews and good *fabada* bubble away at the popular **Mesón del Labrador** on C/ de Argüelles near the cathedral (*inexpensive*) which has a *sidra* bar in a garden downstairs. As for good cheaper places, ring us collect if you find one that's interesting; we certainly couldn't.

Entertainment and Nightlife

Oviedo is one of the few places you will find anything beyond the usual all-night drinking and chattering. It's the centre of Asturian rock, and you can see what the local groups are getting up to in the desperate-looking clubs such as **Padlock,** all along C/ Rosal, one street south of the Campo de San Francisco and the University. Otherwise, the action is on the nearby streets in the old town, with more clubs and bars for the younger set: Pza. Riego, Pza. del Fontan, C/Canóniga and C/ Ildefonso Martínez. Asturian separatists hang out at **Xalabam**, C/ Postigo Alto 8; there are many discos in this area, of which **Berlin** most successfully avoids Spanish pop. One fun place is the **Cervecería Asturianu** on C/ Carta Puebla, with every different kind of beer and whiskey imaginable, with décor that includes pieces of the Berlin Wall. For simply drinking and chattering, the best bet is the informal places around Fontan where tables magically appear on the street every sundown, or else **Salsipuedes**, with an outdoor terrace on Ildefonso Martínez.

Western Asturias

The principality, beyond the coast and the Picos, is terra incognita for most foreigners—a hilly, wooded land of small mining-towns and agricultural villages, crisscrossed with walking paths. Much of it is protected, especially in the national hunting preserves that cover the northern slopes of the Cordillera Cantábrica. The coast is excellent—rugged cliffs, few tourists, plenty of shellfish and beaches everywhere. Public transport is limited throughout the area, and you'd do well to rent a car—and pack a big lunch—before setting out. Be sure to pick up one of the large detailed maps at the tourist office in Oviedo.

Getting Around

By bus: all the main towns can be reached by bus. ALSA buses from Oviedo, Pza. Primo de Rivera, ✆ 528 12 20, go to Salas, Puerto de Somiedo, Cangas del Narcea, Tineo and Pola de Allande. Empresa Fernández, Llamaquique, Oviedo, ✆ 523 83 90, has buses to Mieres, Pola de Lena, and Turón; there are also a half dozen or so a day down the western coast to Cudillero and Luarca, and as many from Gijón. Alcotán, C/ Padre Suárez 27, Oviedo, ✆ 421 76 17, has buses to Pola de Laviana. The RENFE train between Oviedo and León stops at Pajares and Pola de Lena.

By car: if you're driving when the snow is flying, it's essential to call ahead for road conditions, ✆ 525 46 11. If you want to rent a car, the main companies in Oviedo are along C/ Ventura Rodríguez, where you can shop around for the best deal.

Salas: Pza. Castillo ✆ (98) 583 09 88
Tuñón: Santa Adriano, ✆ (98) 576 10 61
Tineo: Calle Mayor, ✆ (98) 580 01 87
Cangas del Narcea: ✆ (98) 581 17 21

There are **markets** in Mieres on Sundays; Pola de Siera on Tuesdays; Tineo on Thursdays, and Cangas del Narcea on Saturdays.

Around Oviedo: Miners' Valleys and More Churches

Southeast of Oviedo, the AS 244 passes **Langreo** and **Pola de Laviana**, both typical Asturian copper-mining towns, on its way to Reres National Reserve and the beautiful mountain pass, **Puerto de Tarna**. From a point just south, a lonely mountain path leads up to **Beleño**, on the edge of the Picos de Europa, where the reward is a fine panorama over the mountains. The next pass to the west, **Puerto San Isidro**, has a major ski installation (both passes can be reached by bus from Pueblo de Lillo in León province). **Coyanzo**, some 12km below the pass, is set near an idyllic little gorge, the **Hoces de Río Aller**.

Black vulture

Directly south of Oviedo, along the train route and recently built highway to León (an engineering marvel Spain is not a little proud of), the views become increasingly magnificent as you the ascend to the dramatic **Puerto de Pajares**, another ski spot on the border with Léon. But before you get there, look for the signs 6km south of **Pola de Lena** for another of Ramiro I's lovely churches, the hilltop **Santa Cristina de Lena**, a cruciform temple built around 845, with blind arches similar to Santa María de Naranco, Visigothic decorations and an intricate iconostasis of Mozarabic inspiration (the key is available in the house below by the bridge). The landmark in this part of the Cantabrian mountains is the jagged-peaked 7855ft **Peña Ubiña**, which sturdy walkers can tackle in around 4 or 5 hours from **Tuiza de Arriba** for incomparable views over the Picos de Europa and Somiedo (to reach Tuiza, take the side road from the highway at Campomanes.) From Pajares, you can make the much shorter climb up the 1861m **Pico de los Celleros**.

Up to the *Cordillera*, and Somiedo National Park

Southwest of Oviedo, in the highest part of the Cantabrian mountains, is the wild **Reserva Nacional de Somiedo**, where boars roam and deer and bears play on the banks of 18 glacial lakes. One approach to it is by way of **Trubia**, a village known mostly for its huge armament works. Ten km south of Trubia on the road to the park you can stop at **Tuñón** for one of the last of the 'Asturian' churches, **San Adrián**, built by Alfonso III (866–910). Sombre in design and Mozarabic in style, it features clerestory windows and pretty lattice-work crosses. Inside are some of the oldest frescoes anywhere in Spain, traces of what seem to be sun symbols over the altar and zig-zag motifs taken straight from the Grand Mosque of Córdoba. The lady in the tobacco shop opposite has the key, but the only guide is the unusually friendly bat that lives in the choir.

The Dress Rehearsal

 The event of the century in Asturias was the epic miners' revolt of 1934, a full-scale battle that eerily prefigured the Spanish Civil War. Because of the large numbers of workers in mining and industry, Asturias in the early part of this century was politically the odd man out, an island of belligerent Marxists with millenarian fantasies in the middle of the arch-conservative northwest. Mining and metalworking go way back in Asturias, but they really took off at the beginning of this century, when *indianos* forced home by Spain's loss of Cuba and the Philippines began to invest their money here. In the First World War, Spanish neutrality made for a boom in the mining areas, one which quickly collapsed in the '20s, leaving Asturias with the angriest, most radicalized proletariat in Spain.

Along with the Basques and Catalans, Asturians were strong supporters of the Republic when it appeared in 1931 but, for many of their leaders, the new regime was only a stepping-stone on the way to Socialism. The depression increased popular discontent, but what really set the workers boiling was the radical right-wing national government elected in 1934. Under Prime Minister Gil Robles, it began dismantling all the reforms of its leftist predecessors, and openly postured for the restoration of the monarchy.

On 4 October 1934, the UGT and CNT trade unions declared a general strike in Asturias in protest. Barcelona and Madrid rose up at the same time but failed to follow through, leaving the Asturians on their own, and in a fighting mood. The main centres of the revolt were Mieres, Sama and Oviedo, but it was the munitions works at Trubia, which you'll pass on the way to Somiedo, that turned the strike into a war. The workers occupied it and seized some 30,000 rifles inside. Soon there was a 30,000-man 'Red Army', and a revolutionary committee was formed to govern the province.

The government sent in a dependable general named Mola, leading a force made up mainly of Moroccan troops—northern Morocco was still a Spanish protectorate. The

Moors were mercenaries who had fought against their own people, but they were fiercely loyal to their commander, a certain Francisco Franco. Franco, a Galician married to an Asturian woman, felt right at home. He had already led troops, using the Spanish Foreign Legion, to crush a general strike in Asturias in 1917. The Legion was also present in 1934. An outfit not much like the romantic French version, this one was now led by a fascist psychopath named Millan Astray, famous for his missing arm and eye-patch. Its motto was 'Long Live Death!' and the legionnaires did their best to live up to it in Asturias. As for the Moors, some of them must have enjoyed the irony of a Spanish commander, an heir to Pelayo, bringing them to a place where they hadn't set foot for a thousand years.

The government had to make its point, and the revolt was crushed quickly and with the utmost ferocity. Many of the mining towns were thoroughly wrecked, and the troops slaughtered nearly 1300 Asturians in reprisals after the surrender on 19 October. A year and a half later, after new elections brought the leftist Popular Front to power, the coup that began the Civil War started with the same cast of characters: General Mola, who was to be the new dictator, but who died in an air crash at the start; the Foreign Legion; and the inevitable Francisco Franco, whose Moroccans won him the title of *caudillo* (leader). The best-equipped and trained forces in Spain, they used their practice in Asturias to get the jump on the disorganized government and citizens' militias, and gained control of much of Spain within a month, an advantage that helped assure the Nationalists' final victory.

Further south, **Proaza** has a number of medieval buildings; it is separated from the next village, **Caranga**, by a pretty gorge you can walk through, the **Desfiladero del Teverga**. The road continues south through **La Plaza**, site of the interesting 12th-century **Colegiata de San Pedro**, where elements of Asturian pre-Romanesque combine with early French Romanesque; on the capitals are sculpted local animals, and there are two 18th-century mummies.

From La Plaza, the road south cuts through a magnificent forest to the Puerto Ventana, perhaps the least-used Asturian mountain pass. Just on the other side of the pass, from the Leonese village of **Torrestio** you can hike in three hours into the lovely heart of Somiedo and its mysterious lakes, where *xanas*, or mermaids, guard the sunken treasures they use to please their lovers on the night of St John. The first lake, **Lago de la Cueva**, is the source of the Río Sil; the third and largest is the eerie, dark **Lago Negro**. Somiedo isn't really a park, but a hunting preserve. Despite all the mining this part of the Cordillera Cantábrica is one of the most unspoiled and natural in Spain. For one thing, it has a healthy population of bears (there are almost none in the Pyrenees) and even a few wolves; both are protected by law though they have few friends among the farmers and shepherds. Somiedo also has plenty of deer and boar, chamois and many species of eagle, kite, harrier and buzzard, including the rare lammergeyer or headed vulture, the largest bird of prey in Europe—a thoroughly startling sight, with its black wings, fierce expression, and habit of dropping bones on rocks from high altitudes to break them open to suck the marrow.

A second approach to Somiedo is via the N 634, the main road west from Oviedo. This will take you through the fat village of **Grado**, where everybody comes on Wednesday and Sunday for the markets, and **Salas**, with its medieval monuments and palaces, as well as the fine Renaissance **Colegiata de Santa María**, where the prize is the beautiful alabaster tomb of the Inquisitor Valdés-Salas. The surrounding countryside is rich in picturesque *hórreos* (granaries), and to the west are the lovely pasturelands and hills around **Navelgas** and **Bárcena del Monasterio**, where the *vaqueros* (*see below*) winter their herds.

From Salas you can head south and follow the valley of the Pigüeña to the Somiedo Park. The big village in this iron-mining area is **Belmonte de Miranda** (C-633); a curiosity in the region is the **Machuco de Alvariza** (near Belmonte village), an oak-built hydraulic hammer used in the 18th-century iron works. Many *vaqueros* still live in the vicinity— some of their conical-roofed *pallozas* (huts), along with several Celtic *castros* (hill-forts) lie further up towards **Pola de Somiedo**, the chief town in the district. Pola de Somiedo stands at the head of the four-hour path to Somiedo's fourth lake, the **Lago del Valle**, passing several *pallozas* on the way. South of Pola are the ancient thatch-roofed hamlets of **Santa María de Puerto** and the remote **La Pornacal** (trail from Villar de Vildas).

West of Oviedo: Ancient Pottery and Primaeval Forests

Back on the main route west from Oviedo, after Salas the next village is **Tineo**, a great trout-fishing area crossed by a branch of the Santiago pilgrimage route. A number of medieval churches survive from that era—Tineo's 13th-century parish church and the ruined monastery and church of San Miguel in nearby **Obona**. Further south a dirt road leads up to the tiny borough of **Llamas del Mouro**, where potters, isolated from the rest of the world, still create the shiny black ceramic jugs and bowls made by their Celto-Iberian ancestors. The pieces are fired in the ancient style, in circular ovens buried in the earth. Three of these are still in use.

Cangas del Narcea, the largest town in southwest Asturias, is modern and has little to waylay you; head instead further south to **Pico de la Masa** (near Puerto del Connio) for the view over the magnificent 5000-hectare **Bosque de Muniellos**, one of Europe's last and most extensive forests of primeval oak and beech. A strictly protected wildlife preserve, the forest is the last refuge in the world of the rare *urogallo*, a funny-looking kind of capercaillie with red eyebrows. The trail through the forest begins at **Tablizas**, a short hike from Moal; the hike takes about five-and-a-half hours and will leave you mourning for the ancient times, when (they say) a squirrel could cross the whole of Iberia without ever touching the ground. Like Altamira, Muniellos is accounted such a threatened treasure that only 20 people a day are allowed in it; write in advance to the Agencia de Medio Ambiente del Principado de Asturias, 1 Plaza General Ordóñez, Oviedo 33007. East of Muniellos lies the **Reserva Nacional de Degaña**, another lovely, wooded area, with pretty meadows and small lakes formed by glaciers. In the Roman era, Degaña was heavily mined for its gold.

Gold was also mined in the most westerly zone of the province, around **Pola de Allande** and **Grandas de Salime**, both enchanting, seldom visited villages. Grandas has a partially

Romanesque church, San Salvador, and a **Museo Etnográfico y Escuela de Artesanía**, with exhibits on country life in old Asturias and craftworkers present weaving, making baskets and carving wood. In **Celón**, 5km from Pola, there's a fine 12th-century church, **Santa María**, with good frescoes and carvings. One of Asturias' best-preserved Celtic *castros* is up on **Pico San Chuis** to the west near Berducedo, whose ancient inhabitants, like the modern, exploited the region's minerals.

✆ *(98–)*   *Where to Stay and Eating Out*

There are hotels and *hostales* in the villages along the N 634, but up towards the Somiedo Park expect only *casas particulares* and not a lot of those.

Mieres

Mieres, on the Oviedo–León road, offers a good stopover at ★★Hs **Villa de Mieres**, C/ Teodoro Cuesta 33, ✆ 546 70 04 (*inexpensive*), and good home cooking in modern, smart surroundings at **Casa Villa**, C/ Aller, ✆ 546 00 33, serving Asturian favourites for around 3000 pts.

Salas

Salas is a convenient stopover on the N 634, with a few inexpensive *hostales* over bars. The ★★**Castillo de Valdés**, Pza. General Aranda, ✆583 10 37, is a restored 16th-century palace (*rooms moderate*); its restaurant is the local dining hot spot, serving imaginative Asturian dishes, including locally fished salmon, for around 2500 pts. There are basic **campgrounds** within the Somiedo Park at Valle de Lago and Saliencia.

Cangas del Narcea

Cangas has the widest range of choices in this region. The best places to stay are the ★**Peña Grande**, out on the main road, ✆ 581 23 92 (*moderate*), with a restaurant; the ★**Hs Acebo**, C/ Hermanos Flórez 1, ✆ 581 00 66; and the small ★★**Hs Virgen del Carmen**, C/ Mayor 46, ✆ 581 15 02, with eight inexpensive rooms.

Tineo

Here you'll find three *hostales*, each with only a handful of rooms: ★★**Don Miguel**, El Viso, ✆ 580 03 25, and ★**Casa Lula**, El Crucero, ✆ 580 16 00; both have rooms for around 7000 pts. The least expensive *hostal* in Tineo, ★★**Hs Casa Sole**, on the main road, ✆ 580 60 44, offers nice rooms with or without baths.

Where to Ski

Valgrande Pajares, 3km from the Busdongo train station, offers 15 slopes from the very difficult to the very easy, 10 lifts and two chairlifts (✆ 549 61 23). The closest hotels are in León province, at La Pola de Gordón and Villamanín. **San Isidro** (León province) is near Puebla de Lillo, and offers three very difficult runs in the Cebolledo circuit, as well as five of average difficulty and four easy ones; there's a chair lift and seven ski lifts, ✆ 73 50 66. There are a couple of hotels at Puebla de Lillo, but no public transport. Other ski installations in the area are at San Emiliano, on the slopes of Peña Ubiña, at **Lietariegos Pass**, and **Maraña**, near Riaño in León.

Asturias' Western Coast

The Asturian coast west of Avilés could well be the best chance in this book for a peaceful and agreeable seaside holiday. The shoreline itself does not seem dramatic until you see it close up—wild cliffs of jumbled, glittering metamorphic rock, mixed in with long stretches of beach where you can easily find uncrowded spots even on August weekends. Cudillero and Luarca happen to be two of the most delightful seaside villages on earth, and there are plenty of isolated beaches all along the rugged coast between them.

Tourist Information

Cudillero: Pza. de San Pedro, ✆ (98) 559 01 18
Luarca: Pza. Alfonso X el Sabio, ✆ (98) 564 00 83.
Navia: El Parque, ✆ (98) 547 37 95
Tapia de Casariego: Pza. Constitución, ✆ (98) 562 82 05
Castropol: Carretera General, ✆ (98) 563 51 13
Taramundi: Hotel La Rectoral, ✆ (98) 564 67 60

There are **markets** in Cudillero and Navia on Fridays; Tapia de Casariego on Mondays and Fridays.

Cudillero and Luarca

The first resort west of Avilés, **Cudillero** is well-protected from the tourist hordes by its geography; the only way into this fishing village is its narrow, cobbled main street, which snakes down almost vertically for two miles before reaching the impossibly picturesque little harbour at the bottom of the cliffs. There are few hotels but, except for the summer days when it fills up with Madrileño day trippers, Cudillero would be a perfect place to hide out for a few days. If you have a car you can find plenty of good beaches nearby, especially the broad **Playa de la Cueva** (visible from a high viaduct on the coast highway, though in fact miles away from it).

Asturias has no shortage of souvenirs. The most common things you'll see are traditional wooden clogs, or *madreñas*, but recently the hot item seems to be whole cow hides; the roadside stand by the viaduct has a wide selection.

Luarca, with its sheltered harbour at the mouth of the Río Negro, is a little more tourist-orientated, but it is still in every respect the most satisfactory place for a holiday on Spain's northern coast. The village was an important place in medieval times, first as a whaling port and then from trade with the Americas. The best way to see it is to follow the first signposted road in from the east—a back road that will take you to the cemetery, high on a cliff with a stunning view over the village below. Luarca is still an important fishing port, mostly for tuna, and the harbourfront ensemble makes a pretty photograph. Old Luarca stretches inland from there, with some stately palaces from the 17th and 18th centuries, and some old quarters with narrow alleys climbing up the steep hills. There is a quite acceptable beach right in the centre of Luarca, but for something special head for **Playa del Barayo**, a beautiful natural area west of Luarca, with many species of waterfowl in the woods nearby.

The *Vaqueros*

The territory around Luarca is the land of the *vaqueros*, one of Iberia's marginal peoples, first mentioned in Middle Ages. The *vaqueros* were cowherds who spent half of the year in the mountain pastures with their cattle, transporting all of their worldly goods in ox carts and building *pallozas* (huts with conical thatched roofs), which you can still see in rural regions further inland. Although ostracized from society (in most parishes they weren't even allowed to hear Mass inside a church or be buried in holy ground), they themselves claimed to be far older than God, and returned disdain for disdain. Recent research based on their dialect places them as first-century AD immigrants from Italy. Those still living around Luarca have traded in their ox carts for pick-ups, though curiously enough, Franco, abolisher of so many ancient Spanish festivals, inaugurated a new one, ostensibly to preserve their customs, in the form of a 'Vaquero wedding' in La Braña de Aristébano, 6km south of Luarca. On the last Sunday in July, prominent citizens are chosen to play the parts of the Vaqueros, who are duly married and escorted home with a procession that includes the neatly made matrimonial bed pulled by oxen.

Continuing westwards, **Navia** is the next fishing village. Southwest of here at **Coaña** you can visit the extensive remains of another Celtic *castro*—foundations of stone walls, paved streets and the circular foundations of houses. The similarity between these and the *vaquero* huts led some to believe that the *vaqueros* were a lost Celtic tribe. Near the main road, there's a monolith carved with the star symbol so widespread in northern Spain. The Asturian coast ends with **Castropol**, another attractive fishing port sheltered on the broad Ría de Ribadeo. Inland, south beyond Vegadeo, tiny **Taramundi** up on the mountains has long been famous for the manufacture of knives; pocket knives with carved and painted wooden handles made here are another popular Asturian souvenir.

Ⓒ *(98–)*   ***Where to Stay and Eating Out***

Cudillero

Cudillero isn't ready to become a resort yet; there are fewer than 150 beds in town and they may all be full in summer. The best place to sleep is an old inn, **★La Lupa**, in San Juan de la Piñera (2km east of the village), Ⓒ 559 00 63 (*moderate*). In the village itself, there's **★San Pablo**, C/ Suárez Inclán, Ⓒ 559 11 55 (*moderate*), and not much else; ask around the bars for *casas particulares*, though if you have a car you'll see plenty of modest *hostales* hanging their signs out on the roads into the village. Restaurants line the tiny harbour: the **Taberna del Puerto**, ℂ 559 04 77 (*moderate*), with excellent seafood, and the less expensive **El Remo**, which does a good *paella*.

In a lovely setting with a view of the sea and mountains, Concha de Artedo has one of the many pretty beaches in the area (off the coastal road west of Cudillero): **Casa Marino**, ℂ 559 01 86, serves top-class seafood, and a memorable *zarzuela de mariscos y pescados* (shellfish and fish casserole) for around 3500 pts. East of Cudillero at Playa de Aguilar, **Azpiazu**, ℂ 558 32 10 (*moderate*) also specializes in seafood, and has a breezy summer terrace where you can tuck into shellfish soup, hake and cider-marinated main courses.

Luarca

The one swanky hotel is the bright, central and airy **★★★Gayoso**, Pza. Gómez, ℂ 564 00 54 (*moderate*). The few others are nearby, including the **★Hs Oria**, around the corner on C/ Crucero; clean rooms with bath (*inexpensive*). A bit dearer but still good, the **★Hs Rico** is nearby on Pza. Alfonso X, ℂ 564 17 19 (*inexpensive*). The closest campground is the inexpensive **Los Cantiles** at Villar, on the cliffs above Luarca, ℂ 564 09 38. As at Cudillero, for dinner you need look no further than the row of seafood restaurants that line the harbour; nearly all of them have outside tables to enjoy the view. **La Mesón del Mar**, on the far end, offers a wonderful seafood *menú gastronómico* with a bit of everything in the day's catch, well worth the 3800 pts. The least expensive on the harbour (no tables outside) is a good one: **La Dársena**, where a full dinner costs about 2100 pts. One of the best hotel-restaurants in the area is 6km west of town on the N 634, the **★★Casa Consuelo** at Otur, ℂ 564 08 44 (*moderate*), where the food served in the large dining-rooms attracts people from miles around with classic Asturian *fabada* and cider (1500-pts *menú*).

Figueras del Mar

At the farthest western limit of Asturias, near Castropol, you'll find the region's loveliest hotel, the **★★Palacete Peñalba**, El Cotarelo, ℂ 563 61 25 (*expensive*). Set in a glorious Art Nouveau mansion designed by a follower of Gaudí, it is a listed monument, and retains its gardens and much of its original furnishings; all rooms have TV and minibar.

Old Castile and León

Burgos cathedral

Old Castile and León encompasses two ancient kingdoms of Spain and the *meseta*—a flat, semi-arid table-top 700–1000m above sea level—where the climate, summed up in an old Castilian proverb, is nine months of winter and three months of hell. It looks like no other place in Europe: endless rolling dun-coloured plains, spotted with scrub and patches of mountains, but few trees; during the mindless free-for-all of the Reconquista nearly all of the forests were axed. Depending on your mood you will find the *meseta* romantic and picturesque, or brooding and eerie, but you'll never forget it. From this unlikely land, however, came the culture, language, and people who would dominate in

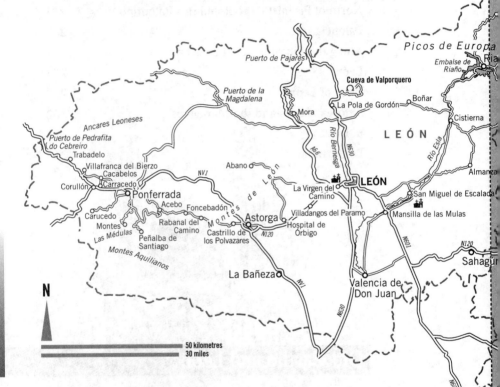

their day not only the nations of Iberia, but a good part of two continents. Even today Burgos, seat of the first counts of Castile, is the headquarters of all that is pure Castilian and *castizo*, down to proper lisping pronunciation of the name of Castile's hero, the Cid, or 'El Theed'.

In early times Castile not only resembled America's Far West, but played the same kind of frontier rôle twice in European history. After the Romans whipped the native Iberians, retired legionaries were given land to raise wheat (any place named *Quintanilla* recalls one of their settlements, as in *quinta*, a rural villa or farm). The Visigoths followed in their tracks, but the Moors found little to like in Old Castile and conquered it without settling it. The Christian kingdoms to the north erected a string of border fortifications that gave the region its name Castile ('land of castles') sometime around 800. In 882 the first part of Castile was reconquered by Alfonso III of Asturias; two years later, Diego Porcelos founded Burgos and became the first count of Castile. According to the medieval *Romance de Fernán González*, the Good

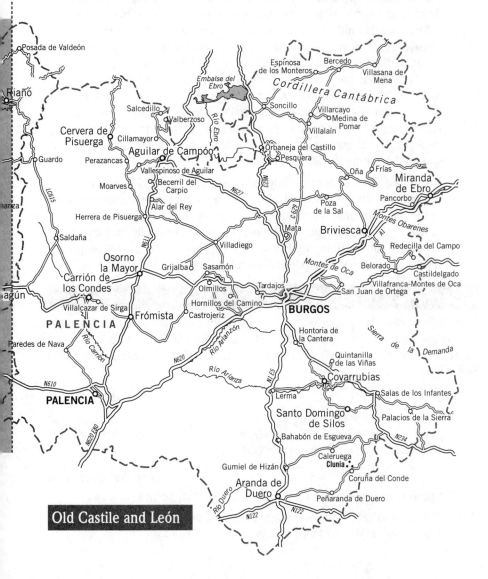

Old Castile and León

Count Fernán González obtained Castile's independence from Asturias-León in the 10th century by selling the king of Asturias a horse and goshawk. The king, lacking any handy cash, promised Fernán González he'd pay him double the price for every day that he didn't pay. The king forgot his promise, but by the time Fernán González reminded him, the sum was so extraordinary that all the king could do was give him Castile.

Fernán González formed his fledging state politically into seven counties, the *Antiguas Merindades de Castilla*. Unlike the feudal Christian kingdoms to the north, where the land was owned by great lords, or the Church, or the military orders, Castile was settled by free men or *hidalgos*, each of whom owned their farms and bore the responsibility for defending them. The difficulties in repopulating vast expanses of empty land was greatly eased by the development of the *camino de Santiago* (the medieval road equivalent of the Union-Pacific, America's first transcontinental railroad), especially after Castile was 'tamed' by the reconquest of Toledo by Alfonso VI and the Cid in 1085. It set off a medieval boom: settlers moved in, churches, hostels, hospitals and towns sprouted all along the length of the road.

Northwest Spain's includes only the oldest parts of Castilla y León, the provinces of Burgos, Palencia, and León, a region that encompasses some of the most striking, weird and unknown landscapes in Spain. In between are picturesque little towns that have been collecting dust since Charles V sucked them dry in the 16th century; others have changed little since the medieval pilgrims wended their way to Compostela.

Approaches To Burgos

This section covers the approaches to Burgos from the east and north, whether you're coming in slowly along the pilgrims' road from La Rioja, quickly on the *autopista* from Bilbao, or through the magnificent mountains scenery of the Cantabrian range from Santander.

Getting Around

There are frequent buses from Burgos to Belorado and less frequently to Miranda de Ebro, a major railway junction. At least one bus a day goes up to Briviesca, Oña, Frías, Espinosa de los Monteros, and Poza de la Sal.

Tourist Information

Miranda de Ebro: on the Madrid–Irún road, ✆ (947) 31 18 86.

There is **market** in Oña on Fridays; in Medina de Pomar on Thursdays; and in Espinosa de los Monteros on Tuesdays

The pilgrimage road follows the N 120 from Santo Domingo de la Calzada (see p.111) and enters Castile at medieval **Redecilla del Campo**, built like an old strip frontier town along the road. Houses still bear their *hidalgos'* crests, but as usual the main focus is the church, **Virgen de la Calle**, not much in itself but containing a sublime 12th-century baptismal font, intricately carved with the towers and windows of a city presumed to be Jerusalem. The church in the next town, **Castildelgado**, has interesting Gothic *retablos*; while beyond, **Viloria de Rioja** conserves the font where Santo Domingo de la Calzada was baptized. Further west, the much larger, leather-making town of **Belorado** (the Belfuratus of the *Codex Calixtinus*) attracts a different kind of pilgrim these days with its factory outlets. Ruins of a monastery and a hospital recall its former vocation, along with two churches, San Pedro and Santa María, built in the 1500s in the wide, airy Catalan Gothic style. Hermits lived in the caves by **Tosantos**, around the church of the **Virgen de la Peña**, built in the wall of a cliff, while to the west, a kilometre from the walking path in Espinosa del Camino, you can see the 9th-century ruins of the Mozarab monastery of **San Félix de Oca**, where the first count of Castile, Diego Porcelos, was buried.

Just west of the Sierra de la Demanda, the deeply forested Montes de Oca (the mountains of the Goose) mark the traditional border of Castile. At their foot, **Villafranca Montes de Oca**, a town settled by Franks, was once a major pilgrims' halt; today both Franks and pilgrims have gone, leaving a church and the 14th-century Hospital de San Antón (currently undergoing restoration) to recall its glory days. A path leads up to the hermitage of the **Virgen de Oca**, a pretty, leafy place with plenty of picnic tables. At Villafranca the N 120 and the walking path split; the latter, heading up the pine-forested slopes (enjoy it: it's the last shade before the mountains west of León) eventually emerges at **San Juan de Ortega**.

San Juan de Ortega is named after Santo Domingo's architecturally-minded sidekick, who, after a pilgrimage to Jerusalem, came back to Spain determined to build chapels, bridges and hostels along the *camino*, especially in places like this, where wolves devoured more than a few pilgrims. A couple of miles from the N 120, the hamlet he founded is all but abandoned, although unlike the hostel (now *parador*) built by Santo Domingo de la Calzada, San Juan's still serves its original purpose, thanks to the local priest who feeds and lodges pilgrims. In 1142 the saint designed the church, of which most notably the apse survives, an original, elegant design of gracefully slender round columns and three receding arches around alabaster windows. Inside, San Juan is buried in a magnificent tomb, with an effigy and delightful cartoon-like scenes from his life carved in the base, crowned by an Isabelline Gothic baldachin, paid for by Isabel the Catholic herself, who got pregnant for the first time in 1477 after praying by the saint's Romanesque tomb (now down in the crypt). At 5pm, on the day of the spring and autumn equinoxes (21 March and 22 September), pilgrims come to see the *Milagro de la Luz*, when a sunbeam illuminates the womb of the lovely Virgin of the Annunciation, carved on a triple capital in the crossing. Isabel also paid for the chapel of San Nicolás, designed to hold the tomb now removed to the old church; in exchange the Renaissance grille from the old church has been installed in the chapel. Just to the west, the walking path continues to one of San Juan de Ortega's bridges in the tiny hamlet of **Agés; Atapuerca,** the next town, has prehistoric caves with simple sculptures. Beyond stretch the sprawling eastern suburbs of Burgos (*see* p.225).

To Burgos from Bilbao: the Gate of Pancorbo

The Bilbao–Madrid motorway A1 runs into Castile near **Miranda de Ebro,** a major town, but with little to see besides the glass balconies of its old houses hanging over the river. It grew up around a medieval bridge, which was replaced in 1777 by the Puente de Carlos III. The 16th-century church of Santa María is Miranda's most beautiful monument, while the Ebro itself sculpted the stunning gorge, the **Hoces del Sobrón** through the nearby Montes Obarenes.

The road, the *autopista,* and train funnel dramatically through the pass at **Pancorbo,** for V. S. Pritchett 'a place of horror, for the rock crowds in, comes down in precipitous, yellow shafts, and at the top has been tortured into frightening animal shapes by the climate'. A ruined Moorish castle and an 18th-century fort that played a role when Wellington's army chased the French through the gorge in 1813 survive above the homely, old town. Most of the Pancorbans work in the big truck stops, where drivers tuck into a bowl of *sopa castellano* to prepare themselves for their long ride in the night to beat the heat of the *meseta* beyond. Or as Pritchett put it: 'Pancorbo is the moment of conversion. Now one meets Spain, the indifferent enemy.'

El Pueblo Querido

You can learn a lot about Pancorbo ('breadbasket') in a surprisingly short time. Downhill from the painful little splotch of bars and restaurants along the N 1, Spain's Main Street, you'll find a proud and venerable *pueblo* at the gateway of Castile. It has a sight of sorts— the parish church of Santiago has a Flamboyant Gothic carved stone *custodio* that is 'probably unique in Spain'.

The centre of Pancorbo is a clutch of half-timbered buildings around a tiny Plaza Mayor. It has one bar, called *El Estrecho,* or 'the Straits' because it is situated at the point on the high street too narrow for two cars to pass; the kids come in in the afternoon to play table football. There is also a bank branch, the *Caja de Ahorros y Monte de Piedad del Círculo Católico de Burgos,* the 'Savings Bank and Holy Pawn Shop of the Catholic Circle of Burgos'. Though no longer performing the functions of an old-time *Monte de Piedad,* they will exchange the most obscure travellers' cheques with a smile, or give you a loan to fix up an old stone house. There is an office of the *Guardia Civil,* and a grocer's, on the edge of town, in a building that looks like a garage. Like every village *supermercado* in Spain, they proudly advertise *ultramarinos,* goods from 'beyond the sea' such as cellophane-wrapped slices of ham and tinned peas.

Pancorbo holds fast to its history and its traditions; every year at the fiesta, they elect a Queen and her Ladies-in-Waiting. Last year, in the *Programa Oficial de Fiestas,* one of the select, the beautiful Raquel Caño Manero, age 15, reports that she hasn't got a boyfriend yet, and there are no places to go in Pancorbo *para diver-*

tirse, to have fun. She likes every sort of music, except jazz and opera. Local poets have penned several odes to this village, including the *Himno a Pancorbo* that figures prominently each year at the fiesta. Its chorus:

> *¡Pancorbo! Lanceremos*
> *acentos de amor*
> *al pueblo querido*
> *al pueblo mejor.*
>
> *Entone Castilla*
> *un himno en su honor.*
> *En él tuvo siempre*
> *un fiel servidor.*

Between Pancorbo and Burgos, **Briviesca** on the river Oca was, until the 11th century, on the *camino francés*, before Sancho the Great prompted a change of route through Nájera. The regular rectangular plan of Briviesca, with its pleasant Plaza Mayor, was the model for several towns founded in South America; its octagonal church, **Santa Clara** (1565), has star vaulting and a florid carved *retablo mayor* (a rare, unpolychromed one, with a central figure dreaming of the tree of Jesse); another fine 16th-century *retablo* is in the Capilla de Santa Casilda in the **Colegiata de Santa María**. In 1388, the Cortes Generales of King Juan I were held in Briviesca, and here he bestowed on his eldest son, Enrique, for his wedding to Catherine of Lancaster the title of 'Prince of Asturias', a title, like that of the Prince of Wales, that has been held ever since by the heir to the Spanish throne. Farther west towards Burgos, and off the road to the right, the Benedictine Monasterio de Rodilla has vanished, leaving only its lovely Romanesque church, **Nuestra Señora del Valle**, set in a meadow with picnic tables.

Northeast Approaches: Oña

Briviesca is the chief town of the Bureba, where the foothills of the Cantabrian mountains begin. This bulge of the map in northeast Burgos province, the cradle of Old Castile, is full of curiosities and remarkable scenery; a good place to start is medieval **Oña**, '*La Villa Condal*', north of Briviesca. Founded by the Romans on the river Oca, Oña had one of the first castles of Castile and was granted its *fueros* or privileges in 950 by Fernán González, Castile's first king. In the early days, the king's travelling court often stayed here; in 1033, Sancho the Great of Navarra, heir of Castile, ordered the old royal stronghold replaced by the Benedictine **Monasterio de San Salvador**. He meant this to serve as a royal pantheon, a status he encouraged by spending his dying days in Oña.

Oña's main plaza is picturesquely laid out on three different levels. Behind an old pilgrims' cross, the monastery, rebuilt in 1640 and decorated with four squat kings who would look perfectly at home on a deck of cards, is now used as a psychiatric hospital. However, the town offers guided tours of its **church**, atop a flight of steps (*open 9–12 and 4–7; adm*). The entrance is through the 15th-century Pórtico de los Reyes, carved with figures of kings and counts, leading into an open atrium; beyond is the oldest Romanesque façade in Castile (1072), with Flemish-Gothic paintings just inside, and a *mudéjar* door. Although the walls of the long narrow church date from the 11th century, the interior was redone in the 15th by Fernando Díaz. The second Baroque *retablo* on the right marks the tomb of Santa Tigridia, San Salvador's first abbess; its expressive Romanesque *Cristo de Santa Tigridia* is attributed to sculptors from the Toulouse school. Further up, charming 14th-century Gothic frescoes depict the legend of St Mary of Egypt (really Isis, they say, dressed in Christian clothing). Fernando Díaz's starry dome measures 400 sq m and is the second largest in Spain after Tarragona; below are filigree choir stalls in walnut, and flanking the ultra-florid 18th-century Baroque *retablo* is the magnificent **Panteón Real**. Sancho the Great (d. 1035) and his wife are here, among others, their tombs arranged by Fernando Díaz into charming little temples, richly carved and decorated with elaborate tracery and Hispano-Flemish paintings by Fray Alonso de Zamora. Behind the *retablo*, the **Capilla de San Íñigo** contains the 16th-century silver reliquary of Íñigo (Eneco), persuaded to be first abbot of Oña by Sancho the Great and whose death, they say, grieved Christian, Jew and Saracen alike.

The **museum** in the sacristy contains the excellent alabaster tomb of Bishop Lope de Mendoza, by Italian Mannerist master Leone Leoni; a fragment of 10th-century cloth once belonging to Sancho the Great, with Arabic writing, the figures of an alchemist and the horse and goshawk of Castile's independence. The **cloister**, built by Simón de Colonia in 1508, is a rich piece of Isabelline Gothic, and presiding over the door is the Gothic statue of Santa María de Oña, whom the poet-king Alfonso the Wise praised in his *Cantiga 221*; when his son Fernando the future saint was given up for dead by his doctors, the statue, brought into his presence, restored him. She was also known as sovereign against worms in Infantes. One wing holds the tombs of the counts of Bureba, cousins to the counts of Castile and the granddaughters of the Cid. One of their classicizing epitaphs translates:

> *Gómez, who defended the Spanish coasts*
> *Like Hector you guarded them, while your faithful wife Urraca*
> *Remained here, and contemplated how the cold winters*
> *and pleasant springs passed*
> *And how nothing under heaven endures.*

Down towards the river, you can see the last of Oña's medieval gates, the **Arco de la Estrella,** and the Gothic church of **San Juan**, with a carved portal under the porch.

Up the Ebro: Frías and Medina de Pomar

East of Oña, built high over the banks of the Ebro, medieval **Frías** looks beautiful on post-cards: a ruined 12th-century castle spirals up a rocky outcrop known as 'the Molar' high above the hanging whitewashed houses, arcaded lanes and intimate vegetable gardens. Because it's on the way to nowhere, few people ever visit, and if it's hot you can join the locals for a dip in the Ebro in the shadow of Frías' magnificent **medieval bridge**, complete with its mighty gate and central guard tower. Between Oña and Frías, turn north 16km at Trespaderne for 12th-century **San Pantaleón de Losa**, site of a curious hermitage set over the village on a huge boulder resembling a capsized boat. Odd carvings decorate the capitals (ships, dragons' heads, masks, and a speak-no-evil figure). Further up the valley, by the Orduña pass, is one of the highest waterfalls in Europe.

Another road north of Trespaderne leads to **Medina de Pomar**, site of a powerful, two-towered castle built in the 14th century by the Velasco family, the hereditary Constables of Castile; a *mudéjar* stucco frieze in the main hall is decorated with inscriptions in Gothic and Arabic letters. The Constables founded the **Convent of Santa Clara** in 1313, and lie buried in tombs with alabaster effigies in its early Gothic church with an octagonal star-vault; Santa Clara's lovely 16th-century Capilla de la Concepción has a Renaissance grille and *retablo* by Diego de Siloé and Felipe de Vigarni. In the convent museum, you'll find paintings attributed to Rogier van der Weyden, an ivory Christ of Lepanto, a dead Christ by Gregorio Fernández, and goldwork. Medina de Pomar is also proud of Juan de Salazar, who went to the New World in 1547 and founded Asunción, the capital of Paraguay.

The Canyons of the Ebro

Up the Ebro from Oña, just outside Puente-Arenas, **San Pedro de Tejada** (*Apr–Oct 9–1 and 4–7, other times 10–2 and 4–6*) is one of the province's finest Romanesque churches, its portal carved with a Last Supper and Ascension of Christ. Its other carvings are flagrantly erotic, in the same vein as the church at Cervatos, just over the mountains in Cantabria (*see* p.176). Further up, above Incinillas, **Villarcayo** (due west of Medina de Pomar), was the capital of the Merindad de Castilla la Vieja, one of Fernán González's original counties, but it was burned in the First Carlist War. Only bits of its medieval past survive, especially in the **Museo-Monasterio de Santa María la Real de Vileña** (*open Sun 10.30–11.30 and 4.30–6.30*), founded to hold the treasures and fragments of the 13th-century Cistercian monastery that burned down in 1970.

Villarcayo is in easy striking distance of a pair of sites associated with the archaic judges of Castile, who in this isolated pocket in the 8th and 9th centuries played a role somewhere between chieftain, lawmaker and general sage. One of them, *juez* Laín Calvo, was buried in the Romanesque hermitage of the Virgen de la Torrentera in **Villalaín**; when disinterred, the chronicles write, all were amazed at the giant stature of his body, which turned to dust on contact with the air. The church, with a square apse and inscription dated 1130, has a lovely portal and interesting murals inside. Sculptures of the five judges of Castille decorate the elegant doorway of the large Renaissance church in nearby **Bisjueces**; one judge, Nuño Rasura, wears a striking Chinese hat. North of Villarcayo in **Torme**, the 12th-century Romanesque church of Butrera is one of the best preserved in the province, with fascinating capitals and an excellent relief of the Three Magi.

To the northwest, you can pick up the 6318 into the mountains (*see* below). For the Ebro Canyons, however, cut over to **Soncillo**, then drive southwest through the Puerta de Carrales towards Ruerrero, at the beginning of the Canyons of the Ebro. The cliffs grow increasingly majestic and fantastical as you drive towards **Orbaneja del Castillo**: vultures and eagles circle high over the ruddy canyon walls, sculpted by eons of wind and rain to form a bizarre natural roof line of soaring bridges, castle walls, haunted towers or hollow snaggle-toothed caves. In Orbaneja an enchanting, lush waterfall cascades, even in August; from here the road does a semi-circle through the canyon before climbing up to the N 623, the main Santander—Burgos highway.

The main highway is not an unattractive route, but for something even better, pass it by and cross the Ebro at **Pesquera de Ebro**, make your way east to Pesadas de Burgos and turn right onto the C 629. For the next 14 km the road is surreal—perfectly straight, in the middle of absolutely no where, yet each kilometre is systematically marked off with an impressive 10ft monument in stone—all identical, all bearing no identification whatsoever. The sensation of wandering across the middle of a bizarre games table for giants is confirmed when, after the last monument, you turn east and it's as if the world has suddenly dropped out beneath your feet, leaving you to wind down, down, down, the edge of the table, with tremendous views across to the **Castillo de las Rojas**, an impressive ruin piled high on a rocky outcrop. The castle, where Charles V shamelessly imprisoned the ambassadors of Pope Clement in 1528, defends **Poza de la Sal**, a town founded by the Romans, who first extracted salt from its marshes along the Río Torca Salada. Fortified in the 10th century, the town and its salt were so important that in 1530 its lord was made Marqués de Poza. In its web of tiny lanes there's a Gothic church with a Baroque façade, the 18th-century salt administration offices, a pair of old gateways and a panoramic view from Plaza Nueva; along the river, the old salt works, abandoned in the mid-19th century, are near an interesting Roman aqueduct that supplied the village wash basin. From here the road continues south towards Briviesca.

The Far Northeast Corner: in the Cordillera Cantábrica

Near Soncillo the 6318 leads into the secret corner of Burgos province; if you're coming from the north, the N 629 from Laredo will take you straight there. Some day, perhaps, the most extraordinary attraction, the massive karstic cave complex of **Ojo Guareña** by Quintanilla-Sotoscueva, with its prehistoric paintings and upper Palaeolithic footprints, will be open to visitors; extending some 40km underground (not all of them yet explored at the time of writing) you can only get as far as the subterranean **Hermitages of SS. Bernabé and Tirso**, set on a panoramic esplanade with their façades built into the cliffs; inside are 17th- and 18th-century paintings and wax ex-votos.

The 6318 continues east to medieval **Espinosa de los Monteros**, the local market town, with its 14th-century Castillo de los Condestables on the far bank of the river Trueba, and the Constable's elegant Baroque palace in town; there are several tower houses, and a good 15th-century *retablo* by Fray Alonso de Zamora in the church of San Nicolás. The fifth of August is the best time to come, when the citizenry indulge in what the tourist office describes with some trepidation as 'strange dances of pagan origin'. Some 15km north there's a small ski station at **Portillo de Lunada**, where the old Roman road once passed between the *meseta* to Cantabria; the views down the valley of the Miera are worth the trouble of visiting any time of year.

On the other hand, if you venture east, interesting Romanesque churches are your reward: San Miguel at **Bercedo**, with a good portal and beams carved into animals; a 12th-century Templar church of Santa María, at **Siones**, with an elegant double archway in the apse, strange and beautiful capitals and other carvings, a 12th-century statue of the Virgin and a Visigothic baptismal font; and the church San Lorenzo at **Vallejo de Mena**, founded by the Knights of St John with a gallery of arcades along the top of the south façade and a handsome apse. The parish church of the big town in these parts, medieval **Villasana de Mena,** has a good relief of the Three Magi.

Ⓣ (947–)	*Where to Stay and Eating Out*

Villafranca Montes de Oca

El Pájaro, Ctra. Logroño–Burgos, Ⓣ 58 20 01 (*inexpensive*), is your best bet for a simple room and a meal along this stretch of the pilgrims' route; there's also the restored Hospital de la Reina for pilgrims, recently inaugurated by Queen Sofia.

Pancorbo/Briviesca

Hotel-restaurants line the highway at Pancorbo, but the best bet is just in on the edge of the old town: **Casa Rural El Ferial,** San Nicolás 59, Ⓣ 35 42 76 (after 9pm), a spanking new inexpensive bed and breakfast overlooking a little garden, but the best thing about it are the owners, Vicente Cardiñanos and his wife, who must be the most hospitable people in Castile. In Briviesca, **★★El Valles,** Ctra. Madrid–Irún km 280, Ⓣ 59 00 25, ◉ 59 24 84 (*moderate*), has long been a favourite stopover for its quiet rooms and good filling food for the road; in town **El Concejo,** Pza. Mayor 14, Ⓣ 59 16 86 (*moderate–expensive*), is prettily set in a 15th-century mansion and serves a tasty leek and prawn *pastel* in cheese sauce and imaginative desserts; good wine list (closed Mon).

Medina de Pomar

★★★Las Merindades, Pza. Somovilla, Ⓣ 11 08 22 (*moderate*), located in a pretty, historical building with the village's best, moderately priced restaurant downstairs; try the *solomillo a los ajos tostados* (sirloin with toasted garlic).

Burgos

First it must be said that Burgos is a genteel and quite pleasant town, its river, the Arlanzón, so filled with frogs in the spring and early summer that they drown out the traffic with their croaking; and that the favourite promenade, the Paseo del Espolón, is one of Spain's prettiest, adorned with amazing topiary hedges. Burgos contains one of the greatest collections of Gothic art and monuments in southern Europe, and it is the city in all Spain where you are most likely to see a nun riding a bicycle. Yet throughout much of its history, Burgos' role has been that of a stern military camp, from the day of El Cid Campeador to Franco el Caudillo who, during the Civil War, made Burgos his temporary capital, the city where, it was said, 'the very stones are Nationalist'. Here, in 1970, Franco held the infamous Burgos trials in which sixteen Basque separatists (two of them priests) were tried in a kangaroo court. Six were sentenced to death, though outraged world opinion convinced Franco to commute the sentences.

The Kingdom of Castile was born in Burgos, and it is fitting that the city itself began as a castle erected on the Moorish frontier in 884. By 926 it was ready to take its first step away from Leonese rule, electing its own judges; in 950, one of the judges' successors, Fernán González, declared his independence as Count of Castile. His descendant, Fernando I, elevated the title to king and married the heiress of León. Burgos remained sole capital of Castile until 1087, when Alfonso VI moved to Toledo (one reason must have been to put some distance between himself and the overbearing Cid). The frontier was moving southwards, and though most Spanish kings managed to spend some time here, this city that had done so much to create the ethos of Spain now found itself something of a backwater. But Burgos has always remained true to the cause. It is still the most aristocratic, the most pious, most polite, most reactionary city in Spain. Franco rewarded it with a big programme of state-financed expansion and industrialization, an attempt to drag the city into the 20th century that may well succeed some day.

Getting There

This is easy in Burgos. Both trains and buses have their stations within easy walking distance of the centre.

By train: RENFE is on Avda. Conde Guadalhorce, across the river from the cathedral, ✆ (947) 20 35 60; tickets are also dispensed from the office at Moneda 21, ✆ 20 91 31. Burgos is on the main rail line from Irún to Madrid (connections to Pamplona, Vitoria, Bilbao, Valladolid, etc.), with less frequent links with Zaragoza, Palencia, León, and A Coruña; also to Salamanca, Barcelona, Málaga, Madrid, Córdoba and Vigo on various *talgos*.

By bus: the bus terminal is on C/ Miranda, across the river from the Arco de Sta María, ✆ (947) 26 55 65; there are daily buses to León (one), Santander (three), Madrid (seven), Soria, San Sebastián and Vitoria (four or more), and the provincial villages. Even if there may be only one bus a day to villages not on a main route, such as Frías, they're often conveniently timed for a day trip.

Tourist Information

Plaza de Alonso Martínez 7, ✆ (947) 20 31 25.

Arco de Santa María

Burgos' glistening white, fairy-tale front door, the **Arco de Santa María**, was originally part of the medieval walls, but after the Comunero revolt it was embellished to appease Charles V; triumphal arches like this were a Renaissance conceit (the first one was made at Naples for a Spanish king), and they were especially favoured by the vainglorious and ambitious Charles. The Emperor himself is portrayed in a Burgos pantheon that includes its first judges, King Fernán González, and El Cid. The arch was designed by Francisco de Colonia and Juan de Vallejo, two artists you are going to know well before you leave Burgos—along with Francisco's father Juan, responsible for the great openwork spires of the Cathedral, looming just behind the arch.

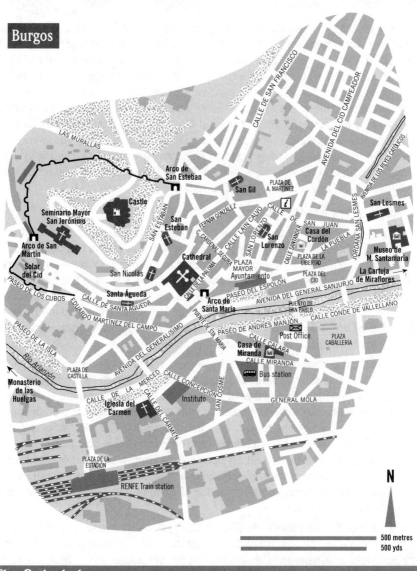

Arco de
San Esteban

San Gil

PLAZA DE
A. MARTÍNEZ

Castle

San Lesmes

Seminario Mayor
San Jerónimo

San
Esteban

Casa del
Cordón

Arco de San
Martín

San
Lorenzo

Museo de
M. Santamaría

Cathedral

PLAZA DE LA
LIBERTAD

La Cartuja
de Miraflores

Solar
del Cid

San Nicolás

PLAZA
MAYOR
Ayuntamiento

PLAZA DEL
CID

Santa Águeda

Arco de
Santa María

PASEO DEL ESPOLÓN

AVENIDA DEL GENERAL SANJURJO

PUENTE DE
SAN PABLO

CALLE CONDE DE VALLELLANO

Monasterio
de las
Huelgas

PASEO DE ANDRÉS MANJÓN

Post Office

PLAZA
CABALLERÍA

Casa de
Miranda

CALLE MIRANDA

PLAZA DE
CASTILLA

Bus station

Iglesia del
Carmen

Instituto

GENERAL MOLA

LAS MURALLAS

CALLE DE SAN FRANCISCO

AVENIDA DEL CID CAMPEADOR

AVENIDA DE LOS REYES CATÓLICOS

JORDANA SAN LESMES

CALLE DE SANTA ÁGUEDA

EDUARDO MARTÍNEZ DEL CAMPO

PASEO DE LOS CUBOS

PASEO DE LA ISLA

Río Arlanzón

AVENIDA DEL GENERALÍSIMO

PUENTE DE STA. MARÍA

CALLE DE LA MERCED

CALLE CONCEPCIÓN

CALLE DEL CARMEN

SAN COSME

CALLE CALERA

FERNÁN GONZÁLEZ

SAN ESTEBAN

C. CARDENAL SEGURA

CALLE DE LA PALOMA

CALLE LAÍN CALVO

CALLE DE SAN JUAN

CALLE SANTANDER

LA PUEBLA

SAN LORENZO

PLAZA DE LA
ESTACIÓN

RENFE Train station

N

500 metres
500 yds

The Cathedral

Along with León and Toledo, Burgos has one of Spain's greatest Gothic cathedrals. Yet while León has an instant, sublime appeal, Burgos' power lies in its awesome number of masterworks and details from the tiniest carving in the choir stalls to its beautiful star-vaulted domes. In 1221, in honour of his marriage to Beatrice of Swabia, Fernando III and the English bishop Maurice laid the first cornerstone. On the north side, a stair leads up to the **Puerta del Sarmental**, its 13th-century tympanum showing Christ and the four Evangelists (sitting studiously at their desk, writing the Gospels). The first portal to be finished, the south-side **Puerta Alta de la Coronería** (1257) is the most interesting, with its Apostles, Almighty, and a peculiar row of mere mortals, the Blessed and the Damned, in between. Around the corner of the transept, the **Puerta de la Pellejería** is part of the original 13th-century work. These doors are hardly ever opened; Burgos is prey to a biting wind in the late afternoon, and the cross-current would blow the congregation away. From up here, though, you can get a good view of the forest of spires, especially on the lantern, adorned with scores of figures. Three generations of the Colonia family devoted themselves to moulding the soft grey stone of Burgos into the cathedral's intricate towers and pinnacles. Colonia is Cologne, in Germany; Hans of Cologne began the works in the late 1400s, and his son Simón and grandson Francisco carried on the job, followed by Juan de Vallejo, who built the Platersque crossing tower. At night these are illuminated along with the Arco de Santo María for a dazzling tour de force.

A Building Trying to Disappear

If you have the time, take a good, long look at the exterior of this cathedral (preferably from up the stairs on the edge of the plaza). This is the Gothic idea stretched to its wildest extreme—in its day it must have looked as outrageous as Gaudí's Sagrada Familia when its first parabolic towers went up in the 1900s. In the first blossoming of Gothic building in the Ile-de-France, they concentrated on the interior—soaring arches and acres of stained glass to make the walls disappear and create a kind of spiritual union of inside and outside.

Spain, the land of extremes, naturally had to take the principle a step further. The virtuoso stone lace spires, finished to Juan de Colonia's design in the 19th century, are only the crowning glory of the most diaphanous church ever built. Note how the windows in the bell towers were made so wide that from most points of view you can actually see through the towers. Hundreds of pinnacles, as electric as any of Gaudí's, pattern out the sky, while between the towers hangs an equally transparent, throughly over-the-top gallery of statues of Spanish kings, under the biggest, most delicate stone traceries ever perched over a façade. Imagine the master mason directing the works in the 1200s, dreaming of a building that would be built half of stone, half of light and air.

The **west façade** incorporates two Stars of David, an unintentional reminder that more than one of Burgos' bishops hailed from a Jewish family before 1492, as did the city's greatest sculptors, Diego and Gil de Siloé, the undisputed masters of Isabelline Gothic. Their work inside makes up one of the cathedral's main attractions. Tragically, the three portals of the west façade were destroyed in the name of improvement, in the 'Age of Enlightenment' of the 18th century, and replaced with pallid substitutes. But around the rear, another monument of late Gothic excess survives, the huge, octagonal, **Capilla del Condestable** (*see* below), attached to the apse.

Along with the cathedral of Santiago, this is one of the two great treasure-houses of Spain. The enclosed **choir** is almost entirely shut off from the rest of the church. You can peer through the grill work to see the magnificent gold-trimmed star vault of Juan de Vallejo's **lantern**, under the central tower, which Felipe II declared couldn't have been built by men, but only by angels. Four stately round piers support a profusion of intricate carved decoration—a Spanish twist on Renaissance styles, married harmoniously into a Gothic building. Underneath its majestic beauty a simple slab marks the **tomb of the Cid and his wife Ximena**, their bones relocated here with great pomp in 1921. The other tomb in the *coro* belongs to Bishop Maurice, topped by his enamelled copper effigy; try to get in to see the magnificent carving on the wood and inlaid stalls—unabashed pagan figures on the seats, New Testament scenes above. They were done by Felipe de Vigarni, who also sculpted the dramatic scene on the ambulatory behind the main altar.

De Vigarni, who also designed the choir, carved the Tomb of *Don Gonzalo de Lerma* in the 16th-century **Capilla de la Presentación**, to the right of the choir. To the left, the **Chapel of Santa Ana** has a wonderfully ornate polychromed altar by Gil de Siloé. One of Diego de Siloé's masterpieces, the diamond-shaped, drippingly Plateresque **Golden Stair** (1523), is the most strikingly original feature of the interior, the perfectly proportioned solution to the Puerta Alta, 7.7m above the floor of the cathedral. The idea of stairways as architectural showpieces was just beginning in 1523; Michelangelo was working on his famous one at the Laurentian Library in Florence at the same time.

Buffalo Jesus and the Fly-catcher

The two features of the interior that everyone remembers, though, are just inside the west door. First, to the right as you enter, is the plainest but most venerated, the glass-doored **Capilla del Santo Cristo**, where ladies in mantillas gather to worship one of the strangest cult idols any religion has conjured up—the 13th-century **Cristo de Burgos**, a figure made of old buffalo hide (long reputed to be human skin), real hair and fingernails (according to an old tale, both had to trimmed every few days) dressed in a green frock and warm to the touch. The idol is made so that both the head and arms can move, like a doll; these were probably somehow manipulated to impress the faithful, back in the age of miracles.

Nearly as famous is the 15th-century mechanical clock across the nave near the roof, the **Papamoscas** ('fly-catcher'), a grinning devil who pops out of a hole in the wall to strike the hour. The second chapel from the Papamoscas, **Santa Ana**, has a *retablo* of the Tree of Jesse by Gil de Siloé and a fine Bishop's tomb by his son Diego. The most spectacular chapel, the octagonal **Chapel of the High Constable of Castile** (*Capilla del Condestable*), was built by Simón de Colonia for Pedro Hernández de Velasco in 1482–94. The tomb, accompanied by that of the Constable's wife, Doña Mencía de Mendoza, faces the elaborate altar by Vigarni and Diego de Siloé. The Constable, the head of the Castilian army, clutches his sword even after death; his lady's little dog sleeps at her feet. Velasco was Constable during the conquest of Granada, whose Moorish craftsmen inspired the great, geometric star-vaulting that crowns the chapel. The chapel has its own sacristy, a treasure chest full of trinkets and a wonderfully voluptuous auburn-haired *Magdalen* by Giampetrino, a pupil of Leonardo da Vinci. This being Burgos, she's usually locked up; you'll have to ask the man in the souvenir shop to open the door. The nearby **Sacristía Mayor**—the cathedral's sacristy—is adorned with one of the cathedral's lighter scenes, a Baroque bubble bath of a heaven.

The **Museo Diocesano** off the cloister (*open daily 9.30–1 and 4–6.30; adm*) contains the famous leather-bound coffer the Cid filled with sand and locked tight, then passed off as gold as security to Raquel and Vidas, two Jewish money-lenders, who made him a sizeable loan; another prized possession is the Cid's marriage agreement.

Around the Cathedral

Just to the northwest of the cathedral on Calle Fernán González, **San Nicolás de Bari** contains an incredible wall-sized alabaster *retablo* by Francisco de Colonia (1505), depicting 36 scenes from the Bible and more angels than could dance on a head of a pin. **Santa Águeda**, a plain 15th-century church on Calle Santa Águeda, is the successor of the church where the Cid forced Alfonso VI to swear on a silver lock that he had nothing to do with the assassination of his brother Sancho—an iron copy of the lock is hung over the door inside.

The Cid's ancestral mansion, the **Solar del Cid**, was demolished in 1771, though two obelisks mark the site. Between his two banishments and innumerable campaigns, he probably had little leisure to enjoy it anyway.

The **castle** was blown up by the French in 1813—an explosion that shattered most of the cathedral's stained glass, and little remains to be seen up here besides the fine view of the city. In its day, however, the castle saw many important events—Edward I of England and Leonora of Castile were married here. It is reached through the horseshoe **Arco de San Esteban**; also near the arch are two 14th-century Gothic churches: **San Esteban** and **San Gil**, both with fine interiors.

Near San Gil, in Plaza Alonso Martínez, you'll notice a grim little building called the **Capitanería**, guarded by military police and adorned with commemorative plaques. This was the Nationalist capital during the Civil War; here Franco assumed total power among the rebels and directed his campaigns in the north. Calle Santander is Burgos' main shopping street; at its head is the **Casa del Cordón**, named after the rope (really a Franciscan monk's belt) carved over the door in honour of St Francis. This palace was built by the Condestable de Velasco in 1485. Fernando and Isabel received Columbus here after his second voyage, and 18 years later, an aging Fernando sent Ponce de León off to discover the Fountain of Youth. His son-in-law Philippe I had died in the same house six years earlier.

Nearby, the attractive, arcaded **Plaza Mayor** has recently been refurbished and pedestrianized, although the shady **Paseo del Espolón** along the riverfront is the city's real centre; at the far end, a mighty equestrian **statue of the Cid** with the flowing beard no one dared to pull seems ready to fly off its base and attack any enemy crossing **San Pablo Bridge** towards the Plaza Primo de Rivera. The bridge itself is embellished with stone figures of the Cid's wife, his companions and a Moorish king.

Across the bridge the lovely **Casa Miranda** (1545) houses the **Museo de Burgos** (*open daily exc Mon 9.45–1.50 and 4.15–7, Sat and Sun 10–2; adm*) with an archaeological collection.

Monasterio de Las Huelgas

On the outskirts of Burgos lie two of Spain's richest monasteries, both well worth a visit. A 20-minute walk to the west will take you to the Cistercian convent of Las Huelgas (*open daily exc Mon, 10.30–1.15 and 4–3.45, Sun am only; adm*), founded by Alfonso VIII in 1187 at the behest of his wife Eleanor, daughter of England's Henry II (*huelga* in Spanish means a strike now, but back then *Las Huelgas Reales*, the monastery's true name, meant 'the royal repose'). The abbess of Las Huelgas enjoyed more power and influence than any other woman in Spain except the Queen herself, until her powers were revoked in the 19th century. In 1219 San Fernando III started the custom of Castilian kings of going to Las Huelgas to be knighted into the Order of Santiago—not by any inferior, mind you, but by Santiago himself; in the cloister you can see the statue of the saint with a moveable arm holding out a sword made especially for the purpose. Guided tours (in Spanish) will take you through the English-Gothic church: statues of Alfonso VIII and Eleanor kneel before the altar, and there's a curious painted iron pulpit of 1560 that gyrated to allow the priest to address the nuns in the choir or congregation. The church also serves as a royal Pantheon of Castilian kings and royal ladies. The French, as usual, desecrated the tombs, though the one they missed, that of Alfonso X's son Fernando de la Cerda, produced such a fine collection of goods as to form the nucleus of Las Huelgas' **Museo de Ricas Telas**, a fascinating collection of fabrics and medieval dress, showing considerable Eastern influences. These are not the only Moorish touches in Las Huelgas: note the geometric tomb of the Infanta Doña Blanca, the peacock and stars in the *mudéjar* cloister, and the **Capilla de Santiago**. The grandest chamber, the **Sala Capitular**, contains a trophy from Alfonso VIII's great Battle of Las Navas de Tolosa—the beautiful silk flap of the Moorish commander's tent—and Don Juan's banner from Lepanto, which he gave to his daughter Ana, abbess of Las Huelgas. If the guide's in a good mood, he'll play a scale on the well-tuned columns in the halls. Some 43 nuns still live at Las Huelgas, painting porcelain and baking cookies.

Noble and wealthy pilgrims would receive a fair welcome at Las Huelgas, but for the needs of poor pilgrims Alfonso VIII also built the **Hospital del Rey**, a short walk from Las Huelgas, facing the road to Léon. Most impressive here are the 16th-century Plateresque gateway and the court.

La Cartuja de Miraflores

Burgos' second great monastery is a half hour's walk to the east, through a lovely park of shady trees. **Miraflores** (*open daily 10.15–3 and 4–6, Sun 11.20–12.30, 1–3 and 4–6*) was founded by Juan II in 1441 and is still used as a monastery, so you can see only the church, built by the Colonia family; yet this alone contains more great art than many a cathedral. Here Isabel la Católica commissioned the great Gil de Siloé to sculpt the **tomb of Juan II and Isabel of Portugal** as a memorial to her parents, and after four years of steady work he created the most elaborately detailed tomb of all time, 'imprisoning Death inside an alabaster star' as a local guidebook poetically put it. Instead of a chisel, it looks as if Siloé used a needle to sew the gorgeous alabaster robes of the effigies—Juan pensive, his wife reading a book. Isabela owed her succession to the death of her brother, and as a posthumous thank-you had Siloé carve his memorial as well. The **tomb of the Infante Don Alfonso** portrays the young prince (1453–68) kneeling at prayer surrounded by a wonderfully playful menagerie of animals, putti and birds entwined in the vines. Master Siloé also did most of the gilt *retablo* of the high altar, said to be made with the gold that Columbus had presented to the Catholic kings at the Casa de Cordón.

There are other works of art: a lovely painting of the *Annunciation* by Pedro Berruguete, the carvings on the stalls of the lay brothers' choir (the middle section of the Carthusian church's traditional three divisions—the monks' choir is in the front, the general public in the back, by the painting of the Virgin sending the infernal spirits packing). In the side chapel there's a wooden polychrome **statue of St Bruno** carved by the Portuguese Manuel Pereira, so lifelike 'it would speak if it weren't a Carthusian monk' as the *burgaleses* like to say.

Below Miraflores and 10km further down the road is the **Abbey of San Pedro de Cardeña**, founded in 899 and now a Trappist monastery *(open 10–1 and 4–6, Sun 12–1.30 and 4–6; adm)*. Here the Cid left his family when banished by Alfonso VI, and here he requested to be buried by his wife Ximena. The French stole the bones and when the Spanish government finally got them back it was to inter them in the more secure precincts of the cathedral. You can visit the original tombs with their effigies in a chapel off the **Cloister of Martyrs**, where 200 Benedictines were beheaded during a 10th-century Moorish raid. The Cid's faithful charger Babieca is buried just outside the gate.

Burgos ℭ (947–)   ***Where to Stay***

expensive

Just outside Burgos on the Madrid road, the ★★★★★**Landa Palace**, ℭ 20 63 43, 🖾 26 46 76, is a member of the prestigious Relais et Châteaux and provides a memorable stay in an over-the-top pseudo-medieval tower furnished with antiques, an indoor atrium and swimming-pool, and beautiful rooms (they may be in a castle, but they have mod cons El Cid would think were sorcery) for 30,000pts. A meal in the Landa's equally palatial restaurant, the region's finest, will set you back some 6000 pts. In the centre of Burgos, the ★★★★**Hotel Condestable**, Vitoria 8, ℭ 26 71 25, 🖾 20 46 65, is the city's long-running traditional favourite in an elegant setting. ★★★★**Hotel Almirante Bonifaz**, Vitoria 22 and 24, ℭ 20 69 43, 🖾 20 29 19, has similar rooms in the centre of town. ★★★**Del Cid**, Pza. Santa María 8, ℭ 20 87 15, 🖾 26 94 60, magnificently located opposite the cathedral, has well equipped modern doubles, garage space and a secret connecting tunnel with their excellent restaurant next door.

moderate/inexpensive

The charmingly old-fashioned ★★**Norte y Londres** on Pza. Alonso Martínez 10, ℭ 26 41 25, 🖾 27 73 75, offer a whiff of charm and elegance in the middle of town; another lovely old building with glass balconies, ★★★**Cordón**, La Puebla 6,

*26 50 00, has rooms bordering on expensive. For fun you can stay near the river in the **Hilton (not related to the chain), Vitoria 165, © 22 51 16, situated near the park (*inexpensive*). Right off the Plaza Mayor, the Hs *Hs Hidalgo, © 20 34 81, a well-kept and old fashioned *hostal*, is on a street that is (at least at night) relatively quiet. The *Hs Victoria, San Juan 3, © 20 15 42, is nothing special but clean and priced right; the same could be said for the faded but tolerable *Castellano on Laín Calvo, just north of the Plaza Mayor. There is also a youth hostel, the **Residencia Juvenil Gil de Siloé**, Avda. General Vigón, © 22 03 62.

Eating Out

For a medieval atmosphere in a 15th-century building facing the cathedral and delicious, roast sucking-lamb, the **Mesón del Cid**, Pza. Santa María 8, © 20 87 15, is the place to go. The dining-rooms are on various levels throughout the building, which held one of Spain's first printing presses (menu 3500 pts). Just inside the Arco de Santa María, the **Corral de los Infantes** offers Castilian specialities like *olla podrida* and 'medieval lentils' for 1600pts; outdoor dining in the summer. The Chinese restaurant next door has inexpensive *platos combinados*. **Gaona**, Virgen de la Paloma 41, near the cathedral, © 20 61 91 (*moderate*), has Basque cooking in a glassed-in terrace; peppers stuffed with cod is a treat. Just north of the cathedral on Huerta del Rey, the **Mesón el Cardinal** has a wide array of fancy *bocadillos*, *tortillas* and seafood tapas. Near the statue of the Cid, the **Casa Alonso** on Calatrava offers a nice 1000-pts menu: *paella*, *merluza*, stuffed pork chops or Castilian snails. The most popular place in town, **Casa Ojeda** on Vitoria 5, © 20 90 52, has the best tapas in its bar and good local cuisine in its dining-room (around 2500 pts).

Southeast of Burgos

The most popular corner for a day's out from Burgos is the mountainous region to the southeast, on or off the N 234 towards Soria where it's hard to tell where one *sierra* begins and another ends. Covarrubias and Santo Domingo de Silos are firmly marked on the tourist map, but you'll need a car to take in the prizes just off the beaten track such as San Quirce or the Visigothic church of Quintanilla de las Viñas.

Getting Around

Transport here is mostly non-existent. There are several buses daily from Burgos to Aranda de Duero, and in general one a day to Santo Domingo de Silos, Caleruega, Lerma, and Covarrubias, but that's about it.

Tourist Information

Lerma: in the centre, © (947) 17 01 43

A Scatological Abbey and a Visigothic Beauty

The **Abadía de San Quirce** is not easy to find; signposts guide you from **Hontoria de la Cantera**. Set in a quiet wooded valley, it was founded by Count Fernán González after his defeat of the Saracens on this spot, in 929. Abandoned in 1835, the church conserves its original structure, with a stout fortified tower in the centre; the west door has 11 modillons showing the Creator, Adam and Eve, Cain and Abel and in between, earthy reliefs of men squatting and defecating, with inscriptions reading *io cago* and *mal cago* (I shit, and I shit badly); one thinks of the anarchical shitting figure, the *cagoter* that accompanies every Catalan Christmas crib. Other reliefs decorate the north door and modillons supporting the charming bubble of an apse, unusually illuminated by two round bull's eye windows and a regular Romanesque window, which was probably originally a bull's eye as well; inside (*open only the first Tues of each month, 9.30–6*) the capitals are carved with the legend of San Quirce and a naked woman who suckles serpents, with lions on either side.

Further south on the N 234, there's an unusual corridor-dolmen at the ghost town of **Mazariegos,** where the big stones are engraved with what could be horses. Aim your next stop for **Quintanilla de las Viñas,** where 4km up under the steel toned Montes de Lara and the ruins of the Castilla de Lara, the gold-stoned Visigothic **Nuestra Señora de las Viñas** drinks up the sun (*open 9.30–2 and 4–8 , winter 9–4; closed Mon, Tues and the last weekend of each month; if no one's there, try the guardian's house, marked Turismo 1km south*). This is nothing less than the last Visigothic basilica in Spain, dated 7th century or just before the invasion of the Moors. Made of large blocks incised with Christian graffiti, only the square apse and part of the transept have survived the past 1300 years: the exterior of the former is beautifully girdled with three friezes, the lowest band of vines and grapes, the middle band decorated with plants and birds: ducks, peacocks, doves, and what are believed to be the monograms of the founders, set in round medallions of curling tendrils. The upper band has a distinct Persian air with griffons, leopards, lions, deer, bulls and rams. Inside, on the triumphal arch, there's another bird frieze and a rare example of Visigothic syncretism: angels with rocket wings, Byzantine in style or perhaps even more like the winged figures on Roman tombs, holding up portraits identifying Christ with the moon (a bearded figure, with a crescent moon LVNA on his head like horns) and the Virgin (or Church) with the sun SOL, topped by a Latin inscription: 'I, modest Flammola, I offer this modest gift.' Blocks in the apse show heavily coiffed, symmetrical but inexplicable 'astral' figures, sculpted by another artist who had trouble getting the arms and hands on right.

Fernán González Country: San Pedro de Arlanza and Covarrubias

South of Quintanilla de las Viñas, the Arlanza river runs east–west through a valley known in the 10th century as the Valley of Towers, the frontier of old Castile, pushed this far south by 'the Good Count' Fernán González, the founder of the realm. His exploits are described in an epic poem, written in the 13th century by a monk in the large, now romantically ruined abbey of **San Pedro de Arlanza**, founded by the count's father, Gonzalo Fernández in 912, below a cave where the hermit Pelagio predicted the illustrious destiny of his line. The guardian will let you in to see what's left of the church, its tower, cloister and nave, where grass grows between the old paving stones.

Medieval **Covarrubias** is Old Castile's half-timbered showcase of porticoed squares and lanes, guarded by the only surviving 10th-century Mozarab tower in the Valley of Towers, the sturdy **Torreón de Doña Urraca**, whose countess was walled up inside in 965 and left to die. The Ayuntamiento has a Romanesque doorway that once belonged to Fernán González's palace. Behind this, the ex-Colegiata, **San Cosme y San Damián** (*open 10.30–1.30 and 4.30–6.30, weekends 10–2 and 4–7, closed Tues; adm*) was rebuilt in 1474 as the pantheon for the count's descendants, the Infantes de Covarrubias, whose tombs line the nave; in 1848, the remains of Fernán González and his wife Sancha were transferred from San Pedro de Arlanza and placed next to the altar in a 4th-century Roman sarcophagus. The 17th-century organ, one of the most beautiful in Spain, still works, although you'll have to attend mass to hear its sweet antique sound. The cloister contains the tomb of a 13th-century Norwegian princess, promised to Alfonso the Wise but married to his ex-bishop brother Fernando (*see p.242*). The prize in the museum is the Flemish-inspired *Triptych of the Magi*, by an unknown 16th-century sculptor.

Santo Domingo de Silos and its Sublime Cloister

South of Covarrubias at **Santibáñez del Val**, the road to Barrious leads 2km to the river Ura and the 10th-century Mozarabic hermitage of **Santa Cecilia de Barriosuso**, with a square apse and window made of five rings and a horseshoe arch inside.The real attraction in these parts, though, and one that brings many pilgrims down on a special detour, is **Santo Domingo de Silos** (*open 10.30–1.15 and 4.30–7, Sun and hols 4.30–7; adm*), a Benedictine monastery founded in 954 by Fernán González and ruled in the next century by the abbot who gave it its name, Santo Domingo. Rebuilt after al-Mansur burned it to the ground, the monastery was refounded in the 19th century by French Benedictines from Solesmes, who have made it famous for Gregorian chant (sung at 9am Mon–Sat and noon on Sun, and at 7pm). They inherited the most beautiful Romanesque **cloister** in Spain, superbly elegant, double-decked and ivory coloured, built around an ancient cypress tree. The lower section dates from the late 11th to early 12th centuries and has fascinating capitals on twin columns carved by a sculptor so well versed in animals and other motifs of the Córdoba caliphate and Middle East that he may have been a Moor himself. On the corners of the cloister, eight large reliefs on the life of Jesus are in a similar style; one shows the only known representation of Christ dressed in pilgrim's garb. The cloister's *mudéjar* **ceiling**, painted with scenes of everyday life in the Middle Ages, has been restored. Off the cloister, the **museum** houses Mozarabic illuminations (Santo Domingo is a study centre of Mozarabic art, liturgies and manuscripts), the Romanesque tympanum from the first church, a 12th-century paten with Roman cameos, an 11th-century chalice, and the 18th-century **pharmacy** (*botica*) with its big jars of potions. After all this, the **church**, rebuilt in the neoclassical style in the 18th century, seems dull.

A mere 2.5km from Santo Domingo towards Caleruega, a narrow gorge, the **Desfiladero de la Yecla**, has been fitted with wooden walkways, making for an easy and spectacular walk; the stair descends just before the tunnel and the end of the walkway emerges just after it. The gorge is part of a Nature Park with a large colony of vultures, hawks and buzzards, the largest *sabina* (shrubby juniper) forest in the world, and remains of a Celtic *castro*. Beyond, attractive hilltop **Hinojar de Cervera**, the Cueva de San García has even older traces of civilization, dating back to the Upper Palaeolithic era. **Caleruega**, further south, was the birthplace in 1170 of yet another canonized Domingo, the one who went into the heavenly big time, Santo Domingo de Guzmán. It was his theological battles against the heretical Cathars in Toulouse that led, in 1216, to Domingo's founding of his preaching order, the Dominicans or Black Friars, who took on the job of the Inquisition. The Guzmán tower house is still intact, and the exact spot of the saint's birth is marked in the crypt of the church of Dominican Madres.

The Bloody Cucumber of Vengeance

East of Santo Domingo de Silos, Salas de los Infantes is named after the legend of the Siete Infantes de Lara, a favourite subject of Spanish ballad and romance. The seven sons of Gonzalo Gustios, the lord of Salas, were known for their chivalry and prowess, in no small thanks to their tutor, the judge Nuño Rasura. In 986, their troubles began at the splendid wedding of their uncle Ruy Velázquez to Doña Lambra, when the youngest of the seven brothers quarrelled with a kinsman of the bride. Doña Lambra took the quarrel as a personal insult, and as the brothers rode away, she ordered her slave to heave a bloody cucumber at them. This was the ultimate deadly insult in 10th-century Castile (discretion forbade the romancers to explain exactly why); the outraged brothers slew the slave, even when he tried to 'hide even in the folds of her garment'.

Now it was Ruy Velázquez's turn to feel insulted by the brothers, and he schemed to avenge himself on the whole family. First he sent the father to Córdoba with a message in Arabic for the king, asking him to slay the bearer; but the Moorish king took pity on Gustios and merely put him in prison,where the king's sister fell in love with him and bore him a son named Mudarra. Meanwhile, Ruy Velázquez plotted an ambuscade with another Moorish king, so that when he sent the seven brothers and Nuño Rasura out to fight the Moors they were headed off at the pass by a far superior force and killed. The Moorish king sent Velázquez their eight heads, and he forwarded them to Gustios as a homecoming present.

After 14 years, Mudarra came north to find his father and promised to avenge the deaths of his seven brothers. When Ruy Velázquez heard of Mudarra, he thumpingly declared, in Lockhart's translation of the *Spanish Ballad*s:

> *Oh, in vain have I slaughter'd the Infants of Lara,*
> *There's an heir in his halls–there's the bastard Mudara.*
> *There's the son of the renegade–spawn of Mahoun:*
> *If I meet with Mudara, my spear brings him down.*

Of course it was Mudarra who brought down Velázquez instead. He then stoned and burned Doña Lambra at the stake for the bloody cucumber insult, and became lord of Salas. The parish church of **Salas de los Infantes** keeps the heads of the Seven Infantes and Nuño Rasura in a reliquary; their trunks are stored in the weird old tombs at San Millán de la Cogolla (*see* p.108).

There are some weird old things around Salas, beginning with a Visigothic hermitage covered with strange symbols on a hill just south of **Barbadillo del Mercado** (on the N 234), under cliffs that provide a refuge for lammergeiers, those Boeing 747s of the bird world. East, in **Palacios de la Sierra**, the parish church keeps a collection of undecipherable palaeochristian tombstones. **Jaramillo de la Fuente**, towards the Sierra de la Demanda, has a fine 12th-century Romanesque church with good capitals.

Way Down South in Burgos Province

The N 1 south of Burgos to Madrid passes through **Lerma**, another town on the Arlanza river, founded by the son of Fernán González in 978. It owes its impressive appearance to the unusually successful Dukes of Lerma, one of whom (Francisco Gómez de Sandoval y Rojas) ruled Spain between 1598 and 1618 for Felipe III. It was the Duke's idea to expel the Moriscos, and devote a part of the proceeds from their expropriated property into making Lerma (effectively, the capital of Spain during his lifetime) a unique monumental complex, with at least six monasteries and a four-towered **Palacio Ducal**, currently undergoing restoration. This is linked by a flying walkway (so the duke could attend mass without mingling with the commoners) to the **Colegiata de San Pedro**, bearing the duke's crest over the door. Inside, the church contains its original organ of 1616 and a statue in bronze of the archbishop of Seville, the uncle of the Duke. The tourist office (*see* above) offers guided tours of the town (*11–2 and 5–7*).

Much further south, **Gumiel de Hizán** has a fine 15th-century parish church with monumental stairs and a beautiful Renaissance *retablo* by an unknown master; the adjacent museum, open when the priest is around, has Romanesque capitals salvaged from its long gone monastery. Gumiel marks the northern limits of D.O. Ribera del Duero, the largest and finest wine region in Castile, producing a variety of reds, especially from a local grape known as *tinto del país*; mixed with garnacha, malbec, merlot and cabernet sauvignon, it becomes a fresh rosé, a purplish young wine or a mellow well aged wine; '81, '86 and '89 are excellent; Vega Sicilia is is the most illustrious name. **Aranda de Duero**, the third town of the province, has a number of old *bodegas* and a pair of good churches: **Santa María** has a beautiful portal attributed to Simón de Colonia and an excellent Renaissance *retablo*.

Downriver, the Augustinian **Monasterio de la Vid** ('of the vine', *open 10–1 and 4–7.30*) boasts an 18th-century Baroque façade with spiralling leaves and roses on the sides of the elegant belfry and octagonal dome. East of Aranda, picturesque **Peñaranda de Duero** is built around the sprawling castle of its medieval lords, the Avellaneda, who in the safer 16th century decided to move down into the arcaded Plaza Mayor. A fine Plateresque portal marks their **Palacio de los Zúñiga y Avellaneda** (*open 10–1.30 and 4–7, closed*

Mon), built around an elegant two-storey patio; rooms are adorned with superb *artesonado* ceilings and plasterwork. Around the corner, a 17th-century **Botica de Jimeno** is the second oldest pharmacy in Spain, in the same family for seven generations; of its original fittings, there are some 230 pharmaceutical jars, stills and books.

North of Peñaranda, the half-ruined silhouette of a castle tops **Coruña del Conde**, where in the 18th century a local inventor named Diego Marín made the first manned flight in Spain. The equally isolated 11th-century **Ermita del Santo Cristo** is made out of stones cannibalized from the Roman city of **Clunia** (just north, near Peñalba de Castro, where the guardian lives; *open 10–2 and 4–8. winter 5–7, closed Sun pm and Mon*). Founded under the reign of Augustus, it counted 30,000 inhabitants at its peak. In AD 69 Galba, Governor of Nearer Spain, rose up here against Nero and was proclaimed Emperor by his legionaries; the Senate concurred, leaving Nero to run himself through. He was the first ruler to come from outside the Julian and Claudian families, although he adopted the names Caesar and Augustus. Managing to displease nearly everybody by the time he got to Rome, he was brutally murdered the next year by Otho, his successor—another, more ominous precedent. Clunia was abandoned with the fall of Rome, leaving the forum, a large if eroded rock-cut theatre, baths, temples, and houses with mosaics dusty and mute.

© *(947–)*   **Where to Stay and Eating Out**

Covarrubias

★★★**Arlanza**, Pza. Mayor 11, © 40 30 25, ✆ 40 63 59 (*moderate*), occupies a handsome old mansion in the centre of town; its restaurant serves medieval banquets of trout and roast lamb every Saturday night with music and ancient Castilian dances; book ahead. Another fine old house contains **Galin**, Pza. Doña Urraca, © 40 30 15 (*inexpensive*), where people come from miles around to tuck into an authentic *olla podrida* and other mainstays for ridiculously low prices (1300-pts *menú*; closed Tues in winter). **Torreón de Doña Urraca**, Pza. Doña Sancha, © 40 31 08 (*moderate*), has a delightful terrace, open only in summer.

Santo Domingo de Silos

The charming ★★★**Tres Coronas**, Pza. Mayor 6, © 38 07 27, ✆ 38 80 25 (*moderate*), is located in a 17th-century house, with 16 intimate rooms; its restaurant, **Casa Emeterio**, features Castilian cuisine (*menú* 2200pts). Near the famous cloister, ★★**Arco de San Juan**, Pradera de San Juan, © 38 07 94 (*moderate*), is quiet and offers a delightful garden; family-run **Méson Asador**, C/ Principal, © 39 00 53, has inexpensive rooms and food. Men 'in need of spiritual exercise' can eat and sleep for a song (well, almost) in the monastery by ringing the Padre Hospedería, © 38 07 68.

Aranda de Duero

Aranda gets plenty of business travellers en route to Madrid and concentrates its functional hotels near the highway; most have cheap weekend rates. ★★★**Los**

Bronces, Ctra Madrid–Irún km 160, ✆ 50 08 50, near the Burgos exit, and
★★★Tres Condes, at Avda. Castilla 66, ✆ 50 24 00, ✆ 50 24 04, are typica (*both moderate*). There are two special places to eat, however: **Mesón de la Villa**, Pza. Mayor 3, ✆ 50 10 25, serves some of the best food around, including poultry and garden vegetables raised on owner Eugenio Herrero's own farm, accompanied by the finest Riojas (around 4000 pts, closed Mon). The second is **Rafael Corrales**, Carrequemada 2, ✆ 50 02 77, an *asador* that opened in 1902 serving baby lamb baked in a wood oven, washed down with Ribera del Duero (closed Thurs).

Along the Pilgrimage Route: Burgos to Carrión de los Condes

Those rayes that do but warm you in England, do roast you here;
those beams that irridate onely, and gild your honey-suckled fields,
do here scorch and parch the chinky gaping soyle, and put too many
wrinkles on the face of your common mother.

Howell

If the medieval pilgrim survived the storms, cut-throats and wolves at Roncesvalles, the Navarrese who exposed themselves when excited, and the dupers and fleshpots of Burgos, then they faced the dustiest, flattest, hottest and most monotonous landscape in Europe. The idea is that with nothing to look at, one becomes introspective and meditative, altogether in a proper state to receive enlightenment. On the other hand, nearly all the route between Burgos and Léon is off the highways, on paths and lonely backroads where 20th-century intrusions are rare; their straggling hamlets of humble adobe houses, church towers crowned with storks and huge dovecotes (pigeon was the only meat the country folk could afford) evoke the Middle Ages as powerfully as any cathedral.

Getting Around

Daily buses run from Burgos to Aguilar de Campóo and Cervera de Pisuerga, to Palencia, Frómista, Sahagún, Saldaña and Carríon (on the Burgos–León route), to Sasamón and Grijalba. Frómista can also be reached by train between Palencia and Santander.

Tourist Information

Frómista: Pso. Central (summer only).
Carrión de los Condes: Pza. Santa María (summer only).

From Burgos to the Puente de Fitero

After Burgos, the pilgrim's path goes straight to Castrojeriz, leaving the N 120 in Tardajos; by car the first important stop is **Sasamón**, 33km west of the capital. This was the Celtiberian Segisamo, where Augustus camped with his Macedonian legions, en route to pummel the Cantabrians. The town's pride is its church of **Santa María la Real**, with an exact 12th-century copy of the Sarmental door on the cathedral of Burgos; it has a good if damaged cloister and a statue of St Michael attributed to Diego de Siloé. The

Ermita de San Isidro Labrador has a superb 16th-century cross, the Cruz del Humilladero. Of the third church, the 15th-century **San Miguel**, only the portal survives with its seven archivaults isolated in a field like a lost triumphal arch (the rest of the church has vanished into thin air). In nearby **Olmillos**, the stately 15th-century castle belonged to the Leví, a noble family of Conversos; the current owner plans to convert it into a pilgrims' guesthouse. A few kilometres east, at **Grijalba**, the 13th-century Gothic church of **Santa María de los Reyes** has plenty of gargoyles and carved capitals with New Testament themes; inside, the ribs of the vaults are painted with alligators with sharp teeth. The font is a pretty 12th-century work carved with interlacings, supported by a lion and serpent.

The main road, however, heads south of Tardajos to pass through the little village of **Hornillos del Camino**, with an old pilgrims' hospital, the Espíritu Santo. After Hornillos the road passes right through the haunting, ravaged remains of the 14th-century **Monasterio de San Antón**, its once magnificent vaults hanging miraculously in the void. Its monks were famous for treating pilgrims afflicted with 'St Anthony's fire' or erysipelas, inflammations on the body, associated with leprosy. What really went on is a medieval mystery. The Order of St Anthony was founded in France in 1093, named after a 5th-century anchorite in the Egyptian desert, often depicted holding fire in his hands, symbolic of spiritual force and energy. His followers went about dressed in blue with the Greek T or *tau*, the cross of St Anthony, sown on their black habits, bearing a staff and bell; they would not only give passing pilgrims a meal but little *tau*-shaped amulets holding 'St Anthony's fire'. As St Anthony was also the patron of domestic animals (if not pictured with fiery hands, Anthony is shown with his pet pig), his monks kept pigs, or rather, let them run wild, a practice that ended when one jaywalking porker in Paris tripped up the horse bearing the Dauphin and caused him to break his neck.

Westward is the medieval castle and village of **Castrojeriz**, an old Iberian settlement that once had seven hospitals and a residence of Pedro the Cruel along its long Calle de los Peregrinos. In 974, Fernán González wrote down its privileges in a charter, giving equal rights to Christians and Jews. Its finest monument is at the village entrance: the Gothic church of **Santa María del Manzano**, named after the apple tree trunk where its statue of the Virgin was found when Santiago himself, on his white horse, leapt from the castle to the tree; note the horseshoes on the door. Inside there are 16th-century tapestries and a *retablo* by Mengs; other tapestries, 17th-century and Flemish, are displayed in the parish museum of **Santo Domingo**; **San Juan**, built next to a 12th-century tower, conserves a half-ruined 14th-century cloister with an *artesonado mudéjar* ceiling. An 8km detour to the south leads to **Celada del Camino**, which recalls a former pilgrimage rôle in its name and in its late Romanesque church, with striking Gothic tombs. Closer to Castrojeriz, **Castrillo de Matajudíos** (apparently not 'Kill Jews' but 'Hill of Jews') was the birthplace of the great Spanish composer of the Renaissance, Antonio de Cabezón.

West of Castrojeriz the ruthless horizons of the *meseta* come into their own. The last hill for miles, the windswept Alto de Mostelares (900m) looks over the Pisuerga river, the traditional frontier between Castile and León, although these days it merely delimits the dotted line between Burgos and Palencia provinces. It is spanned by the handsome

Puente de Fitero with 11 arches, built in the 11th century by pilgrimage-promoter Alfonso IV. Just before the bridge are the ruins of a 13th-century hospital of San Nicolás; just across it begins the Tierra de Campos, the high plains of the Visigoths. Little **Boadilla del Camino**, the first village (9km), has a beautiful 15th-century Gothic column in its plaza decorated with scallops. The parish church has a curious Romanesque baptismal font on twelve baby columns and decorated with swastikas and solar symbols.

Frómista

Six km west, **Frómista** has been a key pilgrims' stop since the days of the *Codex Calixtinus* for its 'perfect Romanesque church', golden **San Martín** (*open 10–2 and 4.30–8, winter 3–6.30*), founded in 1035 by the widow of Sancho the Great. Restored in 1893 with no little controversy by the arch-restorer of France, Viollet-le-Duc, San Martín is now a national monument stripped of all its trappings. Two slender round turrets buttress the west door; inside the proportions of the three-aisled, three-apsed, barrel-vaulted interior crowned by an octagonal tower satisfy the soul, and send shivers of delight up the spine of every architect who has ever entered. But just as noteworthy is the extraordinary amount of sculpted detail inside and out, on the modillons and capitals; the original 11th-century carvings are superb and easy to distinguish from the fond fancies of the restorers, who based their work on medieval sarcophagi and marked their work with an R. The whole is a tantalising, but ultimately inaccessible, book of hundreds of medieval symbols and occult messages; a pair of binoculars comes in handy and a crique in the neck is probably unavoidable. The dedication to Martin, the 4th-century bishop of Tours, is also meaningful: Martin was a strong defender of the Priscillianists when they were persecuted and when Prisciliano was executed for heresy (*see* p.281); not that he supported their gnostic-Celtic beliefs as much as he fought the Church's use of civil means and persecutions to put down heresies. Of Frómista's other churches, note especially the 16th-century **Santa María del Castillo** with its elaborate painted Hispano-Flemish *retablo* with 29 panels. Near Frómista, you can visit four sets of locks of the **Castilian Canal**, dug in the 18th and 19th century and the inspiration for Lesseps' bigger ditch in Panama.

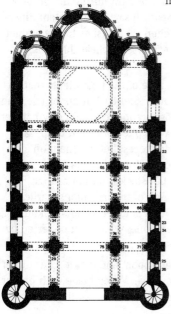

Plan of San Martín

Beyond Frómista, the tawny little villages of Palencia merge into the tawny earth. **Villarmentero de Campos** has a delightful picnic ground, with a lawn for a siesta to prepare yourself for the next stop at **Villalcázar de Sirga**, once a thriving town and key Templar possession. The Knights, at the start of the 13th century, built the enormous church of **Santa María la Blanca**, with what must be the tallest porch in Spain to shelter a richly decorated double portal with a double frieze (if closed, find the sacristan who lives around the corner on the street left of the church). Pilgrims would make a beeline to the Capilla de Santiago and its miraculous Virgin to whom Alfonso X the Wise dedicated his *Cantigas* and who looks a little worse for wear, with her peasant features and headless child, but modern visitors tend to head straight to the beautifully carved tombs sculpted by Antón Pérez de Carrión of the Infante Don Felipe (son of Fernando III the Saint) and his second wife, Leonor Ruiz de Castro, curiously gagged. Don Felipe, fifth of 14 children, was pursuing a meteoric ecclesiastical career and had just been made archbishop of Seville when he reversed course and married the Norwegian princess promised to his brother, the future Alfonso X. The princess died after four years and is buried in Covarrubias; Felipe soon remarried, but not long after, in 1271, was murdered by his brother, the next in line for the throne, none other than Alfonso who got away with it (no wonder he celebrated the Virgin's miracles). Here too is the tomb of a Knight Templar, with his hawk and sleeping lion: a rare burial, as most Templars were buried face down in the earth without a casket. The magnificent *retablo mayor* was painted by the school of Berruguete.

Richard Ford's Recipe for Roadkill

No writer on Spain can ever hope to match Richard Ford, author of the *Handbook for Travellers in Spain*, (1845), the first serious guide to Spain and perhaps the best to any country, ever. No subject daunted him, not even Spanish cuisine. He diplomatically advises his readers to never let mine host's cat out of sight during the preparation of a meal, then quotes the old Spanish saying 'A prudent diner will never look too closely into the things of the kitchen if he wishes to live a quiet life'; after all, Ford reasonably adds: 'it is the knowledge of the cheat that kills, not the cat' simmering away in the *olla podrida*.

Ford goes on to suggest that if you really want to be sure of the ingredients that go into your dinner, the only thing to do is have your own valet cook it up for you, and offers a fine recipe for a *guisado*: 'Take hare, partridge, rabbit, chicken, or whatever you may have foraged on the road; it is also capital with pheasant...cut it up, save the blood, the liver and the gibblets; do not wash the pieces, but dry them on a cloth; fry them with onions in a teacup of oil till browned; take an *olla* (pot), put in the bits with oil, equal portions of wine and water, but stock is far better than water; claret answers well, Valdepeñas better; add a bit of bacon, onions, garlic, salt, pepper pimientos, a bunch of thyme or herbs; let it simmer, carefully skimming it. Half an hour before serving, add the giblets; when done, which can be tested by feeling with a fork, serve hot.

The stew should be constantly stirred with a wooden spoon, and grease, the ruin of all cookery, carefully skimmed off as it rises to the surface. When made with proper care and with a good salad, it forms a supper for a cardinal, or for Santiago himself'.

Castrojeriz (© 947–)

★★El Méson, Cordón 1, © 37 74 00, offers a handful of rooms in an old mill (and a new annex), a peaceful setting and simple favourites like trout stuffed with ham in the dining room (*moderate–inexpensive*).

Frómista (© 979–)

Hostería de Los Palmeros, Pza. San Telmo, © 81 00 67, began its career as a *hostal* for pilgrims, although the medieval has been seasoned with several styles since; furnished with antiques, its 10 expensive rooms are complemented by a fine restaurant with an *artesonado* ceiling; dinners around 3500 pts (closed Tues except in summer). **★Hs San Telmo,** Martín Veña 8, © 81 01 02 (*moderate*), is a good second choice; **Fonda Marisa,** © 81 00 23, costs even less and cooks up good cheap *menús.*

Villalcázar de Sirga (© 979–)

There's nowhere to stay except at the pilgrims' shelter behind the town hall, but a charming old *posada* awaits for lunch or dinner, the very popular **Mesón Villasirga,** Pza. Mayor © 88 80 22, featuring baked sucking-pig with almonds and other Castilian favourites (no cat, we promise) for 2800 pts (open daily May–Oct, other times Fri, Sat, and Sun only; book at weekends).

North of Frómista: the Románico Palentino

If you've the time or inclination, you could do worse than take a wander off the beaten track into the northern part of Palencia province, into the foothills of the Cantabrian mountains, known as the Románico Palentino for its rare collection of some 200 mostly untouched, never remodelled Romanesque churches (nothing less than the greatest concentration in Europe). It seems that masons brought in to build churches along the *camino* came up here to build churches in the new villages, founded to repopulate the region. Aguilar de Campóo, linked by bus from Burgos or Palencia, or train from Santander, makes the best base for exploring, although you really need a car and patience, and that most elusive object of desire: a good map of Spain (but try the Nuevo Atlas de España if you can find one).

Tourist Information

Aguilar de Campóo: Pza. Mayor 33, © (979) 12 20 24 (July and Aug only).

North to Aguilar

Northwest of Alar del Rey (on the Santander–Palencia N 611) you can easily see two of the finest Romanesque works in the region. **San Andrés de Arroyo** (*open summer 9.30–1.15 and 4.15–7.15, winter 9.30–12 and 3.15–6.15*) is a Bernardine convent founded in 1190 with an interesting little museum; the entrance to the chapterhouse is beautiful and the cloister has extraordinary twin columns and capitals, decorated with interlacings and fretwork, zigzags and exotic flora. The second church, golden-stone **Moarves de Ojeda** has a superb portal, with a Christ in a mandorla, four Evangelists and twelve Apostles; the capitals are crowded with people and inside there's a 13th-century baptismal font and a Gothic Virgin and Child. Other prime stops on the Romanesque trail are north of Moarves: **Cozuelos**, with a simple early 12th-century church; **Vallespinoso de Aguilar**, where a fortified 12th-century hermitage on a rock has a cylindrical tower and pretty door; and **Barrio de Santa María**, a handsome village where the Ermita de Santa Eulalia is a pristine example of 13th-century church with a lovely apse and the narrowest windows in Spain, complete with 13th-century murals inside. Barrio de Santa María's parish church underwent a Renaissance remodelling and has good 15th-century paintings inside and a finely carved Renaissance *retablo mayor.* From Vallespinoso the road skirts the Aguilar reservoir to Aguilar de Campóo (*see* below).

Alternatively, if you stick to the N-611, north of Alar del Rey, you'll find (just to the left) **Becerril del Carpio** with two Romanesque churches: one in Barrio de San Pedro with a fine portal; one in Barrio de Santa María, amid the Baroque mansions, where they had enough pesetas to remodel the church and give it some fancy retables. In nearby **Santa María de Mave**, the monastery founded in 1208 has a fine portal, an octagonal lantern and some Renaissance murals in one of its three apses; the monastery building itself has been converted into a charming hotel (*see* below). The church in **Olleros de Pisuerga** to the west is some 300 years older, a rare example of a Spanish church carved into the living rock, with two naves. Further north, only a kilometre from Aguilar, **Lomilla** has a pretty Romanesque church with a 14th-century calvary.

Aguilar de Campóo

Set in the green mountain valley of the Río Pisuerga and next to a large man-made lake, Aguilar de Campóo is a picturesque town of cookie bakers and decidedly leaning, medieval houses with big bold coats-of-arms, founded in the 10th century during the Reconquista resettlement scheme. The Aguilar, or eagle, of its name refers to its rocky limestone outcrop, its eagle's nest, crowned by a ruined but still mighty five-towered castle built in the 11th century. At the foot of the castle, the **Hermitage of Santa Cecilia** (get the key in the *casa rectoral*) was founded in 1041, and has a fine 12th-century tower and exceptional capitals: one shows the Massacre of the Innocents, by 11th-century knights in fishscale armour. The town walls were erected in the 1300s by Pedro I of Castile; one of the surviving six gates has an inscription in Hebrew as well as Spanish, a rare (and unique) souvenir of Aguilar's once sizeable Jewish population. On the arcaded Plaza de España, the **Palacio de los Marqueses** is where Charles V once spent a week; the Gothic **Colegiata de San Miguel** has the Renaissance mausoleum of the Marquesses of Aguilar and a **museum** (*open 10–1 and 5–8*) full of tombs, *retablos* and sculptures. Another square is named after Aguilar native Juan Martín, one of the 18 sailors to return on Magellan's ship around the world. Two km west of Aguilar, the Cistercian monastery of **Santa María la Real** (1213) has more excellent capitals and a good cloister; in 1988 it won a Europa Nostra award for its restoration and now shelters a **Centre of**

Romanesque Studies, with plenty of information on, and a unique collection of, models of the region's churches (*open 10–3 and 4–8, Sat and Sun 11–2 and 5–7*). Tradition has it that Bernardo de Carpio is buried in a cave nearby; offended by Charlemagne's invasion of Spain in the *Chanson de Roland*, Castilian troubadours invented Bernardo as their own hero, a doughty warrior who along with the Castilians joined up with the Saracens and personally slew Roland, the brutish Frank invader. But after the battle of Roncesvalles Bernardo was betrayed by his own king and joined the Moors for good.

Romanesque Routes North of Aguilar

The road directly north of Aguilar takes in more Romanesque charmers: the 12th-century church at **Matalbaniega**, with two decorated portals, carved modillons and unusual caryatids holding up a window. **Cillamayor**'s Romanesque church has a funerary hypogeum; at **Revilla de Santullán**, the church has a handsome portal with its fifteen figures, sitting at desks like members of the board, and other sculptures that verge on the pornographic. Further along, **Valberzoso**'s church has 15th-century frescoes; the village of **Brañosera** claims to be one of the oldest municipalities in Spain, with its charter dating back to 824; its Romanesque church has a good 12th-century portal. **Salcedillo**'s church also has a 12th-century portal; medieval **Villanueva de la Torre** has a 14th-century tower and church. **San Cebrián de Muda**'s 12th-century church has Renaissance paintings and murals.

West of Aguilar, **Cervera de Pisuerga** was once an important frontier settlement, but has retired to its meadows and old family manors, proud of its recently restored 16th-century Gothic church, **Santa María del Castillo**, built on the medieval citadel, with a fine Hispano-Flemish *retablo* by Felipe de Vigarni and a beautiful painting of the *Adoration of the Magi* by Juan de Flandres, both in the Capilla de Santa Ana. Three km away, at **Ruesga**, there are huge views across the mountains, and a *parador* to enjoy them. At the northernmost point of Palencia province, **San Salvador de Cantamuda** is a graceful church with a pretty steeple and altar table. Southeast of Cervera de Pisuerga, **Perazancas de Ojeda** has not only a good Romanesque parish church, but the 12th-century Lombard Romanesque hermitage of San Pelayo with contemporary murals.

© (979–)   *Where to Stay and Eating Out*

Aguilar de Campóo

★★★**Valentin**, Avda. Generalísimo 21, © 12 21 25 (*moderate*), is a scenic mountain hotel in an elegant old building (in need of a lick of paint) with a garden and good restaurant; or there's the less expensive ★★**Villa de Aguilar**, Alférez Provisional, © 12 22 25 (*moderate*) with all rooms with bath. In Santa María de Mave, 12km from Aguilar, the serene ★★**Hostería El Convento**, © 12 36 11 (*moderate*), occupies a lovingly restored Benedictine monastery, the perfect place to sleep in, if you're doing the Romanesque route. Delicious, simple and satisfying food awaits at **Cortés**, El Puente 39, © 12 30 55: menus for under 2000 pts, or you can splurge on the *caldereta de pescados y mariscos* (a huge seafood stew for two) for 8000 pts.

Cervera de Pisuerga

Up on the edge of the Picos near man-made lakes and newborn rivers, the modern ★★★**Parador Fuentes Carrionas**, Ctra. de Ruesga, ✆ 87 00 75, ✉ 87 01 05 (*expensive*), makes a plush headquarters for nature-lovers, with a good restaurant. Plaza España has a couple of inexpensive choices, among them, ★**Siglo XX**, ✆ 12 29 00, with average food. For a meat orgy, **Gasolina**, by Plaza Mayor, ✆ 87 07 13, will fill you up with offerings from its oven and grill for under 3000 pts. For something sweet, **Uko**, Ukaldo Merino 15, is famous across Spain for its puff pastries.

Along the Carrión River

West of Frómista, into the *campos góticos*, the Visigothic plains, the pilgrims' route continues to Carrión de los Condes, which also occupies one of Old Castile's chief north–south arteries. Palencia and environs were more important in Roman and Visigothic times than now; among the things to see are two Roman villas and the oldest dated church in Spain.

Getting Around

Carrión de los Condes is connected by **bus** with Frómista and Palencia at least twice a day. Palencia is easy to leave: there are frequent **trains** to Burgos, Valladolid, Ávila, Madrid and Santander (via Frómista and Aguilar de Campóo); trains to León call at Paredes de Nava. The RENFE station is at Jardinillos, ✆ (979) 74 30 19. The bus station is nearby, on Avda. Dr. Simón Nieto.

Tourist Information

Palencia: Mayor 105, ✆ (979) 74 00 68.

Back on the Pilgrim Track: Carrión de los Condes

West of Villalcázar de Sirga, Carrión de los Condes is named after the river Carrión and not for putrefying nobility, although it can't be denied that the Infantes or Counts of Carrión, who married the Cid's two daughters, were genuinely rotten villains; after picking up their big, glittering dowries, they beat their wives and tied them to oaks and left them for dead. The outraged Cid gathered up a posse, killed the Counts, and found his daughters new, even more princely husbands. The wicked Infantes are buried in the lovely Renaissance cloister of **San Zoilo**, a Benedictine monastery by the river, founded in 1047, when the Emir of Córdoba sent the 4th-century relics of Zoilo to the Count of Carrión. The lower gallery of the cloister is the work of Juan de Badajoz, who began in 1537; the upper bit was added in 1604. It looks its best on Friday nights, when the monastery hosts medieval dinners complete with troubadours; to book, call ✆ 88 00 50.

Over the 16th-century bridge from San Zoilo, the heart of Carrión has two worn 12th-century Romanesque churches that preserve interesting portals: **Santiago**, in the Plaza Mayor, with its Christ in Majesty and apostles and representatives of 22 medieval guilds, including an armourer, scholar, musicians, cooks, tailor, smith, soldiers bashing each other, and contortionists. On the edge of town, **Santa María del Camino** has a capital on the portal depicting the Tribute of 100 Maidens that the Castilians sent yearly to the Moors (probably because they had nothing else the Moors could possibly want); other figures are of Samson fighting the lion and women riding beasts. The interior is out of kilter, although whether it was done so intentionally (like Getaria, for instance) is hard to fathom; it could just be falling over. Lastly, the **Convent of Santa Clara** has just opened a small **museum**, with religious art and a 17th-century organ (*open 10.30–12.30 and 4–6*). During the great days of the pilgrimage, the town produced two men of genius: Rabbi Shem Tov Ardutiel (Sem Tob), author of the *Danza General de la Muerte*, who died in 1370, and Íñigo López de Mendoza, the Marqués de Santillana, the Renaissance poet, not to be confused with the tycoon who bought the title (*see* p.181). Lastly, just off the road before the province of León, you can visit the 3rd-century AD **Roman villa** at **Quintanilla de la Cueza** for its colourful mosaic floors and the heating system or hypocausts, protected by a shelter; there's a small museum on the site with finds.

South along the Carrión to Palencia

Paredes de Nava was the birthplace of two influential Castilian artists, painter Pedro Berruguete (d.1504) who worked in Urbino and introduced the Renaissance style to Spain as court painter to Fernando and Isabel and his son Alonso (d.1561), a pupil of Michelangelo, who brought mannerism back with him and served as court painter to Charles V, although sculpture was his real love. A few of the Berruguetes' paintings, including a *retablo mayor* by Pedro, remain in **Santa Eulalia**, with its delicious bell tower. The adjacent **museum** (*open 11–2 and 4–7*) has an impressive collection of works by other Renaissance masters (Gil de Siloé, Juan de Valmaseda, Juan de Flandres, Juan de Juni, etc.) brought in from little churches in artsy Paredes de Nava. If you can't get enough, more paintings by Pedro Berruguete are in the church in **Becerril de Campos**, 10km south.

Palencia

Palencia is one of the bigger wallflowers in the garden of Spain's provincial capitals, although in 1185 Alfonso VIII made it the site of Spain's first university (in 1239 it was removed to Salamanca). Part of the blame for Palencia's failure to thrive rests squarely on the shoulders of Charles V who, after sucking the city dry to pay for the bribes he needed to be elected Holy Roman Emperor, rubbed out the city's prospects and privileges in revenge for its leading role in the Comunero revolt.

The one thing they couldn't take away from Palencia is its Gothic **cathedral**, nicknamed *La Bella Desconocida* ('the Unknown Beauty'), in Plaza San Antolín (*open 10.30–1 and 4–6.30, Sun and hols 9–2; adm to crypt and museum*). The exterior is austerely plain except for two portals; Juan de Flandres' Renaissance *retablo mayor* is the prize in an interior that has remained more or less unchanged—a lack of Baroque curlicues and rolling eyeballs is a tell-tale sign of decline in a Spanish town. The oldest part of the crypt (673) is the only known surviving example of a Visigothic martyrium, built by King Wamba before he was shuttled off to a monastery (in the 7th century, the Visigothic kings lived in nearby

Pampliega, a little village that time forgot). Among the highlights in the museum is an early *San Sebastián* by El Greco and a fine *Virgin and Child* by Pedro Berruguete. Don't miss the clock in the transept, where a Lion and Knight strike the hours with gusto.

The bridge over the Carrión, the Puentecillas, is contemporary with the cathedral; 11th-century **San Miguel**, further south, is a fine little ogival Romanesque church, where the Cid married his Ximena. East of Calle Mayor, the 16th-century **Santa Clara** has a famous *Cristo Yacente* that elicited the comment from the ultra-pious Felipe II: 'If I had faith, I would believe that this was the real body of Christ.' Until the archaeology museum reopens (ask at the tourist office) you can take some comfort in the privately-run **Museo de la Calzada**, just off C/ Mayor on C/ Barrio y Mier 10 (*open 12–2 and 7–9, closed Thurs and Sun*) where Juan Carlos's personal cobbler displays pairs of his Majesty's shoes, along with other celebrities' footwear.

Ten km south of Palencia in the village of **Baños de Cerrato** (2km from Venta de Baños), the Visigothic King Recesvinto (he of the famous golden crown with dangling letters spelling his name) founded the sturdy church of **San Juan de Baños** back in 661 (*open 10–1 and 4–7, closed Mon; Patricio, the guardian, lives just opposite*), the purest example of Visigothic architecture to come down to us. Fretwork windows like impossible key holes and a carved doorway (and a belfry, added by the restorers) relieve the simple stone exterior. Inside, the nave is divided by rows of horseshoe arches, and the capitals, doorways, and the apse are discreetly decorated with finely carved 8-pointed crosses (*croix pattées*), leaves, scallop shells, solar spirals and palms. Recesvinto's rather complex dedicatory inscription survives intact on the triumphal arch, framed by modillons decorated with diving eagles. In its use of pleasing, robust architectural volumes and the concentration of intricate detail in a few places, San Juan has been called the first Spanish church. Recent excavations uncovered 58 7th-century tombs and the original plan of the church, with its three apses standing out separately like prongs on a fork; in the Middle Ages it was condensed into a more ordinary rectangle. The Baños of its name refers to a nearby curative spring, closed in by two Visigothic arches and restored in 1941.

North of Carrión de los Condes: Saldaña and a Roman Villa

From Carrión de los Condes, the C 615 follows the river Carrión up to **Renedo de la Vega** and the ruins of the monastery of Santa María de la Vega, a *mudéjar* work of 1215; the parish church has a fine Renaissance cross. Further north, towards Lobera, a sign points the way to **Pedrosa de la Vega** (1.5km), where the 3rd–4th-century Roman **Villa of Olmeda** was discovered in 1968 (*open winter 11–1.30 and 4–6, summer 10–1.30 and 5–7, closed Mon*) with its perfectly preserved polychrome mosaic floors, including not only geometric designs, but also mythological and hunting scenes. Nearby, in the pretty medieval village of **Saldaña**, the church of San Pedro houses finds from the ongoing excavations. Saldaña's ruined 11th-century castle was the residence of Doña Urraca, sister and advisor of Alfonso VI; the 15th-century Gothic **San Miguel** has a *retablo* attributed to Gil de Siloé and effigy tombs of the Counts of Saldaña. The holy of holies in these parts is an 8th-century statue of the Virgin in the neoclassical **Ermita de la Virgen del Valle**.

Carrión de los Condes (℡ 979–)

There are simple rooms and a restaurant at the monastery **San Zoilo** (℡ 88 11 45, ✆ 88 10 90), but plans for a fancier future when restoration works are completed; otherwise, there's the pleasant ★**Hs La Corte**, Santa María 34, ℡ 88 01 38 (*moderate*), with a good restaurant or the even cheaper beds at **El Resbalón**, C/ Marqués de Santillana, ℡ 88 00 11, which also serves filling *menús* for around 1000 pts including wine and dessert. South of Carrión in Villoldo,★★**Estrella del Bajo Carrión**, Ctra. Palencia-Riaño, ℡ 82 70 05, ✆ 82 72 69 (*moderate*), is comfortable and modern family hotel with a large garden; good meals at around 3000 pts.

Palencia (℡ 979–)

★★★**Rey Sancho de Castilla**, Avda. Ponce de León, ℡ 72 53 00, ✆ 71 03 34 (*expensive*), has recently been restored and offers a number of diversions—swimming, tennis, TV, bingo—and activities for children. For the same price and facilities (though no pool) ★★★**Castilla La Vieja** is another sound choice on Avda. Casado del Alisal 26, ℡ 74 90 44, ✆ 74 75 77 (*expensive*), with a good restaurant. ★★**Monclús,** Menéndez Pelayo 3, ℡ 74 43 00 (*moderate*), is comfortable and good value. **Lorenzo**, Casado del Alisal 6, ℡ 74 35 45 (*moderate*), cooks up the best and most traditional food in town, cooked by mama 'La Gorda'; among its specialities is *pisto*—creamed tomatoes, peppers, onions; *menús* 3700 pts (closed Sun). **Casa Damian**, Ignacio Martínez de Azcoitia 9, ℡ 74 46 28 (*moderate*), serves up steaming bowls of Castilian *menestra de verduras*, its speciality, and other regional dishes (closed Mon). For something cheaper, there's **Ecuador-Casa Matías**, Martín Calleja 19, with hams, sausages and wines, and **Taberna Plaza Mayor**, for *raciones* of gambas and other nice things.

Along the Pilgrims' Road to León

The *camino de Santiago* continues its flat way towards León, almost imperceptibly rising as it crosses 236km of the largest province in Castile. Framed by the Cordillera Cantábrica to the north and the lower, softer Montes de León to the west, the province was a refuge for Mozarabs from Andalucía in the first days of the Reconquista, and what remains of their monasteries are among the finest monuments along the whole road.

Getting Around

Sahagún is linked by trains between Palencia and León and less frequently by buses between León and Carrión de los Condes.

Tourist Information

Valencia de Don Juan: Pza. del Generalísimo 1, ℡ (987) 75 04 64

Sahagún and its *Mudéjar* Bricks

Sahagún started out as the site of a Roman villa and an early Christian basilica dedicated to San Facundo, a martyred legionary. During the 12th century, when it was the seventh official stop of the *Codex Calixtinus*, it had a population of 12,000 and artificially concentrated so much wealth in the middle of nowhere that it earned the nickname the 'Las Vegas of the Middle Ages'. Today a mere 3000 souls try to fill up the dusty plaza mayor, the darkened old porticoes and forlorn chewed-up houses.

Sahagún's rise and fall went hand in hand with that of Spain's most powerful Benedictine abbey, **San Benito**. In 904, the old Roman road had just started its transformation into the pilgrim's way when the site was purchased by Alfonso III the Great of Asturias for a community of Mozarab refugees from Andalucía. Although twice burned by the Moors, the seeds of its future glory were sown in the 11th century when Sancho III of Castile snatched León, the inheritance of his brother Alfonso, and locked Alfonso up in the abbey. He was about to tear out Alfonso's eyes for good measure when their sister Urraca intervened. Urraca had always liked Alfonso better, and managed to save his eyes by promising nasty Sancho to become a nun. With both siblings locked away, Sancho felt safe on the throne. But Alfonso made a secret pact with the abbot of San Benito, who helped him escape and take refuge with the Moors in Toledo. In 1072, Sancho was assassinated and Alfonso was crowned king of Castile and León.

Like Henry VIII, Alfonso VI married his way through six wives; those from Aquitaine and Burgundy put him into contact with Cluny—the great promoter of the Santiago pilgrimage. Never forgetting the help he received at Sahagún, the king refounded San Benito in 1080 under the new Cluniac reforms and made his personal confessor, Bernard de Sédirac (the future Primate of Spain), its first abbot. Alfonso poured money into the abbey, gave it vast estates, and founded a huge pilgrims' hospital. In its heyday San Benito even minted its own coins; in 1534 its theological school had the status of a university. Felipe II brought it low by moving the school to Navarra's Monasterio de Irache in 1596 and constraining the abbey to pay nearly all of its rents to the crown. In the 18th century two fires finished off what remained, leaving only a 17th-century portal by Felipe Berrojo, now a decorative city gate at the west end of town, an ungainly clock tower and the adjacent ruins of the 12th-century Gothic **Capilla de San Mancio** with its brick arches. Smaller bits of San Benito are in the **museum** in the **Monasterio Santa Cruz** *(open 10–2.30 and 4.30 –6.30, closed winter)*: the tombs of Alfonso VI and a few of his wives and the great silver *custodia* by master Enrique de Arfe, which makes official appearances only for Corpus Cristi but the nuns will show it if you ask (especially if you make a donation); they also run a pilgrims' *hostal.*

What Sahagún never had was a ready supply of building stone, which led to the craftsmen who immigrated here from the Moorish lands to develop an architecture in brick, a medium that permitted new decorative patterns and delicacy. The first example, **San Tirso** *(open 10.30–1.30 and 5–8, Sun 10–1.20, closed Mon)* was built near the monastery in the first decade of the 12th century, with its squat, tapering skyscraper-tower rising out three round apses; recent restoration work unearthed two sculpted Mozarab imposts with floral reliefs from the original monastery. **San Lorenzo** is just a little later and more obviously Moorish in design, but has suffered more changes over time, its interior redone in the 18th century (the chapel has Renaissance reliefs by Juan de Juni); both churches have porticoes along their sides for the famous markets Sahagún held in its boom period. In 1259 the Franciscans founded another monastery and the much damaged **Santuario de La Peregrina**, just outside the town on the N 620, the third and latest *mudéjar* church, applying the new brick techniques to Gothic; inside some lovely bits of the original stucco work survive.

Near the medieval bridge that crosses the Río Cea stands a grove of poplars. According to the *Codex Calixtinus*, these are the lances of Charlemagne's paladins who, awaiting battle with the Moor Aigolando, planted them in the ground before going to sleep. Overnight some of the lances took root and flowered, a sign of impending martyrdom. Thinking to spare the men whose lances had taken root, Charlemagne let them stay in camp when he went off to fight the Moors. But when he returned, victorious, he found that all the men he had left behind had been massacred by a Moorish raiding party. Five km south, on the Cea's bank, two sisters founded **San Pedro de las Dueñas** in the 10th century, with a beautiful Renaissance crucifix by Gregorio Fernández and 18 top-notch Romanesque capitals from the church's 1109 rebuilding, begun in stone and continued in brick by *mudéjar* craftsmen. Another road from Sahagún, the C 611, leads in 6km to the mighty, well-preserved 16th-century castle at **Grajal de Campos**.

San Miguel de Escalada

After Sahagún the pedestrian *camino* parts from the highway, to meet again at **Mansilla de las Mulas** on the river Esla, which has preserved only atmospheric ruins of its 12th-century walls, monasteries and *hostales*. Nearby, between Villamoros and Villasbariego, **Lancia** started out as an *oppidum* (fortified settlement) of the Astures; in 25 BC they were soundly defeated by the Romans after a fierce resistance; a few ruins remains, and to this day farmers uncover antiquities in the surrounding fields.

This was the new frontier back in the early days of the Reconquista, when the kings of Oviedo had just added León to their title. Among the first pioneers on the scene were Abad Adefonso and his companions, refugees from Córdoba, who in 913 founded the beautiful church of **San Miguel de Escalada** (just before Mansilla, take the road northeast 8km). The site, a gentle hill overlooking a valley, previously had a Palaeochristian church dedicated to the archangel. A lovely portico of horseshoe arches, an *ajímez* window and a heavy 11th-century tower mark the exterior, while the interior (hopefully reopened after a major restoration) is proof in golden limestone that the Cordovans never forgot the classic symmetrical Roman basilica form and its proportions. Delicate horseshoe arches divide the three aisles, and separate the transept and triple apse from the main body of the basilica (like the Byzantines, the Mozarab liturgy called for a screen between the holy precinct and the parishioners). The capitals have simple palmette designs; luxuriant floral and geometric reliefs with lions and peacocks eating grapes decorate the chancels and friezes; over the door you can make out the highly elaborate if faint dedicatory inscription. The ceiling, a later *mudéjar* addition, bears the arms of León and Castile.

Southwest of Mansilla, **Valencia de Don Juan** was named after its first duke, the son of Alfonso the Wise, and is worth a detour for a theatrical 15th-century **castle**, which rises from the banks of the Río Esla and is featured on all León's tourist brochures, with its massive walls (on one side only, like a stage set) broken by a series of slender turrets and crenellations. The surrounding Esla *vega* is one of the most fertile swathes of the province, producer of Valdevimbre-Los Oteros, a light, fruity rosé wine with an orangeish rose colour, fermented in curious bunker-like *bodegas*. Its gentle sparkle comes from a technique called *madreo*, in which whole grapes are added to the fermenting must. Only small quantities are produced; Valencia de Don Juan or Villamañán to the west provide your best chances to hunt up a bottle.

✆ (987–)   ***Where to Stay and Eating Out***

Sahagún

The **★Hs Alfonso VI**, C/ Antonio Nicolás 6, ✆ 78 11 44 (*moderate*), is one of the smarter choices in town, or there's the colourful **Fonda Asturiana**, ✆ 78 00 73 (*cheap*), with good inexpensive food. Santa Cruz's **★Hs Hospedería Benedictina**, ✆ 78 00 78 (*moderate*), has sparkling rooms with bath. In summer, the Benedictine nuns at San Pedro de las Dueñas run the serendipitous **★Hospedería Monástica**, ✆ 78 01 50 (*cheap*), with tasty inexpensive meals for the public at weekends.

Valencia de Don Juan

In the centre of town**★★Villegos II**, C/ Palacio 10, ✆ 75 01 61 (*moderate*), is an intimate family hotel with a little garden pool, overlooked by the five pretty rooms. Nearby, in the oldest house in town, **★★Hs El Palacio**, C/ Palacio 3, ✆ 75 04 74 (*moderate*), is a charming little inn, decorated with antiques and a document saying that King Felipe III once slept here (in the bed of the missus). Run by Asturians, it also has an excellent *sidería* and good home-cooking (closed Oct–May).

León

> *León tuvo veintecuatro reyes*
> *antes que Castilla leyes*
>
> (León had 24 kings before Castile even had laws)

Radiant under the famous spires of its cathedral, León is a singularly happy city of clean boulevards shaded by horse-chestnut trees: one of the few places in Spain to achieve modern *urbanización* with grace and elegance. Part of the credit for this must go to its hyperactive City Hall, which blankets the city with posters depicting itself as a friendly lion, advising the Leonese to ride the bus, recycle their glass and not to blaspheme in front of the children. The founding of a University has given the old city a transfusion of young blood and keeps the bars full until the wee hours of the morning.

History

Although the lion has long been the city's symbol, its name actually comes from *Legio Septima Gemina*, the Roman Seventh Legion, established here in AD 68 when Galba built a fort to guard the plain and the Roman road from Zaragoza. Reconquered from the Moors in the 850s by Ordoño I of Asturias (850–66), León changed hands several times again before king Ordoño II (914–24) moved his capital here. Even then, factionalism in the royal family left the city weak and prey to Moorish re-reconquests; in 981 the pious iconoclast al-Mansur grabbed it and his son reoccupied it from 996 until Alfonso V's victory at the Battle of Calatañazor in 1002. After this last Moorish hurrah, León, rebuilt and refortified, reconquered Castile. But just as León eclipsed Asturias, Castile—first a county, then a separate kingdom—eclipsed León. In 1252, under Fernando III el Santo, the on-again off-again union of the two kingdoms was finalized. Castile never looked back, but for León, then one of the largest cities in Spain, the marriage spelt nothing but decline and marginalization: the nobles went off to the court in Burgos and the people left to settle the new frontiers gained by the Reconquista.

Into this vacuum of power and influence stepped the Church: the pilgrims' road became the chief source of income. Medieval pilgrims eagerly looked forward to León, with its Hilton of a *hostal*, where they could shake the dust off their wide-brimmed hats and catch their breath for the last leg of their journey. Broken and crushed during the Comunero revolt against Charles V, León sank into oblivion until the invention of the railway made its mines viable once again. These in turn declined, leaving León its share of modern autonomy atavists who, remembering the good old days of the 10th and 11th centuries preach '*León sin Castilla*' (León without Castile). As yet their movement has little support—it's too much like a mother rejecting her own child.

Getting Around

By train: León's main Avda. de Ordoño II crosses the Bernesga river to meet the RENFE station, ✆ (987) 22 37 04. There are frequent connections with Burgos, Palencia, Medina del Campo, Madrid, Astorga, Ponferrada, Ourense and Lugo. The Transcantábrico journey to Bilbao begins at 8.50am at the FEVE station, Avda. Padre Isla 48, ✆ (987) 22 59 19, stops for a half-hour lunch at Mataporquera near the Picos de Europa and arrives at Bilbao at 7.12pm, stopping everywhere in between; regular trains depart for Oviedo and Gijón nine times a day through some magnificent mountain scenery and at least 500 tunnels.

By bus: buses, ✆ (987) 22 62 00, depart from the terminal south of the RENFE station, on Pso. Ingeniero Sáenz de Miera, for the villages in the province and Oviedo, Burgos, Santander, Salamanca and Madrid.

Tourist Information

Plaza de Regla 4, across from the cathedral, ✆ (987) 23 70 82.

There is a **market** in Plaza Mayor on Saturdays.

San Marcos

PLAZA DE SAN MARCOS

PUENTE DE SAN MARCOS

AVENIDA DE SUERO DE QUIÑONES

FEVE Train Station

AVENIDA DE JOSÉ ANTONIO PRIMO DE RIVERA

JUAN MADRAZO

RAMIRO VALBUENA

AVENIDA DEL

LUCAS DE TUY

PLAZA DE COLÓN

ROA DE LA VEGA

PASEO DE LA CONDESA DE SAGASTA

PASEO DE SALAMANCA

Jardines de la Condesa de Sagasta

COLÓN

PLAZA DE CALVO SOTELO

AVENIDA GENERAL SANJ

Río Bernesga

AVENIDA DE ROMA

SAN AGUSTÍN

ALCÁZAR DE TOLEDO

ALFONSO V

AVENIDA DE ASTORGA

RENFE Train Station

AVENIDA DE ORDOÑO II

GIL Y CARRASCO

GLORIETA DE GUZMÁN EL BUENO

AVENIDA DE PALENCIA

BURGO NUEVO

PLAZA DE LAS CORTES LEONES

AVENIDA DE LA REPÚBLICA ARGENTINA

PASEO DEL INGENIERO SÁEZ DE MIERA

Parque de Papalaguinda

AVENIDA DE LA FACULTAD DE VETERINARIA

BERNARDO DEL CARPIO

VILLA DE BENAVENTE

PLAZA DE FERNANDO MERINO

AVENIDA LANCIA

Bus Station

León

FEVE Train Station

RENUEVA

AVENIDA DEL PADRE ISLA

Telephone Exchange

LA TORRE

LOPE DE VEGA

L. SANJURJO

PLAZA DE SANTO DOMINGO

PLAZA DEL ESPOLÓN

Medieval walls

PLAZA DEL VIZCONDE

CAJAL

RAMÓN Y

Real Basílica de San Isidoro

AVENIDA DE

RUIZ DE SALAZAR

PLAZA DE S. ISIDORO

SERRANOS

Santa Marina la Real

SAN P. ELAYO

PABLO

FLOREZ

CARDENAL LANDAZURI

AVENIDA DE LOS CUBOS

Marqués de Montealegre

EL CID

PLAZA TORRES DE OMAÑA

Tourist Office

PLAZA REGIA

Cathedral

PLAZA DE PUERTO OBISPO

SAN PEDRO ANCHA

Los Botines

C/ GENERALÍSIMO FRANCO

Palacio de los Guzmanes

Ayuntamiento

PLAZA DE SAN MARCELO

CALLE DE LA RÚA

PLAZA DE LO NDE LUNA

Palace of the Condes de Luna

AZABACHERÍA

Old Consistorio

DOM BERRUETA

AVENIDA DE LA INDEPENDENCIA

PLAZA DE S. MARTÍN

San Martín

PLAZA MAYOR

SANTA NONIA

LAS NESAS

PLAZA DE D. GUTIERRA

Post Office

LAS CERCAS

LAS CASTAÑONES

PLAZA DE STA. MARÍA DEL CAMINO

SAN FRANCISCO

Nuestra Señora del Mercado

PASEO FRANCISCO

PLAZA DE SAN FRANCISCO

Convento de San Francisco

N

200 metres
200 yards

The Spaniards call this the most splendid articulation of French Gothic in Spain, *La Pulchra Leonina* ('Belle of León'), a cathedral so remarkable that it would stand out even in France for its daring and superb walls of stained glass. A like amount of glass caused Beauvais, its closest rival in window-acreage, to collapse, a disaster León has managed to avert so far by increasing support to the walls and by maintaining a continual campaign to keep it vertical in the face of subsidence: expect some scaffolding. Although Calahorra in La Rioja claims the most storks' nests, León comes in a close second with some 100 families, to the extent that droppings on the stone have become a problem.

The first church was built by Ordoño II, who donated part of his estates for the construction of Santa María de la Regla. It was twice destroyed before 1204, when Alfonso IX began a new church in warm golden stone in unheard-of dimensions, modelled on the soaring Gothic cathedrals of Chartres and Rheims. His successor, Fernando III, worried by the expense, tried to limit its size, but the Leonese responded by putting up their own money for the construction. The cathedral was more or less completed by the 15th century—the date of the openwork tower of the west façade by Joosken van Utrecht, linked rather oddly to the main body of the cathedral with visible buttresses.

Outstanding 13th-century sculpture decorate the north, south, and especially the **west portal** with its three finely carved tympana—the one in the centre illustrates a lively scene of the Last Judgement, the devils boiling the sinners beneath a triumphant Christ. In between the doors a pillar with a statue of Solomon was the place where the king or his representative would sit in judgement. The exterior, however, pales before the soaring spectacle of the **interior**, stripped in the 19th century of all its Baroque frosting, leaving it bare and breathtaking, especially when the late-afternoon sun streams in to ignite the richest and most vivid stained glass imaginable, 1800 square metres of it, all glowing reds and golds, greens and violets. The oldest glass, in the chapels around the apse and the great rose window in the front of the twelve Apostles, dates from the 13th century; the last is from the 19th, and all made by Spanish artists.

If you can draw your eyes from the soaring walls of glass, note the choir in the centre of the nave, set behind an ornate triumphal arch of a façade and embellished with 15th-century alabaster carvings by Juan de Badajoz the elder; its midsection of glass was added fairly recently so you can see straight through to the altar, swimming in reflections of the windows. The *retablo mayor* contains an excellent Renaissance painting of Christ's Burial by Nicolás Francés. The chapels in the ambulatory house beautiful Gothic tombs, and there's an altar to Nuestra Señora del Dado, at which a disgruntled gambler allegedly once flung his dice, hitting the Christ Child on the nose and making it bleed. Through the Plateresque Puerta del Dado, the **cathedral museum and cloister** (*open Mon–Fri 9.30–1.30 and 4–7, Sat 10–1.30, closed Sun; adm; if the doors are locked, wait for the harried woman with the big keys*) has a big collection of Romanesque Virgin Marys; also a Crucifixion by Juan de Juni and a Mozarabic Bible. The cloister itself was damaged in the 14th century and reworked with classical motives by Juan de Badajoz the elder.

Around the Cathedral: the Barrio Húmedo

Alongside the cathedral run León's **walls**, built by Alfonso XI in 1324 over the Roman and early medieval fortifications; nearly half of the original 80 bastions remain intact. To the east extend the narrow lanes of the old town, where so many Leonese come to wet their whistles that everyone calls it the **Barrio Húmedo** 'the humid quarter'. The elegant **Old Consistorio** (1677) presides in the arcaded **Plaza Mayor**, where a tower belonged to the Ponce family, one of whom went to Florida seeking the Fountain of Youth; the adjacent **Plaza de San Martín** is the most humid corner of the humid quarter. By the market in Gral. Mola, another famous family, the Quiñoneses, had their 14th-century **Palace of the Condes de Luna**, of which only the tower and fine façade remain. The best of the churches is Romanesque **Nuestra Señora del Mercado** (*open 11–12 and 7–8*) in Plaza Santa María del Camino.

From the cathedral, busy Calle General Franco (the old Roman *decumanus*) leads up to Plaza de Botines and Plaza San Marcelo, where all of sudden you come upon León's version of Sleeping Beauty's castle, **Los Botines** ('the spats'). Antoni Gaudí's most conventional work, Los Botines was built in 1891—'in a moment of doubt' according to one of his biographers— as a private residence, with pointy turrets, typically swirling Gaudiesque ironwork and a statue of St George (patron of Gaudí's native Catalunya) over the door, where, by the look on the grinning dragon's face, the saint is scratching him in just the right spot. Two fine Renaissance palaces share the plazas: the arcaded **Ayuntamiento** and the **Palacio de los Guzmanes** (now the provincial Diputación), with a sumptuous façade designed by Rodrigo de Hontañón in 1559.

A Spanish Legend Past its Sell-by Date

An earlier Guzmán palace on this site saw the birth of Guzmán el Bueno, the knight who in 1292 defended the citadel of Tarifa at the southernmost point of Spain against a Moorish army. Fighting with the Moors was the renegade Infante Don Juan, brother of Sancho IV, who had captured Guzmán's young son, took him beneath the walls of Tarifa, and threatened to kill him if Guzmán refused to surrender. Guzmán's response was to toss him a dagger. His son was killed but Tarifa did not fall. During the Spanish Civil War, the Nationalists recycled this legend for the 1936 siege of the Alcázar in Toledo, with the Republicans playing the villain's role. It was a splendid piece of Francoist propaganda—in the war that first used the very word propaganda (from the Church's *Propaganda fide*, or propagation of the faith) as we use it today.

San Isidoro and the Panteón de los Reyes

If León's cathedral is one of the best in Spain, the city can claim a similar pedestal for the Romanesque frescoes in its **Real Basílica de San Isidoro**, north of Plaza de Botines in Plaza San Isidoro. Founded in the 9th century, razed to the ground by al-Mansur, it was rebuilt by Fernando I, the first to unify León and Castile in 1037 and the first to call

Christ Pantocrator, Real Basílica de San Isidoro

himself 'King of the Spains'. In 1063 León bagged the relics of St Isidoro of Seville, that 6th-century, encyclopedia-writing Visigothic nobleman and doctor of the Church whose bones, upon hearing of the Reconquista, started to speak, asking to be transferred to Christian territory. These chattering bones must have driven the Moors in Seville crazy, so they obliged and packed them off to León; the basilica was at once rededicated to him, enlarged and given its lofty bell tower. Once here, the gentle Isidoro, like a half dozen other saints along the road, was conscripted into Reconquista duty; you can see him over the side door, on horseback in his bishop's gear, whacking the Moor with John Wayneish gusto. Specifically, he helped Alfonso VIII reconquer Baeza, and to this day a confraternity from Baeza, in theory, maintains a 24-hour vigil by his relics in the church.

The façade has two entrances; the church is entered through the righthand, 11th-century Puerta del Perdón topped by a tympanum sculpted with the Descent from the Cross, the Three Marys and the Ascension. This is the first Door of Pardon along the *camino de Santiago*; if a pilgrim were too ill or weak to carry on, he or she could touch the door and receive the same indulgence and absolution granted to someone who walked all the way to Compostela. The barrel-vaulted interior with its foiled arches, desecrated by Soult's French army in the Peninsular War, is something of a heavily restored disappointment; of the 12th-century original only the transept capitals and chapel remain.

The more ornate Puerta del Cordero, its tympanum carved with the Sacrifice of Isaac, leads into the original narthex of the church, the **Panteón de los Reyes** (*open 9–2 and 3–8, winter 10–1.30 and 4–6.30, Sun 9–2, closed Mon; adm*), founded by Fernando I for his simple stone sarcophagus and those of his descendants. Its two small groin-vaulted chambers are supported by elaborately carved capitals (Daniel in the Lions' Den, the Resurrection of Lazarus), and the ceiling and walls are covered with extraordinary vivid frescoes from the 12th century, among the best preserved Romanesque paintings anywhere still in their original setting. Stylistically similar to the 5th-century frescoes and mosaics in Santa Costanza (which all the pilgrims to Rome would have visited), Christ Pantocrator and the Evangelists, with human bodies and animal heads (Luke looks like the Minotaur) reign over scenes of the shepherds, the Flight to Egypt, the Last Supper, the Tears of St Peter, the Seven Cities and Seven Lamps of the Apocalypse. Best of all, there's an allegory of the months, beginning with the two-headed Janus, Roman god of the door, who looks both backward and ahead at the 'hinge' of the old and new years.

Although the French desecrated the tombs and burned the library, they somehow missed the treasures displayed in the Pantheon's **museum** (*same hours*) on the first floor, which originally formed part of Fernando I's palace: St Isidoro's original silver reliquary, the gem-studded chalice of Doña Urraca (made from two Roman cups), and lovely Mozarab caskets covered with ivories and enamels. The library, rebuilt in the 16th century by Juan de Badajoz, has an illuminated Bible of 960 that somehow escaped the French firebugs.

The Hospital de San Marcos and the Archaeology Museum

León's third great monument lies at the end of the garden along the riverside Paseo Condesa de Sagasta. The **Hospital de San Marcos** was built in 1173 as headquarters for the Order of the Knights of Santiago, charged with the pilgrims' protection; at their hospital the weary, blistered pilgrim could rest and prepare for the rigours ahead. In 1514, when the powerful Knights were more devoted to their own pleasure and status, they set about rebuilding their headquarters thanks to an enormous donation by Fernando the Catholic—something of a payoff for electing him to the post of Grand Master and surrendering their semi-autonomy to the Crown. Over the 16th to 18th centuries the monastery was given its superb 330ft Plateresque façade, first designed by Pedro de Larrea but altered by many hands afterwards, including those of Juan de Badajoz the younger, its frieze of busts, niches (the statues were never completed), swags and garlands, scallop shells, pinnacles, and intricate lacey reliefs culminating in the portal topped by Santiago Matamoros and the arms of Charles V, who inherited the title of Grand Master from his grandfather Fernando. Used after 1837 as a barracks, the building went quickly to rack and ruin and was several times condemned by the city until 1961, when the government purchased it, and invested a fortune to create Spain's most beautiful luxury hotel. Non guests as usual can partake at the bar, and visit the upper choir of the adjacent **church of San Marcos** with its cockleshell façade.

The chapterhouse and sacristy by Juan de Badajoz the younger contain the **Provincial Archaeology Museum** (*open 10–2 and 5–7.30, Sun 10–2, closed Mon*), with a small but prize collection: the 11th-century ivory Carrizo crucifix, enamels from Limoges, a Mozarab cross given by King Ramiro II in 940 to Santiago de Peñalba, the Corullón calvary, three pairs of beautiful capitals from the first Mozarab church at Sahagún, made by the same craftsmen as at Escalada, medieval weapons and mementoes of the Roman Seventh Legion, portraits of the knights of Santiago, and artefacts discovered in a Punic necropolis near the Maragato village of Santa Colomba de Somoza—a key discovery in unravelling the origins of the Maragatos (*see* below).

León ✆ (987–)   *Where to Stay*

The luxurious *parador*, the ★★★★★**Parador San Marcos**, Pza. San Marcos 7, ✆ 23 73 00, ✉ 23 34 58 (*luxury*), is not only Spain's best hotel, it is a veritable antiques museum in its public rooms—even the bedrooms are furnished with unique pieces. There are less expensive rooms in the modern building behind, with views over the river and gardens. The attractively designed ★★★★**Alfonso V**, C/ Padre Isla 1, ✆ 22 09 00, 🖃 22 12 44 (*expensive*), is the newest hotel in town (and nearly as pricey as the San Marcos). In the new part of town, the very modern ★★**Quindós**, Avda. José Antonio 24, ✆ 23 62 00, 🖃 24 22 01 (*moderate*), is arty and comes with excellent service. By the river, ★★**Riosol**, Avda. de Palencia 3, ✆ 21 66 50, 🖃 21 69 97 (*expensive*), is large and pleasant. León has a good choice of cheaper places, although most are on busy streets: ★**Paris**, Generalísimo 20, ✆ 23 86 00, near the cathedral, is an old palace, though the rooms are modern; ★**Hs Guzmán el Bueno**, López Castrillón 6, ✆ 23 64 12, in the old town is one of the quieter choices (*both moderate*). Within walking distance of the RENFE station, ★**Hs Londres**, Avda. de Roma 1, ✆ 22 22 74 (*moderate*), is comfortable and convenient; ★**Hs Oviedo**, Avda. Roma 26, ✆ 22 22 36, is similar (*cheap*). León's youth hostel, **Residencia Juvenil Infanta Doña Sancha**, Corredera 4, ✆ 20 22 01, is at the south end of town, and has a pool.

Eating Out

León is famous for sweetbreads and black puddings (*morcilla*), game dishes and garlic soup with trout. **Casa Pozo**, Pza. San Marcelo 15 (near the Ayuntamiento), ✆ 22 30 39, specializes in both trout and salmon and prime fresh ingredients (menu 3000 pts, closed Sun eve and 1–15 July). **El Faisán Dorado**, Cantareros 2, ✆ 25 66 09, has a good name for excellent game and lobster dishes, and friendly service; good wine list too (menu 1800 pts, otherwise expensive–moderate, closed Sun eve and Mon). **Bodega Regia**, Gral. Mola 5, ✆ 21 31 73 specializes in simple, traditional dishes at reasonable prices (2000-pts menú, closed Sun). In the Barrio Húmedo, Plaza San Martín is the bopping headquarters not only of bars and tapas but also inexpensive restaurants; try the 12th-century **El Nuevo Racimo de Oro** at No. 8, ✆ 25 41 00, which has a good bar and plenty of atmosphere; good Leonese cuisine as well (around 2500 pts; closed Sun in summer and Wed rest of the year). The same management also runs the less expensive **Mesón Leonés del Racimo de Oro**, Caño Badillo 2, ✆ 25 75 75, specializing in regional dishes like roasts and Serrano ham; the tables overlook a patio and the *bodega* dates back to the 12th century (closed Sun eve and Tues). **Fornos**, C/ Cid 8 (*moderate–inexpensive*), has long been a favourite for its lively atmosphere and delicious food (closed Sun eve and Mon). León's most venerable pastry shrine is **Camilo de Blas**, Generalísimo 13, or try one of the ultra-refined cakes from **Viuda de Pedro Peréz**, Pozo 13.

West of León

Two distinct regions fill the region between León and Galicia: between Astorga and Ponferrada **La Maragatería**, the homeland of the Maragatos, one of Spain's marginal peoples, and west of Ponferrada **El Bierzo**, a unique mountainous region, with some of the province's prettiest wooded valleys, distorted and eroded by mining and a favourite abode for 10th-century hermits.

Getting Around

RENFE links Astorga and Ponferrada with León, Lugo and beyond, four times a day, although note that for Astorga the station is a long hike, while buses go to the centre. Astorga is the point of departure of buses for La Maragatería; Ponferrada for El Bierzo; and León for the villages in the south. The Cueva de Valporquero is accessible only by car, although there are often excursions organized from León.

Tourist Information

Astorga: Ayuntamiento, Plaza de España, © (987) 61 59 47
Ponferrada: Gil y Carrasco 4, © (987) 42 42 36

There is a **market** in Astorga on Tues, and in Ponferrada on Wed and Sat.

North of León

Northern León province encompasses the southern slopes of the Cordillera Cantábrica and the Picos de Europa and one of Spain's best caves, the **Cueva de Valporquero**, 46km from León through the spectacular gorges of the Torio river (*open 10–2 and 4–7; adm; bring non-skid shoes and a jacket*). The caves have no prehistoric art, but 4km of colourful galleries with little lakes, esplanades, a stalactite 'cemetery', chamber of wonders, and striking sheer cliffs. Another beauty spot is the **Puerto de Pajares** (1379m), the lofty pass in the Cordillera Cantábrica used since antiquity as the main gate between León and Oviedo. The Leonese gateway to the Picos de Europa is **Riaño**, from where you can visit the **Valle de Valdeón** and **Valle de Sajambre**.

Along the Pilgrimage Road to Hospital de Órbigo

On the N 120, not far from the industrial sprawl west of León, is, for better or worse, the only modern chapel along the *camino de Santiago*: **La Virgen del Camino**, a concrete box built in 1961 by Brother Coello de Portugal. It has all the air of a middle American college library, but houses a much venerated 16th-century statue of the Virgin, set in a Baroque *retablo*; the stained-glass workshop at Chartres produced the ugly windows and Catalan sculptor Subirachs contributed the weird emaciated bronze figures of the Virgin and the Apostles that cover the front.

One of the bridges the pilgrims crossed, the 13th-century Puente del Paso Honroso, still stands parallel to the N 120, 23km west of León, not far from the long-gone *hostal* that gave its name to **Hospital de Órbigo**; the bridge is well preserved in a tranquil green setting.

Don Quixote's Prototype

Things weren't so tranquil back in July 1434, when Don Suero de Quiñones, a knight from León, placed an iron collar around his neck and with his nine companions vowed to hold the bridge for the 13 days preceeding 25 July, the feast day of Santiago, and challenge every passer-by to declare his lady, Leonor de Tovar, the fairest in the land. If they refused to admit it, they had to joust. As it was a Holy Year, the road was crowded with pilgrims. The bishop of León condemned the enterprise from the start and refused burial in sacred ground for anyone killed, but not even that deterred 727 men from taking up the challenge (no one recorded how many refused). Don Suero and his companions broke over 300 lances, wounded a score and killed one, but at the end of the month retired undefeated. The incident, the last hurrah of Spanish romantic chivalry, has gone down in history as the *Paso Honroso*; many scholars believe the story of Don Suero de Quiñones was an inspiration for Cervantes' Don Quixote.

Astorga, Gaudí and the Maragatos

Roman Astúrica Augusta was an important administrative centre for the Romans, close to the mines and a main station along their celebrated Vía de la Plata, the 'silver road' that ran down to Zamora and Seville and across to Galicia, to transport the gold of the Bierzo, the silver of Galicia and the copper of Asturias. Like León, Astorga had its own bishopric by the 3rd century; like León it remained important in the Middle Ages because of the pilgrimage. It has genteelly declined since the 18th century, helped along by a bit of pillaging and sacking in the Peninsular War.

The best way to approach Astorga is to circle the centre, still belted by half of its robust Roman-medieval **walls**, and enter on the northwest side of town, where the **Catedral de Santa María** and Bishop's palace looming over the walls make a startling impression. Begun in 1451, the cathedral took until the 18th century to complete, with too many cooks along the way; even the colour of the stone in the towers doesn't match. The façade with its flying buttresses between the towers was inspired by the cathedral in León, only here the ornamentation on the façade is floridly Baroque: intricate garlands, cherubs, columns with plump rings of vegetation and reliefs of the Descent from the Cross, the Adulterous Woman, and the Expulsion of the Merchants from the Temple. The interior suffers from a clammy ecclesiastical anomie, with all the interest concentrated in the *retablo mayor*, in marble high relief, by Gaspar Becerra (1520–70), an Andalucian who studied with Michelangelo. Off the neglected, classical cloister, the **Museo Diocesano** (*open daily 10–2 and 4–8; adm*) houses some fine medieval pieces—including a 10th-century casket of gold and silver that belonged to Alfonso III, a figure of Santo Toribio by Gaspar Becerra and a 12th-century painted tomb.

Astorga seemed like a dusty, declining nowhere to Juan Bautista Grau y Vallespinós when he arrived as its new bishop. In 1887, hoping to give his see a dynamic jump start into the 20th century, he commissioned the most imaginative architect he knew, his good friend and fellow Catalan, Antoni Gaudí of Barcelona, to build him a new **Palacio Episcopal.** The rest of Astorga had deep reservations about the *modernista* fairy tale castle that began to sprout on the edge of town and, once the bishop died in 1893, the public's hostility to the project burst open so violently that Gaudí quit and refused to ever return to Astorga. Without his input, this pale asymmetrical castle (completed only in 1963), built more or less in the shape of a Latin cross, with sharp pointed towers and turrets, a moat and a huge sloping front, lacks the extraordinary detail and colour that characterize Gaudí's work, who usually designed everything down to the furniture. Instead of a bishop, the palace now houses the **Museo de los Caminos** (*open daily 11–2 and 3.30–6.30; adm*), a collection of pilgrimage paraphernalia, maps of the routes, Roman remains, art from various churches (note especially the mean-looking she-devil and Santiago in the Renaissance altarpiece from Bécares) along with some mean-looking examples of contemporary provincial art. For a hint of Gaudí's intentions, don't miss the magnificent atmospheric throne room with its discreet stained glass and chapels.

Maragato Mysteries

 Before leaving, look at the top of the cathedral apse, decorated with the figure of a Maragato named Pero Mato, who fought with Santiago at the legendary battle of Clavijo in 844. Astorga is the 'capital' of the Maragatos, who have lived here and in the villages to the west for as long as anyone can remember. Until the 19th century, they were muleteers and carriers, transporting nearly all the goods between Castile and Galicia, a line of work forced on them by their stubborn, almost uncultivatable land; their name has been traced back to the Latin *mercator*, or merchant. Grave and dry in manner, their honesty and industry were proverbial and no one hesitated to trust them with huge sums of money. Until recently they still wore their ancient costumes: huge slouched hats, very broad-bottomed breeches called *zaraguelles* (from the Arabic word for kilts) and red garters for the men; for the women, a crescent-shaped cap covered with a mantle and heavy earrings. They kept very much to themselves, marrying only other Maragatos, and twice a year, at Corpus Christi and the Ascension, all would gather in Astorga and exactly at 2pm would begin a dance called El Canizo and finish at exactly 3; if any non-Maragatos attempted to join in the dance would stop immediately. In the kitchen they are known for their cakes called *mantecadas* (available in every Astorga pastry shop) and for the odd custom of eating their Maragato stew backwards: first they would eat the meat, then the vegetables, then the soup.

Who were the Maragatos? Common beliefs that they were Celts, Visigoths or Berbers who came over in the 8th century and managed to hold on to this enclave after converting to Christianity have been called into question by Dr Julio Carro, who in the late 1950s discovered a Punic necropolis near the village of Santa Colomba de Somoza west of Astorga—hardly where you'd expect to find one, because the Phoenicians were sailors and León isn't exactly on the coast. Among the finds were figurines nearly identical to those found at Punic sites in Ibiza and dressed in a style very similar to the Maragatos. Carro's conclusion, based on his discoveries and on Maragato cultural traditions, was that the Maragatos descended from Phoenicians and Iberians enslaved by the Romans to work the gold mines of El Bierzo. The Maragatos themselves agree, and to thank Carro for discovering their true origins, they put up a stone plaque to him in the village of Quintanilla de Somoza. These days the Maragato traditions and insularity has practically vanished; although you can still recognize a Maragata at once by her lime green stretch slacks and horn-rimmed glasses.

In reality, the only other Maragatos you're likely to notice as such are the two *jacquemart* figures, Zancudo and Colasa, who bang the hour atop the attractive 17th-century

Ayuntamiento at the east end of Astorga; in front of it you can descend into the Roman slaves' prison, the **Ergástula**, where the Maragatos' ancestors languished. In **Plaza Roma** you'll find ruins of Roman houses, some with pretty mosaics.

West of Astorga: Villages of the Maragatería

The mostly ruined villages of the Maragatería have been in decline ever since the railway took over the Maragatos' ancestral occupation, but **Castrillo de los Polvazares** (6km from Astorga, just off the Pilgrims' Way), has been restored to the verge of being twee, with old stone houses now mostly holiday homes, a score of roadside crosses and a main cobbled street built wide for mule trains. Further west, only a handful of people remain at **Santa Catalina de Somoza**, with its monument to a Maragato musician, while up from El Ganso ('the Goose'), down-at-heel **Rabanal del Camino** was the ninth stop on the pilgrimage in the *Codex Calixtinus*, a spot safeguarded by the Templars: now only a few people remain to tend its little Romanesque church.

After Rabanal, pilgrims tackled the wild Montes de León, climbing up to **Foncebadón**: 'Who hasn't passed by way of Foncebadón doesn't know solitude nor sadness' is an old saying, especially true now that the village is abandoned. Just beyond, at the top of the 1504m pass, stands the spindly **Iron Cross**, planted by a pilgrim untold years ago. Later pilgrims have added, one by one, the huge mound of slate stones at its foot, just as the Celts would 'give' stones to roadside shrines to placate the dangers ahead. To the left rises **El Teleno** (2188m), one of the two holy mountains of the Celts in El Bierzo.

Ⓒ *(987–)*   *Where to Stay and Eating Out*

Astorga

> ★★★**Hotel Gaudí**, Pza. Eduardo de Castro 6, Ⓒ 61 56 54, ✆ 61 50 40 (*expensive*), is by far the finest place to stay, not far from the cathedral; its good, moderately priced restaurant with a fancy marble floor features several Maragato dishes and fish. ★★**Hs La Peseta**, Pza. San Bartolomé 3, Ⓒ 61 72 75 (*moderate*), is central and boasts the best restaurant in Astorga, where you can sample the generous wines of El Bierzo with heaping plates of *pulpo a la Gallega* (octopus) or *congrio al ajo Arriero* (conger eel in a paprika sauce); 3000 pts and closed Sun eve. except Aug.

El Bierzo

In the old days the Romans dug for gold in these hills; the modern Leonese extract the iron and cobalt. El Bierzo has bleak mining towns, lovely mountain scenery, vineyards, orchards and tobacco fields, charming villages that time forgot, and ancient hermitages— its isolation and warm climate (the mountains shield it from the worst of the *meseta* and Atlantic)—attracted so many anchorites early on that it was known as the Thebaid of Spain. Its inhabitants feel closer to their neighbours in Galicia than to León, and make half-serious murmurs about autonomy, mostly expressed in the venerable Spanish spraypaint tradition of changing the spelling on signs.

After the Iron Cross the pilgrims' road descends into the fertile valleys of El Bierzo by way of **Manjarín**, another abandoned hamlet, and **Acebo**, with its still flowing pilgrims' Fountain of the Trout along its one street. From Acebo it's 5km south to **Compludo**, a tiny isolated hamlet, where San Fructuoso, the first holy man in El Bierzo, founded his first monastery in 614. Although this is now long gone, San Fructuoso's forge, the remarkable **Herrería de Compludo** (now a national monument) still works as well as it did in the 7th century using the stream to turn its great wheel.

Ponferrada

Both the easy N VI or the dramatic, lonely (but well-signed) pilgrims' track over the Montes de León lead to **Ponferrada**, originally a Roman mouthful known as Interamnium Flavium. It is the largest town of El Bierzo, and sums up the region's split personality, part of it mine- blackened, slag-heaped and shabby, the other half medievally pretty. The town's name

Castillo de los Templarios, Ponferrada

comes from a long-gone bridge with iron balustrades, erected over the Río Sil for the pilgrims by the local 11th-century pontifex, Bishop Osmundo. On the east bank of the Sil stands Ponferrada's proudest monument, the 12th-century **Castillo de los Templarios** (*open 10.30–1.30 and 4–7, Sun am only, closed Mon*), its triple ramparts built to defend the pilgrims from the Moors; its fairy-tale gate and towers were added later, in 1340. In 1811 the French went out of their way to vandalize it, resulting in heavy restoration. Here and there you can see Templar crosses and *taus* carved on the walls. While building the castle, the Templars discovered a statue of the Virgin in the heart of a holm oak tree, now enshrined in the **Basílica de Nuestra Señora de la Encina** (1577), with a good *retablo mayor* by the school of Gregorio Fernández. Elsewhere in the old town, look for the medieval gate, the **Puerta del Reloj**, and the early 17th-century **Ayuntamiento**. Sitting on a hill, 2km south on the Madrid road, the minute church of **Santo Tomás de las Ollas** ('St Tom of the Pots'—there used to be a pottery workshop next door) is a curious Mozarabic church built by the monks of San Pedro de Montes, with horseshoe arches and best of all, an elliptical ten-sided apse encircled with blind arcading.

Into the Valley of Silence

South of Ponferrada, the Oza river winds through the beautiful **Valle del Silencio** where, from the 7th century to the 10th, hermits took up their abode under the dramatic white flanks of Monte Aquiana, a mountain sacred to the Celts. Most of the hermits were Visigoths from Andalucía, come to spread the writings of San Isidoro of Seville. One of these was San Fructuoso, founder of the monastery of **San Pedro de Monte** in the village of **Montes** (to get there, take the road to San Esteban de Valdueza for 8km, then turn left 14km on a narrow, hairpinning road that follows the river Oza; at the end of the road, it's a steep 500m walk up). Reinhabited in 890 by St Genadio of Andalucía and his monks, the ruins are mostly 12th century, although Genadio's 919 dedication is still embedded in the wall and some of the original Asturian style capitals are intact. Despite an 18th-century restoration, the whole complex is on the verge of collapse.

The real jewel of El Bierzo, the little Mozarabic church of **Peñalba de Santiago** (*open 10.30–1.30 and 4–7, closed Sun afternoon and Mon*) is a bit farther on in a spectacular setting at the head of the valley (take the left turning over the river, and leave your car at the entrance of the little medieval hamlet). Founded by Saint Genadio and dedicated in 913, its perfect proportions are reminiscent of Palaeochristian basilicas in Africa, as is its shape: rectangular with three cupolas and two apses rather oddly facing one another. The rough stone and slate exterior doesn't prepare you for the refinement and fine craftsmanship inside, beginning with a pretty double-arched portal crowned by two horseshoe arches. A track leads up to the hermit's cave of San Genadio for the magnificent view down onto the church and its tower, surrounded by a huddle of slate roofs.

Las Médulas

Carucedo, 20km southwest of Ponferrada, is the point of departure for an unusual journey through an ancient ecological disaster, **Las Médulas**. In the first century AD, the Romans noted the soft red soil was sprinkled with gold and minium (or red lead, used for painting), but to extract it meant sifting through thousands of tons of earth. Labour back then was no problem: some 60,000 slaves were brought in to dig a complex network of galleries, wells, dams and canals—one over 40km long—to erode away the soil. The work was gruelling and dangerous, and thousands died over the next two centuries in moving an estimated 300 million tons of earth to extract 90 tonnes of gold. Whole hills collapsed in the process, and new ones of left-over tailings were piled up by the slaves, leaving behind a landscape like a row of jagged red spinal cords—or medullas. There's a natural balcony over Las Médulas from Orellán; from the village of Las Médulas, 4km from Carucedo, you can take a stroll (bring sturdy shoes) past the ancient canals, galleries, rock needles and surreal caves—a natural disaster perhaps, but a strangely beautiful one.

North of Ponferrada: the Ancares Leoneses

North of Ponferrada, a lonely road heads north to Vega de Espinareda and the beautiful, densely forested, mountainous Ancares Leoneses, now under the jurisdiction of the National Park. The park not only protects a number of endangered species—a few brown bears, Iberian wolves, roe deer, and capercaillie—but also a dying way of life in its 27 remote mountain hamlets, with their traditional architecture and *pallozas*, straw-topped round stone huts first built by the Celts. The best examples may be seen along the tiny roads up the Ancares river valley. Nearly all the hamlets are cloaked in chestnut groves, which until a couple of decades ago provided much of their food.

D.O. El Bierzo

After Ponferrada the pilgrimage route enters the Valley of Bierzo, the bed of a dried-up lake, surrounded by a ring of mountains and criss-crossed by trout streams. Its microclimate is warm, damp yet shot with sunlight, with few frosts, ideal for cultivating vines, both on steep slopes and on the riverbanks. The finest, D.O. El Bierzo reds, are made entirely from the native Mencía grape and have a personality all their own, although this is diluted when Prieto Picudo and Garnacha are added. The less interesting whites are made from Malvasia and Valenciana. Three of the top producers are Valdeobispo, Casar de Valdaiga and Palacio de Arganza (try their red Almena del Bierzo).

Carracedo

Cacabelos, 12km west of Ponferrada, was another important stop on the *camino*, although these days it's best known for its wines and its church of Las Angustíar, where there's a famous scene of baby Jesus floating on a cloud playing cards with St Anthony. Don't miss a brief detour 3km south to the **Monastery of Santa María de Carracedo**, founded in 990 in a pastoral setting, this time by Bermudo II the Gouty of León. In 1138 it came under the patronage of Doña Sancha, sister of Alfonso VII, who built a new church and monastery. At the end of the 18th century the monks decided it was time for a change and began a large neoclassical church. It was only partially finished in 1811 when the French marched through and effectively put an end to the project, leaving half of a new church and much of the old intact, pieced together, restored and roofed over for the monastery's 1000th birthday. By the church are the remains of a little **palace** built by Alfonso IX in the early 1200s, to house his wife Teresa of Portugal and his two daughters when the Pope annulled his marriage. The claims of the princesses to the throne was a powerful reason behind the union of León and Castile declared by Fernando III el Santo—Alfonso IX's son from his second marriage. The palace has a fancy Gothic room known as the 'Queen's kitchen', the Queen's Mirador, and a relief by the door of a mysterious woman on a bed surrounded by attendants, including the Virgin.

Villafranca del Bierzo

The *Codex Calixtinus*' tenth stop on the *camino de Santiago*, **Villafranca del Bierzo**, is one of the most attractive small towns along the whole road, embraced on all sides by mountains, built at the confluence of the Burbia and Valcarce rivers. As its name suggests, the town was founded by the French in the 11th century and in its heyday it had eight monasteries and six pilgrims' hospitals; today it makes wine and lodges visitors to the region. On the hill where pilgrims entered Villafranca is the well-preserved 16th-century **Castillo de los Marqueses de Villafranca** and the 12th-century **Santiago**, a simple Romanesque church but an important one, with the second Puerta del Perdón along the road. Pilgrims too weary or ill to continue had only to touch the door to achieve the same indulgences as they would at Compostela. Some then keeled over dead and were buried in the adjacent cemetery. All of the church's unfortunately eroded decoration is concentrated around the Puerta del Perdón; you can see three kings on horseback, a Crucifixion and Christ in Majesty.

The pilgrims would descend from the church and castle to walk along wide, atmospheric **Calle del Agua**, 'Water Street', lined with blazoned 16th- and 17th-century palaces with iron balconies that often looked over a real street of water, so often has the Burbia flooded it. The Plaza Mayor was set higher up away from danger, and near this you'll find the church of **San Francisco**, all that remains of a monastery founded by St Francis himself during his pilgrimage. It has a magnificent 15th-century *mudéjar artesonado* ceiling, much of which has been recently restored. Down on the banks of the Burbia, **La Colegiata de Santa María** (*open 10–2 and 4–8*) stands on the site of the 11th-century monastery founded by the monks of Cluny. It fell into ruins and was rebuilt from scratch in 1544 to designs by Rodrigo Gil de Hontañón. Construction continued into the 18th century, when the money ran out, leaving the nave cut short and the west façade closed by a simple wall, although what was completed of the part-Gothic and part-Renaissance interior is uncommonly grand; note especially the chapel of the Trinity and a reliquary by Juan de Juni.

Just to the south of Villafranca, **Corullón** has two more lovely Romanesque churches: **San Esteban** and the recently restored **San Miguel**, adorned with leering and grinning funny faces. Corullón's ivy-smothered **castle** affords an excellent view of the Bierzo valley. West of Villafranca, the pilgrims' road passes through the narrow valley of the Valcarce dotted with tiny old fashioned villages. At **Herrerías**, with its old Hospital de los Ingleses (English Hostel) the road and pilgrims' route divide; the latter, rising to the pass at Cebreiro and hence into Galicia, was as dangerous and dreaded as it is beautiful.

© (987–)   *Where to Stay and Eating Out*

Ponferrada

The largest and best-endowed hotel is ✶✶✶✶**Del Temple**, Avda. de Portugal, © 41 00 58, ✉ 42 35 25 (*expensive*), located in a pseudo-Templar castle, with a swimming pool; beware that it can be noisy. ✶✶✶**Bérgidum**, Avda. de la Plata 2, © 40 15 12 (*expensive/moderate*), offers contemporary comforts and friendly service. Most of the cheaper choices are in the new town: ✶**Madrid**, on main Avda. de la Puebla 44, © 41 15 50 (*moderate*); ✶✶**Hs Marán**, Avda. A. López Peláez 29, © 41 63 51 (*inexpensive*); and ✶**Hs La Madrileña**, on the same street at no. 4, © 41 28 14 (*cheap*). In Pza. Ayuntamiento, **La Fonda**, © 42 57 94 (*moderate–inexpensive*), uses local ingredients to create some interesting dishes (try the *gambas* with bacon); menus 1600 pts. (closed Sun eve).

Villafranca del Bierzo

The ✶✶✶**Parador de Villafranca del Bierzo**, Avda. de Calvo Sotelo, © 54 01 75, ✉ 54 00 10 (*expensive*), is not one of the chain's showcases, but more like a comfortable motel in a scenic locale. Family-run ✶**Hs Casa Méndez**, Pza. de la Concepción, © 54 24 08 (*moderate*), has good home cooking to go with its inexpensive rooms with bath; ✶**Hs Ponterrey**, Dr. Arén 17, © 54 00 75 (*inexpensive*), is also reliable. The excellent **Eurbia**, La Granja, © 54 05 85 (*moderate–inexpensive*) serves delicious *cocidos*, roasts and fish.

Galicia

If Asturias is Spain's Wales, then Galicia is in many ways its Ireland, for many years so far removed from the mainstream of Spanish life and history it might just as well have been an island. Here the Celtic invaders of 1000 BC found their cosiest niche, in the same kind of rain-swept, green land facing the setting sun that their brethren had settled farther north in Brittany and Cornwall. The Moors left no mark in Galicia, having been expelled in the 8th century by the kings of Asturias—who promptly turned their attention to the richer spoils of the south. While

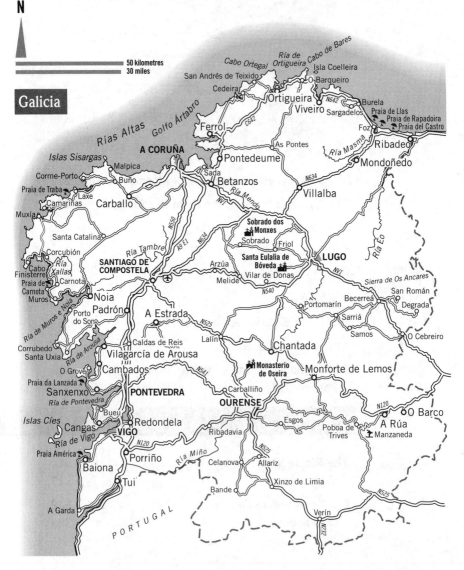

the rest of the north expanded into the newly won lands of the Reconquista, the Galicians, or Gallegos, were hemmed in by Portugal and forced to turn inwards, dividing their land into ever smaller and smaller holdings with every generation. Famines were common, and as soon as the New World was discovered, they emigrated in droves—there are more Gallegos in Buenos Aires alone than in all of Galicia. Even today Galicia is one of the poorest regions in Spain.

Yet few places in Spain have such a lasting charm. The coastline is pierced by a dozen estuaries, or *rías*, wild and scenic in the north, and in the south, sheltering serene beaches (Galicia has some 772 of these) and tiny coves, perfect for the smuggling that has long been a mainstay of the economy. Rivers in deep, narrow valleys with fantasy names—the Éo, the Ulla, the Lor, the Sil and Jallas—spill down wild mountains on their way to the sea. Bright green gardens cover every inch of cultivable land, although a third of the acreage is wasted by the granite walls each Gallego has erected around his own little plot. Each farm, however small, has a sturdy, self-sufficient air, with its cow and conical hayrack, its trellis of vines (producing excellent white wines similar to Portugal's 'green' wines) and tiny plots of turnips, peppers, maize, cabbage, peas and Spain's finest potatoes. Many cottages have granaries *(hórreos)*, monumental pieces of granite set up on pillars to protect the grain from rodents and wet, with window-like vents to permit air to circulate, topped by a gabled roof with crosses. Early travellers mistook them for hermitages. Chestnut, oak and furze forests cover the hills, while in sheltered spots the Gallegos grow kiwi fruit, oranges, palm trees and camellias, which have been the rage since their introduction from Japan.

Because of the endless division of land, much of Galicia is covered higgledy piggledy with farms and houses in some 31,000 'villages' (most with populations of 100–200), sprinkled here and there with the showy bungalows of the *americanos* who made their fortunes in Argentina. Many older houses, especially in A Coruña, have balconies closed in by glass 'crystal galleries', adorned with elaborate white mullions. Another distinctive feature of Galicia are the sculpted granite crosses at the crossroads. Some apparently guided pilgrims, or marked out the high roads, or fulfilled vows, or perhaps even served the same geomantric organization as Neolithic menhirs and dolmens, only carved into acceptable Christian forms. In the Rías Baixas, and especially along the rivers leading into them, you'll see the stately manor country villas the Gallegos call *pazos*, from the Roman *palatio*.

Galicia's language, Gallego, is chock-full of x's (pronounced 'sh') and closely related to Portuguese, and spoken by a greater percentage of the population than Basque or Catalan are in their respective regions. Even García Lorca penned verses in Gallego, inspired by the language of Alfonso the Wise's masterpiece, the *Cantigas de Santa María* and the evocative poetry, reminiscent of Emily Dickinson's, by Rosalía de Castro (1837–85; especially her *Cantares Gallegos*). Rosalía was a key figure in the *Rexurdimento* (literary renaissance), inspired by the Catalans, and like theirs, a forerunner of Spain's nationalist movements.

Culturally, Galicia has always looked to its ancient roots. The national instrument, the *gaita*, is very similar to Breton or Irish bagpipes, and Gallegos like nothing better than to blow it at festivals. Celtic influences are also strong in Galicia's festivals (many associated with death, witches and evil spirits); you can buy a 400-page book that lists every one of them. Irish immigrants in the 16th century introduced lace-making (*camarinhas*), still done by older women all along the coast.

Galician Cuisine

Eating is one of the great pleasures of Galicia; in Spain, Gallego restaurants command as much respect as the Basque. The estuaries are rich in an extraordinary array of seafood, from the famous scallops of Santiago and lobster, mussels, shrimp, oysters, razor shell clams, squid, crab, to some creatures unique to Galicia such as *zamburiñas* scallops, lobster-like *santiaguiños*, and ugly *percebes*, that have no names in English. Quantity is matched by quality: Galician seafood is considered the best in the world and preparation is kept as simple as possible. Another favourite served in every town are *empanadas*, large flat flaky pies filled with eels or lamprey (the most sought after; try it before you knock it), sardines, pork, or veal. Turnip greens (*grelos*) are a staple, especially in *Caldo Gallego*, a broth that also features turnips and white beans; in winter, the heartier *lacón con grelos*, pork shoulder with greens, sausages and potatoes, holds pride of place. Galicia produces Spain's best veal and good cheeses, such as Roquefort-like *cabrales* and *gamonedo*, both mainly from cow's milk mixed with smaller quantities of ewe's or goats' milk; birch-smoked pear-shaped *San Simón*; or mild, soft *ulloa* or *pasiego*. A tapas meal to make a Gallego weep includes grilled sardines, *pulpo a la gallega* (tender octopus with peppers and paprika), roasted small green peppers (*pimientas de Padrón*), with chewy hunks of bread and lightly salted breast-shaped *tetilla* cheese, washed down with white Ribeira wine. For dessert try *tarta de Santiago* (almond tart), and to top it all off, a glass of Galician fire water, *aguardiente*—served at night after a meal to ward off evil spirits—properly burned (*queimada*), with lemon peel and sugar.

The Coast West of Asturias: As Mariñas de Lugo

In the Spanish drive to leave no coast unchristened, this wild Atlantic-thundered northern-most stretch of Galicia is known as As Mariñas de Lugo after the provincial capital Lugo. It surrenders every so often to admit sandy beaches decorated with storm-chiselled cliffs and rocks; until very recently, deplorable slow roads conspired to keep it a secret.

Besides buses originating from Lugo, Gijón and A Coruña, the slow FEVE choo-choo from Gijón or Oviedo makes several leisurely trips a day along the coast to Ferrol, stopping at Ribadeo, Foz, Burela, Viveiro, Covas, O Barqueiro and Ortigueira.

Ribadeo: Praza de España, ✆ (982) 11 06 89.

Viveiro: Praza Maior, ✆ (982) 56 01 10

There are **markets** in Mondoñedo on Thursdays and Sundays; in Foz on Tuesdays; in Viveiro on Mondays, Thursdays and Saturdays; and in Cedeira there is a fish market daily, and a market for other food Wednesdays and Saturdays.

Ribadeo and Foz

Galician *rías*, or estuaries, are usually named after their largest towns. The first *ría* west of Asturias, **Ribadeo**, is named after a piquant old fishing town that staggers up to a dusty main **Praza de España**, where palm trees and the delightfully eclectic **Casa Morena** of 1905 lend it a lost Californian air. The 18th-century town hall was built as the home of the Marqués de Sargadelos, a liberal-minded reformer and philanthropist who was tied to the tail of horse and dragged to his death for his beliefs. The hermitage atop **Monte de Santa Cruz**, 2km south of Ribadeo on LU 133, offers splendid views of the Galician-Asturian coastline, guarded by a folksy monument to the Galician bagpiper; in early August Santa Cruz pipers from across Galicia gather here in an ear-splitting eisteddfod called the *Xira a Santa Cruz*. West, the tiny lobster fishing village of **Rinlo** is the gateway to the long sandy beach known either as the **Praia del Castro** or **As Catedrais** after its rock formations in the sea. Other pretty beaches dwarfed by towering cliffs, **Praia de Rapadoira** and **Praia de Llas** lie further west by **Foz**, a workaday industrial fishing port at the mouth of the Rio Masma. Only a lonely pile of stones, the Peña do Altar, recalls Foz's illustrious Celtiberian origins.

Inland: Mondoñedo

If Foz is no prize, Mondoñedo,18km to the south up the Masma valley offers some consolation. Mondoñedo was founded in 1117, when the diocese of San Martín de Mondoñedo (*see* below) was relocated inland; it received a second boost in its fortunes in the 15th century, when it was chosen as capital of its own little province, a distinction that lasted until 1834 and witnessed the construction of many proud houses of provincial barons, some with the glassed-in balconies or *solanas* typical of Galicia. Mondoñedo's granite **Cathedral** was begun in 1219 and when the time came to slap on a Baroque façade, it was done with surgical discretion, preserving the Romanesque portal and Gothic rose window in harmonious blind arches. The interior is still late Romanesque and decorated with remarkable 14th-century frescoes of the *Massacre of the Innocents*; there's a wonderful organ with trumpets (1710), and a painted Gothic statue known as the *Virgen*

Inglesa, brought over from St Paul's in London for safekeeping during the Reformation. The 17th-century cloister's **Museo Diocesano** displays paintings from Sevilla, furniture, and fancy liturgical bric-à-brac. The cathedral square is Mondoñedo's best, and there's a pretty *Alameda* before the Baroque church **Os Remedios**, decorated with grand Churrigueresque *retablos*, 'that sculpture of emblazoned tripes' as Pritchett calls it, and lots of candles, too, for the remedies in its name are said to be usually granted.

Between Mondoñedo and Foz, the Benedictine **Monasterio de Vilanova de Lourenzá** dates from the 10th century, but became wealthy enough in the 17th and 18th centuries to finance a major rebuilding programme so ambitious that the fancy façade of the church by granite wizard Fernando de las Casas y Novoa was never quite finished. The graceful interior gives the lie to the idea that Spanish Baroque means dark, gloomy and heavy. Don't miss the exquisitely carved altarpiece in the sacristy (1680); in the chapel of Santa María de Valdeflores you can make a wish while stroking the bones of the monastery's founder, Conde Gutierre Osorio.

Las Rías Altas: West of Foz to Viveiro, O Barqueiro and Ortigueira

From Foz, a brief inland detour will take you to the impressive, mightily buttressed 11th-century **San Martín de Mondoñedo**, a rare Romanesque church left untampered over the centuries, mainly because it was abandoned by its parishoners, leaving intact and uncovered fine 13th-century murals and the original capitals and the tomb of San Gonzalo, who sank a belligerent Norman fleet with a single prayer. Heading west on the coast, you can pay your respects to the **Citania de Fazouro**, a well-preserved Celtic *castro*; the similar Castro do Chan, near the pretty fishing-port of **Burela**, yielded the unique golden torques in the Lugo museum. Just inland from Cervo, **Sargadelos** had one of Spain's earliest ironworks and a famous Royal Ceramics Factory. The latter closed in 1860, but reopened in 1970 as the **Cerámica de Sargadelos** (*open Mon–Fri 8.30–1 and 4.30–6*) manufacturing traditional blue and white jugs and avant-garde works; if you're sticking around the area you can take a ceramics course in August by writing ahead.

Beyond Cervo and Sargadelos, the Rías Altas, or Upper Estuaries, begin in earnest, offering some of the best wild and windy coastal scenery in Iberia. Fragrant eucalyptus groves dot the coast around **Viveiro**, at the head of its lovely *ría*. Viveiro is the choice place to stay in the Rías Altas, sheltered by its partly ruined medieval walls from the ravages of the Atlantic, automobiles, and time itself. In the 18th century it imported linen from the Baltic in exchange for Galician agricultural goods but these days its outer fishing port **Celeiro**, on the opposite side of the estuary, deals mostly in sardines. Three medieval gates survive, along with the fancy **Puerta de Carlos V** (1548) on Avda. Galicia, erected to curry favour with Charles V. Inside, the narrow lanes and pretty **Praza de Pastor Díaz** are paved in granite and lined with medieval houses sucking in light through their *solanas*, while the austere but pure 12th-century Romanesque **Santa María del Campo** provides a town centrepiece. Viveiro has some ravishing beaches: the sand plain of **Covas** sweeping out to a treetop rock 'castles', **O Faro** facing the ocean, and **Xilloi** and **Ares** near Celeiro, where legend has it an ancient city sank into the sea for refusing to hear the preaching of St James. You can get a good overview from the mirador atop **San Roque**, the mountain just behind Viveiro. Off to the west, the rugged **Isla Coelleira**— 'rabbit island'—has been forlorn and desolate ever since the Templars, who took refuge there from the pope's pogrom, were massacred one night in 1307 by the lord of Viveiro.

The next estuary west, the Ría do Barqueiro, provides a magnficent setting for the little hamlet of **Vicendo** and its azalea gardens, the wide beach at **Arealonga** and, over the *ría*, for **O Barqueiro,** a picture-postcard amphitheatre of white, slate-roofed houses cupped around a bijou lobster port, in a landscape of piney fjords. A road leads down the *ría* to more beaches and to the tiny fishing hamlet and fabulous curling sandy beach of **Bares,** the northernmost settlement in Spain, marked by a lighthouse and blocks of walls from the days when it served as a port for Phoenician ships en route to the tin mines of Cornwall.

The next estuary, Ría de Santa María de Ortigueira, takes a veritable network of rivers. **Ortigueira,** on the pine-wooded east bank is a peaceful, unremarkable town (except during its annual Festival del Mundo Celta) with narrow streets running down to the waterfront and white sandy beaches that never get too crowded. On the west bank of the *ría* (cross the river at Mera) the long toes of the Sierra de Capelada extend down to Cape Ortegal, where the fishing village of **Cariño** is the last to look over the Cantabrian sea.

Cliffs, Lizards and Cedeira

West of Cariño the road takes in spectacular views of the 612m cliffs of the **Garita de Herbeira** en route to the village and tiny sanctuary of **San Andrés de Teixido,** perched on savage, wave-battered cliffs. Wild horses roam the meadows and woodlands here, and pilgrims flow in year round, for as the saying goes '*A San Andrés de Teixido, que no vai vivo vai morto*' 'if you don't go while alive, you'll go dead'—reincarnated as a lizard or toad, creatures which are never harmed in the village. On 8 September, the dead are given a formal invitation to the festival, when colourful, archaic dough figures are baked to be consumed before mass, and pilgrims who over the past year had a close brush with the Grim Reaper are carried to the church in coffins. Buy an amulet or *santera* of the saint, or enquire about San Andrés' famous love herb, which in the good old days was consumed in large quantities after mass as a prelude to a general orgy. A corniche road continues to the lovely town and port of **Cedeira,** which marks a series of stunning beaches, dunes and and lagoons that stretch all the way to Ferrol. The Ría de Cedeira is lined with beauty spots: the lofty **Mirador de Peña Edrosa,** the lighthouse at **Punta Candelaria,** and to the west, the gorgeous setting of the hermitage of **San Antonio de Corveiro.**

West of Asturias © (982–)   *Where to Stay and Eating Out*

Ribadeo

In a scenic, quiet spot overlooking the *ría*, the ***Parador de Ribadeo,** C/ Amador Fernández, © 10 08 25, ✆ 10 03 46 (*expensive*), won't win any prizes for atmosphere but is comfortable and homey, and has fine views over the working harbour; the restaurant features the day's catch. The cheapest decent place in Ribadeo is the *Hs Galicia,** C/ Virgen del Camino 1, © 11 07 77 (*cheap*), with 10 rooms. The beaches west towards Foz are well supplied with campsites. At **O Xardín**, C/ Reinante 20, ✆ 11 02 22 (*moderate*), you can sit amid greenery and feast on delicacies such as baked oysters or turbot cooked with razor-shell clams (*longueirós*); closed Mon in winter.

Mondoñedo

★Montero, Avda. San Lázaro 7, ✆ 52 17 51 (*moderate*), has pleasant doubles, although for character, opt for the recently restored **★Montero II**, across from the cathedral at C/ Candido Martínez 8, ✆ 52 10 41 (*moderate*), decorated with antiques. The small, simple **★Hs Padornelo**, C/ Buenos Aires 1, ✆ 52 18 92, has cheap rooms with or without bath. For a simple, filling, inexpensive dinnter try **A Voltiña**, Ctra. Lorenzana.

Viveiro

Note that most places offer big discounts off season. There's a clutch of hotels along Covas beach, among them, the smart **★★Las Sirenas**, ✆ 56 02 00, ✉ 55 12 67 (*expensive*), with rooms, and flats and studios sleeping up to four, open year round. Little **★Hs As Arenas II**, Avda. de Santiago 22, ✆ and ✉ 55 05 23 (*moderate*), is another comfortable choice, all rooms with bath; cheapest of all by Covas is **Camping Viveiro**, ✆ 56 00 25. The newly built **★★★Ego**, 3km from the centre on Praia de Area, ✆ 56 09 87, ✉ 56 17 62 (*expensive*), has fine views and most other creature comforts. In the centre, **★★Hs Vila**, C/ N. Montenegros 57, ✆ 56 13 31 (*moderate*), has rooms with bath, while the **Nuevo Mundo**, C/ Teodoro de Quirós 14, ✆ 56 00 25 (*inexpensive*), has rooms with pretty balconies over a good, afford-able seafood restaurant. The best place to tuck into a plate of shellfish, **Nito**, by the Praia de Area, ✆ 56 09 87, has a 2400-pts menu; **Vivero**, in the centre at C/ Melitón Cortiñas 16, ✆ 56 00 18, also deals out plates of *mariscos*, for slightly less; for tapas in a friendly atmosphere, try **Pepe** in the same street.

The Galician Interior: the Road to Santiago

Pilgrims who made it as far as Villafranca del Bierzo (*see* p.267) had to gird their loins for one last trial: the Puerto Pedrafita in the Sierra de Ancares. This is Galicia at its wildest, driest and bleakest, deceptively covered with blooms in the spring, but the haunt of were-wolves and witches in the evening—a zone apart, bound in dreams and legends. The regional government, the Xunta de Galicia, has recently restored the atmospheric old *camino francés* and placed yellow scallop-shell markers every 500m. The *camino* itself rarely coincides with the highways, making this last leg of the journey especially pleasant for walkers; to really maintain the medieval mood, Galicia's fierce sheepdogs are still in place with medieval sheepdog attitudes, just asking for a buffet from a stout pilgrim's staff.

Getting Around

The towns in this section are served by bus from Lugo (the station is just outside the Roman walls in Praza de Constitución, ✆ (982) 22 39 85; buses from Lugo to León pass through Becerreá and Pedrafita. Lugo and the junction at Monforte de

Lemos are linked by rail to León, A Coruña, Ourense and Vigo, with speedy Talgos to Zaragoza, Barcelona, Bilbao and Irún. Lugo's station is in the new part of town on Pza. Conde de Fontao, ✆ (982) 22 00 25; take the steps down and walk along Rúa de Castelao to the walls. There's a RENFE office at Pza. Maior 27, ✆ 22 55 03.

Tourist Information

Lugo: Praza Maior 27, ✆ (982) 23 13 61

O Cebreiro, Os Ancares, and the Pilgrim's Road

After Villafranca, the *camino* (and the road) pass through the narrow valley of the river Valcarce, ascending relentlessly to the 1100m pass at **Pedrafita**, the boundary between Léon and Galicia. Here, in 1809, Sir John Moore's troops fleeing to A Coruña, with Marshal Soult's terrible army in hot pursuit, nearly rebelled. Discipline had already vanished in Villafranca, where the soldiers had sacked, raped and looted the homes of their Spanish allies; at Pedrafita and at **O Cebreiro**, another 200m up and a famous brunt of blizzards, hundreds of men froze to death. Such was their haste that the soldiers threw thousands of pounds in gold—the army's pay—over the cliff, along with hundreds of horses, while all the women and children campfollowers were abandoned in the icy wilderness. It was one of the blackest pages in the history of the British army, and it was almost miraculous that Moore was able to restore order and continue to the coast.

Today O Cebreiro has a huge parking lot to allow everyone to enjoy the tremendous views (in good weather) and have a look at the village's Celtic *pallozas*, oval stone huts topped with conical straw roofs where man and beast lived side by side. One has been set aside as a Spartan pilgrim's refuge, while a cluster of four *pallozas* now houses the **Museo de Artes y Costumbres Populares** (*usually open 12–2 and 5–7*). A Benedictine monastery, **Santa María del Cebreiro,** contemporary with the Asturian churches of the 9th century, was built over an old Celtic temple (note the carved stone reused in the entrance). Pilgrims never failed to pay their respects in its squat slate church, where one of the greatest miracles of the road took place: in the late 13th century, an old priest, tired of celebrating mass for just one shepherd in the winter, was grumbling away during the Transfiguration when he and his parishioner were astonished to see the host transformed into flesh and the wine into blood. The chalice in which this miracle happened is a fine example of Romanesque gold work and displayed in the right aisle; legend identifies it with the Holy Grail, left here by a pilgrim (compare it to other Grails in the cathedrals of Genoa and Valencia); next to it in the case are the miraculous paten and a silver reliquary for the blood and flesh donated by celebrity pilgrims Fernando V and Isabel I in 1489.

O Cebreiro and the mighty mountains to the north form part of the **Reserva Nacional de Os Ancares**, part refuge of the rare capercaillie (especially around Degrada) and part hunting reserve of roebuck and boar. Several of the tiny villages lost in the bosom of the range also have *pallozas*, a few still inhabited by diehards—**Villarello, Cervantes, Doiras** and, best of all, **Piornedo**, which can only be reached by foot from Donís. **Becerreá**, on the Lugo road, is the main base for excursions into Os Ancares.

From O Cebreiro, the *camino* ascends vertiginously to **O Poio** pass (1337m), but from here it's all downhill through mountain meadows, chestnut groves and tiny hamlets, where most of the pilgrims' chapels and hostals have survived only in name. The exception, **Triacastela**, huddled under an old *castro*, still has its Romanesque church of Santiago, with a simple Baroque tower; by the river Ouribio a pilgrims' fountain and monument. During the construction of the cathedral of Santiago at Compostela, every medieval pilgrim would pick up a chunk of limestone in the quarries outside Triacastela, and carry it 100km to the Castañeda kilns to be melted into mortar. Modern pilgrims sometimes continue the custom, but now that the cathedral is finished they leave their stone atop Monte de Gozo.

At San Xil, the *camino* splits, the right branch heading prettily over hill and dale, while the other, longer, passes down the narrow wooded Ouribio valley to the huge Benedictine **Abadía de San Xulián** at **Samos** *(open 10.30–1 and 4.30–7)*, where the hospitable old monks always seem glad to see visitors. Founded in 655, abandoned with the arrival of the Moors but rebuilt a few years later, the abbey had a famous library in the Middle Ages. The intellectual tradition continued in the 1700s, when Samos was the home of Padre Feijóo, the 'Spanish Voltaire', a major figure in the Spanish Enlightenment. The tiny slate chapel of San Salvador is from the 9th century, but the medieval monastery burned down in the 16th century and its replacement in 1951, leading to the reconstruction of the two cloisters, one late Gothic and the other, larger, very strict and buttoned-down Spanish Baroque, decorated with frescoes of St Benedict (as truly awful as only modern religious art can be); in the centre flows the lovely Fountain of the Nereids, said to be the work of Velázquez. There's a recent statue of Padre Feijóo, who founded the monastic **church** with profits from his essays. Designed by monk Juan Vázquez, the west façade has a cool elegance, even minus its planned towers. The interior is austere and virtuous, the only sign of playfulness— *trompe l'oeil* doctors of the church—tucked in the pendentives of the dome.

The two branches of the *camino* meet in **Sarriá,** a bustling cement-making town on the rail line. In its quietly aloof medieval core, there's a ruined castle, the little Romanesque church of San Salvador and a pilgrims' hostel in the **Convento de los Mercedarios**, where the church has Isabelline Gothic frills. Ten km west, **Portomarín** was a pilgrims' halt protected by the Templars, but even they couldn't have fended off the waters of the Minho, when the river was dammed in the 1960s to form the Embalse de Belesar, submerging the medieval bridge and village. However, old Portomarín's porticoed main street plan was salvaged in a new Portomarín, along with the pretty façade of **San Pedro** and the Romanesque tower church of **San Nicolás**. The latter has a rose window like a telephone dial and Romanesque portals so fine that they were long attributed to Master Mateo, one decorated with the 24 Elders playing their rebecs and the other with a charming scene of the Annunciation; step inside to see the stately single aisled interior. The adjacent monument is to the electrical engineer who helped the villagers with their request to relocate rather than simply receive an indemnity for their property. And they continue to do what they've always done best: supply Galicia with excellent *aguardiente*—firewater which they not only distil but drain during the nightly *marcha*.

And the Last Leg of the *Camino*

At **Vilar de Donas**, 'Ladyville' (just off the pilgrim's road 15km west of Portomarín), the 13th-century granite church of **San Salvador** merits a detour. From the exterior you can see the ruined Gothic cloister of the long-gone monastery and the pretty Romanesque-Gothic portal, decorated with reading and praying monks; inside the tall granite walls are emerald green from the damp, while those in the rounded apse are embellished with 15th-century paintings: the Resurrection, Annunciation, the queen of heaven and the noble ladies who gave their name to the village. The altar stone is carved with the miracle at O Cebreiro, with Jesus in person emerging out of the chalice; the 15th-century baldachin in the transept is one of the few to survive intact in Galicia. San Salvador was once the seat of the Knights of Santiago in Galicia (note the crossed swords, the symbol of the order, on the tombs).

If it weren't for the proximity of Santiago itself, the last two days' march along the *camino* would be disappointing, especially for the modern pilgrim. The Códice Calixtino advised pilgrims to say the rosary at **Palas do Rei**, the penultimate stop, although only a few medieval traces remain in its church. The old road passes over a medieval bridge at **Furelos**, before arriving in **Melide**, where the church of Sancti Spiritus decorates the endearing Praza do Convento and the roadside cross, marking the geographic centre of Galicia, is one of the oldest. Just outside Melide, you'll find a dolmen, the **Pedra de Raposo** and the crumbling church Santa María with 15th-century murals in the apse, perhaps by the same artist as Vilar de Donas. **Arzúa** was the traditional last overnight stop, 30km from Compostela.

These days Santiago's airport is the dominant feature of **Labacolla** ('Wash Arse'), 8km from Compostela where 'for the love of the Apostle' the pilgrims would bathe in the stream flowing by the church. Sentries were posted to make sure they performed the ritual, as much against lice as for the sensibilities of St James. Another 5km would take them up to the now rather desolate hill (km 717 along the *autopista*), **Monte del Gozo** or Mountjoy, and the tremendous, long-awaited sight of the towers of Santiago. The first member of each pilgrimage band to sight the cathedral towers was called the 'King', a proud title that was passed down as a surname; if yours is King, Leroy or Rey, the chances are you had a sharp-eyed ancestor. These days you can barely make them out; Santiago's sprawl and traffic conspire to make the last few kilometres a hellish welcome to a heavenly goal (*see* p.283).

℗ *(982–)*   *Where to Stay and Eating Out*

O Cebreiro and Os Ancares

Near the *pallozas*, **★★Hs San Giraldo de Aurillac**, ℗ 36 71 25 (*inexpensive*), now a *mesón*, offers 6 authentically medieval rooms in a Benedictine convent founded by monks from St Géraud d'Aurillac in France in 1072. Sturdy stone **★★Hs Piornedo**, in Cervantes, ℗ 36 83 19 (*moderate*), has lovely views over the mountains. Other lodgings in Os Ancares are in Becerreá: **★Hs Herbón**, G. Jiménez 8, ℗ 36 01 34 (*inexpensive*), and the **★★Hs Rivera**, Avda. Madrid 86, ℗ 36 01 85 (*moderate*), outside town. Both are basic *hostales* open all year; a couple of bars in town serve meals as well.

Sarriá

Sarriá has plenty of choices, starting with ★★★**Alfonso IX**, Peregrino 29, ✆ 53 00 05, ✉ 53 12 61 (*expensive*), with a good restaurant; for less, ★★**Hs Londres**, Calvo Sotelo 153, ✆ 53 24 56, ✉ 53 30 06 (*moderate*), has doubles with baths.

Detours off the *Camino*: Lugo

Many pilgrims made the detour to **Lugo**, the capital of Spain's poorest province but happily dozing away in cosy retirement on the banks of the Minho after a career of some consequence, the kind of town 'where an ill poet would feel happy,' according to one French observer. Its Celtic name *lug* means either the sun god or sacred forest, and when the Romans took it over in the 2nd century AD, they renamed it Lucus Augusti, made it the capital of their province of Gallaecia and endowed it with a remarkable dark slate corset of **walls**, the best preserved ancient fortifications in Spain, just over 2km long and 28ft (9.2m) high and interspersed with 85 rounded towers. For all that, Lugo was grabbed by the Suevi in the 5th century, the Visigoths in 585, and the Moors in the 8th century. The bastions now defend historic Lugo from its own modern sprawl; for a good view of both, take the promenade along the top of the walls.

Four ancient gates (and six modern ones) pierce the dark fastness. Pilgrims would enter the southern Santiago gate to visit Lugo's **Cathedral**, built in 1177 and encased in a Baroque skin that offers a modest prelude to the great façade and three towers at Santiago de Compostela. On the west front note the figure of Lugo's patron San Froilán with his wolf: the story goes that the saint was travelling with a well-laden mule when a ferocious wolf ambushed him and killed the mule. The angry saint scolded until the beast repented and agreed to bear the mule's load himself. Only the north, 14th-century, Gothic portal survived the Baroquers, with its fine Romanesque Christ in Majesty and a capital carved with a Last Supper. Inside there are fittings from every century: a Romanesque chapel and another from 1735, lavish and Baroque in the shape of a rounded Greek cross, dedicated to the Virgen de los Ojos Grandes, 'Our Lady of the Big Eyes', designed by Fernando de las Casas, master of the Obradoiro façade at Compostela. Glass protects a beautiful walnut *coro* carved with a proto Art Nouveau flair by Francisco Moure (1590–1621), whose detailed scenes include an anatomy lesson. The Renaissance *retablo mayor* survives in two bits, filling the transepts; there's a pretty Baroque cloister off the south transept. Since the miracle of O Cebreiro, the Cathedral has had the rare privilege of *manifestado* (having the Host on permanent display), an honour depicted on Galicia's crest.

Next to the cathedral, elegant Praza Santa María holds the handsome 17th-century **Bishop's Palace**, built in the style of a typical Gallego *pazo*. Just west, **Praza do Campo** with its fountain was the Roman forum; Lugo's medieval neighbourhood, **La Tinería**, extends here around Rúa Cruz and Rúanova. Just north of Prazo do Campo, the formal Alameda gardens give onto the Praza Maior, site of Lugo's rococo Ayuntamiento. Rúa da Raiña heads north to big and busy **Praza de Santo Domingo**, dominated by a big eagle on a column suffering from midriff bulge, dedicated to Augustus. The square has two Gothic churches: 14th-century **Santo Domingo** and 16th-century, *mudéjar*-influenced, **San Francisco**, formerly part of a 12th-century monastery founded by St Francis on his return from his pilgrimage to Santiago. The delicate cloister and refectory now house the interesting **Provincial Museum** (*open Sept–June 10.30–2 and 4.30–8.30, closed Sun; July and Aug 11–2 and 5–8, Sat 10–2, closed Sun*) containing Celtic and Roman finds—a golden, winged ram from the 2nd century BC, gold torques, jet figures from Compostela, the biggest collection of sundials in Galicia, ceramics from Sargadelos and folk art; if you like what you see don't miss the Sargadelos shop in the square. Lugo's beauty-spots are along the Río Minho, the most beautiful of Galicia's rivers; in the **Parque Rosalía de Castro**, just outside the Santiago gate and a favourite rendezvous during the evening *paseo,* the *mirador* has magnificent views of the valley. Near here are the brick vaults of the **Termas Romanas**, or Roman hot baths, now part of a modern complex.

Santa Eulalia de Bóveda, and a Mystery

Some 16km southwest of Lugo (take the Ourense road for 4km, then bear right towards Friol and follow the signs) is the extraordinary 4th-century subterranean chapel of **Santa Eulalia de Bóveda**, built over a Celtic temple as a Roman nymphaeum, and later as a mausoleum (*open for guided tours in Spanish, Oct–May 11–5, June–Sept 11–7; Sun and hols 11–2, closed Mon*). Discovered in 1962, steps lead down to what must have been an antechamber of some kind. A brick horseshoe arch with mysterious reliefs of female dancers on one side and the healing of a man on the other leads into a vaulted room with a shallow pool in the centre (perhaps used for immersion baptisms by the early Christians), decorated with colourful winsome murals of birds and trees, variously dated 4th or 8th century—just predating the pre-Romanesque churches of Asturias. The columns by the pool were found nearby and re-erected around the rim; under the pavement, an efficient drainage system kept the water clear and clean. According to the guide, stones carved with the sun, moon and stars were found here and taken to Rome, and the only known building similar to Santa Eulalia is in the Ukraine, and just as mysterious.

Heresy, Galician Style

 According to popular belief, the right wall of Santa Eulalia once contained the tomb of Galicia's first 'saint', Prisciliano, whose doctrines, a syncretism of old Celtic and Christian beliefs, attracted many followers in Galicia and León but upset the church. For one thing, Prisciliano believed works of the spirit obliterated sexual differences, and that monks and nuns should live together. His followers walked barefoot to stay in contact with the earth's forces, were vegetarians, did a bit of sun-worshipping on the side and retreated to hermitages (alone or with their families and servants) in the holy mountains of the Celts. The counsel of Zaragoza (380) interdicted him, and when that had no effect, the bishop of Triers had him beheaded five years later—making Prisciliano one of the first holy men to be martyred by the Church instead of by Romans. His death only increased the popularity of what became known as Priscillianism in Galicia until the early 9th century, when, by an extraordinary coincidence, the head and body of St James was discovered in Santiago. Galician nationalists know they really belonged to Prisciliano, and that the holy heretic now has the last laugh in the venerated crypt in Compostela.

Another rewarding excursion from Lugo and another popular detour for pilgrim is northwest to the evocative ruins of **Sobrado dos Monxes** (*open 10.15–1.30 and 4.15–6.45*), Galicia's greatest monastery, founded by the Cistercians in 1142. Although the original building, by an architect from Clairvaux specially sent over by St Bernard, hasn't survived, a fresh handful of monks have been doing what they can with government funds to preserve the massive towered Baroque church, the lovely if rotting choir stalls, originally in the cathedral of Santiago, and the monumental, ogival **kitchen** where pilgrims once cadged meals; also intact are the 13th-century chapel dedicated to the Magdalen, a sacristy (1571) by Juan de Herrera, a 12th-century chapter-house or Sala Capitular, and three 17th- and 18th-century cloisters, wreathed in lichens and wildflowers.

Villalba, farther north,was the capital of the Terra Cha, ruled by the Andrade family, who left behind their powerful 15th-century octagonal castle, now an exceptionally nice *parador.*

A Detour South: Monforte de Lemos

If you're driving, consider a detour south to **Monforte de Lemos**, dominated by a Homage tower, all that remains of the medieval castle of the counts of Lemos. It had two important monasteries: Benedictine **San Vicente del Pino**, founded in the 10th century, with a late Romanesque church, sheltering a 15th-century statue of St Anne; and, near the medieval bridge, the colossal 16th-century Jesuit **Colegio de la Compañía**, inspired by the geometric Baroque of Herrera. Look in the chapel for a beautiful Renaissance *retablo* in walnut carved with the life of the Virgin by de Moure, two El Grecos painted before the Cretan reached the flaming summit of his style, and a lovely triptych attributed to Hugo van der Goes. The area south of here towards the river Sil contain the vineyards of Amandi, one of Galicia's finest reds, grown in a village named, of all things, **Sober**.

Lugo and Around ✆ (982–)　　　　　　　*Where to Stay and Eating Out*

Lugo

At the top of the scale, the ★★★★**Gran Hotel Lugo**, Avda. Ramón Ferreiro 21, ✆ 22 41 52, ✉ 24 16 60 (*expensive*), offers a pool, piano bar, air conditioning, a good seafood restaurant (Os Marisqueiros) and a pizzeria. Within the walls, the ★★★**Méndez Núñez**, Reina 1, ✆ 23 07 11, ✉ 22 97 38 (*moderate*), has modern rooms, or you can have a view of the walls at the ★★**Hs Mar de Plata**, Ronda Muralla 5, ✆ 22 89 10. ★**Hs Parames**, Rúa do Progreso 28, ✆ 22 62 51 (*inexpensive*), is decent and central, and has a popular restaurant with a 900-pts menu. Although Lugo boasts of quirky delicacies such as pancakes with pig's blood, it has a good seafood restaurant; two of the best are nearby in Rúa da Cruz, **Alberto** ✆ 22 83 10 (closed Sun), and the older **Verruga**, ✆ 22 98 55 (closed Mon); both have good 2300-pts menus. **Campos**, Rúa Nova 4, © 22 97 43, has traditional Gallego sucking-pig, octopus and delicacies such as *pimientos del Piquillo* filled with seafood (menus from 1300 pts).

Vilalba

The crenellated ★★★**Parador Condes de Vilalba**, Valeriano Valdesuso, © 51 00 11, ◙ 51 00 90 (*expensive*), bestows on its visitors feudal fancies—the windows in the 3m-thick walls were made to shoot arrows at attackers far below. Book early to nab one of its 6 rooms, all centrally heated, with modern necessities like TVs and minibars. The restaurant in the cellar offers baronial dining on free-range capons, fresh Galician produce and wine (closed Dec). For half as much, check into modern, functional ★★★**Villamartín**, Avda. Tierra, © 51 12 15, ◙ 51 11 35 (*moderate*).

Monforte de Lemos

The most pretentions are on offer at the ★★**Hs Puente Romano II**, Paseo del Malecón, © 41 11 68 (*moderate*), but there are also nicely priced rooms at the ★★**Hs Río** near the centre at R. Baamonde 30, © 40 18 50 (*cheap*). For reliably delicious Gallego cuisine, try **O Grelo**, Chantada 16, © 40 47 01 (*moderate*).

Santiago de Compostela

The original European tourist destination, Santiago de Compostela still comes up with the goods. Not only does it boast a great cathedral where pilgrims are promised 50 per cent off their time in Purgatory, but the moss-stained Baroque city is pure granite magic, a rich grey palette of a hundred moods crowned with curlicues. Any tendency towards atrophy into a Euro-tourist museum shrine is thwarted by the university, which keeps the ancient streets and especially the bars full of life year round and fuels the raw *urbanización* that engulfs the perimeters, swelling the population to more than 90,000. Expect rain—the city, the 'Urinal of Spain' never fails gently to remind you that the showers are good for granite, fostering the elegant patina on its monuments and the micro-gardens that sprout out of the stone, an especially appropriate flourish to the Competelan Baroque of Simón Rodríguez and Fernando de Casas y Novoa with its 'vegetative impulse of verticality'. But on a cold winter's twilight you may see it stripped as bare as García Lorca did in one of his Galician poems:

> *See the rain on the streets,*
> *a moan of glass and stone,*
> *See in the failing wind*
> *The dust and ashes of your sea..*

History

The story goes that in the year 813, a bright star led Pelayo, a hermit shepherd of Iria Flavia (Padrón), to the forgotten tomb of St James the Greater, the legendary apostle of Spain. The place was named Compostela, a corruption of the Latin *Campus stellae* 'Field

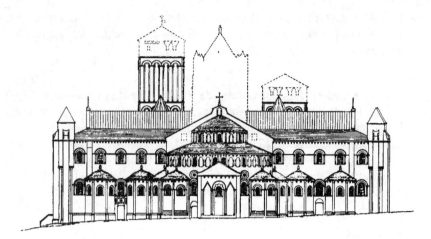

A reconstruction of the Romanesque apse of Santiago de Compostela cathedral

of the star', although some say that Pelayo's discovery merely happened in the Roman cemetery, or *compostum*, where bodies decomposed. This theory was given a boost in the late 1940s when excavations in the cathedral's foundation revealed Roman graves over a Celtic *castro*. Of course apostles don't compost like everyone else, and the remains of James were just what Christian Spain required at the dawn of the Reconquista. Local bishop Theodomir confirmed the relics' authenticity and built a chapel; in 829 Alfonso II the Chaste of Asturias built a much larger chapel over the tomb. So many pilgrims began to arrive that an even larger church was needed and supplied by Alfonso III the Great in 896. This in turn fell to Al-Mansur and his Moorish armies when they swept through in 997; Al-Mansur took the bells as a souvenir for the Great Mosque at Córdoba, where they were turned upside down to hold oil, but he left the Apostle's tomb alone, awed, they say, by the piety of a single monk, who fearlessly knelt there and prayed during the battle.

Sometime in these early days James the humble fisherman with a voice of thunder was given a new posthumous role as Santiago Matamoros, a fierce Moor-thumping Generalísimo, the hero of the entirely apocryphal Battle of Clavijo of 844. This legend was 'confirmed' in a 12th-century document known as the *Privilegio de los Votos de Santiago*, purporting to be by Ramiro I of Asturias, the grateful victor of Clavijo, vowing a tax in perpetuity to the saint's church in Compostela (a tax that continued to be imposed in Spain until 1834).

After Al-Mansur, church and town were soon rebuilt, this time with walls. In 1075, thanks to the new tax, the present Cathedral was begun to accommodate the massive flow of pilgrims from all over Europe. By 1104, Compostela was made an archbishopric, under the feisty Diego Gelmírez; in 1189, Alexander III decreed it a Holy City, on a par with Jerusalem and Rome. In 1236, Fernando III the Saint brought back Santiago's bells from the Great Mosque. In 1589, with Drake (a pirate and worse, a Protestant) ravaging the coast, Santiago was tucked away for safekeeping, but in a fit of amnesia, no one could remember where. Still, the pilgrims came, and only in the 19th century, when numbers declined drastically, did a cathedral workman stumble across the most important relics in Spain (1879). How to make sure they were genuine? An authenticated apostolic bone chip from Pistoia was sent over and fitted the notch in the skull like a hand in a glove.

Getting Around

Santiago's airport, ✆ (981)59 74 00, is at Labacolla, 11km to the east. It has regular flights to Barcelona, Madrid, Sevilla, Santa Cruz de Tenerife, Bilbao, Santander and San Sebastián, as well as direct flights to London, Paris, Amsterdam, Geneva and Frankfurt. Iberia's office is at Gral. Pardiñas 36, ✆ 57 20 24; there are buses to the airport from the station run by the Empresa Freire, ✆ 58 81 11.

Santiago's train station is a 10-minute walk from the centre at the end of Rúa do Hórreo, ✆ 52 02 02, with daily connections to Madrid, Ourense, A Coruña, Vigo, Zamora and other points. The bus station is way out on San Cayetano, ✆ 58 77 00, at the opposite end of town from the train station; city bus 10 links it to Praza de Galicia. Buses go to nearly all points in Galicia, especially the Rías Altas.

Tourist Information

Rúa de Vilar 43, ✆ (981) 58 40 81. There is a daily market (exc Sunday), in the covered market in Praza de San Félix.

The Praza do Obradoiro

Irresistibly all roads in Compostela lead up to the towering granite magnet of the Cathedral of Santiago, the town's *raison d'être* and culmination of the pilgrim's journey. Approach it from the enormous Praza do Obradoiro, the 'Square of Works,' also known as Praza de España, where for centuries the cathedral's stone masons liberated the soul of Galicia's stone and made it sing and blaze like a Baroque bonfire. In the rain and mists, at morning or sunset or the heat of the day, the cathedral façade changes its tune; it cries out for a new Monet to paint its moods during the course of the day or, perhaps even better, a composer.

Before going in, pause for a look over the Praza do Obradoiro itself, where a colourful carnival of pilgrims, students, Gallegos holding demonstrations, vendors of postcards and plastic birds with flapping wings all play out their rôles before a prize collection of civic monuments, erected over the last six centuries. Left, and adjacent to the Cathedral, the rather plain **Pazo de Gelmírez** was built in the 12th and 13th centuries by the two Archbishops whose worldly aplomb helped make Santiago great: Diego Gelmírez, the first to hold the job, who received a licence to mint money when he oversaw the forgery of the *Votos de Santiago* and used the funds to build the Cathedral, and Arias, reputedly 'one of the great ecclesiastical pirates of 13th-century Spain'. They didn't build their own palace as well as they might have: new walls had to be added between the 16th and 18th centuries to keep it from collapsing. Although the upper section is still the archbishop's palace, you can visit the lower medieval rooms, especially the huge Romanesque dining-hall, where the corbels under the vaults are carved with delicious scenes of a medieval feast, complete with musicians; one trencherman is tucking into an *empanada..*

Santiago de Compostela

N

100 metres
100 yards

CAMPO DAS HORTAS

CRUZEIRO DO GAIO

RÚA DAS HORTAS

RÚA DAS CARRETAS

AVENIDA DE COMPOSTELA

Hospital Real
Hostal de los
Reyes Católicos
(H)

San Fructuoso

Pazo
de Rajoy

PRAZA DO OBRADOIRO

RÚA DO POMBAL

PASEO DE FERRADURA

Colegio de
San Jerónimo

Santa Susana

Colegio
Mayor de
Fonseca

CAMPO DE SAN CLEMENZO

TRAVESA DE FONSECA

Post Office

Iglesia del Pilar

Colegio de
S. Clemenzo

RÚA DA RAIÑA

RÚA DO VILAR

AVENIDA DE FIGUEROA

RÚA DO FRANCO

RÚA NOVA

i
Tourist
Information

CARREIRA DO CONDÉ

PRAZA
DO TORAL

Santa María
Salomé

RÚA DA SENRA

RÚA DAS ORFAS

RÚA DE MONTERO RÍOS

FONTE DE SANTO ANTONIO

PRAZA DE
GALICIA

Train
Station

Santa María
del Sar

Convento de San Francisco

RÚA DOS CASTIÑEIROS

AVENIDA DE XOAN XXIII

RÚA DOS XASMÍNS

COSTA VELLA

RÚA DOS LOUREIROS

Convento de Santa Clara

RÚA DE SAN FRANCISCO

RÚA DE SAN ROQUE

San Martiño Pinario

PRAZA DE SAN MARTIÑO

RÚA DE SANTA CRISTINA

PRAZINA DE SAN ROQUE

Convento de San Martiño Pinario

ABRILARES

Museo de Santiago y de las Peregrinaciones

Pazo de Gelmirez

PRAZA DE SAN MIGUEL

RÚA DE SAN MIGUEL

RÚA DAS RODAS

SAN XOAN

CAMPAS

PRAZA DE LA AZABACHERÍA

Casa da Troya

RÚA DE TROIA

RUELA DE XERUSALEN

San Miguel dos Agros

RÚA DA ALGALIA DE ARRIBA

RÚA DA ALGALIA DE ABAIXO

Casa da Parra

RÚA DA AZABACHERÍA

Cathedral

Iglesia de las Ánimas

RUELA DAS ANIMAS

PRAZA DAS PLATERÍAS

PRAZA QUINTANA

Convento de San Paio de Antealtares

Ayuntamiento Antiguo

PRAZA DE CERVANTES

RÚA DAS CASAS REAIS

Convento de Santo Domingo de Bonaval/Museo do Pobo Galego

RÚA DA CONGA

RÚA DO PREGUNTOIRO

RÚA DE SAN BIEITO

RÚA TRAVESA

PORTA DO CAMINO

SANTO DOMINGO

Casa do Dean

RÚA DE GELMIREZ

Santa María do Camino

PRAZA DE SAN AGOSTIÑO

NOVA

PRAZA DE ABASTOS

RÚA DA VIRXE DA CERCA

RÚA DA CALDERERÍA

TRAVESA DA UNIVERSIDADE

University

Convento de las Mercedarias

Continuing around the square, the Plateresque **Hospital Real** (1501–09) was constructed for poor pilgrims by Fernando and Isabel with the booty from taking Granada in 1492. Built by Enrique de Egas on Filarete's design for the Ospedale Maggiore in Milan, its façade, typical of Plateresque, concentrates its embellishments in a few key spots, in its long Baroque balconies added in 1678 but especially in the crowded triumphal Gothic Renaissance altarpiece of a doorway. Medallions of the founders glower at each other in the corners of the arch, while a Christian's Who's Who from Adam and Eve on up fill the chiselled niches. The building was used as a hospital until 1953, when it was converted into a five-star *parador*: at least have a drink down in the bar (the former hospital morgue!) and try to visit the four elegant courtyards and beautiful late Gothic chapel along the way.

Tucked at the bottom of the stairway to the left of the Hospital, the little church of **San Fructuoso** by Lucus Caaveiro (1757) is a good introduction to Compostela's special Baroque and its fondness for heavy geometrical forms. The enormous 18th-century **Pazo de Rajoy**, designed as a seminary and now the town hall, is pure Parisian neoclassicism, by French architect Charles Lemaur; on top note the proud figure of Santiago Matamoros. Next, the 16th-century **Colegio de San Jerónimo** was founded as a university, where priests could learn languages to hear the pilgrims' confessions; its curious portal was reused from a 15th-century *hostal* and is often pointed out as an example of Renaissance retro. Classes were held just behind in the **Colegio Mayor de Fonseca**, built by Juan de Álava (1546) around a lovely, peaceful cloister with a beautiful *mudéjar* ceiling, still a favourite place for weary scholars to enjoy a breath of fresh air; the college is now used as a library.

The Cathedral of Santiago

And back to that Baroque firecracker, the Obradoiro façade of the cathedral where the two towers shoot like huge flames to heaven. On the right, the Tower of the Bells was built by José Peña de Toro in the 1600s, while the left hand one was added by Fernando Casas y Novoa in1750s, when he tackled the main façade. A lively triple ramp stair leads up to a pair of doors, arranged to form a cross in stone work; stacked above are two calm windows in a shallow arch like the eye of a hurricane just before the front peaks in a flickering crest of granite fire.

At the foot of the steps a door leads into the delightful **crypt of Master Mateo** or 'Catedral Vieja' (*10.30–1.30 and 4–6.30, Sun 10.20–1.30, adm; keep your ticket for the treasury, cloister and museum*), built by the great master builder to distribute the weight of his Romanesque façade, but so elaborately, with ancient columns, capitals, and fine sculpture under the vaults that people used to think this was the first cathedral.

Inside the Cathedral: the Pórtico de la Gloria

Perhaps the most startling surprise for many visitors awaits just within the busy Baroque doors up the staircase, where the original 12th-century façade of the cathedral survives perfectly intact. This is the sublime **Pórtico de la Gloria**, nothing less than the greatest single piece of Romanesque sculpture, anywhere. Sculpted in warm brown granite between 1168–88 by Master Mateo (dated and signed on the lintel of the central arch) its three doorways are dedicated to the Triumph of the Apocalypse, a theme that decorated many churches along the *camino*, but here, at the very end of the road, it reaches an apogee of joy and mirth, full of movement, life and rhythm; if the end of the world is like this, you want to be there. Nearly all the 200 or so figures are smiling or laughing, beginning with St James himself, welcoming you from his perch on the central pillar, carved with the tree of Jesse, showing the genealogy of Christ from Adam to the Virgin Mary; so many millions of pilgrims have put a hand on the pillar while bending to kiss the base in

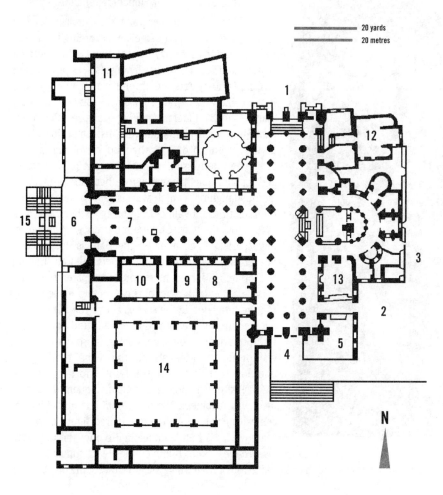

20 yards
20 metres

N

1	Puerta de la Azabachería	5	Torre de la Trinidad	11	Pazo de Gelmírez
2	Praza da Quintana	6	Obradoiro façade	12	Capilla de la Corticela
3	Puerta Santa	7	Pórtico de la Gloria	13	Capilla del Pilar
4	Puerta de las Platerías	8	sacristy	14	cloister
		9	treasury	15	crypt of Master Mateo
		10	reliquary chapel		

thanksgiving that the stone has the five worn indentations from their fingers. Originally it was even brightly painted, and traces of a 17th-century touch-up remain.

Above St James in the central arch, Christ in Majesty appears 'like jasper and carnelian' according to the text in Revelations, raising both hands in blessing, surrounded by the four Evangelists, Apostles and angels. 'And round the throne was a rainbow that looked like an emerald', an ogival rainbow of musicians—the 24 Elders of the Apocalypse (plus a few stand-ins), each with a different instrument on his lap as they seem to discuss their hopes for another gig during an intermission. On the two side pillars apostles and prophets chat pleasantly together, among them the famous laughing Daniel, who is said to owe his good humour to the loveliness of Queen Esther, whom he eyes across the way; Chinese monsters grimace on the lowest frieze. The door on the right is dedicated to heaven and hell, mostly, and depicts children suffering the torments of the damned with their parents—on the surface a powerful psychological trick to make parents toe the line—while the scenes above the left door are even more elusive and food for all kinds of esoteric interpretations; note the benign portrayal of Jews waiting for the Messiah and the twins, recalling the tradition that St James was Jesus' mortal twin (*see* p.313). After drinking in this most eloquent draught of medieval happiness, pilgrims would line up behind the central pillar before the curly-haired figure of Master Mateo, who is humbly kneeling to offer the Cathedral to God; his nickname, '*O Santo dos Croques*' 'Saint Bump-on-the-Head' comes from the millions who have bowed their heads to touch Mateo's in the hope that some of his genius would rub off.

The **Romanesque interior** of the cathedral is essentially as Master Mateo left it, a long, majestic, barrel-vaulted, nave lined with galleries, although it takes your eyes some time to get used to the mystic gloom; the cathedral's Baroque coating blocked out much of the original light, including that which once poured in an unusual nine-sided rose window over the Pórtico de la Gloria. The huge, silver high altar glimmers in the penumbra, visible since the 1940s when the enclosed Baroque choir was removed. Of the chapels along the nave the most important is the first on the right, the 16th-century **reliquary chapel** and Royal Pantheon, with medieval tombs of Galicia's royal family, and reliquaries containing bits of the True Cross and the head of St James the Lesser, who was occasionally purposefully confused with James the Greater for propaganda ends. Next on the right is the cathedral **Treasury,** aglitter with the silver hammer used to pound open the Holy Door in Holy Years, silver scallop shells, a score of other showy religious trappings and a celebrated 16th-century monstrance decorated with scenes from lives of Jesus and St James.

Thou shield of that faith which in Spain we revere
Thou Scourge of each foeman who dares to draw near
Whom the Son of the God whom the elements tames,
Called Child of the Thunder, Immortal Saint James!

Pilgrims' hymn, translated by George Burrows

Actually, when you get right up to it, the glow-in-the-dark 17th-century high altar, lavishly coated with Mexican silver, turns out to be a pointless piece of tomfoolery, its cast of knick-knack characters borrowed from a giant's Christmas tree. On top Santiago Matamoros cuts down the Moors, but what goes around comes around; in the Civil War, bedsheets had to be draped over the trampled Moors when Franco came with his crack Moroccan troops to vow to liberate Spain from the godless Republicans. Just over the altar itself sits a stiff idol, a 12th-century statue of Santiago, the Patron Saint of Spain, his clothes and throne later tricked out lavishly by a Mexican archbishop. The thing to do is climb the narrow stairway behind the altar, kiss the statue's robe and receive a holy card (for the certificate of indulgence, the *compostellana*, pilgrims should apply with their documents to the *Oficina arzobispal*, in the back of the cathedral). Below the altar you can pay your respects to the saint's bones in the 19th-century silver crypt; the outer, rounded wall here survives from Alfonso III's 9th-century church, while the inner wall is believed to be Roman.

To the side of the high altar, notice the ropes and pulleys suspended from the octagonal dome or *cimborio*, from which, on high feast days, the **Botafumeiro**, the world's largest censer, is suspended and swung with terrifying force across the entire length of the transept in a comet-like arc of perfumed smoke and sparks. Weighing in at 54kg, the Botafumeiro is a smaller brass version of the original silver model made in 1602 and pilfered by Napoleon's troops: it takes eight men, the *tiraboleiros*, to swing it on a system invented in the Middle Ages. Don't miss it if you're in town on a holy day, and try not to think about the time when Catherine of Aragón attended Mass and the Botafumeiro broke loose and flew out of the window. The Botafumeiro sweetened the air in the cathedral, where many medieval pilgrims slept at night (until a few behaved scandalously and doors were added to the previously wide-open Pórtico de la Gloria); others say the Botafumeiro was invented as a public-relations gimmick to upstage the pilgrimage to Rome.

The ten chapels radiating like petals from the ambulatory are all worth a look, especially the one straight behind the altar, the Romanesque **Capilla de San Salvador**, where pilgrims received Communion. Off the north transept, a doorway topped with a 13th-century relief of the Magi leads into the church-sized three-aisled Romanesque **Capilla de la Corticela.** Off the south transept, a 16th-century Gothic-vaulted **cloister** big enough for a football match was designed by Juan de Álava and Gil de Hontañón to replace Master Mateo's Romanesque original, and holds the **Cathedral Museum** and **Library**; the former has an illuminated 12th-century *Codex Calixtus* and the latter contains the

Botafumeiro when it's not in use. The archaeological section is of special interest for the fragments of Master Mateo's cloister, while the **Sala Capitular** contains the Cathedral's impressive collection of tapestries, including 17th-century Flemish scenes of Hannibal crossing the Alps and Scipio with his Romans, along with others, some remarkably insipid even if designed by the likes of Rubens and Goya. There are, however, pretty views to be had from the upper rooms across the Praza do Obradoiro.

Around the Cathedral

Although low key after the Obradoiro façade, the cathedral's other entrances each deserve a look. Circumnavigating the Pazo de Gelmírez, you'll come first to the split-level **Praza das Platerías**, named after the silversmiths whose shops once filled the arcades of this jewel-like square. The double **Puerta de las Platerías** is the only one to remain essentially unchanged from the Romanesque cathedral: the tympanum on the right has scenes from the Life and Christ and the Passion, and the one on the left features winged monkeys and a woman giving birth to a skull, while below, King David plays the fiddle; some of the figures were salvaged from the demolished French door and the cathedral's stone Romanesque choir. Locals use the doors as a short cut across town, as their ancestors did in the Middle Ages, when cathedrals were covered public squares as much as religious shrines. From here you can gaze up the Cathedral's highest tower, the ornament-laden 80m **Berenguel** designed by Galician humanist Domingo de Andrade in the 1710s to hold the town clock. The *praza*'s geometric Baroque **Chapter House** and the **fountain of the horse** were both designed by Fernández Sarela.

Continuing past the bulk of the Berenguel is the enclosed **Praza da Quintana**, an inviting place to sit on the steps and linger; the upper level is named 'of the living' and the lower 'of the dead', recalling the Roman cemetery that once occupied the spot. In the Middle Ages this was the square of cheap food, ladled out from the stalls. Alongside the square runs the stern, unforgiving façade of the **Convento de San Paio de Antelares** 'Pelayo before the Altars' containing a **Museo de Arte Sacro** (entrance around back, *open summer only 10–1 and 4–7*), where a celebrity Virgin holds the Child in one hand and thumps a devil with the other. The cloistered nuns keep up the square's culinary tradition with their famous almond and coconut tarts. In the lower square is the **Puerta Santa**, opened only during a holy year, or Año Xacobeo, when St James' Day—25 July—falls on a Sunday; the next one will be 1999. The doorway of 1611 consists of 24 compartments, each pigeon-holing a carved figure from the Romanesque choir, which may have been the work of Master Mateo. In the upper level of the square, the handsome 17th-century **Casa de la Parra** is one of the prettiest in Santiago, decorated with stylized bunches of grapes.

The north façade faces **Praza de la Azabachería** ('of the jet-makers'),where pilgrims bought souvenirs; you couldn't have your photo taken next to St James back then, but you could get little black figures of the Apostle with yourself praying at his feet. The use of jet (hard black polished lignite) is said to be in memory of a local coal-worker, Contolay, who helped St Francis of Assisi on his pilgrimage. Two jet-makers are still in business, although they now specialize in jewellery and works of art: Regueira, at Azabachería 9, and Mayer, Platerías 6. In the Middle Ages, the square was the favourite rendezvous for French pilgrims, who would bathe in the long-gone Fountain of Paradise, before entering the Cathedral for the first time through the French Door, unfortunately obliterated by the dullest of the 18th-century facelifts the Cathedral underwent.

The Gallop to the Scallop

The very first thing a medieval pilgrim did upon arriving in the city was stop in the Barrio de los Conchieros, buy a scallop, eat it (this is where French pilgrims learned to make *coquilles St Jacques*, after all) and stick the shell on the turned-up brim of his or her hat—visible proof that they had made it at last; strict laws forbade the selling of scallops anywhere else along the *camino*. By the 16th century, the real shell was replaced by a fancy souvenir replica, either in silver or in jet.

The scallop, that tasty bivalve that thrives in the *rías* of Galicia, has been associated with the Santiago pilgrimage since the early Middle Ages. In Compostela, as usual, they can explain it with a miracle: a young Gallego, on the eve of his wedding, was spirited into the sea by his wayward horse and believed drowned, although in truth the horse was running along the waves to meet the stone boat bringing the body of St James to Galicia. When the bridegroom returned, escorting the boat, his body was covered with an armour of milk-white shells, so amazing the locals that they converted at once to the new faith. Its Spanish name, *venera*, calls up associations with the vagina and Venus, the goddess of love, who was born of the seafoam and surfed ashore on a giant scallop shell. For pilgrims, the shell also symbolized the end of the journey, the resurrection and unity in the world—the sea from which it came, the earth in its stony hardness, and the sun in its radiant lines. It's hard to think of another symbol so polyvalent, embracing sex, death, dinner and spiritual wholeness—not to mention a multinational company peddling the Super or Unleaded souls of the dead dinosaurs that fuel the way.

San Martín Pinario

Another attraction in Praza de la Azabachería was the chance for destitute pilgrims to hang their rags on an iron cross, the *Crus d'os farrapos*, and pick up new clothes from the Benedictines at San Martín Pinario. San Martín, one of the most venerable monastic institutions in the city, was founded in 912 as the special protector of the Apostle's tomb. In the 1400s, the two other Benedictine houses in Santiago joined San Martín to form an institution powerful enough to challenge the Inquisition. In spite of complaints that it would compete with the Cathedral just opposite, they commissioned an elaborate top-heavy façade by Gabriel Casas in the 18th century; note on top the monks' vocation reflected in the statue of St Martin of Tours sharing his cloak with a poor man. Inside, the vast Claustro de la Portería with its elegant fountain was completed by Casas' more famous follower, Casas y Novoa, while just beyond is an extraordinary, floating 17th-century staircase with Aztec decorations under a fancy Baroque dome. Beyond, the huge barrel-vaulted church is the stage for Casas y Novoa's *retablo mayor*, one of the most overripe pieces of flummery ever produced, a feverish blast of intricate gilded detail, a nightmarish vision of total paradise marked by the merciless destiny of the unbelieving Moors stage left and stage right. Casas y Novoa was also responsible for the almost as frantic Capilla del Socorro on the right side of the nave, and the rather more restrained Sacristy; the elaborate 17th-century choir stalls are also well worth a leisurely look. The stately, colonnaded 18th-century church façade facing Praza San Martín grows like an altarpiece above a sunken Baroque staircase designed by a Dominican named Manuel de los Mártires, all granite ribbons squirming below the level of the pavement, like nothing else in Spain.

In Praza San Miguel (in front of Praza San Martín) the 14th-century Gothic Pazo de Don Pedro contains the **Museo de Santiago y de las Peregrinaciones**, slated to open in 1996; opposite, **San Miquel dos Agros** is another product of Santiago's 18th-century boom. But for a real eyeful of local Baroque, continue along to Rúa da Algalía de Arriba and walk north to Rúa de San Roque, where the startling façade of **Santa Clara** by Simón Rodríguez almost jumps out at you, its fat, abstract almost mechanical-looking volutes culminating in a trio of huge unadorned cylinders that look as if they could roll off the roof any second, altogether more 1930s in effect that 1730s.

Elsewhere in Santiago

Like any natural, organic medieval city, Santiago is a delight to wander in, its narrow, arcaded streets and intimate squares paved with granite flagstones, lined with old palaces, churches, and monasteries, tinged with green and gold from moss and lichens. The founders of the two great mendicant orders of the 13th century both made pilgrimages and personally founded monasteries. In 1214, St Francis founded the **Convento de San Francisco**, in Rúa de San Francisco, under the Hospital de los Reyes Católicos; the Benedictines were impressed enough with Francis' preaching to give him the land, in return for an annual basket of fish. Rebuilt in the 18th century, the convent has a fine granite cross sculpted by Caaveiro with scenes of Francis' life. St Dominic's rather larger **Convento de Santo Domingo de Bonaval**, founded during his pilgrimage in 1220, is due east on the Puerto del Camino at the end of Rúa das Casas Reais. Behind the Baroque façade hides a handsome Gothic church from the 1300s and the chapel of the Pantheon of Illustrious Gallegos, last resting-place of poet Rosalía de Castro and the caricaturist Castelao (died 1950), the Goya of the Civil War. The convent and cloister house the **Museo do Pobo Galego** *(open 11–1 and 4–7, Sun, am only; adm)* with a good collection of folk items, rural tools and other odds and ends, although most memorable of all is the **triple spiral staircase**, a stunning architectural *tour de force* by Domingo de Andrade, where three different, unsupported granite stairways interlace almost as if by magic in a single tower, each leading to different doors.

Off the Azabachería, Rúa de Troya is named after the venerable **Casa de la Troya**, base for the local *tunas*, not fish but bands of student minstrels in capes and ribbons, who play Galician-Celtic music around the Praza da Immaculada. The Azabachería leads into Praza Cervantes and a street called Preguntoiro ('questioning') after all the pilgrims who asked for directions here. This curves around to arcaded Rúa Nova, site of the little church of

Santa María Salomé with a Romanesque door under a Gothic arcade. Parallel extends **Rúa do Vilar**, Santiago's delightful, arcaded main shopping street, where the **Casa do Dean** has a fine Baroque portal; at the Confitería Mora (No. 60), pick up a delicious *tarta de Compostela,* made with chocolate bumps in honour of the Santo dos Croques. For the classic view of Santiago's towers and roofs, walk along the **Paseo da Ferradura** just east to the cathedral, a leafy 19th-century park where old men will take your photo with cameras nearly as old as themselves. The ornate iron pavilion on the Alameda where bands often play on Sunday afternoons is all that survives of the 1909 Exposicíon Regional Gallega.

Santa María del Sar

After being thoroughly Baroqued by the centre of Santiago, take a Romanesque break at the 12th-century Santa María del Sar, a mile south of yet another stately Baroque confection, the **Convento de las Mercedarias**. Set all alone in its meadow, Santa María is a jewel of Spanish architecture, with a different slant—literally. The piers and arches along the high barrel-vaulted nave have leant back at a startlingly precarious angle as long as anyone can remember; although the common explanation is that the tilt was caused by the subsidence of the soil, it may well have been done intentionally—like the *campanile* of Pisa or the leaning towers of Bologna, along with many other pieces of crooked bravura from the same period. A rakish tilt would be entirely in the imaginative and often outlandish spirit of the brilliant 12th century. The buttresses had to be added only after the great Lisbon earthquake of 1755. Don't miss the remarkable carvings by Master Mateo along one gallery in the **cloister** (*open Mon–Sat 10–1 and 4–6, summer til 10pm*).

Santiago de Compostela ℭ (981–)   *Where to Stay*

Finding a place to stay at any price is easy in the city that has received visitors for 1100 years; even during the high holy day of 25 July you'll probably be met at the bus or train station by landladies luring you to their *hostales* or *casas particulares* for around 2000 pts a head.

luxury/expensive

Poor pilgrims used to stay in the magnificent 15th-century ★★★★★**Hs Los Reyes Católicos**, Praza del Obradoiro, ℭ 58 22 00, ✆ 56 30 94, but since 1954 it has been reserved for visitors with well-padded wallets, the luxurious *ne plus ultra* of Spanish *hostales* and one of Europe's best hotels. Plushly furnished with antiques, art, and fountains, most rooms look onto one of four shady patios; some are simple, while the bridal suites have been enjoyed by VIPs from Franco on up; with the typical double at 25,000 pts, it's the most pricey *parador* in Spain. The trendiest place to stay, central ★★★★★**Araguaney**, Alfredo Brañas 5, ℭ 59 59 00, ✆ 59 02 87, offers every conceivable service, except perhaps easy parking—a headache in the *casco viejo*. ★★★★**Hotel Compostela**, Hórreo 1, ℭ 58 57 00, ✆ 56 32 69, is a grand old granite hotel still offering a touch of class for 14,000 pts.

For a cheerful Catholic atmosphere near the centre, get a room at the former Franciscan Missionary College, ★★★**Hogar San Francisco**, Campillo de San Francisco 3, ✆ 58 16 00, 📠 57 19 16. ★★**Hs Universal**, Pza. de Galicia 2, ✆ 58 58 00, is a solid no-surprises provincial hotel only 100m from the *casco viejo*.

Located on Santiago's prettiest street, ★★**Hs Suso**, Rúa del Vilar 65, ✆ 58 66 11, is run by a jovial fellow who knows everything and probably has something to do with the tasty tapas in the bar downstairs. A lovely patina of age adorns the friendly and charming ★**Hs La Estela**, by the cathedral on Raxoi 1, ✆ 58 27 96. If you'd like to do some of your own cooking, **Hospedaje Rodrigues**, Pinos 4, ✆ 58 84 08, offers kitchen privileges to guests.

Eating Out

Eating in Santiago is a pleasure—competition is keen and the food has to be good to succeed. Rúa del Hórreo has the biggest concentration of restaurants—one window of tempting seafood after another. Classic eateries include **Anexo Vilas** on the outskirts at Avda. de Villagarcía 21, ✆ 59 86 37, where an informal tapas bar serves delicious seafood and *empanadas*, while a dining room upstairs produces uncomplicated fresh food and shows Gallegan cuisine at its very best. For pudding, try the *Postre Xacobeo*, followed by a local digestif made from apples or peaches (menu 4000 pts, closed Mon); another brother runs the equally worthy bastion of Gallego cuisines, **Vilas**, at Rosalía de Castro 88, ✆ 59 21 70; similar prices, closed Sun). For tradition mixed with international, seasonal dishes, try **Don Gaiferos** (*expensive*) in a beautiful vaulted dining room in Rúa Nova 23, ✆ 58 38 94 (closed Sun). **Tacita de Juan**, Hórreo 31, ✆ 56 20 41 (*expensive*) offers *nouvelle cuisine* made from the freshest Galician ingredients (menu 4500 pts, closed Sun).

For a special treat, drive out 8km to Vedra in the Valle de Ulla, where **Roberto**, San Xulián de Sales, ✆ 51 17 69, prepares some of the most delicious, imaginative dishes in all Galicia in a lovely country villa (*expensive*, but not outrageous; closed Sat and Sun eve).

Alameda, San Clemente 32, ✆ 58 81 00 (*moderate*), has been serving up hearty Galician fare for more than 30 years—all types of *empanadas*, some filling stews and dishes hot from the oven, and local wines. For good value, **A Roda**, Rodríguez de Viguiri 7, ✆ 58 70 50 (*moderate/inexpensive*) is one of the best. The oldest restaurant in Santiago, going on 120 years of business, **Asesino**, Pza. Universidad 16, ✆ 58 15 68 (*inexpensive*), still packs them in and fills them up for around 2000 pts (closed Sun). For a feast of fresh seafood that won't break the bank, drive out to **Pampín**, Puente Espino at Calo-Teo on the Padrón road, ✆ 80 31 70 (*inexpensive*).

bars and nightlife

Santiago's lively bars offer a wonderful way to eat and drink a rainy night away. The area around Rúa Franco is the centre of the evening *marcha*, where **El Franco** at No. 28 is typical place to start with your first *aperitivo*. *Raciones* or tapas of octopus with peppers and paprika are the speciality at the **Mesón do Pulpo**, Vista Alegre 30; **O Gato Negro**, Raiña has delicious eel pies and peppers. **Bodeguilla de San Roque**, San Roque 13 (near Santa Clara) serves wine with plates of delicious breast-shaped *tetilla* cheese and ham. For jazz with your drinks, try **La Borriquita de Belém**, San Paio, near the cathedral, while chocolate lovers should try the hot chocolate or chocolate cocktails served nearby at **Metate**, Colexón de San Paio, a former chocolate factory. The prettiest café in town, **Derby**, Huérfanos 29, hasn't changed its décor since the 1920s. Live music and readings often happen at **Bellas Farto**, San Miguel 3. When you can't eat or drink any more, you can dance: the beautiful people of Santiago meet at the disco in the aforementioned hotel **Araguaney**; **Duque**, at Santiago de Chile 15, has a fun atmosphere and plenty of pop for a bop. **Peregrino**, Rosalía de Castro, is trendy and usually packed.

Back to the Rías: the Golfo Ártabro

Two of Galicia's most important ports, Ferrol and A Coruña, occupy either end of the 20km Golfo Ártabro, savagely bitten out of the northwest coast, with four teeth marking the four estuaries that flow into it. You can get there by dawdling west along the Rías Altas (*see* p.274) or by racing up the A 9 motorway from Santiago.

Getting Around

By air: A Coruña's airport is 9km away at Alvedro, ✆ (981) 23 22 40, with connections to Madrid, Barcelona and Sevilla. There's an airport bus into town.

By train: Ferrol and A Coruña are linked by RENFE with Pontedeume and the main junction at Betanzos, Santiago, Ferrol, Lugo, Vigo, Padrón and Villagarcía de Arosa. In A Coruña the station San Cristóbal is a bit out of the way on Marqués Figueroa, ✆ (981) 15 02 02—best to take bus no. 1 from the nearby bus station to the historic centre. There's also a RENFE travel office on Fontán 3, ✆ 22 19 48. In Ferrol, RENFE and FEVE share the same station ✆ (981) 31 46 55.

By bus: A Coruña's bus station is on Caballeros near the RENFE station, ✆ 23 96 44; El Rápido buses serve Betanzos and Monfero. Ferrol's buses leave from the train station, ✆ 32 47 51 and go to Betanzos, Viveiro, Foz, Ribadeo and Lugo.

Tourist Information

Ferrol: Magdalena 12, ✆ (981) 31 11 79.
Pontedeume: Avda. Saavedra Meneses 2, ✆ (981) 43 02 70.
A Coruña: Dársena de la Marina, ✆ (981) 22 18 22.

There are **markets** in Pontedeume on Saturdays; in Betanzos on Tuesdays, Thursdays and Saturdays; in A Coruña Monday–Fridays (Mercado San Agustín).

Ferrol and Pontedeume

Plump on the big fat Ría de Betanzos, swollen by four rivers, the salty city of Ferrol was named after its lighthouse (*faro*) and counts some 90,000 souls, many of whom work for or depend on the Spanish navy. Gently, slowly, the port city has dropped the article 'El' from the front of its name and the 'del Caudillo' stuck on the back in honour of Francisco Franco, born here in 1892, son of a naval supply officer who grew up to be the youngest general in Spanish history before his career as dictator, never losing his Gallego roots in his maddening stubbornness and inscrutability—earning himself the nickname 'the Sphinx without a secret'. Besides the enormous docks, navy yards and sailors' red light gauntlet, Ferrol has a pretty enough medieval core, a large planned 18th-century geometric, neoclassical quarter, the legacy of Felipe V who greatly boosted Ferrol's fortunes, and a modern quarter that looks like a Simcity computer game. The best thing to do is just wander among the pretty houses with 'crystal galleries' and the casino and gardens. A pair of castles on the slender waist of the *ría* defend the naval base. Five km from Ferrol, at the bottom of the estuary, **San Martín de Xubia** was founded as a monastery way back in the 9th century. It was the only one in Galicia adopted by Cluny (1113) but all that survives is the Cluniac church with its three apses and excellent carved capitals.

South of Ferrol, the charming medieval town of **Pontedeume** was once the preserve of the Counts of Andrade, who built and collected the tolls from their great bridge over the Ría Eume, once supported by 58 arches; some 15 arches still remain, as well as a 14th-century palace and tower emblazoned with the family's huge crest. The tolls financed the Andrades' hunts; note the weathered stone boars standing guard by the bridge. The parish church, the late-Gothic Santiago, is a trove of minor art. There are a couple of beaches along the *ría* (the Praia Perbes is a good one) and off the N VI to Betanzos, **San Miguel de Breamo** (1137), with its façade pierced by a window in the shape of an 11-point star and capitals to warm the cockles of any Romanesque diehard's heart.

If you have a car, two ruined monasteries beckon inland from Pontedeume, as much for their architecture as for their lovely settings. Up the Eume river, the Benedictine **Monasterio de Caaveiro** was founded in 934 by San Rosendo, who became a bishop at 18 and defended Compostela from the Normans and Saracens. Although renowned as a stickler for the rules, Rosendo could hardly have founded Caaveiro in a more evocative place, and to this day the ruined, overgrown 12th-century church perched over the river is exceedingly romantic. Twenty km south of Pontedeume, the 12th-century Cistercian **Monasterio de Monfero** with its two cloisters is equally derelict, even if more recently rebuilt in the 17th century, unabashedly grandiose for its remote rustic setting; only the church, with a singular chequer-board façade of granite and slate blocks, is still in use.

Betanzos

Rising steeply over the head of yet another small estuary, lovely Betanzos is a far more ancient place, a Celtic village that grew into the Roman port of Brigantium Flavium. It thrived into the 18th century, when the Mandeo and Mendo rivers washed in so much silt that they stole Betanzos' seacoast. Progress stopped, leaving a time capsule: houses and mansions of all sizes with wrought iron balconies or *solanas* line the narrow lanes that wind up the hill from the habour's medieval gates. Life revolves around the charming, monumental **Praza de García Hermanos**, its central ornament a statue of two Indianos and a replica of Versailles' Fountain of Diana. Most of the surrounding buildings are from the 18th century, including a neoclassical palace now used as the National Archives of Galicia; this runs a small but interesting historical **Museo de las Mariñas** (*open 5–8, Sat 11–1*). The three attractive churches are just off the square: the 14th-century **Santa María del Azogue**; 15th-century **Santiago,** with a figure of Santiago Matamoros on the tympanum; and Gothic **San Francisco**, inspired by the basilica at Assisi and its door topped with a bizarre figure of a boar with a cross rising out of its back. Inside, don't miss the delightful 14th-century *tomb of Fernán Pérez de Andrade O Boo* (the Good), who paid for the church and whose sarcophagus, supported on the backs of a boar and a bear, is covered with hunting scenes, perhaps in the hope that there'd be plenty of game in heaven. Take time to walk along the Ría Mandeo, one of Galicia's prettiest.

Rather than take the N VI directly to A Coruña, follow the pretty scenery along the Ría de Betanzos up to the local resort of **Sada**, to see its boardwalk and **La Terraza**, the finest *modernista* building in Galicia, designed by López Hernández, a curious pavilion made of glass and giant music stands. The road to A Coruña passes the **Pazo de Meirás**, residence of Galicia's greatest novelist, Countess Emilia Pardo Bazán, and later Franco, whose descendants still own it; further along, just offshore on a wooded islet, the 17th-century **Castillo de Santa Cruz** once defended A Coruña and now awaits a new rôle. Inland, south of the A 9, **Cambre**'s late 12th-century Romanesque church of Santa María has five sweet little chapels around its apse, decorated with good carvings and sculpted columns.

A Coruña

Occupying the length of the Ría da Coruña and the southwest fringe of the Golfo Ártabro, A Coruña is the liveliest city in Galicia, its big (pop. 230,000), exuberant, commercial capital with character to spare. Sprawling over a peninsula and attached to the mainland by a thin neck of land, it has beautiful windswept beaches facing the Atlantic and a magnificent sheltered harbour in the estuary that has made its fortune and paid for all its hypnotic wall of windowed balconies or *solanas* that gave A Coruña its nickname 'Crystal City'.

A Coruña's relationship with Britain goes back to its first settlers, Phoenician merchants who imported tin from Cornwall. The Romans called it Ardobicum Corunium, and tenuously associated it with Hercules, who performed one of his Twelve Labours (stealing the cattle of Geryon) down in Cádiz on the other side of Spain and reputedly had a hand in building the lighthouse. The Suevians and the Moors took turns running the show until 1002; in the Middle Ages, English pilgrims to Santiago often landed here, among them Chaucer's Wife of Bath and his patron John of Gaunt, who arrived in 1386, though unsuccessfully, to claim the Spanish throne for his wife, daughter of Pedro the Cruel.

Felipe II and the Invincible Armada

 Some 200 years later it was Spain's turn to invade England. The pious royal bureaucrat Felipe II had more than one bone to pick with Queen Elizabeth's England in the 1580s: Elizabeth had recently invented the Bloody Mary by lopping off the head of Mary Queen of Scots, Felipe's favourite candidate for the throne of England, and England was helping the Protestants of the Netherlands in their revolt against Spain; Spanish trade routes were threatened but most of all Elizabeth had confirmed the country's Protestant orientation. To solve all of his problems and force England back into the Catholic fold, Felipe decided on what seemed to be a foolproof plan: to build up the biggest fleet of warships in Spanish history, and coordinate this Invincible Armada with an invasion of England by his army in the Netherlands. Francis Drake got wind of Felipe's plans and in 1587 sailed into Cádiz 'to singe the king's beard' by burning the parked fleet and setting the invasion date back by a year.

Finally, in 22 July 1588, an Armada of 130 enormous galleons, manned by 10,000 sailors and 19,000 soldiers set sail from A Coruña. The great mastodons were inter- cepted near Plymouth by the faster ships of Lord Howard, who continued to hound Felipe's majestic fleet for the next week in various sea battles, without inflicting much damage or causing any fissures to the Armada's formation. England's stroke of luck came when the Armada set anchor near Calais, where it was to meet with the invasion fleet from the Netherlands. Howard sent fireships against the Armada, which panicked the Spaniards into breaking up their formation; soon after, on 8 August, in a battle that raged up and down the Channel, the quick English defeated the lumbering Armada at Gravelines, the score one English ship to two Spanish. When the Spaniards tried to sail home to regroup, the wind and luck against them, the English forced them to sail home the long way around Scotland, where appalling storms wreaked havoc; by the time the Invincible Armada limped back to Spain, only 76 half-wrecked galleons pulled into port, minus 15,000 soldiers. Although the war between England and Spain dragged on until 1604, the repercussions of the defeat of the Armada endured for centuries. Spain was demoralized, Felipe's trea- sury was empty, but in cocky Elizabethan England the party had just begun.

In the 'Groyne'

The classic view of A Coruña is of its harbour along **Avenida de la Marina**, lined with a solid wall of crystal galleries set in white balconies, a window cleaner's vision of hell. It is magical to sail into, just as Drake fearlessly did in 1589, swooping down in the night with 30 ships to rub salt in Felipe's wounds. Only a young girl named María Pita stood in the way, not only raising the alarm to save the city but somehow swiping Drake's flag in the process. In gratitude A Coruña gave her name to its biggest, busiest square, **Praza María Pita**, where the bars under its porticoes stay packed until the wee hours of the morning. One side is taken up with the city hall, the eclectic *modernista* **Palacio Municipal** (1907) by Pedro Mariño, decorated with symbols of A Coruña (*open Mon–Fri 5–7*).

A Coruña harbour

The older part of A Coruña—what old British seadogs called 'the Groyne'—begins at Praza María Pita, a labyrinth of winding streets squeezed around a hill. Near the harbour at Rúa Tabernas 13, Countess Emilia Pardo Bazán was born in 1851; the mansion now houses the **Royal Gallego Academy** and a small **museum** dedicated to the novelist (*open Mon–Sat 10–12*). Nearby Rúa Santiago leads into little Praza A. Fariña (or de Azcárraga), its bright flower beds covering the spot where gallows once stood. For pilgrims who sailed into A Coruña, the 12th-century over-restored Romanesque church of **Santiago** was their first stop; one door has a carving of Santiago Matamoros at Clavijo, another the Lamb of God; its 16th-century tower once defended the city from English pirates. The **Colegiata de Santa María del Campo**, begun in the 1210s and finished in the 1400s, stands at the top of the square. Its sculptors were star-struck: star decorations run along the roof and on the west façade; the triple portal has a carving of the Three Magi. Over the north door two angels stand by as someone seems to fall out of the sky with either star symbols or perhaps Ezekiel's wheel of fire, whirling up in the cosmos. Inside are some fine Romanesque tombs, polychrome statues and just to the left of the altar, another star, carved on a capital. Just down from here, the little Plazuela de Santa Bárbara is A Coruña's most charming, site of the **Convento de Santa Barbara** (1613), where cloistered Poor Clares live behind the portal, carved with SS. Barbara, Catherine, and the Virgin, while over the door there's St Michael, God holding a pilgrim in his hand and a sun and another star. Behind this, the **Convento de Santo Domingo** has two excellent Baroque chapels from the 17th century, especially the Capilla de la Virgen del Rosario, sheltering the Crystal City's patroness.

Santo Domingo stands on the edge of the evocative **Jardín de San Carlos**, set in the walls of the old fortress of San Carlos. It contains the granite tomb of Sir John Moore, who in 1809 led the routed, dispirited British army across Galicia with the French on his tail. At Elviña, just before A Coruña, he sent most of his troops ahead to board ships for home, just as Marshal Soult launched into a vicious attack; Moore managed to stall the French long enough for 15,000 of his men to embark under Soult's nose, an operation that has been called a precursor to Dunkirk. Casualties were high on both sides (Moore died pierced by a cannonball) and the British lost at Elviña, only to return under a new commander, the Duke of Wellington. Moore earned some verses in Gallego by Rosalía de Castro and some in a more Kiplingesque vain from Rev. Charles Wolfe:

> *Lightly, they'll talk of the spirit that's gone,*
> *And o'er his cold ashes upbraid him—*
> *But little he'll reck, if they let him sleep on*
> *In the grave where a Briton has laid him*

Just opposite, A Coruña's busy military history is remembered in the **Museo Militar** (*open 10–2*) in the old church of San Francisco. From here, bus no. 3 will take you out 2km to the northernmost tip of the peninsula and the 104m **Torre de Hércules**, A Coruña's proudest symbol (*open 10–2 and 4–6, closed Sat afternoon and Sun*). Built in the 2nd century AD in the time of Trajan, it's the oldest continuous working Roman light-house, but with an external skin from 1791. Bring a pep pill: it's 242 steps to the top for the splendid view of the city and ocean from 300ft up. Within walking distance from the Jardin de San Carlos, the Paseo do Parrote leads out to **Castillo de San Antón**, last rebuilt in 1779. It now defends artefacts from the Iron Age, the Celtic *castros*, Romans, and Middle Ages in the **Museo Arqueológico** (*open 10–3 and 4–9, closed Mon; adm*).

In the newer part of A Coruña (beyond Praza de María Pita) the ex-Maritime Consulate in Praza do Pintor Sotomayor (off the Rúa Panaderas) houses the **Museo de Bellas Artes,** with a collection of European paintings, sculptures, ceramics and coins dating from the 17th century (*open 10–2, in summer also 4–6, closed Mon; adm*). Near the Mercado San Agustín, the old Plaza dos Ovos has been converted into a charmingly goofy square devoted to comedians. A completely different atmosphere reigns in spooky Praza de España a block up from the market, with its soldiers and monument to José Millán Astray, the one-armed, one-eyed head of the Spanish foreign legion who taught his troops to cry '*¡Viva la Muerte!*' in the Civil War. The **Casa de las Ciencias** in Parque de Santa Margarita has a planetarium and museum dedicated to the world of science, technology and nature (*open 10–7, Sun 11–3, closed Mon*).

On the other side of the isthmus lie A Coruña's beaches: the **Praias de Ríazor** and **Orzán** fill up in summer. Quieter (except in August), cleaner and prettier strands are outside the city at **Santa Cristina, Bastiagueiro, Santa Cruz, Mera** and **Lorbe** (this last is the farthest from town, 16km away).

Ferrol

Franco saw to it that his home town got a ★★★**Parador do Ferrol**, Almirante Fernández Martín, ☎ 35 67 20, ✉ 35 67 20 (*expensive*); its ageing nautically decorated rooms have handsome views over the *ría*. If you're driving, little ★★★ **Pazo da Merce**, Ctra. Fene at Neda, ☎ 38 22 00, ✉ 38 01 04 (*expensive*), is a prettier place, a 17th- and 18th-century manor with *ría* views and a pool. ★★**Hs Almendra**, Almendra 4, ☎ 35 81 90, is a good moderate choice; cheaper rooms are concentrated on Pardo Bajo near the station. Along the waterfront at Neda, a 10-minute drive out towards Ortigueira, **Casa Tomás**, ☎ 38 02 40, is a favourite with specialities straight from the *ría*: *jurelos en escabeche* (fresh sardines in oil, garlic, basil and wine vinegar) and crayfish from the grill (*menú* 3800 pts; closed Sun eve and Mon). In town, **Borona**, Dolores 52, ☎ 35 50 99 (*moderate*) isn't much to look at but serves delicious *nouvelle cuisine* (closed Sun). **Pataquiña**, Dolores 35, ☎ 35 23 11, offers heaps of good, well-prepared Gallego specialities; try their *salsa Pataquiña*, a delectable mixture of shrimp and crab cooked in brandy and garlic (*menú* 2000pts).

Betanzos

★**Los Ángeles**, Los Ángeles 11, ☎ 77 15 11, ✉ 77 12 13 (*moderate*), is modern, but not exactly full of character, while the best bargain, ★**Hs Barreiros**, Argentina 6, ☎ 77 22 59 (*cheap*), has simple rooms and a good cheap restaurant, Mesón dos Arcos. **Casanova**, Pza. García Hermanos 15, ☎ 77 06 03 (*moderate*), in a rustically romantic setting, serves up tasty salmon and lamprey dishes for the bold.

A Coruña

A Coruña fills up in the summer, so arrive early or book ahead. The best-located and most luxurious hotel in the city, ★★★★**Finisterre**, Pso. del Parrote 20, ☎ 20 54 00, ✉ 20 84 62 (*expensive*), overlooks the sea and has a pool, tennis courts, nursery and children's pool, playground and a casino for adult games. ★★★**Riazor**, Avda. Pedro Barrié de la Maza 29, ☎ 25 34 00, ✉ 25 34 04 (*expensive*), is a pleasant, less costly alternative with a fine beachside location and modern rooms. Near the Torre de Hércules, with frequent buses into the centre, ★★★**Ciudad de La Coruña**, Polígono Adormideras, ☎ 21 11 00, ✉ 22 46 10 (*expensive*), has modern rooms, all with sea views. ★★**Hs Mar del Plata**, Pso. de Ronda 58, ☎ 25 79 66 (*moderate*), has pleasant rooms with bath; ★★**España**, Juan de Vega 7, ☎ 22 45 06, ✉ 20 02 79 (*moderate*), is central if a bit noisy; all rooms with bath. Cheaper central places include the well-kept ★**Hs El Parador**, Olmos 15, ☎ 22 21 21 (*moderate*); ★**Hs Palacio**, Pza. de Galicia 2, ☎ 12 23 38 (*inexpensive*); ★**Hs Centro Gallego**, La Estrella 2, ☎ 22 22 36 (*inexpensive*), and two no-name *hostales* on Zapatería by Santa María do Campo.

Seafood rules menus here and two of the best places to eat it are **Coral**, near the port at La Estrella 2, ✆ 22 10 82, for exceptional, delicately prepared shellfish and a classy setting (*menú* 4000 pts; closed Sun, exc in summer), or the long-established **Casa Pardo**, Novoa Santos 15, ✆ 28 00 21 (*moderate*), famous for melt-in-your-mouth monkfish dishes (closed Sun). **A La Brasa**, Juan Flórez 38, ✆ 26 54 57 (*moderate*) as its name implies, specializes in meat and fish sizzling from the grill; if there are two of you, work up an appetite and order the *punta trasera de ternera a la parrilla*, a whopper of a succulent steak with baked potatoes. **La Marina**, Avda. de la Marina 14, ✆ 22 39 14, is a popular place offering solid fish and regional dishes for around 2800 pts (closed Sun eve, Mon and June), or for less try old-fashioned **O Piote** on the same street (1750-pts *menú* with wine). The bar zone around Rúa Franja and Praza María Pita keeps going well into dawn when the fishing fleet pulls in and everyone goes down to watch the auctioning of the catch, the Muro, a strange ritual featuring fast-talking Gallegos and fish you've never seen before.

West of A Coruña: A Costa da Morte

Before tourism invented the Costa del Sol and the Costa Blanca, the Galicians dubbed this region down to Finisterra the 'Coast of Death' after its number of drownings, shipwrecks and ancient Celtic memories; from the end of the west, from the end of the Milky Way, Celtic warriors would sail out to their reward in the seven-towered castle of Arianrhod. The scenery along this wild land of the setting sun is romantic, the waves are dramatic, and the beaches pale and inviting; only the water is icy cold.

Getting Around

A Coruña and Santiago are the main bases for transport to the Costa da Morte, but buses are not all that frequent, and if you intend to visit more than one destination in a day, study bus schedules before setting out. Carballo, 35km southwest of A Coruña, is the main bus junction for the coastal villages.

Ría de Corme e Laxe

Heading west of A Coruña and Carballo, **Buño** is Galicia's traditional pottery town *par excellence*, manufacturing yellow and brown earthenware crocks in the shape of pigs and plates for as long as anyone can remember, readily purchasable along the main street. The road north of Buño ends up at **Malpica**, where the granite cliffs west of A Coruña first relax their vigilance. A former whaling-port, Malpica is partly sheltered by the windswept Sisargas islets, populated only by a large seabird nursery. Appropriately enough, the Costa da Morte has some fine dolmens, or Neolithic tombs, beginning with Malpica's **Pedra de Arca**. The nearest swimming is to the southwest, at the sheltered **Praia de Niñons**, passing by way of the romantic little ivy-shrouded castle known as the **Torres de Mens**, next to a tiny Romanesque chapel decorated with erotic figures.

Corme Porto, a picturesque fishing village to the west, has a reputation for being a law unto itself, a nest of resistance to Franco's Guardia Civil goons even into the 1950s, perhaps because they tried to get in the way of Corme's main industry: smuggling. Ask directions to the **Pedra da Serpe** at Gondomil, a snake carved in the stone believed to date from Phoenicians and connected to the legend of St Adrian, the local St Patrick, who is said to have gathered all the snakes in Galicia here and given them a mighty kick into the ground, where they disappeared. It has a fine white beach and dunes and a more sheltered strand, the **Praia de Balarés** just before the medieval bridge to **Ponteceso**, birthplace of poet Eduardo Pondal (1835–1917). **Laxe**, a pleasant fishing village across the estuary from Corme, has a white beach, safe even for children; for something more remote, continue south along the coast past Pedreira to the enormous **Praia de Traba**. There's a 14th-century church dedicated to Santiago and two intriguing dolmens on the road to Bayo, 5km inland: signs point the way to the **Dolmen of Dombate**, with engravings of a ship inside on the right and the **Pedra Cuberta**, another kilometre south, with a 6.2m chamber.

Ría de Camariñas

After some very rugged coast, the rocks relent to admit another *ría* shared by the remote fishing hamlets of Camariñas and Muxía, both renowned for intricate bobbin lace. From little, white, and increasingly trendy **Camariñas** you can walk 5km to Cabo Villán and its lighthouse, a wild piece of savage, torn coast, which makes you feel small and that civilization is far away, perhaps less so now that a set of experimental windmills have been erected to harness the wild winds that whip the cape. **Muxía** has always been a bit more important, as the proud escutcheons on the houses testify. It is also the holy city of the Costa da Morte, with its seaside sanctuary of **Nostra Señora de la Barca**, where the Virgin Mary herself is said to have sailed in a ship of stone when Santiago was preaching in these parts (it wasn't her only Spanish holiday: she made a similar appearance riding a stone pillar in Zaragoza). Ship-shaped votive offerings dangle throughout the church. Parts of the Virgin's own magic boat may be seen around the church, including the hull, the Pedra de Abalar, which moves whenever a person completely free of sin stands on it. If you suffer from colic or gastritis, a walk under the stone keel, the Pedra dos Cadrises (the stone that looks like a stylized dinosaur) should fix you up nicely.

Four km from Muxía, in Moraime the Benedictine church of **San Xián** (Julian) is mostly from the 12th century, but was founded in the 900s as a shelter for pilgrims; although humidity has blasted away most of the frescoes, 26 (again, two extra) Elders of the Apocalypse survive on the main portal. Inland, along the C 552, the 16th-century **Castillo de Vimianzo** (*open Tues–Sat 10–1 and 4–7*), once home to the cruel Álvaro Pérez de Moscoso, has just been lovingly restored to house a collection of paintings, photos and crafts.

Ría de Corcubión and the End of the World

Further south, a by-road off the C 552 leads up to the lighthouse at **Cabo Touriñán**, where, as the plaque states, and notwithstanding Finisterre, you are standing on the westernmost point of continental Europe. Another branch of the road leads to the huge (and hugely exposed) beach, the **Praia do Rostro**, before continuing south to the little industrial port of **Cée**, defended by the 18th-century Castillo de Cardenal. Cée has practically merged with **Corcubión**, an old fishing village sprinkled with manor houses and *solanas*. The parish church has a curious statue of St Mark, brought from Venice by a ship that refused to budge until the saint was taken ashore. White beaches are sprinkled under the pines, among them **Praia Sardiñeiro** with a few bars and restaurants.

Beyond lies the traditional westernmost point of Europe, the granite houses of **Finisterre** (or Fisterra) huddled like barnacles on the rocks around the church of the miracle-working Christ of the Golden Beard, who came out of the sea. According to tradition, these same waters contain the city of Duyo (or Dugium), which sank beneath the waves at the same time as Pompeii went under the lava; but sunken cities are a wide-ranging Celtic conceit, like Ys in Brittany that hark back to the Hesperides, the Blessed Isles beyond the West. Two km beyond is **Cape Finisterre** with its lighthouse, the world's end, where the Roman legions and pilgrims from Santiago came to gaze at the sun sinking into the limitless horizon. Often at other times the cape is bleak and wrapped in fog, when it's easy to imagine wandering souls flitting mournfully along the savage coast before taking their last step into the Beyond. At the foot of the cape, pilgrims would visit the Romanesque church and the '**Ara Solís**', evoking the mysteries of life, death and resurrection. For the best overviews, take the road up to **Vista Monte do Facho** where sterile women used to rub up against a menhir until an 18th-century bishop ordered it destroyed.

From Cée, the C 550 follows the coast around to **Ezaro**, a wild, picturesque place where massive granite boulders of 600m Mount Pindo, 'the Celtic Olympus', have mysterious engravings and ruins of ancient shrines. Unable to erode an estuary of its own through the mountain, the Río Xallas instead tumbles down in a dozen shimmering waterfalls to the sea, polishing the multi-coloured stones as it washes over them. Some of its wild charm has been sacrificed to a hydroelectric plant, but a wander upstream reveals the tumbling Xallas in a more pristine state. South, beyond the cute granite port of **Pindo**, the dune-backed beach of **Carnota** is the longest in Galicia (it also holds a more gloomy record for drownings: even if you think you're a strong swimmer, beware). Carnota also claims Galicia's largest *hórreo*, over 30m long and made entirely of granite. Although the surrounding valley is fertile, this 18th-century *hórreo* was moved here from elsewhere and extended to win the title, which doesn't seem quite fair.

A Costa da Morte © *(981–)* **Where to Stay and Eating Out**

The gastronomic prize of the the Death Coast is barnacles, or *percebes*, which look and may well taste just like Napoleon's pickled member recently auctioned off in London. They cost a fortune; people who gather them from the shore are washed away so often that they can't buy insurance.

Malpica

By the beach, **★★Hs J.B.**, © 72 02 66 (*moderate*), is comfortable enough and open all year; in the centre, **★Hs Panchito**, Pza. Villar Amigo 6, © 72 03 07 (*moderate*), is adequate. For reasonable fresh seafood, **San Francisco** is inexpensive and good. In Laxe, **★Hs Beiramar**, Rosalía de Castro 32, © 72 81 09 (*moderate*), is the only place to stay.

Camariñas

Of the *hostales*, ★Hs La Marina, M. Freijó 4, ✆ 73 60 30 (*inexpensive*), is nearest the sea and has the best views and restaurant; both ★Hs Plaza, Real 12, ✆ 73 61 03 (*moderate*), and ★Hs Triñares II, Area da Vila, ✆ 73 61 08 (*moderate*), have a handful of rooms with bath.

Corcubión

Beautifully located near the sea, ★★★El Hórreo, Sta Isabel, ✆ 74 55 00, ✆ 74 55 63 (*expensive*), is the largest and most pretentious hotel on the Costa da Morte; it has a pool and garden, open all year round. Minute ★Hs La Sirena, Santa Isabel, ✆ 74 50 36 (*cheap*), has 3 simple rooms. For fresh fish and simple good food Casa Leston, Ctra. Finisterre, at Sardiñeiro, ✆ 74 73 54 (*moderate*), can't be beaten.

Finisterre

At the end of the world ★Finisterre, Federico Ávila 8, ✆ 74 00 00 (*moderate*), is the largest and nicest place to check into; the same owner runs the cheaper ★Hs Cabo Finisterre. Cheapest of all is ★Hs Rivas, Ctra. Faro, ✆ 74 00 27 (*inexpensive*). In Pindo, A Revolta, ✆ 85 80 64, serves up filling dishes of hot seafood for around 2500 pts.

Into the Rías Baixas

The Lower Estuaries, or Rías Baixas/Bajas, almost at once have tamer, greener scenery than their wild cousins to the north; here the ocean is predictably warm enough to maintain a regular holiday trade. These less exposed, less continuously 'flushed' *rías* can, however, get a bit dirty if you swim in the innermost coves.

Getting Around

RENFE trains between A Coruña and Vigo pass through Padrón and Vilagarcía. There are hourly buses (7am–9pm) from Santiago to Noia and O Grove. From Vilagarcía buses leave for Isla de Arousa.

Tourist Information

Vilagarcía de Arousa: Avda. Juan Carlos I, 37 baixo, ✆ (986) 50 15 68.
Cambados: Rúa Novedades.
O Grove: Pza. Corgo, ✆ (986) 73 09 75

There are **markets** in Noia on Thursdays and Sundays in Rúa do Mercado; in Vilagarcía on Tuesdays and Saturdays; in Cambados on Thursdays.

The Ría de Muros e Noia

Under Monte Costiños on the north edge of the *ría,* **Muros** is a fine, old-fashioned, granite Gallego town, with narrow, arcaded lanes, a palatial market, and fountain with a stone turtle, all stacked under its Gothic parish church. This contains a startling crucifix found in the sea, the Cristo de la Agonía, with long, flowing hair that grows like his counterpart in Burgos and a stone serpent coiled in the basin of the holy water stoup. There's a good beach at **Louro**, 'the golden', 1.6km from Muros on the tip of the cape. Inland, past Ponte-Outes, **Entines** has the shrine of miracle-working **San Campio**. After making the ritual walk around the crucifix (six times clockwise, three counterclockwise) you can pay a visit to Campio in person, or so it seems; an early Christian martyr brought from Rome in the 18th century by a bishop of Santiago, his skeleton has been lovingly covered with wax and dressed in a centurion's costume and a garland so that he looks as if he were sleeping.

To reach Noia, cross over the medieval **Ponte Nafonso**, named after its master builder who lies buried under the 14th-century cross at the end, having laboured 30 years without seeing the bridge completed. **Noia** (or Noya) is full of legends, beginning with its name, after Noah, whose dove is said to have found the olive branch here—a scene depicted on the town's arms—while his ark found a solid base to anchor on the holy Celtic mountain of Barbanza just south. This local Mt Ararat is adorned with numerous dolmens and in Noia itself you can visit the mysterious cemetery next to the Gothic **Santa María a Nova** (1327) where guildsmen between the 10th and 16th centuries left headstones carved with symbols far more pagan than Christian; some 200 have symbols and designs relating to the trades of the deceased. Others are a total enigma. Another church, early 15th-century **San Martín**, has a good rose window carved into its fortress-like façade, and fine carvings on the portal; opposite, the **Pazo de Tapal** dates from the same period.

Often windy beaches and lagoons dot the coast of the *ría* south from Noia. The main village, **Porto do Son**, lies between the state-of the-art defensive outpost of NATO atop Mount Iroite and its rather more picturesque Celtic equivalent at the **Castro de Baroña**, located on an outcrop over the sea. From **Oleiros** you can drive up to a pair of miradors (498m) on the Montes Barbanza, for great views from Cabo Finisterre to Vigo on a clear day. Oleiros also an exceptional dolmen, **Axeitos**—an enormous rock measuring nearly 16 sq. m, supported by eight smaller ones. At the tip of the headland, **Corrubedo** has a proud set of dunes, the highest in all Galicia, constantly sculpted by the wind.

Ría de Arousa to Pádron

The shore-hugging C 550 first runs into the Ría de Arousa, touristically the most developed of all Galicia's estuaries, although this hardly means anything remotely like Benidorm or Torremolinos. The first town you come to, **Santa Uxia** (or Eugenia) **de Ribeira**, combines tourism with its status as Spain's top coastal and underwater fishing port. Remains of a Phoenician port are nearby at Aguiño, while further south, the **Isla de Sálvora** is a haunt of mermaids; a 16th-century *hidalgo* married one, and gave birth to a dynasty named Mariños de Lobeira. Locally a whole science has evolved to distinguish mermaids in case of doubt: they have smooth soles on their feet and no belly buttons. The rest of this shore has quiet beaches; **A Póboa do Camaniñal** has some stately homes.

At the head of the estuary, at the mouth of the blood-sucking lamprey-rich river Ulla, **Padrón** is the raggle-taggle capital of Galicia's favourite vegetable tapa, midget green *pimientas de Padrón*, roasted in oil and salted and astonishingly tasty, although occasionally one packs the same wallop as a *jalapeño*. Padrón has plenty of legendary baggage to accompany its peppers: it is ancient *Iria Flavia*, the port where Santiago's disciples sailed with their precious cargo, anchoring their stone boat to a stone 'memorial pillar' (*pedrón*), now displayed under the altar in the 17th-century church of **Santiago**. The stone boat was met by a pagan queen, Lupa, who mockingly gave the Christians two wild bulls to transport the coffin. When yoked the bulls turned into peaceful oxen; the astonished Lupa converted at once and was baptized by Saint James himself, who popped out of his coffin in the oxcart to do the job. On the Carretera de Herbón on the fringes of town, the **Casa-Museo de Rosalía** (*open 9–2 and 4–8, adm; closed Mon*) was the home of Galicia's favourite poet Rosalía de Castro (1837–85), the illegitimate daughter of a priest, who unhappily married historian Manuel Murguía, had six children, wrote beautiful poetry in Gallego and died young of cancer. Another house is covered from top to bottom in bleached scallop shells. The bridge over the Ulla to Puentecesures is attributed to Master Mateo.

Vilagarcía to Isla A Toxa

From Padrón the C 550 continues south past **Catoira** and the romantic remains of Alfonso V's Towers of the West, part of the front line defences of Santiago against the Normans (and scene of the annual Fiesta Vikinga). The big town on the south bank is **Vilagarcía de Arousa**, the glossy base for Galicia's drug-smuggling barons. After a drink and a look at all the suspicious types in a fancy pants café, perhaps the best thing to do is leave and drive up to the home of the pagan queen, Castro Lupario, atop **Monte Lobeira** (5km from Vilagarcía) for the extraordinary views, or visit the woodsy, sand-fringed **Isla de Arousa**, reputedly the chief drop-off point for Colombian cocaine in Europe. All this nefarious underworld activity seems far away in **Cambados**, an atmospheric noble town with plenty of old family crests and a lovely granite paved square; note the Italianate details on the balconies around the 17th-century Praza de Fefiñanes. The cemetery church, **Santa Mariña Dozo**, on Camino de la Pastora has carvings on its vault of the allegory of the man who ate his own excrement(!); if you know where that comes from, please drop us a line.

The Perfect Accompaniment to Fish

 As if seafood lovers didn't have enough to rave about in Galicia, the *rías* also supply Albariño, the ideal dry, fruity white wine to go with their heaving plates of *mariscos*. Cambados is the capital of Albariño, and the first Sunday of every August the lovely gardens of its *parador* hosts a wine festival. Burgundian monks at the Cistercian monastery of Armentería (*see* below) introduced Albariño vines in the 12th century and they thrived; if most other vineyards in dry hot Spain produce red wines, the humid Atlantic coast and sunnier sheltered slopes of the *rías* provide the ideal climate for aromatic whites. In 1988, the growing region do Rías Baixas was given its demarcation status, divided into the subzones of O Rosal, Val do Salnés (around Cambados), Condado de Tea (which also produces some reds) and the Zona del Albariño. Like its cousin, Portuguese Vinho Verde, Albariño is ever so slightly

sparkling, sending a gentle trail of bubbles to the top of your glass (for lots of suds, go for the Albariño del Palacio). Although usually best drunk as young as possible, Cambados' Albariño Fefiñanes is stored in oak barrels for a few months to give it more flavour. Other recommended Albariños are Lagar de Cervera, Castelo de Fornos (from Bodegas Chaves) and Martín Codax, from Valariño-Cambados. Nothing goes to waste: the stems, seeds, and other leftovers (*oruja*) are distilled into fiery *aguardiente*.

Galicia has two other demarcated wine regions: do Ribeiro, the largest, is just west of Ourense, where production is dominated by the large Bodega Cooperativa do Ribeiro, producer of whites (light Viña Costeira, or the rare celebrated Brandomín) and some reds; the newly popular Armandi and Telura reds come from Ribeiro's new Bodegas Lapatena. The third region, do Valdeorras, is out east of Ourense and produces as many red wines as whites. The latter are of interest for their recent revival of the native godella grapes (Viña Guiran and Viña Abad are two leading labels).The best reds probably come from Bodegas Jesús Nazareno, with Valdoura its most reputed wine.

From Cambados, the C 550 circles down to the family resort of **O Grove**, linked by a bridge to **Isla A Toxa** (de la Toja), a sand-rimmed, pine-clad islet that first became famous when a donkey left for dead was miraculously restored after a few days. Now adorned with a casino (one that Franco always turned a blind eye to), shell-coated church, spa, nouveau-riche estates, sports complex and 9-hole golf course, A Toxa is designed for people with bags of money, leaving O Grove for those who don't, but know how to have a good time.

An Excursion Inland from Vilagarcía to the Manor of the Goose

From Vilagarcía, the N 640 leads in 12km to the old spa town of **Caldas de Reis**, founded by the Romans. If you forego drinking the waters, which promise marriage within a year, at least take a walk through the charming *alameda* and botanical gardens. Farther along, 8km east of the centre of **A Estrada** (the largest rural municipality in Spain, no less), you can visit the exterior of the most lavish country villa in all Galicia, the sumptuous 18th-century **Pazo da Oca** with its ancient trees, arcaded patio, pond and chapel in the gardens, a thoroughly enchanting mix of granite, lichens and greenery.

Muros/Noia (✆ 981)

★★Hs La Muradana, Avda. de la Marina, ✆ 82 68 85 (*moderate*), is a good place to eat and sleep, although the best value for money must be ★Hs Ría de Muros, Calvo Sotelo 53, ✆ 82 60 56 (*moderate*). In Noia, the friendly ★★Hs Ceboleiro, Avda. Galicia 15, ✆ 82 05 31, has the best restaurant, with meals at around 2500 pts.

Padrón (✆ 981)

Fanciest here is ★★★Scala, Pazos, ✆ 81 13 12, ✉ 81 15 50 (*moderate*), but of all the places to stay, ★★Hs Casa Cuco, Avda. de Compostela, ✆ 81 05 11 (*moderate/inexpensive*), has the best name going, and rooms with or without bath. The culinary star of Padrón, the superlative **Chef Rivera**, Enlace Parque 7, ✆ 81 04 13, is your chance to dine on José Rivera Casal's superb, seasonal dishes (if you're not squeamish, the lamprey *empanada* is exquisite) and a delightful mix of traditional Gallego and international cuisine; (menu 2700 pts). On a back street by the river, **Pulperia Réal** has big plates of tender octopus.

Vilagarcía de Arousa (✆ 986)

Prices here are over the odds. Set in a pine wood, the 17th-century ★★★★**Pazo O Rial**, O Rial, Ctra. Vilagarcía-Cambados, ✆ 50 70 11, 🖷 50 16 76 (*expensive*), is sweet and quiet and near the sea, with a pool and satellite TV. ★**Hs 82**, Pza. de la Constitución 13, ✆ and 🖷 50 62 22 (*moderate*), is small but more than pleasant, and there are several others along the waterfront. For dinner, splurge on a memorable experience at **Chocolate**, located 2km away in Villajuán (Vilaxoán), ✆ 50 11 99 (*expensive*), Galicia's most famous restaurant, where divine grilled fish or tender Texas-sized steaks are prepared by the flamboyant owner, accompanied by famously bad service; tributes to the restaurant from celebrities and VIPs line the walls. There are also 18 attractive rooms that will set you back 7000 pts a double. The day's catch gets the home-cooked treatment at **Loliña**, Alameda 1 in Carril, ✆ 50 12 81, served in a sun-baked courtyard (*moderate*; closed Sun eve, Mon and Nov).

Cambados (✆ 986)

The ★★★**Parador de Cambados**, Paseo de Cervantes, ✆ 54 22 50, 🖷 54 20 68 (*expensive*), occupies an old country *pazo* (manor house) with a beautiful garden and a restaurant featuring seafood. ★**El Duende**, Ourense 10, ✆ 54 30 75, 🖷 54 29 00 (*moderate*), offers a nice, cheaper alternative by the sea, or for a bit more, there's ★**Hs Europa**, Ourense 12, ✆ 54 37 25, 🖷 54 37 61 (*moderate*), with a bath in every room. **O Arco**, Real 14, ✆ 54 23 12, remains the classic place to dine, with a good 1700-pts *menú*, or surrender to the tender loving culinary care of **Maria José**, Pza. das Rodas 6, ✆ 54 22 81 (*moderate*), who makes a mean *sopa de mariscos*.

O Grove/A Toxa (✆ 986)

You can rub shoulders with the likes of Julio Iglesias at the ★★★★★**Gran Hotel La Toja**, Isla A Toxa, ✆ 73 00 25, 🖷 73 12 01 (*luxury*), and enjoy golf, tennis, a spa, heated pool and everything else in a park setting, for 27,000 pts a night in the summer; for less than half as much, you can bask in almost as much luxury at ★★★★**Louxo**, ✆ and 🖷 73 02 00 (*expensive*). In O Grove proper, ★★★**Bosque Mar**, Reboredo 93, ✆ 73 10 55, 🖷 73 05 12 (*expensive*), is a pleasant family place with a garden and pool; ★★★**Mar Atlántico**, Pedras Negras San Vicente do Mar, ✆ 73 80 61, 🖷 73 82 99 (*moderate*), is similar, with tennis courts. ★**El Besugo**, González Besada 102, ✆ 73 02 11, 🖷 73 07 87 (*moderate*), on the road to Toxa, has simple, clean rooms with bath, open all year round; nearby, **Posada del Mar,**

Rúa Castelao 202, ✆ 73 01 06 (*moderate*), has fine views from its dining-room and good seafood croquettes, now served by its third generation; a similar pedigree accompanies the slightly cheaper **Casa Pepe**, Rúa Castelao 149, ✆ 73 02 35, again specializing in seafood.

Caldas de Reis (✆ 986)

Attached to the spa, **★★Acuña**, Herrería 2, ✆ 54 00 10 (*moderate*), has not refurbished its charming *modernista* air, with *solanas* overhanging the river. Just east of A Estrada, **O Antejo** (*moderate*), on the N 640, has great views and a good seafood grill.

As Rías Baixas: Pontevedra to Tui

Nothing to the south is as tourist-orientated as the Ría Arousa, though the hotels of the Ría de Pontevedra fill up fast enough in the summer with vacationing Spaniards and Portuguese. The scenery is domesticated, green and pretty. Most of the beaches are safe even for the kids. Pontevedra, the provincial capital, is a handsome confection of granite, the best urban architecture in Galicia after Santiago itself.

Getting Around

In Pontevedra the RENFE station, ✆ (986) 85 13 13, and bus station, ✆ 85 24 08, are next to each other, but a long walk along Alféreces Provisionales; a municipal bus can take you into town. Frequent buses serve the main *ría* villages.

Tourist Information

Sanxenxo: Consistorio 2, ✆ (986) 72 00 75.
Pontevedra: Galerías Oliva 1, ✆ (986) 85 08 14.

There is a **market** in Pontevedra in the Mercado by the river, daily exc Sunday.

The Ría de Pontevedra

The end of the Salnés peninsula dividing the Arousa and Pontevedra estuaries is occupied by the tremendous sweep of the **Praia da Lanzada**, one of Galicia's finest beaches, the delight of windsurfers, and in the old days, of family planners: hoping to get pregnant, women would flock to Lanzada and wade into the sea, lifting up their skirts and letting nine waves (one for each month of gestation) rush against their privates.

Nearby **Portonovo** and its neighbour **Sanxenxo** are jumping little resorts, with beaches like sugar and a chamber of commerce claim that they get more sun than the rest of Galicia; on summer evening everyone for miles around descends on its clubs for a bop.

Combarro has a famous view of its *hórreos* lined up along the shores of the *ría*. Roads from Sanxenxo or Combaro go up to the abandoned medieval **Monasterio de Armenteira**, where the Virgin favoured a monk named Ero: one morning, while listening to the song of a bird, he was granted a look into eternity. To him the ecstasy lasted but a few minutes, but upon returning to the monastery he found that centuries had passed (if the story sounds familiar *see* Leyre, in Navarra, p.88). The story is the

A hórreo

subject of King Alfonso the Wise's Cantiga CIII, and of the carvings on the entrance to Armenteira. The rose window on the main façade of the church is believed to have been a mandala for meditation, the carved archivaults around the door are *mudéjar*, and the guardian will show you the unusual octagonal cupola inspired by Islamic architecture. Look for peculiar masons' marks on the walls.

Just before Pontevedra, the **Monasterio de Poio** was founded in the 7th-century by San Fructuoso, a member of the Visigothic royal family, who caused a sensation by walking across the water to the islet of Tambo to rescue a sinking boat. In the oldest part of the church is the tomb of yet another unorthodox Galician saint, Santa Trahamunda, whose body floated to Galicia in a stone boat from Córdoba; note her statue, clutching an Andalucían palm tree.

Pontevedra

Pontevedra is nothing less than the perfect genteel granite Gallego town. Its streets are shaded with arcades, its squares are marked with stone crosses. Ancient tradition states that it was first called *Helenes*, founded by Teucer (Teucro), who fought at Troy. *Teucro* means 'Trojan' in Castilian, and there is, in fact, a Teucro who fits the bill, a son of Scamander and a nephew of Priam, who is recorded as leading a band of Cretans to western Spain to found a colony. It's also significant that he named the city after Helen, the sister of the twins Castor and Pollux, the favourite gods of Roman warriors. The cult of the warrior twins inspired the soldiers of the Reconquista in the apocryphal tradition that St James was the twin brother of Jesus. As if this weren't enough, Pontevedra also (along with Mallorca, Barcelona and Corsica) claims to be the birthplace of Columbus; there's a statue to him at the west end of the Alameda looking towards the ocean and the Americas.

Pontevedra's promising mythological progress was stymied back in the Middle Ages, when the Río Lérez silted up the port. By the time of Columbus, all the marine business had moved south to Vigo, leaving a compact, endearing and exceptionally vibrant **Zona Monumental**, its showcases all within a stone's throw of the Praza da Peregrina. Here is the tall, twin-towered 18th-century **Virgen La Peregrina** church, built in the shape of a scallop, to house a statue of the city's patroness. It was one of the few instances where the Virgin had any rôle at all to play in the pilgrimages (Pontevedra lies on the *camino* from

Portugal); during our most recent visit in August her feast day was celebrated with folk dances and a procession of hundreds before a crowd so thick you could scarcely breathe, while the 18- to 30-year-olds indulged in an all-out red wine war. And this was one of Pontevedra's *minor* holidays.

Behind the Virgen La Peregrina, there's a lovely 16th-century fountain in a small garden and the 13th- and 14th-century church of **San Francisco** with some good tombs, while across the street arcaded Praza da Ferrería is a favourite hangout for Pontevedrans. From here, Calle Pasantería descends to Pontevedra's most perfect little granite square, the **Praza da Leña**, with its granite porticoes and an ancient cross as its centrepiece. On one side two old houses have been joined to form the **Museo Provincial** (*open 10.30–1.30 and 4.30–8, Sun 11–1, closed Mon*), with an excellent collection of jet figures from Santiago, Celtic gold work, ancient headstones, paintings (by the likes of Zurbarán and Murillo) and works by the talented Gallego caricaturist Alfonso Castelao.

There are other pretty little squares tucked in the streets to the northwest, among them **Praza de Teucro** with its crystal galleries, named after the city's putative father. Just below, where Rúa Isabel II intersects with four other streets, there's a fine stone cross portraying Adam, Eve and the serpent—the numerous tapas bars in the vicinity are also tempting. Rúa Isabel II cuts across the Zona Monumental to the **Basílica de Santa María la Mayor**, constructed in the 16th century by the local Seafarers' Guild, with a Plateresque façade by Cornelis of Holland, with scenes of the Assumption and Death of the Virgin; two cannons still defend the church from incursions up the river. Inside there's a wooden Gothic *retablo* and some relief comic strip-like carvings on the back wall.

On the corner with Praza de España and the Alameda are the romantic, ivy-draped late 13th-century ruins of the **Convento de Santo Domingo** (*open Tues–Fri 10–2*); the leafy Alameda and adjacent **Jardines de Vincenti** are favourite spots from the evening's *paseo*. Out on a little promontory, a granite statue called the Emigrant's Wife, looking out forever across the *ría*, was erected by the people, for the people, honouring the earthy, independent, hardworking women who ran families and farms on their own for years.

Along the South Bank of the Ría de Pontevedra

If Pontevedra has a drawback it tends to be olfactory, a strong smack-in-the-gob pong which wafts in when the wind's up from the massive paper mill to the south. Usually it doesn't hit you until you start down the *ría*, and usually it puts people off from exploring further; this coast, in spite of its green garden charm and sandy coves, has scarcely any tourist facilities. Persevere. One of the chief curiosities is just past **Marín** and its naval academy, by the newish fishing hamlet and beach of **Mogor**: here are some of the most important petroglyphs in Spain, a labyrinth and spirals carved by the Celts. Their presence inspired a local retiree to carve his own petroglyphs, some less than perfect spirals and symbols of God and Country. Another 15km further down the C 550s, **Bueu** is a sleepy fishing village with two *hostales*, a great base from which to explore the surrounding beaches. The sands continue 12km west, down towards the tip of the cape, **Hio**, site of Galicia's most elaborate stone crucifix, sculpted out of a single block of granite in the 19th century by José Cerviño of Pontevedra, with a Descent from the Cross and souls in Purgatory.

Sanxenxo/Sangenjo

There are scores of places, but just try to get one in the summer without a reservation. Some of the best are along Praia de Silgar, such as the modern fashionable ★★★**Rotilio**, Avda. do Porto 7, ℭ 72 02 00, ☞ 72 41 88 (with a superb seafood restaurant), and the welcoming, recently renovated ★★**Hs Minso**, Avda. do Porto 1, ℭ 72 01 50, ☞ 69 09 32 (*both moderate*). ★**Montalvo**, Praia Montalvo, ℭ 72 30 28 (*moderate*), is a reasonable if unremarkable place, although the restaurant is more than adequate. ★**Panadeira**, Praia da Panadeira, ℭ 72 37 28 (*moderate*), is a friendly little establishment in a pretty spot.

Pontevedra

In the centre, ★★★★**Galicia Palace**, Avda. de Vigo 3, ℭ 86 44 11, ☞ 86 10 26 (*expensive*), is comfortable but not that luxurious, although it does have a garage; prices are only a smidgeon higher than the ★★★**Parador de Pontevedra**, Barón 19, ℭ 85 58 00, ☞ 85 21 95 (*expensive*). This offers a chance to sleep in a Gallego *pazo*, with a magnificent stone staircase and a garden. For something less, try ★★★**Virgen del Camino**, Virgen del Camino, ℭ 85 59 00, ☞ 85 09 00 (*expensive*), comfortable and with a garden. ★**Comercio**, A. González Besada 3, ℭ 85 12 17, ☞ 85 99 91 (*moderate*), is adequate and central, with a better than average restaurant. ★**Madrid**, Andrés Mellado 10, ℭ 85 10 06 (*moderate*), is near the centre, but rooms are on the dingy side. The Mercedarian monks up at the **Monasterio de Poio**, 2km from Pontevedra, run an inexpensive guesthouse, ℭ 77 00 00.

Pontevedra has one of the leading restaurants in Galicia, **Casa Solla**, 2km out of town on the road at San Salvador de Poio, ℭ 85 26 78 (*expensive*), famous for its great devotion to traditional recipes, the freshest seafood and meat dishes, matched by excellent service (closed Thurs and Sun eve). In town, **Doña Antonia**, Soportales de la Ferrería 4 (on the first floor), ℭ 84 72 74 (*expensive*), has a well-deserved reputation for imaginative dishes, with duck breasts, baked honeyed lamb and seafood salads; also a delicious chocolate *Tarta de trufa* with coffee cream (closed Sun). **Casa Román**, Avda. Augusto García Sánchez (south of the centre), ℭ 84 35 60, prides itself on select ingredients, especially shellfish (*menú* 3500 pts, closed Sun eve). **Castaño**, Rúa Sapos 8 (by the Alameda), ℭ 85 09 52, is famous for its *empanadas*; full meals cost just over 2000 pts. For less, choose one of the four daily dishes prepared at **Chipen**, Rúa de la Peregrina (1400 pts). Pontevedra has plenty of opportunities to eat economically in the bars in the Zona Monumental: **La Navarra**, Princesa 13, serves a range of wines and snacks; **A. Picota**, Rúa de la Peregrina 4, serves tasty charcuterie and cheese; **O Merlo**, Santa María 2, and **Rianxo**, on Panantería, have great tapas to go with your carafe of chilled Albariño.

The Ría de Vigo

The Ría de Vigo is the economic star of Galicia's estuaries: where all the others get narrower and shallower as they cut into land, the Ría de Vigo narrows at Rande (site of a huge suspension bridge), then widens again to form the sheltered inlet of San Simón, site of one of Europe's largest oyster beds. At the mouth of the estuary, the enchanting Cíes islets (now a national park) protect the port from tempests off the Atlantic and enable mussels farmers to moor their wooden platforms or *bateas* safely in the estuary, where the little molluscs incubate on long ropes suspended in the water. Vigo itself has grown to become the largest city in Galicia with a population of 250,000.

Getting Around

By air: Vigo's airport is 8km from town, with connections to major Spanish cities and Lisbon, ✆ (986) 27 40 49.

By bus and train: this sector of the coast is well served by buses, and there are several trains daily between Pontevedra and Vigo and beyond. The train station is at the top of Rúa Alfonso XIII, a 15-minute walk uphill from the port, ✆ (986) 43 11 14. Frequent buses (to Tui, A Garda, Baiona, Pontevedra, O Grove, Vilagarcía, Santiago and A Coruña) depart from the bus station near Praza de España, a couple of blocks down from the train station; for information, ✆ (986) 37 34 11.

By boat: weekdays from 6am to 10pm and Sundays from 9am–10.30pm, ferries (taking foot passengers only) sail every half hour to Cangas, every hour to Moaña and 6 times daily from mid-June to mid-Sept to the Islas Cíes from Vigo's Estación Marítima near El Berbés (Vapores de Pasaje, ✆ 986–43 77 77). For the Cíes, buy your ticket to the islands as soon as you arrive; by law only 2200 people a day can make the crossing and boats fill up fast. In the summer, there's also a morning boat from Cangas to the Cíes.

Tourist Information

Cangas: Rúa Real, ✆ (986) 30 00 50.
Vigo: Las Avenidas, by the port, ✆ (986) 43 05 77.
Tui: Avda. Portugal, ✆ (986) 60 07 57

There are **markets** in Cangas on Fridays; in Baiona on Mondays; and in Tui there is a Gallego/Portuguese market on Thursdays.

The North Bank of the Ría and the Islas Cíes

From Hio (*see* above) the road crosses the dolmen-dotted promontory for the pleasant small resort of **Cangas**, stretching along the coast with a lively port in its centre and a pleasant beach at the end. In a pirate raid in the 17th century, nearly the entire male population was massacred, leaving the women, they say, to go mad, slowly; accused of witchcraft, they would meet on Areas Gordas beach on St John's Eve, and get into trouble; many ended up in the Inquisition's dungeons, including María Soliña, the subject of a famous Gallego nationalist song. Five km east, **Moaña** is another if quieter resort in the Cangas mould, with an even better beach.

From Cangas or Vigo, the summer-only excursion to the two **Islas Cíes** (the third is off limits as a bird sanctuary) is a delight. Linked by a lick of sand that forms a sheltered lagoon of calm crystal water, the islands offer a perfect lazy day out on the beach, with a couple of cafés and restaurants; alternatively take a picnic and wander along the oceanside paths. It is a National Park, and the only place to stay is a campsite with limited space; ring ahead (**©** 27 85 01) to see if there's a place and buy a voucher with your boat ticket.

Vigo

Nothing less than Spain's premier fishing port, Vigo occupies a privileged hillside spot that attracted both ancient Phoenician and Greek seamen. Its name comes from the Roman *Vicus Spacorum*, but the city claims that its true founder was an early 12th-century troubador, Martín Codax, who, as he describes in his most famous poem, liked to hang out with the boys where Vigo stands today and watch their lady-loves bathe in the estuary. The city's history is full of unwanted English visits; two by Sir Francis Drake (1585 and 1589) and in 1702, when the English surprised a joint Spanish and French treasure fleet just returned from the New World, in the Battle of Rande. The English captured some of the ships but 11 were sunk or run aground near the tiny islets by the suspension bridge, the Puente de Rande; some sources say the silver had already been unloaded, but they haven't stopped treasure-seekers from looking. If they found any, they haven't told.

For all that, there's not much to 'see' in Vigo beyond the fine views towards the sea, although the old part of town hugging the fishing port, the **Barrio del Berbés**, is thick with atmosphere and rough, cobbled streets. As in A Coruña, there's a lively fish auction by the waterside at the crack of dawn; if you've had a rough night you'll have no problem finding a dozen supremely fresh oysters on the half shell from the fishwives along Rúa Teófilo Llorente or in the **Rúa da Pescadería** morning market. Look at the noblemen's palaces in López Puigcerver (**Calle Real**); from **Parque del Castro**, on top of the city, enjoy a great view of the *ría* from the modern monument to the Galeones de Rande: the Celts had their settlement in this commanding position. The municipal museum is in the 17th-century **Pazo de Castralos** (*open Tues–Sat 10–8, Sun 10–1, closed Mon*) in the southwest of town, in the geometric gardens of the **Parque Quiñones de León**. The museum contains antique furniture, folk paintings, local history, all beautifully displayed. Vigo also claims Galicia's sole **zoo**, along the road to the airport (*open 10–1.30 and 3–7*).

South of Vigo to the Ría de Baiona

Vigo's main beaches, white **Praia de Canido** and **Praia Samil**, are just west and often crowded, but the main lure in this neck of the woods is **Baiona** (Bayona), down the coast, one of Galicia's choice resorts, topped by the walls of the medieval **Castillo de Monterreal**. The grounds are occupied by a ravishing *parador*; fork out the 100 pts asked to tour the grounds and walls. The coast is embellished with little beaches of soft sand, namely Ladeira, Santa María and the magnificent crescent of **Praia América**; the latter is named after the fact that Baiona was the first place in Europe to learn that Columbus had discovered a New World, back on 10 March 1493, when the little *Pinta* sailed into its port. The 13th-century church of **Santa María** (*open 10–1 and 4–8*) is a good example of transitional architecture; more contemporary religious art is 1km south of town in the form of a huge granite sculpture of 1910, a sailors' ex-voto to the **Virgen de la Roca**. Wild horses have a free rein in the hills here, rounded up once a year in a *rapa das Bestas*, or *curros* when Gallego cowboys tame them, run a race or two, and let them go again. In **Oya**, 16km south along the pretty and wild coastline, there's a lonely 18th-century Baroque monastery.

To the south, **A Garda**, at the mouth of the Río Minho, perhaps looks more intriguing on the map than it does in the flesh, with its clutch of nouveau-riches *americanos'* bungalows. People have lived there for much longer, however, up in the excavated Celtic *castro* on **Monte Santa Tecla**, a 40-minute walk up from the village. With over 100 houses, this was one of the most important *citanías*, or fortified hill settlements, in Spain, inhabited from the 7th century BC up to the Roman period. Some of the huts have been reconstructed, others are mere foundations, linked by cobbled lanes and encircled by walls. From the top of Monte Tecla there are fine views over the Valley of the Minho into Portugal. Farther up there's a cromlech, or Neolithic stone circle, and at the very top a church with a small **archaeological museum** (*open 11–2 and 4–7.30, closed Mon*) where you can learn about the strange carving discovered on the site, believed to be a map; if true, it would be one of the oldest ever found in the West. The nearest beach is at **Camposancos**, 3km from A Garda, overlooking the mouth of the wide, wooded Río Minho, Galicia's prettiest river and the frontier between Spain and Portugal.

Tui

From A Garda the best thing to do is follow the course of the river Minho up to Tui (or Tuy, pronounced *twee*), a rare frontier town worth visiting in its own right. One of the seven ancient capitals of Galicia, Tui is picturesquely piled upon its acropolis; like Pontevedra, it claims to have been founded by wandering Greeks after the Trojan War. It was the capital of the Visigoth King Witiza in 700, and has seen many battles and border skirmishes with Portugal, defended by the walled city of Valença.

Tui's granite lanes and houses are crowned by the military profile of the **Catedral de San Telmo** with its powerful walls and keep; until the 13th century it did double duty as Tui's castle. Construction began in 1120 and, although not completed until much later, the stone has mellowed into a grey, vertical garden of wild flowers. It has a fine Romanesque porch and a portal of 1225, carved with the Adoration of the Magi, one of the first and finest Gothic works in Galicia, by French-trained sculptors; be sure to note the lovely but strange coat-of-arms on the side wall, with five stars and a crescent moon, said to symbolize the burning of the town by Al-Mansur. The interior is also heavily fortified— against earthquakes—and contains the relics of San Telmo, otherwise known as Pedro González of Astorga (confessor of King Saint Fernando of Castile), who died while working among the seafolk of Galicia in 1246. He is the patron saint of Spanish sailors, who confused his name with their first patron St Elmo (or Erasmus), who sends sailors his lucky fire to light upon their masts, igniting even their finger-tips without burning them. His tomb, accredited with 203 miracles, oozes a vinegary gunk much prized as a cure-all.

Among Tui's smaller churches are **Santo Domingo** (1415), its interior a mix of pre-Romanesque and Gothic; there are finely carved effigies on the tombs and the stone pulpit; **San Francisco** has a Portuguese Baroque chapel to St Telmo. In half an hour you can walk from the centre of Tui to the lovely Portuguese walled town of **Valença do Minho**, crossing an iron bridge built by Gustave Eiffel. The views from Valença to Tui are lovely, as is Valença, blanketed in bright towels, which Spaniards flock over to purchase. The Portuguese, on the other hand, seem to come to Tui for salt cod and toys, especially during the Thursday market. If it's hot, there are a couple of small river beaches perfect for a dip.

Ría de Vigo © (986–)   ***Where to Stay and Eating Out***

Vigo

Luxuriate on the beach in the ★★★★**Gran Hotel Samil**, Apartado 472, 5km south on the Praia de Samil, © 24 00 00, ✉ 23 14 19 (*expensive*), with a pool and tennis courts. Modern ★★★**Ensenada**, Alfonso XIII 7, © 22 61 00, ✉ 43 89 72 (*expensive*), is in the centre and has fine views across the bay. ★★**Nilo**, Marqués de Valladares 8, © 43 28 99, ✉ 43 44 74, is a good moderate choice, just up Rúa Carral, which is a good place to look for cheap sleeps: try ★★**Hs Saboy**, Carral 20, © 43 25 41 and ★**Hs Carral**, Carral 18, © 33 49 27 (*both inexpensive*).

Eating out is an excellent reason for sticking around Vigo. To every kind of seafood and shellfish add the delicacies from the river Minho: salmon, lamprey and baby eels, *anguillas*, the latter two favourite stuffings for *empanadas*. **Síbaris**, Avda. García Barbón 122, © 22 15 26 (*expensive*), gets kudos for its first quality land and sea cuisine in an upmarket, intimate setting (closed Sun). Up at **El Castillo**, Monte del Castro, © 42 11 11, you can dine with a superb view; exquisitely grilled fish and meat are the specialities (menu 4200pts, closed Sun eve and Mon). Out near Praia Samil, **Timón Playa**, Canido 8, at Corujo, © 49 08 15, looks across to the Islas Cíes, and specializes in seafood, rice dishes and *empanadas* (menu 3800 pts, closed Sun). For piles of good old fashioned seafood (and some beef dishes), go to **Puesto Piloto Alcabre**, Avda. Atlántida 98, © 29 79 75 (*moderate*), overlooking the sea (closed Sun eve). For seafood or roast leg of lamb, the long-established people's choice in Vigo is **El Mosquito**, Pza. da Pedra 4 (near the port), © 43 35 70 (*moderate*). For something different, **José Luis**, Avda. Florida (out by the stadium; take a taxi), © 29 95 22 (*moderate*), serves excellent mushroom, game and Basque dishes and a good list of Riojas to wash them down (closed Sun). Good cheap food is plentiful in the bars of El Berbés and along the Gran Vía in the centre; when you get sick of fish try the delicious hams and cheeses at **Bodegón Centro** in Manuel Núñez.

Baiona

The ★★★★**Parador Conde de Gondomar**, Monte Real, ✆ 35 50 00, ✉ 35 50 76 (*expensive*), is Galicia's finest, housed in a modern reconstruction of a typical Galician *pazo* within the medieval walls of Monterreal, in a lovely park; it offers a pool, tennis, children's recreation, and a short walk to the beach. ★★**Hs Tres Carabelas**, Ventura Misa 72, ✆ 35 54 41, ✉ 35 59 21, is a fine old inn on a narrow cobbled lane in the middle of town, with prices at the top of this category. Baiona has wide choice of cheaper options, among them ★**Hs Mesón del Burgo**, Barrio del Burgo, ✆ 35 53 09, and ★**Hs La Anunciada**, Elduayen 16, ✆ 35 55 90, ✉ 35 55 34 (*both moderate*). **O Moscón**, Alférez Barreiro 2, ✆ 35 50 08, is known for its lobster (*bogavante*); otherwise prices are moderate; **Naveira**, on the same street, ✆ 35 50 35, has good home cooking for around 3000 pts; **El Mosquito**, Ventura Misa 32, has good tapas and wine.

A Garda

★★**Convento de San Benito**, Pza. de San Benito, ✆ 61 11 66, ✉ 61 15 17 (*moderate*), is set in a renovated 16th-century monastery with a lovely garden in the cloister; its restaurant, **Os Remos**, serves a delicious lobster and rice dish. Stay near the top of Monte Tecla in the delightful ★**Pazo Santa Tecla**, ✆ 61 00 02 (*moderate*; open June–Sept), with views in every direction, or try portside ★**Hs Martirrey**, José Antonio 8, ✆ 61 03 49 (*inexpensive*). Good fish soups and seafood wait at **El Gran Sol** (*inexpensive*) a friendly family-run taberna at Malteses 32 (closed Sun).

Tui

Overlooking the Minho, the refined ★★★**Parador San Telmo**, Avda. Portugal, ✆ 60 03 09, ✉ 60 21 63 (*expensive*), is located in a large reproduction of a typical Gallego *pazo* 1km below town, with a garden, tennis and pool; ★★★**Colón Tuy**, Colón 11, ✆ 60 02 23, ✉ 60 03 27 (*moderate*), offer similar facilities for less. ★**Hs Generosa**, Calvo Sotelo 37, ✆ 60 00 55 (*cheap*), has fine rooms without bath, or try ★**Hs San Telmo 91**, Avda. de la Concordia 88, ✆ 60 30 11 (*moderate*), all rooms with bath. **O Cabalo Furado**, Pza. Generalísimo, ✆ 60 12 15 (*moderate*), offers good homecooking (closed Sun).

Up the Minho to Ourense

Galicia's least known and only land-locked province is an introspective place, with more valleys, they say, than towns, descending to form the *rías* from the great tableland of Castile. The province is famous for wine (Do Ribeiro, Do Valdeorras, Verín and Monterrey), hot springs, and Spain's walking sarcophagus, Julio Iglesias.

Getting Around

Ourense is the main hub here, with trains to Santiago, Lugo, A Coruña, Vigo, Ribadavia, León and the rest of Spain. RENFE's Estación Empalme is across the river, ✆ 21 02 02 ; tickets also on sale at Rúa Calvo Sotelo 15, ✆ (988) 21 46 04 . The bus station is 1km from the centre on the Vigo road, ✆ (988) 21 60 27.

Tourist Information

Ribadavia: Ayuntamiento, ✆ (988) 47 00 02.
Ourense: Curros Enríquez 1, ✆ (988) 23 47 17.

There are **markets** in Ourense on the 7th and 17th of each month; in Allariz on the 1st and 15th of each month; in Ribadavia on the 10th and 25th of each month; and in Verín on Wednesdays and Fridays.

From Tui to Ribadavia

Both the train and road follow the wooded banks of the Minho, offering one more chance to cross into Portugal, on the ferry from Salvaterra do Minho to the delightful walled city of Monção. To the east, past the first dam, the river takes on a wide and elegiac quality, around the beginning of the wine-growing region of Ribeiro. Ribeiro's charming 15th-century capital, **Ribadavia**, has the best preserved Jewish *barrio* in Galicia, a web of narrow lanes around the church of Santiago; even after the expulsion of the Jews by the Catholic kings, many remained here, hidden with the connivance of the Christian population. Ribadavia has a beautiful **Praza Mayor** and interesting Romanesque churches: a tree grows out of the belltower of the **Oliveira** church, **San Juan** has a 13th-century *cruceiro*, while the **Convento de Santo Domingo**, occasional residence of the kings of Galicia, has a fine Gothic church and simple cloister. You can learn about the local wines at the **Museo del Ribeiro** (*open 10–1 and 5–8*) or visit the ruined **Castillo de los Condes de Ribadavia**, still an impressive pile of walls, gates, towers, and tombs carved into the rock. From Ribadavia, it's 5km to the curious hilltop **Monumento de Beade** (or **Calvario**), with three granite crosses, overlooking a cluster of *hórreos*, and a bit further to the 8th-century, the Asturian-style church of **San Ginés (Xens) de Francelos** with a unique decorative programme by the entrance arch, a mix of Mozarabic and Visigothic elements: rude scenes on the capitals, reliefs of the Flight in Egypt and Christ's entrance into Jerusalem and silhouettes of birds inside.

The Minho and its tributary, the Sil, are the 'holy rivers' of Galicia, their banks thick with churches and hermitages. South of Ribadavia, the village of **Celanova** is built around a vast **Praza Mayor**, with a fountain in the middle (where you mustn't drink from the north spout, at the risk of going mad) and a Cecil B. de Mille Baroque façade of 1681, pasted on the venerable **Benedictine monastery of San Salvador**. The church's Capilla Mayor holds a gargantuan *retablo* of 1697 and the choir is a masterpiece of Gothic carving. Although the monastery itelf is occupied by a school (after having served as a prison in the Civil War) you can pick up the key to see the elegant Renaissance cloister full of dancing light, a Baroque cloister, and the garden at the back, the setting for the diminutive (25 by 10ft) **chapel of San Miguel**, a Mozarabic jewel with a roof that looks like a Chinese hat. Founded by St Rosendo in 936 in memory of his brother Froila, the chapel to this day bears an inscription over the door, asking visitors to pray for Froila's soul.

An even older church is 26km to the south on the N 540 in **Bande**: the rural Visigothic chapel of **Santa Comba,** overlooking the reservoir of Limia. Built with a Byzantine plan around the year 700, Santa Comba is remarkably well-preserved with its borrowed late Corinthian marble columns supporting a horseshoe arch. The rest of the decoration is quite sober, but there are traces of frescoes, including a man in the moon.

East of Celanova (and south of Ourense on the N 525) the medieval town of **Allariz** is a monument in itself and site of two more Romanesque churches: **Santiago** with an unusual round apse and **San Esteban,** on the way to the ruins of the castle. The **Convento de Santa Clara** was founded in 1282 by Violante, the wife of Alfonso X, who is buried in the enormous Baroque cloister. Between Allariz and Ourense, the ruined 12th-century **Santa Mariña das Aguas Santas** (a 15-minute walk from the village; bring a flashlight) has steps down to its crypt—actually a corridor dolmen, constructed of boulders.

Ourense (Orense)

Continuing up the Río Minho, Ourense puts its best face forward, greeting visitors with a graceful **Ponte Romano,** its seven ogival arches striding over 100ft above the Minho. The bridge—the biggest stone bridge in Spain—was built by the Romans and rebuilt on the ancient piers in the 13th century by Ourense's bishop. It is still used, to put it mildly: traffic is Ourense's day-in day-out nightmare, funnelled down the discouraging main street, Rúa do Progreso, cut through the city in the 19th century. Equally discouraging *urbanizaciones* housing Ourense's 100,000 souls take up most of the rest of the space.

If you can find a place to park, or don't mind walking a mile in from the bus or train stations, you can see what first attracted the Romans: the steaming hot springs, *Aquae Urentes,* known by the Visigoths and Suevi as Worm Sea (hence *Ourense*). The main source, **Las Burgas,** still steams out of the neoclassical fountain at a constant, nearly boiling temperature midway down Rúa do Progreso. The locals have invented a hundred uses for the hot water—stick a dead chicken in it, they say, and you can pluck it in two minutes flat. During 1386–7, when Ourense was John of Gaunt's capital during his attempt to claim the throne of Castile, many Englishmen here had the first hot baths of their lives.

Up from here, the arcaded **Praza Maior** and its charming little annex, **Praza de la Magdalena,** is Ourense's historic core and hub of its social life. The old episcopal palace in Praza Maior houses the **Museo Arqueológico Provincial,** (*open 9.30–2.30, closed Mon*) with a collection of finds from the Neolithic era to the Bronze Age, as well as *retablos* and other bits of art salvaged from the province's churches. In the corner of Praza Maior, the **Cathedral** was begun in the 12th century and is entered by way of the **Pórtico del Paraíso,** a 13th-century (and rather naive), brightly painted reproduction of Santiago's great Pórtico de la Gloria.The high altar contains the reliquary of St Martin of Tours, while the florid Baroque chapel by Francisco Castro Canseco houses Ourense's oddest attraction, the Santísimo Cristo who, like the Christ of Burgos, has real hair and a beard and a wood and fabric body; according to legend it was made by Nicodemus and floated ashore near Finisterre. The **Museo Catedralicio** (*open 11.30–1 and 4.30–7*) off the 12th-century cloister has one of the first books printed in Galicia and the 'Treasure of San Rosendo'—rare 10th-century chess pieces carved of rock crystal.

Around Ourense

From Ourense, take the N 525 north to the turn-off to Cobas, and continue beyond to the monumental Cistercian monastery of **Oseira** (*open daily 9.30–12.30 and 3–5.30*), where the late Graham Greene spent time with his heretical thoughts on Catholicism and wrote *Monsignor Quixote* (1982). He certainly came to the right spot; founded in 1137 by four hermits, Oseira was famous for producing monks who dallied in alchemy and magic cures. The monastery façade has a gigantic Churrigueresque doorway and the odd crest of two bones with the tree of knowledge. The massive church dates from the 12th century, and has seven chapels around its altar, with the Virgen de la Leche, supposedly an alchemist's idol, in the main one. Don't miss the curious faces carved in the Claustro de los Medallones.

The most majestic scenery in these parts begins just east of Ourense, heading up the Minho along the N 120, where the cliffs over the river rise ever steeper. At **San Esteban**, dominated by its Romanesque **Monasterio de Ribas de Sil** and its three atmospheric cloisters) the Sil flows into the Minho, and along the latter are wild gorges to walk along. The nearly as dramatic C 536 east of Ourense goes up to **Esgos**, where a small by-road leads to the ruined, abandoned monastery and church of **San Pedro de Rocas**, founded by followers of Prisciliano (*see* p.281) in 573, its three apses excavated in the rock. Abandoned in the Muslim invasion, the spot was rediscovered in the 10th century by Gemondo, a noble hunter lost in the forest; there are some curious old tombs and a little monolithic Mozarabic altar in the in the centre apse. The road continues to rise up higher and higher to **Puebla de Trives**, where there's even a ski resort, **Manzaneda**, with 10 different pistes of all degrees of difficulty, served by a chair lift and three other ski lifts (✆ 31 08 75 to see if there's any snow).

If you're heading southwest from Ourense towards Bragança or Zamora, you may want to stop in the old walled town of **Verín**, capital of the wine-growing Monterrey valley; high up on one side of the valley looms the **Castle of Monterrey**, built in the 16th century, part of it converted into a *parador*. Don't pass up the chance to try a bottle of Verín red— as long as you aren't driving anywhere. This highest-octane Galician wine can pack 14°.

Ourense and Around ✆ (988–)   **Where to Stay and Eating Out**

Ribadavia

★Hs Evencio, Avda. R. Valcárcel 30, ✆ 47 10 45, has a swimming-pool and garden to delight its guests. **★★Hs Oasis**, Ctra. N 120, ✆ 47 16 13, has pleasant rooms with views and a no-frills but fine, inexpensive restaurant (*both moderate*).

Ourense

In the old part of Ourense, **★★★★Gran Hotel San Martín**, Curros Enríquez 1, ✆ 37 18 11, ✉ 37 21 38 (*expensive*), has recently been completely renovated with large, air-conditioned rooms. A few paces away, **★★★Sila**, Avda. de la Habana 61, ✆ 23 63 11, ✉ 23 60 25 (*moderate*), is well-run and has cheerful rooms, TV included. If you've got a car, the new ★★★**Auriense**, at O Cumial Xeixalbo, ✆ 23 49 00, ✉ 24 50 01, is a few minutes from the centre and offers a pool and tennis in a quiet setting. Cheaper choices in the centre are ★**Río Minho**, Juan XXIII 4, ✆ 21 75 94 (*moderate*), and ★**Hs San Miguel II**, San Miguel 14, ✆ 23 92 03 (*cheap*), next door to one of Ourense's best restaurants, **San Miguel**, San Miguel 12, ✆ 22 07 95 (*moderate/expensive*), specializing in seafood fresh from the coast, accompanied by Galicia's finest wines, served in the traditional *taza* (closed Tues). Choose one of three dining rooms at **Martín Fierro**, Sáenz Díez 17, ✆ 37 26 43 (*expensive*), and tuck in to the surf or turf delicacies from the grill, or try the tasty 2900-pts pilgrims' menu (closed Sun). **Carroleiro**, San Miguel 10, ✆ 22 05 66, offers a simple, good 1500-pts *menú* (closed Mon). For tapas stick around the Cathedral; **Queixo, Pan, e Viño**, Pza. Flórez, has good hams and farm cheeses.

Poboa de Trives

The 18th-century ★★★**Pazo Casa Grande**, Marqués de Trives, ✆/✉ 33 20 66 (*moderate*), has 7 atmospheric rooms that share a private chapel. Up at the ski resort of Manzaneda, the ★★**Queixa** is open all year, ✆ 30 97 47, ✉ 31 08 75, offering a heated pool, tennis, children's activities and more (book ahead; 7500 a double, and 14,000 pts for a bungalow for 6).

Verín

Four km outside Verín, the ★★★**Parador de Verín**, ✆ 41 00 75, ✉ 41 20 17 (*expensive*), is located next to the 13th-century castle, with lovely views of the valley below; its restaurant has seafood and other Gallego treats. You can look up at the castle and *parador* from the inexpensive ★**Dos Hermanas**, Avda. de Sousas 106, ✆ 41 02 80 (rooms with bath).

Castellano, as Spanish is properly called, was the first modern language to have a grammar written for it. When a copy was presented to Queen Isabel in 1492, she quite understandably asked what it was for. 'Your majesty', replied a perceptive bishop, 'language is the perfect instrument of empire'. In the centuries to come, this concise, flexible and expressive language would prove just that: an instrument that would contribute more to Spanish unity than any laws or institutions, while spreading itself effortlessly over much of the New World.

Among other European languages, Spanish is closest to Portuguese and Italian—and of course, Catalan and Gallego. Spanish, however, may have the simplest grammar of any Romance language, and if you know a little of any Romance language you will find much of the vocabulary looks familiar. It's quite easy to pick up a working knowledge of Spanish; but Spaniards speak colloquially and fast, and in Andalucía they do it with a pronounced accent, leaving out half the consonants and adding some strange sounds all their own. Expressing yourself may prove a little easier than understanding the replies. Spaniards will appreciate your efforts, and when they correct you, they aren't being snooty; they simply feel it's their duty to help you learn. There are dozens of language books and tapes on the market; one particularly good one is *Teach Yourself Spanish*, by Juan Kattán-Ibarra (Hodder & Stoughton, 1984). If you already speak Spanish, note that the Spaniards increasingly use the familiar *tú* instead of *usted* when addressing even complete strangers.

Pronunciation

Pronunciation is phonetic but somewhat difficult for English speakers.

Vowels

a	short *a* as in 'pat'	**u**	silent after *q* and gue- and gui-;
e	short *e* as in 'set'		otherwise long *u* as in 'flute'
i	as *e* in 'be'	**ü**	*w* sound, as in 'dwell'
o	between long *o* of 'note'	**y**	at end of word or meaning *and*, as **i**
	and short *o* of 'hot'		

Dipthongs

ai, ay	as *i* in 'side'	**ei, ey**	as *ey* in 'they'
au	as *ou* in 'sound'	**oi, oy**	as *oy* of 'boy'

Consonants

Language

c   before the vowels *i* and *e*, it's a *castellano* tradition to pronounce it as *th*; many Spaniards and all Latin Americans pronounce it in this case as an *s*

ch   like *ch* in 'church'

d	often becomes *th*, or is almost silent, at end of word
g	before *i* or *e*, pronounced as **j** (*see below*)
h	silent
j	the *ch* in loch—a guttural, throat-clearing *h*
ll	*y* or *ly* as in million
ñ	*ny* as in canyon (the ~ is called a tilde)
q	*k*
r	usually rolled, which takes practice
v	often pronounced as *b*
z	*th*, but *s* in parts of Andalucía

Stress is on the penultimate syllable if the word ends in a vowel, an *n* or an *s*, and on the last syllable if the word ends in any other consonant; exceptions are marked with an accent.

If all this seems difficult, consider that English pronunciation is even worse for Spaniards. Young people in Spain seem to be all madly learning English these days; if your Spanish friends giggle at your pronunciation, get them to try to say *squirrel*.

Practise on some of the place names:

Madrid	ma-DREED	**Trujillo**	troo-HEE-oh
León	lay-OHN	**Jerez**	her-ETH
Sevilla	se-BEE-ah	**Badajóz**	ba-da-HOTH
Cáceres	CAH-ther-es	**Málaga**	MAHL-ah-gah
Cuenca	KWAYN-ka	**Alcázar**	ahl-CATH-ar
Jaén	ha-AIN	**Valladolid**	ba-yah-dol-EED
Sigüenza	sig-WAYN-thah	**Arévalo**	ahr-EB-bah-lo

Useful Words and Phrases

yes	*sí*	please	*por favor*
no	*no*	thank you (**very much**)	*(muchas) gracias*
I don't know	*No sé*	you're welcome	*de nada*
I don't understand Spanish	*No entiendo español*	It doesn't matter	*No importa* *Es igual*
Do you speak English?	*¿Habla usted inglés?*	all right	*está bien*
		OK	*vale*
Does someone here speak English?	*¿Hay alguien que hable inglés?*	excuse me	*perdóneme*
Speak slowly	*Hable despacio*	Be careful!	*¡Tenga cuidado!*
Can you help me?	*¿Puede usted ayudarme?*	maybe	*quizá(s)*
		nothing	*nada*
Help!	*¡Socorro!*	It is urgent!	*¡Es urgente!*

How do you do?	*¿Cómo está usted?*	**How ...?**	*¿Cómo ...?*
or more familiarly	*¿Cómo estás?*	**How much?**	*¿Cuánto/Cuánta?*
	¿Qué tal?	**How many?**	*¿Cuántos/Cuántas?*
Well, and you?	*¿Bien, y usted?*	**I am lost**	*Me he perdido*
or more familiarly	*¿Bien, y tú?*	**I am hungry**	*Tengo hambre*
What is your name?	*¿Cómo se llama?*	**I am thirsty**	*Tengo sed*
or more familiarly	*¿Cómo te llamas?*	**I am sorry**	*Lo siento*
My name is...	*Me llamo.../*	**I am tired** (man/woman)	*Estoy cansado/a*
	Mi nombre es...	**I am sleepy**	*Tengo sueño*
Hello	*¡Hola!*	**I am ill**	*No siento bien*
Goodbye	*Adios/Hasta luego*	**Leave me alone**	*Déjeme en paz*
Good morning	*Buenos días*	**good**	*bueno/buena*
Good afternoon	*Buenas tardes*	**bad**	*malo/mala*
Good evening	*Buenas noches*	**slow**	*despacio*
What is that?	*¿Qué es eso?*	**fast**	*rápido/rápida*
What ...?	*¿Qué ...?*	**big**	*grande*
Who ...?	*¿Quién ...?*	**small**	*pequeño/pequeña*
Where ...?	*¿Dónde ...?*	**hot**	*caliente*
When ...?	*¿Cuándo ...?*	**cold**	*frío/fría*
Why ...?	*¿Por qué ...?*		

Numbers

one	*uno/una*	twenty one	*veintiuno*
two	*dos*	thirty	*treinta*
three	*tres*	thirty one	*treinta y uno*
four	*cuatro*	forty	*cuarenta*
five	*cinco*	forty one	*cuarenta y uno*
six	*seis*	fifty	*cincuenta*
seven	*siete*	sixty	*sesenta*
eight	*ocho*	seventy	*setenta*
nine	*nueve*	eighty	*ochenta*
ten	*diez*	ninety	*noventa*
eleven	*once*	one hundred	*cien*
twelve	*doce*	one hundred and one	*ciento-uno*
thirteen	*trece*	five hundred	*quinientos*
fourteen	*catorce*	one thousand	*mil*
fifteen	*quince*	first	*primero*
sixteen	*dieciséis*	second	*segundo*
seventeen	*diecisiete*	third	*tercero*
eighteen	*dieciocho*	fourth	*cuarto*
nineteen	*diecinueve*	fifth	*quinto*
twenty	*veinte*	tenth	*décimo*

Time

What time is it?	¿Qué hora es?	morning	mañana
It is 2 o'clock	Son las dos	afternoon	tarde
... half past 2	... las dos y media	evening	noche
... a quarter past 2	... las dos y cuarto	today	hoy
... a quarter to 3	... las tres menos cuarto	yesterday	ayer
		soon	pronto
noon	mediodía	tomorrow	mañana
midnight	medianoche	now	ahora
month	mes	later	después
week	semana	it is early	está temprano
day	día	it is late	está tarde

Days

Monday	lunes	Friday	viernes
Tuesday	martes	Saturday	sábado
Wednesday	miércoles	Sunday	domingo
Thursday	jueves		

Months

January	enero	July	julio
February	febrero	August	agosto
March	marzo	September	septiembre
April	abril	October	octubre
May	mayo	November	noviembre
June	junio	December	diciembre

Shopping and Sightseeing

I would like...	Quisiera...	money	dinero
Where is/are...?	¿Dónde está/están ...?	museum	museo
How much is it?	¿Cuánto vale eso?	theatre	teatro
open	abierto	newspaper (foreign)	periódico (extranjero)
closed	cerrado	pharmacy	farmacía
cheap/expensive	barato/caro	police station	comisaría
bank	banco	policeman	policía
beach	playa	post office	correos
booking/box office	taquilla	postage stamp	sello
church	iglesia	sea	mar
hospital	hospital	shop	tienda

Do you have any change?	¿Tiene cambio?	supermarket	supermercado
		toilet/toilets	servicios/aseos
telephone	teléfono	men	señores/
telephone call	conferencia		hombres/caballeros
tobacco shop	el estanco	women	señoras/damas

Accommodation

Where is the ... hotel?	¿Dónde está el ... hotel?	... with 2 beds	con dos camas
Do you have a room?	¿Tiene usted una habitación?	... with a double bed	con una cama grande
		... with a shower/ bath	con ducha/baño
Can I look at the room?	¿Podría ver la habitación?	... for one person/ two people	para una persona/ dos personas
How much is the room per day/ week?	¿Cuánto cuesta la habitación por día/ semana?	... for one night/ one week	una noche/ una semana

Driving

rent	alquiler	driver	conductor, chófer
car	coche	speed	velocidad
motorbike/moped	moto/ciclomotor	exit	salida
bicycle	bicicleta	entrance	entrada
petrol	gasolina	danger	peligro
garage	garaje	dangerous	peligroso
This doesn't work	Este no funciona	no parking	estacionamento prohibido
road	carretera		
motorway	autopista	narrow	estrecha
Is the road good?	¿Es buena la carretera?	give way/yield	ceda el paso
		road works	obras
breakdown	avería		
(international) driving licence	carnet de conducir (internacional)	Note: Most road signs will be in international pictographs	

Transport

aeroplane	avión	platform	andén
airport	aeropuerto	port	puerto
bus/coach	autobús/autocar	seat	asiento
bus/railway station	estación	ship	buque/barco/ embarcadero
bus stop	parada		
car/automobile	coche	ticket	billete
customs	aduana	train	tren

Directions

I want to go to...	Deseo ir a...
How can I get to... ?	¿Cómo puedo llegar a... ?
Where is... ?	¿Dónde está... ?
When is the next... ?	¿Cuándo sale el próximo... ?
What time does it leave (arrive)?	¿Parte (llega) a qué hora?
From where does it leave?	¿De dónde sale?
Do you stop at ... ?	¿Para en... ?
How long does the trip take?	¿Cuánto tiempo dura el viaje?
I want a (return) ticket to...	Quiero un billete (de ida y vuelta) a..
How much is the fare?	¿Cuánto el billete?
Have a good trip!	¡Buen viaje!
here	aquí

there	allí
close	cerca
far	lejos
left	izquierda
right	derecha
straight on	todo recto
forwards	adelante
backwards	hacia atrás
up	arriba
down	abajo
north (n./adj.)	norte/septentrional
south (n./adj.)	sur/meridional
east (n./adj.)	este/oriental
west (n./adj.)	oeste/occidental
corner	esquina
square	plaza
street	calle

Eating out

Hors d'oeuvres & Eggs — Entremeses y Huevos

aceitunas	olives
alcachofas con mahonesa	artichokes with mayonnaise
ancas de rana	frog's legs
caldo	broth
entremeses variados	assorted hors d'oeuvres
huevos de flamenco	baked eggs in tomato sauce
gambas pil pil	shrimp in hot garlic sauce
gazpacho	cold soup
huevos al plato	fried eggs

huevos revueltos	scrambled eggs
sopa de ajo	garlic soup
sopa de arroz	rice soup
sopa de espárragos	asparagus soup
sopa de fideos	noodle soup
sopa de garbanzos	chickpea soup
sopa de lentejas	lentil soup
sopa de verduras	vegetable soup
tortilla	Spanishomelette, with potatoes
tortilla a la francesa	French omelette

Fish — Pescados

acedías	small plaice
adobo	fish marinated in white wine
almejas	clams

anchoas	anchovies
anguilas	eels
angulas	baby eels
ástaco	crayfish

atún	tuna fish	lenguado	sole
bacalao	codfish (usually dried)	mariscos	shellfish
		mejillones	mussels
besugo	sea bream	merluza	hake
bogavante	lobster	mero	grouper
bonito	tunny	navajas	razor-shell clams
boquerones	anchovies	ostras	oysters
caballa	mackerel	pejesapo	monkfish
calamares	squid	percebes	barnacles
cangrejo	crab	pescadilla	whiting
centollo	spider crab	pez espada	swordfish
chanquetes	whitebait	platija	plaice
chipirones	cuttlefish	pulpo	octopus
… en su tinta	… in its own ink	rape	anglerfish
chirlas	baby clams	raya	skate
dorado, lubina	sea bass	rodaballo	turbot
escabeche	pickled or marinated fish	salmón	salmon
		salmonete	red mullet
gambas	prawns	sardinas	sardines
langosta	lobster	trucha	trout
langostinos	giant prawns	veneras	scallops

Meat and Fowl

Carnes y Aves

albóndigas	meatballs	lomo	pork loin
asado	roast	morcilla	blood sausage
bistec	beefsteak	paloma	pigeon
buey	ox	pato	duck
callos	tripe	pavo	turkey
cerdo	pork	perdiz	partridge
chorizo	spiced sausage	pinchitos	spicy mini-kebabs
chuletas	chops		
cochinillo	sucking-pig	pollo	chicken
conejo	rabbit	rabo/cola de toro	bull's tail cooked with onions and tomatoes
corazón	heart		
cordero	lamb		
faisán	pheasant	riñones	kidneys
fiambres	cold meats	salchicha	sausage
filete	fillet	salchichón	salami
hígado	liver	sesos	brains
jabalí	wild boar	solomillo	sirloin steak
jamón de York	raw cured ham	ternera	veal
jamón serrano	baked ham		
lengua	tongue		

Note: *potajes, cocidos, guisados, estofados, fabadas* and *cazuelas* are various kinds of stew.

Vegetables

alcachofas	artichokes
apio	celery
arroz	rice
arroz mariner	rice with saffron and seafood
berenjena	aubergine (eggplant)
cebolla	onion
champiñones	mushrooms
col, repollo	cabbage
coliflor	cauliflower
endibias	endives
ensalada	salad
espárragos	asparagus
espinacas	spinach

Verduras y Legumbres

garbanzos	chickpeas
guisantes	peas
judías (verdes)	French beans
lechuga	lettuce
lentejas	lentils
patatas (fritas/salteadas)	potatoes (fried/sautéed)
(al horno)	(baked)
pepino	cucumber
pimiento	pepper
puerros	leeks
remolachas	beetroots (beets)
setas	Spanish mushrooms
zanahorias	carrots

Fruits

albaricoque	apricot
almendras	almonds
cerezas	cherries
ciruelas	plums
ciruela pasa	prune
frambuesas	raspberries
fresas	strawberries
(con nata)	(with cream)
higos	figs
limón	lemon

Frutas

manzana	apple
melocotón	peach
melón	melon
naranja	orange
pera	pear
piña	pineapple
plátano	banana
pomelo	grapefruit
sandía	watermelon
uvas	grapes

Desserts

arroz con leche	rice pudding
bizcocho/pastel/torta	cake
blanco y negro	ice cream and coffee float
flan	crème caramel
galletas	biscuits (cookies)
helados	ice creams

Postres

pajama	flan with ice cream
pasteles	pastries
queso	cheese
requesón	cottage cheese
tarta de frutas	fruit pie
turrón	nougat

Drinks

water with ice	agua con hielo
mineral water (without/with fizz)	agua mineral (sin/con gas)

Bebidas

milkshake	batido de leche
coffee (with milk)	café (con leche)
Spanish champagne	cava

beer	cerveza	wine (red, rosé, white)	vino (tinto, rosado, blanco)
chocolate	chocolate	orange juice	zumo de naranja
sherry	jerez	slush, iced squash	granizado
milk	leche		
tea (with lemon)	té (con limón)		

Other Words

(olive) oil	aceite (de oliva)	sandwich (made from English-type bread)	sandwich
marinade	adobo		
garlic	ajo	toast	tostada
sugar	azúcar	vinegar	vinagre
sandwich (made from French-type bread)	bocadillo	breakfast	desayuno
		lunch	almuerzo/comida
savoury pie	empanada	dinner	cena
ice	hielo	knife	cuchillo
butter	mantequilla	fork	tenedor
marmalade	mermelada	spoon	cuchara
honey	miel	cup	taza
bread	pan	plate	plato
roll	panecillo	glass	vaso
ground pepper	pimienta	napkin	servilleta
(without) salt	(sin) sal	table	mesa
sauce	salsa		

Restaurant

menu	carta/menú	Can I see the menu, please?	Déme el menú, por favor
bill/check	cuenta		
change	cambio	Do you have a wine list?	¿Hay una lista de vinos?
set meal	menú del día		
waiter/waitress	camarero/a	Can I have the bill (check), please?	La cuenta, por favor
Do you have a table?	¿Tiene una mesa?		
... for one/two?	¿... para uno/dos?	Can I pay by credit card?	¿Puedo pagar con tarjeta de crédito?

Historical, Architectural, Geographical Terms

Ajimez	in Moorish architecture, an arched double window
Alameda	park or promenade
Ambulatory	semicircular aisle around the high altar of a church
Artesonado	*mudéjar*-style carved wooden ceilings
Atalaya	Phoenician word for tower
Ayuntamiento	city hall
Azulejo	painted glazed tiles, popular in Moorish and *mudéjar* work and later architecture
Baldachin	canopy on posts over an altar or throne
Barrio	city quarter or neighbourhood
Bóveda	vault
Calvario	calvary, or outdoor Stations of the Cross
Capilla Mayor	seat of the high altar in a cathedral
Cartuja	Carthusian monastery
Caserío	Basque country house or chalet
Castizo	anything purely Spanish (from the Castilian point of view)
Castro	Celtic or Iberian fortress settlement
Castrum	Roman military camp
churrigueresque	florid Baroque style of the late 17th and early 18th centuries in the style of José Churriguera (1650–1725), Spanish architect and sculptor
Ciudadela	citadel
Converso	Jew who converted to Christianity
Coro	walled-in choir in the centre of a Spanish cathedral
Corregidor	royal magistrate
Cortes	Spanish Parliament
Cromlech	circular ring of stones
Diputación	seat of provincial government
Embalse	reservoir
Ermita	hermitage
Fueros	exemptions, or privileges of a town or region under medieval Spanish law

Granja	farm or farmhouse
Hidalgo	literally 'son of somebody'—the lowest level of the nobility, just good enough for a coat-of-arms
Homage tower	the tallest tower of a fortification, sometimes detached from the wall
Hórreo	Asturian or Galician granary or corn crib
Isabelline Gothic	late 15th-century style, roughly corresponding to the English Perpendicular
Judería	Jewish quarter
Mirador	a scenic overlook or belvedere
Modernista	Catalan Art Nouveau
Morisco	Muslims who submitted to Christianization to remain in Spain after the Reconquista
Mozarabic	referring to Christians under Muslim rule in Moorish Spain
Mudéjar	Moorish-influenced architecture; Spain's 'National style' in the 12th–16th centuries
Ogival	pointed (arches)
Pallazo	circular, conical-roofed shepherd's hut in Asturias and Galicia
Patio	central courtyard of a house or public building
Pazo	Galician manor house
Plateresque	16th-century style; heavily ornamented Gothic
Plaza	a town square
Plaza de Toros	bullring
Plaza Mayor	square at the centre of many Spanish cities, often totally enclosed and arcaded
Posada	inn
Pronunciamiento	a military coup
Puerta	gate or portal
Reja	iron grilles, either decorative ones in churches or those covering the exterior windows of buildings
Retablo	carved or painted altarpiece
Sala Capitular	chapterhouse
Transitional	in northern Spanish churches, referring to the transition between Romanesque and Gothic

Further Reading

Borrow, George, *The Bible in Spain* (various editions, first written in 1843). A jolly travel account by a preposterous Protestant Bible salesman in 19th-century Spain.

Brenan, Gerald, *Spanish Labyrinth* (Cambridge, 1943). Origins of the Civil War; *The Literature of the Spanish People* (Cambridge, 1951).

Carr, Raymond, *Modern Spain 1875–1980* (Oxford, 1985). A confusing period, confusingly rendered.

Casas, Penelope, *The Foods and Wines of Spain* (Penguin). The best Spanish cookbook in English, with great regional recipes.

Castro, Américo, *The Structure of Spanish History* (E. L. King, 1954). A remarkable interpretation of Spain's history, published in exile during the Franco years.

Elliot, J. H., *Imperial Spain 1469–1714* (Pelican, 1983). Elegant proof that much of the best writing these days is in the field of history.

Epton, Nina, *Navarre: the Flea between Two Monkeys*, and *Grapes and Granite* (on Galicia); good reads but out of print, available only in libraries.

Ford, Richard, *Gatherings from Spain* (Everyman). A boiled-down version of the all-time classic travel-book *A Handbook for Travellers in Spain*, written in 1845. Hard to find but worth the trouble.

Harnilton, R. and Janet Perry, translators, *The Poem of the Cid*, (Penguin).

Hemingway, Ernest, *The Sun Also Rises*, (*Fiesta* in the UK) and *Death in the Afternoon* (various editions). The former put Pamplona on the map, the latter is Hemingway's book on bullfighting.

Hooper, John, *The Spaniards* (Viking, 1993). A comprehensive account of contemporary Spanish life and politics. Well done.

Lee, Laurie, *As I Walked Out One Midsummer Morning* and *A Rose for Winter*. Very well-written adventures of a young man in Spain in 1936, walking from Vigo to Málaga and his return 20 years later.

Lojendio, Louis, *Navarre Romaine* (Zodiaque, 1967), one of the excellent illustrated volumes in the French Zodiaque series on medieval art; other pertinent volumes for northern Spain are *Le Pré-Romaine Hispanique* (on the Visigoths and Asturian churches) and *Le Mozarabe*.

Michener, James A., *Iberia* (Fawcett, 1984). 950 pages of windy bosh, but full of fascinating sidelights just the same.

Morris, Jan, *Spain* (Penguin, 1982). A little disappointing considering the author; careless generalizations and dubious ideas sustained by crystalline prose.

Mitchell, David, *The Spanish Civil War* (Granada, 1982). Anecdotal; wonderful photographs.

Mullins, Edwin, *The Pilgrimage to Santiago* (Secker & Warburg/Taplinger). Perhaps the most colourful and wide-ranging account of the journey.

Reilly, Bernard F, *The Medieval Spains* (Cambridge University Press, 1993). Dry but painstakingly detailed account of the origins of Spain.

Thomas, Hugh, *The Spanish Civil War* (Penguin, 1977). The best general work.

Note: page numbers in *italics* indicate maps; **bold** entries indicate main references.

Index